THE
FORTY-EIGHTH YEARBOOK

OF THE

NATIONAL SOCIETY FOR THE STUDY
OF EDUCATION

PART I

AUDIO-VISUAL MATERIALS
OF INSTRUCTION

Prepared by the Society's Committee

FLOYDE E. BROOKER, STEPHEN M. COREY *(Chairman)*, EDGAR DALE,
CHARLES F. HOBAN, JR., ERNEST HORN, WILLIAM B. LEVENSON,
AND FRANCIS W. NOEL

Edited by
NELSON B. HENRY

Distributed by
THE UNIVERSITY OF CHICAGO PRESS
CHICAGO 37, ILLINOIS
1949

Published by

THE NATIONAL SOCIETY FOR THE STUDY OF EDUCATION

5835 KIMBARK AVENUE, CHICAGO 37, ILLINOIS

COPYRIGHT, 1949, BY
NELSON B. HENRY
SECRETARY OF THE SOCIETY

No part of this yearbook may be reproduced in any form without written permission from the Secretary of the Society

The responsibilities of the Board of Directors of the National Society for the Study of Education in the case of yearbooks prepared by the Society's committees are (1) to select the subjects to be investigated, (2) to appoint committees calculated in their personnel to ensure consideration of all significant points of view, (3) to provide appropriate subsidies for necessary expenses, (4) to publish and distribute the committees' reports, and (5) to arrange for their discussion at the annual meetings.

The responsibility of the Yearbook Editor is to prepare the submitted manuscripts for publication in accordance with the principles and regulations approved by the Board of Directors in the "Guide for Contributors."

Neither the Board of Directors, nor the Yearbook Editor, nor the Society is responsible for the conclusions reached or the opinions expressed by the Society's yearbook committees.

Published 1949
First Printing, 6,000 Copies

OFFICERS OF THE SOCIETY
1948-1949

Board of Directors
(Term of office expires March 1 of the year indicated)

WILLIAM A. BROWNELL (1952)*
Duke University, Durham, North Carolina

HARL R. DOUGLASS (1950)
University of Colorado, Boulder, Colorado

FRANK N. FREEMAN (1951)
University of California, Berkeley, California

ERNEST HORN (1949)
State University of Iowa, Iowa City, Iowa

T. R. MCCONNELL (1952)*
University of Minnesota, Minneapolis, Minnesota

RUTH STRANG (1951)
Teachers College, Columbia University, New York, New York

RALPH W. TYLER (1950)
University of Chicago, Chicago, Illinois

NELSON B. HENRY *(Ex-officio)*
University of Chicago, Chicago, Illinois

Secretary-Treasurer
NELSON B. HENRY (1949)
University of Chicago, Chicago, Illinois

* Elected for three years beginning March 1, 1949

THE SOCIETY'S COMMITTEE ON AUDIO-VISUAL MATERIALS OF INSTRUCTION

FLOYDE E. BROOKER, Chief, Visual Aids to Education, U. S. Office of Education, Washington, D. C.

STEPHEN M. COREY *(Chairman)*, Professor of Education and Executive Officer, Horace Mann-Lincoln Institute of School Experimentation, Teachers College, Columbia University, New York, New York

EDGAR DALE, Professor of Education, Ohio State University, Columbus, Ohio

CHARLES F. HOBAN, JR., State Teachers College, West Chester, Pennsylvania

ERNEST HORN, Professor of Education, State University of Iowa, Iowa City, Iowa

WILLIAM B. LEVENSON, Assistant Superintendent in Charge of Elementary Schools, Cleveland, Ohio

FRANCIS W. NOEL, Chief, Bureau of Audio-visual Education, California State Department of Education, Sacramento, California

ASSOCIATED CONTRIBUTORS

JAMES W. BROWN, Supervisor, Instructional Materials Center, University of Washington, Seattle, Washington

AMO DEBERNARDIS, Director of Instructional Materials, Portland Public Schools, Portland, Oregon

JAMES D. FINN, Assistant Professor of Education, State Teachers College, Greeley, Colorado

ELIZABETH GOLTERMAN, Director, Division of Audio-visual Education, St. Louis Public Schools, St. Louis, Missouri

WILLIAM G. GNAEDINGER, Head, Bureau of Visual Teaching, State College of Washington, Pullman, Washington

L. C. LARSON, Associate Professor of Education and Director of Audio-visual Center, Indiana University, Bloomington, Indiana.

CHARLES FREMONT MILNER, Associate Director, University Extension Division, University of North Carolina, Chapel Hill, North Carolina

A. W. VANDERMEER, Associate Professor of Education, Pennsylvania State College, State College, Pennsylvania

WALTER A. WITTICH, Director, Bureau of Visual Instruction, University Extension Division, University of Wisconsin, Madison, Wisconsin

EDITOR'S PREFACE

The timeliness of this yearbook is evidenced by the rapid increase in the production and use of audio-visual materials for educational purposes in the brief period that has elapsed since the close of the last war. It is generally agreed that the conspicuous success of the armed forces in the use of audio-visual methods in their emergency training programs contributed notably to the heightened interest of leaders in education in more extensive and more systematic exploration of the values of these procedures in normal classroom situations. But it is likewise a familiar fact that, for a quarter of a century preceding the war, the continuing studies in curriculum and in learning were steadily guiding theory and practice in education toward the currently approved standards involving a variety of materials and procedures in all areas of instruction. In this connection it is interesting to note that more than half of the substantial list of references presented in chapter xii of the yearbook, selected as representative of productive research on audio-visual materials, were published prior to 1940.

The apparent need for a yearbook in this field was pointed out by Mr. Horn at the meeting of the Board of Directors in February, 1944. At subsequent meetings in 1944 and 1945, the problem was given further consideration in light of memoranda prepared at the request of the Board by both Professors Corey and Dale. In all these deliberations there was general agreement that an appropriately designed yearbook might well provide effective guidance for teachers and supervisory officers in their planning for the improvement of their instructional programs and procedures through the introduction of or greater emphasis on audio-visual materials. Under the chairmanship of Professor Corey, the yearbook committee developed the preliminary outlines of the various chapters so as to achieve this essential purpose of the publication in marked degree. The considerations underlying the organzation of the volume and the specific aims of the authors in their treatment of the selected topics are briefly characterized in the introductory chapter.

NELSON B. HENRY

TABLE OF CONTENTS

	PAGE
OFFICERS OF THE SOCIETY FOR 1948-1949	iii
THE SOCIETY'S COMMITTEE ON AUDIO-VISUAL MATERIALS OF INSTRUCTION	iv
ASSOCIATED CONTRIBUTORS	iv
EDITOR'S PREFACE	v
INTRODUCTION	1
STEPHEN M. COREY	

CHAPTER

I. COMMUNICATION IN THE MODERN WORLD 4
    FLOYDE E. BROOKER
    The Social Significance of Communication 4
    Analysis of Languages, Media, and Forms of Communication 6
    The Communications Revolution 10
    The Development of Pictorial Forms of Communication and Their Application to Education 14
    Education and the Crisis in Communication 19

II. SCHOOL USE OF AUDIO-VISUAL INSTRUCTIONAL MATERIALS .. 28
    JAMES W. BROWN and A. W. VANDERMEER
    Introduction 28
    Audio-visual Materials and Learning Experiences 29
    Integration of Audio-visual Instructional Materials with the School Curriculum 35
    Present Practices in the Use of Audio-visual Instructional Materials and Methods in the Schools 38
    Some Encouraging Trends 45
    Some Deterring Factors 49

III. OBSTACLES TO THE USE OF AUDIO-VISUAL MATERIALS 53
    CHARLES F. HOBAN, JR.
    Introduction 53
    Characteristics of Audio-visual Materials 53
    More General Educational Deterrents 64
    Implications for Teaching 68

CONTENTS

CHAPTER	PAGE
IV. THE TEACHERS' DECISIONS	72
STEPHEN M. COREY and EDGAR DALE	
Introduction	72
The Four Instructional Questions	77
Overloading the Teacher	93
V. PRESERVICE TEACHER EDUCATION FOR USE OF AUDIO-VISUAL INSTRUCTIONAL MATERIALS	95
WILLIAM G. GNAEDINGER	
Introduction	95
The Content of Preservice Audio-visual Courses	96
Teachers' Needs in Audio-visual Training	99
The Place of Audio-visual Training in the Teacher-training Program	100
The College Audio-visual Center	105
VI. IN-SERVICE TEACHER EDUCATION FOR USE OF AUDIO-VISUAL INSTRUCTIONAL MATERIALS	108
AMO DeBERNARDIS	
Introduction	108
Factors Which Contribute to a Successful Program of In-service Teacher Education for Audio-visual Aids	110
Methods and Techniques for Facilitating Teacher Growth in the Use of Audio-visual Aids	112
Evaluating the Results of the Program of In-service Education	121
Summary	123
VII. THE PROGRAM OF AUDIO-VISUAL EDUCATION IN CITY SCHOOL SYSTEMS	127
ELIZABETH GOLTERMAN	
Introduction	127
The Roots of Visual Education in St. Louis	127
Fundamental Principles: Guide to Development of Audio-visual Education Patterns	129
Administration and Personnel of the Division of Audio-visual Education	130
Co-ordinated Long-Term Planning	132
Selection of Visual Materials	132
Preparation, Inspection, and Repair of Materials	134
Cataloguing, Ordering, and Delivery	141
In-service Education in Utilization	143

CONTENTS ix

CHAPTER PAGE

VIII. THE PROGRAM OF AUDIO-VISUAL EDUCATION IN RURAL
SCHOOLS 145
CHARLES FREMONT MILNER
What Are Adequate Objectives for the Rural Audio-visual
Program? 146
What Methods Have Been Suggested for Reaching These
Objectives? 149
What Is the Status of Audio-visual Programs in Rural
Areas? 152
What Improvements Are Feasible in These Programs?.... 160

IX. STATE PROGRAMS OF AUDIO-VISUAL EDUCATION........... 162
FRANCIS W. NOEL
Principles Directing the Operation of a State Audio-visual
Unit 163
Present Status and Trends of State Programs........... 165
Description of the Initiation and Operation of a State
Program of Audio-visual Education................. 168

X. PRINCIPLES OF ADMINISTERING AUDIO-VISUAL PROGRAMS... 180
FRANCIS W. NOEL
Why Should a Department of Audio-visual Education Be
Established? 181
What Should Be the Functions of an Audio-visual Department? 184
What General Principles and Procedures Underlie the Administration of a Department of Audio-visual Education? 192

XI. SUGGESTED ANSWERS TO SOME PERTINENT QUESTIONS IN THE
AUDIO-VISUAL FIELD 201
L. C. LARSON
Introduction 201
Role in Education 203
Materials 209
Utilization 216
School Preparation of Materials..................... 225
Physical Facilities 232
Administration and Finance 237
Responsibilities of State Agencies and Higher Institutions 248

CHAPTER	PAGE
XII. RESEARCH ON AUDIO-VISUAL MATERIALS	253

EDGAR DALE, JAMES D. FINN, and
CHARLES F. HOBAN, JR.

General Aspects of Research	254
Audio-visual Materials in World War II	254
Instructional Motion Pictures	261
The Theatrical Motion Picture	273
Field Trips	277
Still Pictures, Filmstrips, and Lantern Slides	279
Museum Materials	280
Graphic Materials	282
Radio and Recordings	283
XIII. SO THE CHILDREN MAY LEARN	294

W. A. WITTICH

INDEX	311
INFORMATION CONCERNING THE SOCIETY	315
LIST OF PUBLICATIONS OF THE SOCIETY	317

INTRODUCTION

STEPHEN M. COREY
Professor of Education and Executive Officer
Horace Mann-Lincoln Institute of School Experimentation
Teachers College, Columbia University
New York, New York

Audio-visual instructional materials are difficult to define precisely. Too, the large group of men and women who have a specific interest in these materials defy classification in the well-established "fields" of educational specialization. Some are administrators, some are supervisors, some are psychologists, some are creative producers of materials. All of these persons have in common, however, a major concern with types of teaching aids that are not exclusively verbal.

Because of the diversity of aims among audio-visual specialists, the contributions of this group to the improvement of instruction are guided by principles derived from a variety of areas of scholarship. This is evident in the present yearbook. The production, administration, and utilization of audio-visual instructional materials involve no new administrative or psychological principles. The contribution the present authors have made is to elaborate the implication for such teaching aids of theories and principles that have been developed in the study of other phases of the educational program.

Planning for this yearbook began early in 1946 with a series of outlines and supporting memorandums which were criticized by the Board of Directors of the National Society as well as by a number of other persons.[1] In February, 1947, the yearbook committee met in Chicago and reached a substantial concensus on the general nature of the yearbook. The major interest of the committee was in preparing a volume that would answer questions that practitioners might ask. It was agreed that the arguments and illustrations should be mainly

---

[1] The following individuals contributed to the development of the initial outline: James W. Brown, Edgar Dale, Amo DeBernardis, Virgil Herrick, Miss Marguerite Kirk, L. C. Larson, Francis Noel, Joe Park, Robert Schreiber, Lyle Stewart, Paul Wendt, and Paul Witty.

appropriate for classroom teachers but should not exclude the inquiries that might be made by administrators, supervisors, and producers. It was further agreed at this meeting that the yearbook should be organized so as to bear upon clusters of practical problems, rather than upon the different audio-visual mediums.

Following this February meeting various individuals in addition to the members of the central committee were requested to accept responsibility for specific chapters. The initial drafts were prepared by April, 1948. The central committee read these manuscripts and reported their criticisms and suggestions to the authors. The final drafts were received for editorial revision late in the summer of 1948.

The first four chapters of the yearbook provide the orientation for a consideration of the practical problems with which teachers and school administrators are confronted in the use of audio-visual teaching aids. The initial chapter, "Communication in the Modern World," is intended to provide a broad frame of reference for the consideration of the educational values of audio-visual materials. Chapter ii then introduces the kinds of materials that are to be considered in subsequent chapters of the yearbook and describes the present status of their utilization in schools. In chapter iii the major obstacles to a more widespread use of a variety of teaching aids and possible ways of overcoming them are explained. Chapter iv deals with the general problems faced by teachers in all sorts of instructional situations. In this discussion, specific attention is given to the relationship between the decisions teachers reach when facing these instructional problems and their ideas about instructional materials.

Chapters v and vi describe the present status of preservice and in-service education with respect to audio-visual instructional materials and suggest needed developments. The next four chapters describe what is being done and what should be done in audio-visual instructional materials programs involving geographic and political units of various types and explain the responsibility of the administrator in any type of instructional materials program.

In chapter xi, Mr. Larson and his associates have attempted to identify the questions that are asked most frequently about audio-visual materials and programs, and they have furthermore indicated what they believe to be reasonable answers. These answers are based upon research data when available; otherwise, they represent the best judgment of experienced practitioners. This discussion is followed by a summary of the major investigations involving audio-visual instructional materials—their production, utilization, and administration.

The final chapter, prepared by Mr. Wittich after reading the final draft of the yearbook in galley-proof form, represents the author's unique way of summarizing the essential contributions of the yearbook and of attempting (to borrow his own explanation) "to build a more favorable attitude toward the relationship which a whole array of audio-visual materials may have in building the kind of a learning environment through which our children may learn."

CHAPTER I

COMMUNICATION IN THE MODERN WORLD

FLOYDE E. BROOKER
Chief, Visual Aids to Education
U.S. Office of Education
Washington, D. C.

THE SOCIAL SIGNIFICANCE OF COMMUNICATION

Introduction

This is the problem of the classroom today: Can the teacher teach as much as he is supposed to teach—as he must teach—with the methods he is using? Can he compete with the modern media of communication, the comic-book, the motion picture, the radio, so that the schools can perform their basic role in the world of today? Can he be certain that, with the methods now in use, the school of today will graduate students who can cope with and even lead the world they will inherit?

Everyone has heard that civilization has now at its command a power so great that it can destroy itself. The teacher knows, as teachers everywhere have always known, that a civilization can destroy itself just as effectively, if less dramatically, by the failure to educate the younger generations in managing the world they inherit.

It is the purpose of this chapter to study the problem of communication as a social institution, to describe briefly its historical background, to trace the development of pictorial forms of communication, and then to consider the implications for education of some aspects of the developing crisis in communication.

The Aims and Methods of Communication

Teachers "tell" their students something by every movement of their bodies and every expression of their faces. And the students respond to these messages. Every teacher teaches what he says, but, even more effectively, he teaches what he is. We tend to think of communication as being a matter of words, and of words alone. This, in spite of the fact that every people has adages to the effect that "actions speak louder than words," that "seeing is believing."

Communication may be defined as anything that conveys meaning, that carries a message from one person to another. The "message" exchanged may be an idea, a feeling, an attitude, a philosophy of life, a skill—anything that one person believes is important to tell another.

The pitch of a baby's cry is a message for its mother, the wink that accompanies a bit of conversation may change its entire meaning, a railroad watchman may hold his hand to his nose and so bring a passing train to an emergency stop, a mother and father exchange glances at the dinner table and the children await the decision of the united front they know has just been formed. The picture of a girl on the lighted screen moves, her hair falls down bewitchingly over one eye, and a million girls go out and have their hair cut in the same style. A man sits in his home and gives the whole nation "a fireside chat." The teacher frowns, and the students become quiet.

All this is the subject matter of communication. In every case a message has been expressed, received, and understood. In every case a new relationship has been established. People communicate when they feel the need to secure a new adjustment to other people or when they wish to influence other people. Communication is successful to the degree that it effects the desired adjustment or influences other people.

Importance of the Study of Communication

Communication is thus the very essence of education, of religion, and of all the other institutions basic to society. The group, the community, the nation, the civilization exist only by virtue of the means of communication. For, without communication, common action by the group would be impossible. Thus, when a revolt takes place or a nation is overwhelmed, the first target is the key communications center. The world knew when Warsaw fell, for it no longer heard the "Polonaise."

The word *communication* is used throughout this discussion. The frequency with which the term is used indicates that it needs to be studied with reference to its role in the processes of education and to the changes that have happened within the lifetime of the present generation. Had this chapter been written fifty or sixty years ago, the word *communication* would hardly have been used, for verbal language was almost the only means of conveying messages to any large group of people. The use of printed material or travel were the only ways that space could be overcome for the masses of people.

But times have changed. The motion picture and all the related forms of pictorial communication have provided us with a new way to convey messages. Television marks a further step in man's mastery of time and space. The radio enables millions to hear a single voice and makes the people of the world onlookers at events of national importance. The mass duplication of pictures, the making of pictures that move, the showing of pictures of events as they happen, the opening of the living room to the voices of the world—these have changed the scene in the past generation, and it is time that we consider some of the implications of that change.

There is no longer a "single" way of conveying subject matter. The advent of the motion picture, of television, and of radio have given us a wide choice of media, of ways of conveying a message. And the problem of the teacher today is that of making a choice. A study of the media of communication is, therefore, of primary concern to all educators. For education is effective to the degree that the media of communication are effective. The school has lagged badly in the use of these new media and finds itself in competition with other enterprises that influence populations. It is a characteristic of the times that the amount of teaching the schools must do is increasing rapidly. This responsibility, the schools cannot safely disregard. The challenge to the schools is envisioned in the following commentary.

New millions of participants in the control of general affairs must now attempt to form personal opinions upon matters which were once left to a few. At the same time the complexity of these matters has immensely increased. The old view that the only access to a subject is through prolonged study of it, has, if it be true, consequences for the immediate future which have not yet been faced. The alternative is to raise the level of communication through a direct study of its conditions, its dangers, and its difficulties. The practical side of this undertaking is, if communication be taken in its widest sense, education.[1]

ANALYSIS OF LANGUAGES, MEDIA, AND FORMS OF COMMUNICATION

Definition of Language

A study of communication begins with the understanding that verbal language is only one of many ways of conveying a message. In the course of history, man has used almost everything in his environment, and almost every power of his physical being, as a

---

[1] C. K. Ogden and I. A. Richards, *The Meaning of Meaning.* p. x. New York: Harcourt, Brace & Co., 1936.

vehicle to carry his messages and to receive messages from others. He grunted his way to phonetic speech, fingered and daubed his way to art, used his muscles to develop the many forms of the dance, and learned to give meaning by the pitch of his voice and by the way he used the muscles of his face. He gathered pieces of sticks and layed them in his track, blazed trees to tell others of the path, used the smoke of his campfires to carry his messages, used his hands to talk with strangers, developed rituals to tell the story of the tribe; and, finally, like Prometheus, reached into the clouds to make his messages ride the lightning.

Thus languages developed, for a language is a system of signs on which there is general agreement as to the meaning. This agreement is seldom complete. Even with all the refinements of the English language, there is disagreement at times over the meaning of rather common words, for example, the word "education."

It is a significant fact, too, that no single language ever expresses satisfactorily the whole of experience. Every individual needs and uses more than one language. No language ever duplicates another, for each language is an art form and exists only because it can express an area of experience better than other languages can. Dewey makes an interesting observation on this point:

> The needs of daily life have given superior, practical importance to one mode of communication, that of speech. This fact has unfortunately given rise to a popular impression that the meanings expressed in architecture, sculpture, painting, and music can be translated into words with little if any loss.[2]

It is as fallacious, therefore, for the teacher to teach the motion picture, "Jane Eyre," and think he is teaching the English classic as it would be for someone to teach a poem named the "Fifth Symphony" in the belief that he is teaching Beethoven.

Again, all languages are constantly growing and undergoing changes. Music, for example, has its "modern" and its "classical" school, with the devotees of each claiming they cannot "understand" the other.

Finally, no language is a pure type of expression of ideas. Gestures may accompany speech, songs combine words with music, rituals usually combine many languages, and the sound motion picture is probably the most eclectic of all, using motion pictures, words, music, and an infinite variety of sound effects.

---

[2] John Dewey, *Art as Experience*, p. 106. New York: Minton, Blach & Co., 1934.

Significant Trends in the Use of Language

As we consider the various types of languages some trends may be observed which have importance for the teacher. These trends can be only briefly outlined here, but the individual teacher can extend the outline in terms of her own subjects and experience.

Trend To Reach Ever Larger Groups of People. This reflects the basic needs of the group, which could not grow larger until a common means of communication made group action possible. Provence could not become a part of France until all France, including Provence, was speaking the same language.

This need motivated the application of the fruits of the industrial revolution to communication and gave us, in turn, the printing press, cheap paper, the postal system, the telegraph, the telephone, the still picture, the wireless, the motion picture, the radio, and television.

As populations grew, the need for everyone being literate became ever more important, so there developed a tremendous impetus for popular education, which the printing press now made possible.

Trend from the Transitory to the Permanent, from the Face-to-Face to the Distant. As the group grew beyond the size which a single individual could address, and as group action followed from directions (royal edict, for example), it became more desirable to have a "record" of messages that might be important to the masses, in order that the audience might be extended geographically and in terms of time; for example, what the Pope said to a group might be read in Paris and studied during the months to come.

When we come to the development of pictorial forms of communication, more will be said on this point. It remains here, however, to indicate one implication of this trend for the classroom teacher. When the development of permanent records started, there followed a new and major task for teachers. If printing had not developed an almost universally available medium of mass communication, our English-literature texts would be much smaller than they are now. The primary task in the teaching of English literature is that of selection. The same will be true of the social studies, and, indeed, of many other areas of the curriculum when the collections have grown more extensive and when the teachers become aware of the implications. For what has already happened in English literature will happen in other areas as the sound motion picture, radio transcriptions, recordings, and other forms of records become more widely used.

As the Audience Increased, the Ratio of the Number of the People Who Could Receive a Message to the Number Involved in Sending It

Was Increased. The number of those who express themselves and those who receive the message is equal only in the intimate face-to-face languages. With the advent of the printing press, the number who received the communication increased over those who expressed it. Even the early publications, however, permitted some form of "letter-to-the-editor," and it was not too difficult for the individual to get his own press. Modern mass media permit little talking back. The individual may take his own amateur movies, but only his friends will see them. Few individuals will ever have access to the radio, television, or motion picture for self-expression.

This centralization of mass media, with its paramount importance in terms of group action, gives us the dictator who controls minds by controlling the material, the knowledge, and the information others are allowed to receive. It is also the key to the concern of many governments over the mass media. Most governments exercise a rigid control over the entire output of their radio and motion-picture studios.

As the Mass Media Reached an Ever Greater Audience, the Training Required To Understand Them Decreased. In general, it is easier to understand oral than written English. Hitler, in *Mein Kampf*, mentioned the power of spoken words. Certainly pictures are the most easily understood of all communication media. Few people would require eight years of schooling to understand a motion-picture communication. Approximately this period is required to attain an acceptable mastery of the English language. Whether or not an individual understands a given paragraph is another matter.

This fact constitutes one of the bright hopes of the mass media, that through them we may be able to jump centuries in creating a genuine world literacy and in bringing every hamlet of the world into the stream of world affairs.

The full implication of this fact regarding pictures has not been understood by educators. It is in this medium that we have our greatest potential in enabling the schools to impart more knowledge to more people more quickly.

Modern Mass Media Recapture the Characteristics of Intimate Face-to-Face Communication. Mention has already been made of this, but it should be noted that the need for the intimate overtones of face-to-face communication gave the spur to invention until this intimacy could be captured and the final mastery of time and of space could be achieved in communications. Television is, as yet, so new that we cannot assay its effect, and we can only guess at its power.

Modern Mass Media Tend To Combine Several Languages To Con-

vey Their Message. In addition to recapturing the power of the intimate face-to-face languages, modern mass media tend to form combinations with other languages, such as music. Television and the motion picture exploit the advantages of the dance, of painting, and of all the other graphic arts. This enables them to carry a richer load of meaning than any previous language or other medium of communication. It also introduces a new dimension in the total task of understanding them, learning how to put them to better use, and appreciating their full impact on civilization.

Summary

Language is a system of signs, each with a generally agreed-upon meaning. Man, during the centuries, has developed many languages and uses many of them today. Each has separate characteristics; each communicates different messages; no two of them duplicate each other. Much of the power of mass-communication systems today lies in their use of many languages to convey their meaning, in recapturing the power of the intimate face-to-face languages, in the size of the audience they reach, and in the fact that ever less training is required to understand their message.

THE COMMUNICATIONS REVOLUTION

Relation between the Industrial Revolution and the Communications Revolution

How did this happen to us—this creation of the mass media that enables dictators to sway millions, that enables public-relations experts or a single man to "engineer consent"? To understand this, we must also understand the industrial revolution.

Mention has been made in the previous section of the need to teach larger groups of people. Some indications have also been given of how that need led to the application of the fruits of the industrial revolution to communications. Space will not permit more than a brief outline of this development and of its present-day implications.

The industrial revolution itself created great demands for better communication and for communication with ever larger groups of people. Capitalism required strict accounting of time and money; people could not be induced to do the same thing at the same time, as is required by the machines, until there was a common language of communication; payment could not be separated from point of time and work done until a strict accounting of both was commonly understood and mutually accepted. The factory made mass production possible, and, as markets close at hand were saturated with the product, new markets became necessary. This demand for wider markets also created a demand for wider spread of a common means of communication. The fluctuation of markets created a simultaneous demand for quicker communication. Lloyds of London, for example, used carrier pigeons and a special courier to inform them of the results of the Battle of Waterloo.

These demands of the industrial revolution led to the increasing application to communication of new techniques, new inventions, and new scientific knowledge. It is interesting to note how often artists played a role in this. Morse and Daguerre, for instance, were both artists who played key roles in the communications revolution, giving us, respectively, the telegraph and the basis for photography.

Recency of the Communications Revolution

It cannot be stressed too often that the real flowering of the communications revolution, if one can presume to look into the future, has come in the lifetime of people now living. The telephone, the automobile, the airplane, the wireless, the still camera, the motion picture, color photography, mass reproduction of color pictures in national magazines, mass reproduction of picture, radio, facsimile, television, and telefax have all come since 1870. The development of hard-rubber records and the phonograph and the use of wire and tape recorders are additional illustrations.

Implications of the Communications Revolution

The very recency of the full impact of the communications revolution has created a world in which we as teachers are still "not at home." Some of the impact of the communications revolution have been felt for centuries and have created the world in which we find ourselves today. In the main, these are the direct results of the development of the printing press and of the production of cheap paper. Among the results of these early aids to communication may be listed the following:

The Impetus Given to Modern Science and Technology. The avenues of cheap diffusion of knowledge, opened by the printing press, gave a tremendous impetus to science and technology. Skills and knowledge were no longer confined to the few; they could be put on paper and learned by many. Men, thousands of miles apart in space and centuries apart in time, could read of the experiments of others and then begin their own work where others had stopped.

The craft mores of a thousand previous years were changed. The tradition of the medieval guildsman was the careful maturing of special skills and processes, keeping the secret of them, and then passing them down within the family from father to son. The mores of the scientist were now developed whereby prestige came to the man who published most, who told the world his secrets.

Impetus to Political Democracy. Again the development of cheap printing that could be disseminated far and wide planted the seed of political democracy. If it were necessary for men to act together in the factory, it was also possible for them to act together politically. Men who act together do better when they understand "why"; hence, mercenary armies gave way to citizen armies who demanded of their government a "fourth estate" and to know "why."

This trend continues today. Time is given on the radio and full-page advertisements appear in the newspapers for the candidates of the political parties. The same media are also being used to plead before the public the case of the comic-book publishers, the stock market, the unions, and the action of a foreign power.

Impetus to Popular Education. It was only a short step from political democracy to popular education. Democracy requires that as many people as possible be able to understand group communication. Schools were therefore established for the primary purpose of developing literacy.

The growth of the schools and the application to the problem of education of the developments of the industrial revolution aptly illustrated the characteristics of the communications revolution. The printing press was developed in the middle of the fifteenth century, but the full fruits of this development could not come until a plentiful supply of inexpensive paper was available. Paper in England cost roughly fifty cents a sheet in 1500 and, a hundred years later, still cost forty cents. As late as the end of the seventeenth century the records show that the books were still chained at the Bolton Literary School.

The high cost of paper stimulated the use of substitutes—the wax tablet, the slate, the smooth wooden board, as well as the board painted black. Even these developments were slow. Brinsley mentions the blackboard in his *Ludus Literarius* of 1612, Comenius had pictured one in 1658, but we have no record of its use in schools until about 1800, and no mention is made of slates for individual pupils until about 1815. Again and again the records of the early schools disclose the complaints of the parents over the cost of each new innovation, and the introduction of student slates was the cause of public disturbances.

In spite of the slowness of these developments, the printing press opened channels for the wider diffusion of knowledge. As new information and knowledge became available to the mass of people, the developing political democracy provided them with a constantly expanding means of applying this new knowledge to their daily lives. This impetus continues in the development of adult education and of kindergartens. And in spite of the complaints often registered against the practices of the commercial mass media, it must be remembered that many radio and television programs, films, and publications are highly educational in character. It is unlikely that any battle in all history was so real to so many people as the landing of the troops on the Normandy Beaches on D-Day, or that the life of the Navy personnel was ever more real than that presented in "Fighting Lady."

Impetus to the Generalization of the Interests of People. As the mass media have flooded the country with news of the other nations of the world, there has followed a generalization of the lives of people unprecedented in all history. News from all the world is available. As events remote in terms of space become increasingly important in our daily lives and as the mobility of the population increases, people tend to find their chief interests in societies and events that lie outside their community.

With this lessened concentration of interest in the community, there follows a gradual breakdown in the force of conventions, traditions, group mores, and customs. The ancient boundaries and molding forces of the personality tend to blur, and many individuals have feelings of insecurity.

This feeling is enhanced by the world-wide news service dumping the problems of the entire world into the lap of the average citizen. The frown of a man thousands of miles away, artillery fire in Jerusalem, and the elections in Italy are all news and are the concern of the man on the street. They are remote, yet they add to the feelings of frustration and helplessness of the modern man; their remoteness makes teaching about them in the school both difficult and important. No man today can live in isolation, for this is the world which affects our daily lives, the world we must live in, the world we must teach.

Mass Media Have Created a New Cultural Force. If, on the one hand, the modern media create feelings of insecurity and frustration, they offer, on the other hand, escapist entertainment. They give reality to fairy stories, they create dream creatures who live as all of us want to live, dream creatures that are so very real because we "see" and "hear" them. We know how they hold their hands, brush their teeth, accept or give a kiss—and knowing these things we, too, become a part of the dream.

It is indicative of these, our times, that the people who entertain us draw the highest salaries of our society. The very details that we can see and hear of these dream creatures have given us a new cultural force. For countless centuries groups have been held together by mores, customs, or traditions. These decided the really important things of living—when a girl "dated," what was the status of divorce, the hopes and dreams of the people. These things were never taught in school, they were absorbed as a part of living in the group.

Now, however, the films are bringing life from the outside world. They make it possible by their very specificity to develop a new set of mores, and the films are becoming a cultural force which may provide their own mores and customs.

This new force is one that must be reckoned with. For, as Sherif and Sargent have indicated:

> Thus the mass media, by selecting and stressing certain themes at the expense of others, have the effect of creating and perpetuating ego-involvements which will not endanger the status quo. The values stressed are typically those which make no contribution to the processes of social change.[3]

The Mass Media also Offer Bright Hopes for the Future. If they provide a new cultural force and if, perchance, this is a conservative one, they also provide educators with an opportunity to jump generations in the teaching of those areas where emotional involvement has prevented instruction in the past. They offer a most powerful tool for teaching man really to "know himself" and, thus, to stay the disruptive forces of our times which have already created so great a problem of emotional maladjustment.

THE DEVELOPMENT OF PICTORIAL FORMS OF COMMUNICATION AND THEIR APPLICATION TO EDUCATION

Early Uses of Pictorial Forms

The use of pictures to communicate is as old as history. Our earliest records are the paintings of the cave-dwellers. Our earliest written languages were picture signs. Even after the development of phonetic language, when masses of the people could neither read nor write, the picture symbols (the cross, the wedding ring, the flag) were used to hold the group together. The picture tapestries, the picture symbols of heraldry and of the medieval guilds (barber pole), were used

---

[3] Muzafer Sherif and Stansfeld Sargent, "Ego-involvement and the Mass Media," *Journal of Social Issues,* III (Summer, 1947), 16.

to inform and to teach. From the earliest writings, pictures were also a part of the literature, if we count the illuminated manuscripts and the woodcuts used in many of the early products of the printing press.

The printing press permitted the mass mechanical duplication of words, but pictures were still done by hand and still had to be individually pasted into the book. With the growth of modern languages and the development of mechanical printing, practical supremacy of the verbal forms of communication became complete. As Mumford states it:

> More than any other device, the printed book released people from the domination of the immediate and the local. Doing so, it contributed further to the dissociation of the medieval society: print made a greater impression than actual events, and by centering attention on the printed word, people lost that balance between the sensuous and the intellectual, between image and sound, between the concrete and the abstract. . . . . To exist was to exist in print: the rest of the world tended gradually to become more shadowy. Learning became book-learning and the authority of books was more rapidly diffused by printing, so that if knowledge had an ampler province so, too, did error.
>
> . . . .
>
> Paper removed the necessity for face-to-face contact: debts, deeds, contracts, news were all committed to paper, so that, while feudal society existed by virtue of customs that were rigorously maintained from generation to generation, the last elements of feudal society were abolished in England by the simple device of asking peasants who had always had a customary share in the common lands for some documentary proof that they had ever owned it. Custom and memory now played second fiddle to the written word: reality meant "established on paper." Was it written in the bond? If so, it must be fulfilled. If not, it could be flouted. . . . . A paper world came into existence, and putting a thing on paper became the first stage in thought and action: unfortunately also often the last.[4]

This paper world is still with us. We can remember the shock after World War I when we read how we had been tricked—that what we had read was not so but was deliberate propaganda. We know that we are geared verbally to handle "declarations of war" and "strikes," but we falter when a nation takes over another nation without a "declaration" and when men simply walk off the job.

The impact of the "paper world" was even greater on education. "The divorce between print and firsthand experience was so extreme that one of the first great modern educators, John Amos Komensky

---
[4] Lewis Mumford, *Technics and Civilization*, pp. 136-37. New York: Harcourt, Brace & Co., 1934.

(Comenius), advocated the picture-book for children as a means of restoring the balance and providing the necessary visual association."[5] This revolt against "book learning" was central in the teachings of Froebel, Pestalozzi, and others, continuing down to our own time.

Always the teacher who sought to use the specificity of pictures was handicapped by the difficulties of picture reproduction. Many tried it, such as Robert Owen, who in 1816 was using "painted examples from Natural History framed so as to pass before the children on rollers." The application of pictures to playing cards (the game of "Authors" is an example) came early in the sixteenth century, as did the use of puppets; and the jigsaw puzzle to teach geography came about 1850. But it was not until the development of the half-tone process that pictures could be incorporated in the mechanical processes of producing a book. So it was not until after 1880 that pictures could become an integral part of texts that were inexpensive and available to all.

With the advent of the motion picture, many thought first of all of its usefulness in education. Edison predicted that it was "destined to revolutionize our educational system. . . . . The education of the future, as I see it, will be conducted through the medium of the motion picture, a visualized education." Actually many problems had to be solved, such as safety films and smaller and less expensive projectors, before films could be genuinely applied to the problems of education. These are problems which we have not as yet completely solved.

Recent Developments

No discussion of pictorial media of communication would be complete without a brief discussion of their role in the training of the armed forces, their use in the commercial world, and their modern role in education. The fuller discussion of their role in education will be left to subsequent sections of this division.

The Role of Pictures in Training of the Armed Forces. Perhaps the most significant program in the use of these media was in the training program of the armed forces. They faced the task of training over twelve million men and women in over fourteen hundred specialized jobs, in a wide variety of educational objectives to be served in a wide variety of subject matter. To do this, the armed forces produced many differing types of audio-visual aids. Among these were over five thousand sound motion pictures and over three thousand filmstrips.

---

[5] *Ibid*, p. 136.

This was in addition to a wide variety of other forms of visual aids. The success of this program is reported in chapter xii of this yearbook.

It can be said that the experience of the armed forces differed from that of the usual school in that they had unlimited funds, the use of training aids could be "commanded," and the strongest motivation of all could be employed, namely, to learn how to keep alive. But in spite of this, there is much in the armed forces' experience that has benefited education. Among these could be listed:

1. A body of over one thousand films remained and are in use in the schools today.
2. New cinematic skills and new experiments are used in adapting films to new and, hitherto, untried areas of educational objectives.
3. A pioneering effort is being made with many visual-aids devices and the different ways of using them.
4. Millions of men and women who experienced training through films, and who in the main liked it, came to regard films in training as customary and to be expected.

In the long run the period of World War II will mark the crossover from regarding films as an educational luxury to regarding them as a necessity. It is likely, also, that, as World War I gave great impetus to the testing movement in education, World War II may give the same impetus to audio-visual education.

The Use of Pictures in the Commercial World. We need not discuss this in much detail here, since the facts are well known. It is of importance to all teachers to note, however, that increasingly the large audiences of the world are picture audiences. Eighty-five millions of people attend the theatrical motion picture weekly; five hundred million comic-books are published annually; the magazines which have the largest circulations are, with few exceptions, essentially picture magazines; the newspapers are constantly increasing the space given to pictures; and television, in competition with radio, gains the attention of an audience.

The same thing is true but with less force in the nontheatrical field. Practically all of the national industries and business organizations are using films for the training of their employees, for advertising their products, and for institutional public relations. The public audience viewing these films each year will run approximately a hundred million, and five to ten million dollars are being spent annually on their production. These figures, compared with the theatrical audience of the film, are small, but they are still much larger than those for strictly educational films.

The Use of Pictures in Education. It is in formal education that the use of the new mass media has lagged the most. Some comfort can be gleaned from the fact that within a period of ten years the number of 16-mm. sound projectors leaped from less than five hundred to well over twenty-five thousand, but even this loses some of its force when we consider that we have over two hundred thousand school buildings with over seven hundred thousand classrooms in this country. Compared with the average expenditure of the school child for theatrical films, for comic-books, and for candy, the average annual expenditure for audio-visual materials of instruction of approximately twenty cents per school child per year shrinks to insignificance.

Again, and over great handicaps, progress is being made. New and more convenient projectors are available, films are being geared in with textbooks, and, increasingly, teacher-training institutions are giving courses in audio-visual education.

Unique Values in Pictures

The real significance of visual aids taken as a whole can be best comprehended by considering their basic nature. The entire gamut of pictorial forms of communication, including the poster, the chart, the graph, the still picture, the slide, the filmstrip, and the motion picture, constitute competitive media of communication as complete potentially as the all-of-life they can express. By analogy, we may compare the possible message of a poster to that carried by a single word or sentence, the message of a filmstrip to that carried by a paragraph or series of paragraphs, the message of a motion picture to that of an entire chapter or book. The charts and graphs constitute the quantitative aids of pictorial communication as the Arabic numbers constitute the quantitative expression of the English language.

We have spoken of the mass media and indicated the press, the radio, and the motion picture. This should not hide the fact that communication via the motion picture is primarily based on a different language than that used on the radio. This difference is obscured by the fact that the distinctions between picture language and verbal language are disregarded because television, the newspaper, and the motion picture all use pictures and words in combination. Throughout this discussion the terms "film" and "motion picture" have often been used as a species of shorthand to denote the whole field of picture language.

This new language, as yet, lacks the basic structure that is necessary to make it a full language, although there are signs that this is being achieved. The achievement of its full potential awaits a broader realization that it is in reality a new language, a better understanding of its forms of expression, and a more complete application of its possibilities.

Pictures have yet to find their appropriate place among the media of communication. It may be said that the development of the educational and other types of films, such as the documentary and training, mark the first crude refinements. In the development of the automobile, we had first a crude model; now there are many different forms of the automobile, as the touring car, the station wagon, the truck, and the roadster. So we may expect many additional refinements of the motion picture, each refinement being more sharply focused on serving a specific kind of educational purpose. Because the motion picture is new and because it still requires refinement, we do not yet know fully the role of this new language in the total job of instruction. It will suffice to say that we know, in some instances, that pictures, and pictures only, will suffice to communicate the necessary ideas. For example, a simple line will give a better impression of the irregularity of the eastern seacoast of the United States than any amount of words could do. On the other hand, there are areas where pictorial forms of communication have little to contribute.

EDUCATION AND THE CRISIS IN COMMUNICATION

A Challenge to Teachers

The doctor who knows nothing of sulfa drugs or of penicillin is hardly likely to be the kind of individual to whom we would entrust the medical care of our children. The fact that these drugs did not exist when he went to school, or that their use was not taught in the medical schools he attended, would not serve as an excuse nor would it justify his continuing in practice.

Should we expect any less of the teacher? Do not the members of the teaching profession have the same responsibility for keeping up to date in that knowledge and those developments which relate to their own profession? Do we have the right to continue to use the methods employed ten, twenty, thirty years ago, to continue teaching with a training that, in many instances, is out of date?

The concern of this chapter has been the outlining of the developments in communication to the end that teachers may see the whole range of languages and media of communication that the modern world has made available and to the end that they may be better able to trace the implications of recent developments in terms of application to their own classroom. In the ensuing paragraphs the discussion will be continued in terms of the current problems of education and in terms of the crisis in communication.

Problems of Education

It is obvious that the worlds of 1929 and 1949 are so different, the outlook of the future in each instance so different, that the education provided by the schools for these two worlds could not be the same. Education must change even as the times change, for education is preparation for effective and happy living as a wage-earner, citizen, and parent. The adjustment of education to the needs of life is always slow and always presents a series of problems. The problems that will be considered here are the teaching of the other languages of communication, the teaching of experiences that are ever more remote, and the necessity of teaching more learning experience more quickly. These do not constitute all the problems nor does this classification meet the requirements of logic, but an understanding of these problems and their implications will do much to develop the understanding requisite for the handling of other and related problems.

The Teaching of Other Languages and Skills of Communication. The schools, from their beginning, have stressed the three r's, reading, 'riting, and 'rithmetic. Two of these deal with the essentials of literacy and, if we consider arithmetic as the quantitative side of the English language, all three contribute to the mastery of communication.

There are few areas of the curriculum in which the lag of the schools is more apparent than in the development of literacy in the other languages of communication. And these other means of communication affect the lives of the students almost as much, if not as much, as does the English language. What of literacy in oral communication, in the pictorial forms of language? What of listening habits, of critical comprehension, of self-expression, of picture language?

Nothing written here should in any way minimize the importance of the mastery of the English language nor the importance of verbal language. We will always have words, and words will, as far as we can see in the future, remain the basic, practical medium of communication. The emphasis here is the failure to recognize other languages to the extent that they influence action and offer effective alternatives and the failure of the schools to consider them.

Can we complain of the poor quality of radio, television, or motion-picture programs until we have accepted the responsibility of teaching standards of taste, of discrimination, of appreciation?

The Schools Must Increasingly Teach Experiences That Tend To

Be More Remote. The riots in Bombay, the strife in Indonesia, the conflict over the government of Berlin, the choice of the ruler of China, the spread of disease in Mexico or North Carolina are all the concern of the citizens of this nation, for they all have a direct bearing on the actions of our government.

Even more important than these rather dramatic illustrations is the steadily increasing need for teaching the geography, economics, and politics of the entire world, as the world community develops. This is in keeping with the generalizing influence of modern communication which was discussed earlier.

All of this means that the things which the schools must teach will be increasingly remote from the day-by-day experience of the student in his home community. In part, this derives from the ability of modern communication systems to bring the entire world into the living room; in part it derives from the fact that in terms of military power, economics, health, and politics we live in a world community. If we are to give the student a real understanding and appreciation of the meaning of the hoof-and-mouth disease in Mexico, the failure to develop international control of the atomic bomb, the world conflict of ideologies, or the interdependence of nations, we are not likely to find experiences in the local community that will serve our educational purposes, nor are we likely to do it effectively in verbal terms.

The Need to Teach More Subject Matter. Both of the previous points could be repeated here, for both have implications for increasing the amount of teaching the schools must do. We need, however, to give special consideration to one of the most basic problems facing education, that of teaching an ever increasing body of subject matter.

Basically, education is a short cut whereby we teach to the younger generation all that preceding generations have learned and which is still relevant. If the school or educational system fails to pass on what has been previously learned, then the new generation must begin where the older generation started.

This risk is one that has been brought into sharp focus by the developments directly related to World War II. The amount of content that the schools must teach has increased greatly during the past two decades. Three factors have contributed to this need: (1) the increase of knowledge; (2) the increased scope of our concern politically and geographically; and (3) the increased scope of our concern with the personality of the child.

The amount of new knowledge accumulated during the past twenty years is startling. This increase has come about largely through scientific and technological advances, which have been so great that no phase of our life has remained untouched. Imagine the competency of a physicist who had not heard of nuclear fission, a radio repairman who had not seen television, a housewife who did not know the meaning of "frozen foods." Whole new areas of subject matter as in physics, chemistry, medicine, law, and engineering developed during these decades. All such increases in the body of knowledge relevant to life increase the amount of subject matter that the schools must teach.

We have during these same years increased the scope of our concern with the world. In terms of military power, economics, and health, we live in a world community. In the schools of yesteryear, the emphasis was largely on the history and development of the Graeco-Roman world. This is understandable since most of our own traditions are so largely based on that world. The fact remains that the majority of the peoples of the world live in the Far East, in Oceania, in India, in the Islamic world, and in China. Few of us can name any of the great poets, artists, craftsmen, rulers, or leaders of these cultures, and we are poorly equipped for the development of an intelligent understanding of these people. Yet, how else can we hope for that sympathetic understanding so necessary for the development of the world community and of international peace? Taking on this task, inevitable and necessary as it is, increases the body of subject matter which the schools must teach.

Finally, the schools of today are more concerned with the personality of the student. The school is finding it necessary to be as concerned with the emotions of the students as it has been traditionally concerned with their minds. Recent figures of the numbers of our youth rejected by the armed services for emotional maladjustments, the increasing number of patients in our mental hospitals, and the increased concern with problems of juvenile delinquency are all indications that the schools will take increasing cognizance of this problem.

The problem of more teaching is not entirely a new problem in education. The schools have had to meet it ever since their beginning, and, traditionally, they have met it by increasing the period the child remained in school, by increasing the burden of the instructors, and by starting specialization earlier.

It is unlikely that any of these traditional solutions can continue to meet the problem. We have increased the number of days of the school year, the number of hours in the school day, and the number of years of required school attendance. The voluntary increases—the requirements of advanced institutions—have been even greater until a person studying for a profession is likely to be twenty-five years of age before he is ready to earn a living. We have increased the size of our textbooks and increased the number of subjects until the average instructor feels he is burdened beyond the point where an effective job can be done. One textbook has so many concepts in it that the instructor is expected to teach a concept every three to four minutes of classroom time, an expectation that cannot be realized. Finally, we have already started specialization of preparation so early that it is suggested we have too many butchers, bakers, and candlestick-makers and too few citizens. The increase of specialization in the vocational aspects of life came largely through a lessening of the concern with the individual as a parent and citizen. We have thus strengthened the divisive elements of our society at the expense of the integrative elements.

The Task of the Teacher

The meeting of these problems is the critical task of the teacher of the present day. They are problems faced daily in the classroom, and they are further the problems the teacher faces in his own personal life as an individual and as a citizen.

The crisis in communication affects us all and, in terms of the individual teacher, the resulting problem can be stated simply. What teacher can say he has read all the necessary reading? Who has the time to hear all the radio programs he would like to hear, to see all the motion pictures he would like to see, or to do all the other things he feels would be good to do? What teacher believes he knows all he needs to know to cast his ballot on the issues that affect this country today? What teacher today believes he has the time, the tools, or the skill to teach well all that he is supposed to teach?

Among teachers a common complaint is, "I do not have enough time to teach well what I am supposed to teach." The problem that faces the teacher is the realization that verbal language is no longer enough; he must master the other languages and media of communication and learn to apply them to the problems of the classroom. Thus, he will need to re-think the whole problem of communication and to examine learning situations to determine whether words or pictures will be more effective. For example, we know that a million words will never be as effective as a glance of two seconds at a rock, if the problem is developing an idea of the shape of the rock. But pictures are likely to prove of little value in the development of an understanding of mathematical formula. Yet we have considered that verbal language was the only language. Today our texts are filled with words straining to do what pictures can do more effectively and more quickly.

Our basic task is to discover whether words, pictures, recordings or some combination thereof will serve best, and then, using the media at our command, make education more effective by building a curriculum which will use each medium to the best advantage.

This will not be easy, for it makes a break with tradition. It means starting all over again to learn to listen, and to read pictures. It means using pictures not as illustrations, not as designs to break the monotony of printed pages, but as a language.

It means a curriculum that must be implemented largely in terms of the teacher's own ideas. It cannot consist of assignments of a given number of pages a day. But it means a curriculum in which, in terms of the objectives to be served, the teacher may use a film one day, a chapter in a textbook the next day, a demonstration the next, and a discussion the next.

It means putting to work in the classroom the media that have done so much to produce this modern world. It means that, in the teaching of experiences which are remote in space and time, we will have to use the media that have already brought the entire world into our living-room and made that world live. It means experimentation, it means hard work, but it is the task to which every teacher interested in being as effective and up to date as possible must put his hand.

The Role of Education in Communication

No group, no culture, no nation can be formed until the adequate means of communication make the formation of that group possible. Once the group is formed, communication is equally important in enabling the group to function as a group on matters of common concern. Group action is possible only so long as all the members of the group have free access to the necessary information, can develop opinions and judgments through the free interchange of views, can listen to or have available the judgments of their leaders. "Communication is more than the connective tissue of society; it is the nervous system as well." [6]

As the thirteen colonies became the United States and developed and grew into the world power with armies of occupation thousands of miles beyond the national boundaries, the burden on communication was continually being increased. This is a simple illustration, but it does serve to point up one of the problems of our times, as the group

---

[6] W. Hayes Yeager and William E. Utterback, "Foreword," *The Annals of the American Academy of Political and Social Science*, CCL (March, 1947), vii.

increases in size, the problems requiring group action increase in number and in complexity. Furthermore, as the group grows in size, the members of the group cease to be concerned with the group alone, and become interested in the entire world.

The increase in the number of problems, the complexity of these problems, and the increase in problems which require information and understanding relating to the entire world—all constitute additional burdens on communication. It becomes critical when the media of communication can no longer transmit all the information the citizens need for intelligent group action or when the citizens can no longer assimilate all the material that is available.

In the past, communication has with difficulty kept pace with the growing demands made upon it by social evolution. The resulting chronic maladjustment has now reached the dimensions of a crisis. Despite the remarkable contribution of science to the rapid transmission and appeal, it is a fair question whether modern man will succeed in understanding his world and his neighbors well enough and quickly enough to escape disaster. His struggle to understand has become a race between communication and disaster.[7]

If we are going to prove able to develop a world ruled by law with disputes being solved by judicial processes, if we are to develop adults who can master the technological world we have created, if we can solve the problems posed by a world in which joint action is required between nations of unequal development socially, educationally, and politically, if we can solve the problem posed by the fact that no modern, sovereign nation can any longer guarantee its citizens life, liberty, and the pursuit of happiness—it will have to be by education, and by education alone. To seek world unity and world peace by force is the denial of the very basis of our national existence, the democratic way of life.

This is the problem of today, and it comes to a sharp focus in the classroom and in the person of the teacher. He must acquire more knowledge in order to continue to be a good teacher and a good citizen, and he must constantly teach more subject matter to give his students an adequate education for a modern world. All this at a time when there are not enough hours in the day or days in the year to teach well what we know must be taught. We know that the "minds of men" are the first objective of the modern dictator, that the domination of the minds of men is the aim of the cold war, and that the minds of men must be made the first concern of the teacher.

One answer to this problem is the study of verbal language

---

[7] *Ibid.,* p. 7.

(semantics) to the end that verbal language may become a more efficient instrument of communication. Verbal communication will remain in textbooks and in oral English to structure our thinking, our course of study, and even our society.

Another answer is the continued use of the new media—the film, the radio, and television—in order that the advantages and powers of these media of communication may be applied to the problems of education, and that the power to present subject matter remote in time and space in a living manner may be utilized in the effort to teach more effectively.

REFERENCES

BEARD; DONCASTER; MCALLISTER; MCGLASHAN. *The Growth of Visual Education*, Parts I and II. London: Common Ground, Ltd., (Sidney Place), 1946.

BENT, SILAS. *Machine Made Man*. New York: Farrar Rinehart, 1930.

"Communication and Social Action," *Annals of the American Academy of Political and Social Science*, CCL (March 1947), 1-129.

DEWEY, JOHN. *Art as Experience*. New York: Minton, Blach & Co., 1934.

Films for International Understanding. A Project of Educational Film Library Association, Curriculum Service Bureau for International Studies. Edited by Elizabeth Flory. New York: Curriculum Service Bureau for International Studies, Inc., 1947.

GIPSON, HENRY C. *Films in Business and Industry*. New York: McGraw-Hill Book Co., Inc., 1947.

HAMPTON, BENJAMIN B. *A History of the Movies*. New York: Convici-Friede, 1931.

HOBAN, CHARLES F.; HOBAN, CHARLES F., JR.; ZISMAN, SAMUEL B. *Visualizing the Curriculum*. New York: Cordon Co., 1937.

HUXLEY, JULIAN. *UNESCO: Its Purpose and Its Philosophy*. Washington: American Council on Public Affairs, 1946.

INGLIS, RUTH A. *Freedom of the Movies: A Report on Self-regulation from the Commission on Freedom of the Press*. Chicago: University of Chicago Press, 1947.

JEWETT, FRANK B. *Science and Life in the World*, Vol. III: *A Challenge to the World*. Chapter on "Horizons in Communication," pp. 29-41. New York: Whittlesey House, 1946.

MACLEISH, ARCHIBALD. "The People's Peace," *Atlantic Monthly*, CLXXX (July 1947), 54-58.

"Mass Media: Content, Function, and Measurement," *Journal of Social Issues*, III (Summer, 1947).

MILES, J. R., and SPAIN, C. R. *Audio-Visual Aids in the Armed Services*. Washington: American Council on Education, 1947.

"The Motion-Picture Industry," *Annals of the American Academy of Political and Social Science*, CCLIV (November 1947), 1-172.
MOTT, FRANK LUTHER. *Golden Multitudes*. New York: Macmillan Co., 1947.
MULHERN, JAMES. *A History of Education*. New York: Ronald Press, 1946.
MUMFORD, LEWIS. *Technics and Civilization*. New York: Harcourt, Brace & Co., 1934.
NEBLETTE, C. B. *Photography Principles and Practice*. New York: D. Van Nostrand Co., 1939 (third edition).
"Neglected Areas of Curriculum Implementation," *Educational Record*, XX (April, 1939), 241-55.
OGDEN, C. K., and RICHARDS, I. A. *The Meaning of Meaning*. New York: Harcourt, Brace & Co., 1936.
SHERIF, M., and CANTRIL, H. *The Psychology of Ego-involvements*. New York: John Wiley & Sons, 1947.
SHERIF, MUZAFER, and SARGENT, STANSFELD. "Ego-involvement and the Mass Media," *Journal of Social Issues*, III, (Summer, 1947), 16.
YEAGER, W. HAYES, and UTTERBACK, WILLIAM E. "Foreword, *Annals of the American Academy of Political and Social Science*, CCL (March, 1947), vii.

CHAPTER II

SCHOOL USE OF AUDIO-VISUAL INSTRUCTIONAL MATERIALS

JAMES W. BROWN
Supervisor, Instructional Materials Center
University of Washington
Seattle, Washington

A. W. VANDERMEER
Associate Professor of Education
The Pennsylvania State College
State College, Pennsylvania

INTRODUCTION

Analysis of functions of various communications media in the modern world as developed in the preceding chapter is logically followed, for purposes of this yearbook, by a consideration of the present school use of audio-visual instructional materials. This chapter aims to do four things: (1) to explain the logical relationship of these materials to the learning process; (2) to emphasize the need for their integration with some of the more traditional instructional materials in use in schools; (3) to describe the present use of audio-visual materials at different school levels and in different areas of the curriculum; and (4) to indicate some of the observable trends in the development and use of these materials.

To define the term "audio-visual methods and materials" is difficult because all teaching materials and experiences involve either an "audio" or a "visual" factor or both. The *Dictionary of Education* (**16**) defines visual education as "all education based on the use of materials (other than books) that appeal directly to the sense of sight." Dale (**8**) does not define the term in his textbook,[1] but it may be

---

[1] On page 308, Dale writes, "Textbooks are insured of an important and honored place in teaching materials .... *despite the increasing use of audio-visual materials.*"

inferred from the title of his publication and from the materials and techniques he discusses that the only material excluded is the textbook. For purposes of this chapter, *audio-visual* instructional materials and methods are defined as those which do not depend exclusively upon comprehension of words or similar symbols.

AUDIO-VISUAL MATERIALS AND LEARNING EXPERIENCES
Types of Materials and Procedures

In this section, the major types of audio-visual materials will be described in connection with types of learning situations in which they are most useful. A final paragraph will be concerned with verbal symbols and their relationship to audio-visual materials and methods.

Direct experience is purposeful participation in a real-life situation in which the learner accepts responsibility for the outcome of the experience. All learning and understanding is rooted, directly or indirectly, in firsthand perceptual experiences. Direct experiences are generally indicated early in the course of the individual's instruction. They are the basis of so-called "work experience," apprenticeship, and man-to-man training in industry. In general education, construction activities, group and individual projects, laboratory work, and community surveys usually involve direct experiences for students. Work-experience or "work-study" programs, in which pupils spend part of their time in school-supervised work in industry and part of their time in organized classes, obviously rely heavily on direct experience. Members of a science class who developed their own formula for tooth powder and prepared some for their own use illustrate this type of learning experience.

Dramatic participation consists of taking part in or observing dramatizations and differs from direct experience in that in the former (a) the settings and properties of the real-life situation are usually fictitious, and (b) the pupils are less interested in the intrinsic outcomes of the activity than in what they will learn. High-school students may dramatize a scene in Congress, for example, or they may participate in legislative activities in their own student council. In the former case, the characters, setting, and properties are substitute, unreal, or make-believe, and the purpose is to learn and to convey to others the opinions and considerations influencing congressmen. In the latter case, the setting is real, the characters "play" themselves, and the passage or rejection of the legislation constitutes the primary purpose in the minds of students.

Dramatization provides an effective learning experience in certain areas of the curriculum at all levels of education in the form of plays, pageantry, puppetry, tableau, pantomime, and less formal dramatic situations and activities.

Contrived experiences differ from direct experiences in that, for reasons of economy or safety, the learner's activity involves only the "essential elements" of the corresponding environment for a direct, purposeful experience. A paper representation of the keyboard may be used in group instruction in piano, for example; or a mock-up of the driver's seat of an automobile may be used until the learner is sufficiently familiar with brakes, accelerator, and other features to be trusted at the controls of a real car. Contrived experiences may involve working models (as of a steam engine in physics), mock-ups (as of an office or store in business education), or cut-away models (as in automotive mechanics).

In *observational situations* the learner becomes a somewhat detached onlooker, and his participation in the situation is more imaginative and symbolic in contrast to the techniques described above which involve a high degree of direct interaction between the individual and a defined learning environment. The field-trip, school journey, or excursion is perhaps the most concrete of the observational techniques. Dale (8) defines it as "a planned visit to a point outside the regular classroom." Field trips may range from visits to the school boiler-room to a journey of several days' duration to Washington, D. C.

In *demonstrations,* some authority shows the learners an action or process. Since what is shown is usually removed from its natural environment, the demonstration is somewhat more abstract than the field trip. Demonstrations show how things are done, as for example, a method of proving a theorem in geometry or of turning an Acme thread on an engine lathe. The learner is usually expected to practice what he sees demonstrated. Demonstrations also show or explain principles or processes which the learner is expected only to understand, such as electrolysis of water.

Sometimes students learn by observing and examining objects, specimens, or models. Such experiences usually do not involve action "here and now" as do demonstrations. Exhibits consisting of an arrangement of objects, specimens, or models are used to show interrelationships and to suggest, in a static way, processes. Examples of observational activity range from visits to highly organized museums to the simple examination of frog-egg collections brought to a biology class.

The television broadcast is essentially two-dimensional and presents a learning situation which is, in reality, a representation of something spatially remote from the learner. In return for these limitations, television can bring the learner into somewhat intimate contact with situations which would otherwise be inaccessible. In so doing, television may provide timeliness, as does radio; and dual sense impressions, as does the sound film (41). Mechanical and legal limitations have, up to now, prevented general use of television in schools. For the three years preceding March, 1948, union musicians did not appear in television (40). Regulations regarding the televising of motion pictures are still in the process of being clarified. The limited geographic area covered by television stations and the relatively small size of viewing screens which constitute present-day mechanical deterrents to the widespread school-use of television are rapidly being overcome. As television becomes technically perfected it will develop tremendous potentialities because of its ability to create for the viewer an illusion of being present at the time and place of important events and performances.

Motion pictures have been in use in schools for approximately thirty years. During this time technological changes have tended to make them more economical and capable of presenting situations more realistically. Earlier motion pictures lacked sound; therefore, they were often necessarily more abstract as teaching materials than some of the more recent films. Development of various processes for photographing in natural color and for synchronized sound reproductions have made it possible for films to portray scenes, processes, events, and actions more nearly as they appear in real life. Postnarrated commentary may be timed with the pictorial element to present an effective audio-visual stimulus pattern. Indigenous sound in which the audience hears the sounds produced by the subject being pictured adds realism, as does lip-synchronized sound in which characters are seen and heard speaking. Probably the height of motion-picture realism is seen in full-color films with indigenous sound.

Motion pictures are inherently capable of unique abstractions which contribute to the communication of certain types of ideas. Among these abstractions are: (*a*) animation in which things that are difficult or impossible to see are presented in graphic form, (*b*) time-lapse and slow-motion photography in which action is speeded up or slowed down by means of varying camera speeds in relation to projector speeds, (*c*) telephotography by which distant objects are made to appear nearer, (*d*) photomicrography in which small subjects are made to appear larger, (*e*) microphotography in which large subjects are made to appear smaller, (*f*) coincidental photography in which two or more scenes are made to appear on the screen side by side (or in other nonsuperimposed positions) for purposes of comparison or contrast, (*g*) double exposure in which two or more subjects are more or less superimposed to create an effect of the supernatural, or other special effects, and (*h*) montage in which a variation of coincidental photography and/or rapid kalaedoscopic transitions from one scene to the next are combined with variations of camera angle and other techniques to create general emotionalized impressions. By means of the foregoing techniques and certain others, the unique mechanical features of the motion picture may be utilized to produce impressions of real-life situations which are abstractions in the sense that they may not be gained through direct observation and in that they require some degree of understanding of the symbolism of the motion-picture art.[2]

Still pictures may be divided into two classes: projected and nonprojected. Among the former are the filmstrip, the lantern slide, and the 2" x 2" slide. Nonprojected pictures include the pictorial print and the stereograph. All types of still pictures could, under certain conditions of projection or viewing, show the third dimension and color, but this is infrequently done in schools.

Filmstrips, sometimes termed "slidefilms" or "stripfilms," are usually made up of twenty to one hundred or more individual pictures printed on a roll of film of 35-mm. width. Verbal explanations of the pictures and sometimes continuity are provided by (*a*) titles which are superimposed on the pictures or printed on separate frames, (*b*) an accompanying "teacher's or leader's guide" in pamphlet form, or (*c*) a recorded lecture. The latter may sometimes include also dialogue and indigenous sound. Some filmstrips utilize combinations of the foregoing verbal accompaniments.

Lantern slides are the oldest form of projected picture. A photographically sensitive glass plate 3¼ by 4 inches may be used to record the positive pictorial image. Teachers and students often make their own lantern slides by drawing or printing on etched glass, clear plastic, or the gelatin-coated surface of plain glass. A number of companies have developed projectors which make it possible to project drawings on a screen while they are being made.

"Two-by-two" slides usually consist of individual positive trans-

---

[2] Ninth-grade general science pupils in Bellefonte, Pennsylvania, who had seen a motion picture of a puff adder were uncertain about the identification of a live specimen because "the one in the movie was so much larger." This is a clear example of an audience being misled by a "camera abstraction" (42).

parencies on 35-mm. film, masked and mounted in cardboard or between glass. Much of the popularity of the 2" x 2" slide can be traced to the fact that natural-color photographic processes now make feasible and economical the local production of full-color pictures for projection. Thus, students and teachers alike can make their own color slides. It is equally possible, too, to produce 2" x 2" slides in black and white.

Projected pictures are well adapted to use with groups. For individual use and for bulletin-board and other display purposes, photographs or pictorial prints are often more convenient, although there are available devices for the semipermanent display of 2" x 2" and 3¼" x 4" slides.

By means of an opaque projector, photographs up to 8½" x 11" can be projected for group use. Such a device is of value in using the rich resources of flat pictures that may be obtained from illustrated magazines, from certain picture publishers, and from other sources. Whenever a small picture, diagram, or similar device is of sufficient importance to serve as part of a basic classroom experience, the use of the opaque projector is indicated. This is true of textbook illustrations, even though a copy may be available to each child; for only when all students are looking at the same picture can the teacher be reasonably sure of directing attention accurately.

Collections of still pictures are valuable not only for presenting information but also for developing powers of observation and description, stimulating interest, and promoting growth in inference and awareness of interrelationships.

In past decades, collections of stereographs were popular instructional devices, especially in elementary schools. The three-dimensional effect achieved by means of a stereoscope, which splits the vision of the two eyes, is considered valuable in viewing landscapes, architecture, solid geometry diagrams, and for other instructional purposes. Recent improvements in 35-mm. stereoscopic cameras make possible local production of natural-color pictures which can be seen in the third dimension through inexpensive viewers.

Radio broadcasts, transcriptions, and recordings which portray auditory concepts may be considered as analogous to still pictures which are used for portraying visual concepts. However, except for the field of music, radio and recordings tend in practice to depend more upon verbal symbols and, hence, to be more abstract than still pictures.

Sporadic attempts to use radio programs in education began in the early twenties, and by 1936 broadcasting licenses had been granted to 202 educational institutions. By 1944 less than 25 noncommercial stations were still licensed to broadcast (**41**). National and regional networks and local commercial stations have broadcast a consistently large number of educational programs, however. Early attempts by commercial broadcasters to produce radio programs for classroom listening met difficulties in matching school curriculums and time schedules. Most such programs have now given way largely to programs of broad educational value for out-of-school listening. Certain larger school systems, such as Cleveland, Ohio, have broadcast to their own classrooms for a number of years (**27**).

Radio programs may be either "live" (using flesh-and-blood actors at the time of the broadcast) or transcribed (broadcast from recordings). News commentaries are typically in the former category and dramatic programs frequently are. Transcriptions, which are usually 16-inch discs recorded at $33\frac{1}{3}$ revolutions per minute, are frequently by-products of "live" radio programs. An example is the NBC "University of the Air," which is transcribed and released to schools through the Federal Radio Education Committee (**13**). It is sometimes said that a loss of timeliness results in recorded programs and that this is a distinct limitation of their usefulness. On the other hand, radio and recordings often provide the only means whereby students may hear the voices of important personages and authorities, or learn how the greatest artists interpret masterpieces of music and literature.

Ordinary phonograph records have a maximum diameter of 12 inches and are played at 78 revolutions per minute. Excellent recordings are plentiful in the areas of children's literature, dramatics, poetry, and music.

Recording devices utilizing disc, wire, film, or tape are being used with increasing frequency in schools. Such equipment may help (*a*) diagnose individual difficulties in speech and music, (*b*) provide "reference points" for self-evaluation by students of speech and music, and (*c*) preserve radio programs for repeated playings throughout the school day or term.

Graphic materials include maps, charts, graphs, diagrams, cartoons, posters. According to Hoban (**23**), the common characteristic of all these materials is their *selective representation* of forms, shapes, color, and relationships. The process of selection to which Hoban refers is, in reality, abstraction. Well-designed graphs and charts facilitate emphasis on comparisons and contrasts, quantity, proportion, and trend. Maps emphasize the contours and forms of the earth's surface and the location of resources, cities, and so on. Diagrams indicate space relationships and the sequence of operatons or occurrences. Cartoons and posters give importance to selected features of concepts and situations and, thereby, tend to create emotional dispositions toward their referents. For purposes of conveying a general idea dramatically and clearly, graphic representations bring some elements into bold relief and eliminate or subordinate others.

Graphics, as a class, constitute an excellent illustration of the truism that pupils should be considered as both "consumers" and "producers" of audio-visual instructional materials. In the sense that graphics are utilized for motivation, presentation, or testing, the pupil is a "consumer." It is equally important, however, that pupils learn to express themselves through making their own graphs or cartoons. The drawing of a diagram or the development of a table or chart may be a fruitful means for a student to learn a process or a set of statistics. In this sense, the pupil is a producer of audio-visual materials.

The Role of Verbal Symbols in Learning

Verbal symbols, including the spoken and written word and numbers, are the most abstract of instructional materials. The connection between such symbols and their meanings is usually arbitrary. Symbols used in graphs, diagrams, and posters usually retain some resemblance to the concepts they represent, but the meaning of verbal and numerical symbols must be learned without perceptual links to reality. However, once these abstractions are learned they often provide the most economical means of communicating ideas. The "tyranny of words" stems from the assumption that all people have learned to associate the same realities with verbal abstractions. A person cannot accurately communicate his ideas to another unless both attach the same meanings to the words or symbols used.

INTEGRATION OF AUDIO-VISUAL INSTRUCTIONAL MATERIALS
WITH THE SCHOOL CURRICULUM

Fundamentally, the tasks of the teacher are to select and to manipulate instructional materials and experiences so as to promote desirable changes in the total behavior of pupils. If in attempting to carry out these fundamental tasks the teacher is guided by an understanding of the interrelations between types of instructional materials on the one hand and types of learners and learning goals on the other, he must, by definition, integrate audio-visual materials with the organized curriculum. Integration is the process of selecting and arranging the order and method of use of all instructional materials in a manner which is appropriate to the nature of the teaching objectives to be achieved, the experiential level of the pupils, and the special aptitudes and interests of the pupils. The following illustration includes a brief description of instructional materials and procedures used in a representative teaching unit and an analysis of the psychological and pedagogical factors relating to the process or condition of integration. In this description the materials are mentioned in the order in which they were introduced.

UNIT ON THE SOLAR SYSTEM
Grade VII

1. Viewed 16-mm. sound film, "Trip to the Sky."
2. Discussed film, bringing out "fact and fancy" about our solar neighbors, and setting learning goals such as: What are names, sizes, motions, positions, and conditions of our neighboring planets?
3. Consulted textbook, encyclopedia, and reference works. (At this point students began to realize that the facts and figures like, "The earth is 93,000,000 miles from the sun" were not completely understood. From this point on, however, these works were continually consulted.)
4. Dramatized motion of planets around the sun. (One child was the sun; others, representing planets, "revolved" around him. Accurate relative distances, of course, were out of the question.)
5. "Built" a scale model of the sun and planets. (A large ball placed on the athletic field represented the sun. The earth was a medium-sized pea near the other end of the field. It was a three-mile jaunt by bicycle and on foot to locate Pluto, the outermost-known planet.)
6. Made drawings showing orbits of planets, and charts showing size, distance from sun, and period of rotation.
7. Located Venus, Jupiter, and Saturn during a night's "star-gazing" outing.
8. Viewed and discussed another 16-mm. sound film, "The Solar Family."

Curricular integration of audio-visual materials was achieved in this lesson, which involved the foregoing list of activities and materials, because certain psychological and pedagogical principles were applied:

1. No single type of material was considered to be basic. None stands out as essential to the success of the whole unit; none could be omitted without detracting seriously from the unit's success.
2. The sequence of events was built upon the necessity of arousing and maintaining interest; for providing a logical progression from goal setting, to related activity, to checking, and on to the next goal; and for summarizing. The film, "Trip to the Sky," had an emotional appeal which stimulated interest. The discussion following the film brought out conflicting opinions requiring reconciliation. Subsequent activities provided acceptable answers and cues for further activity. "The Solar Family" was a factual, "summing-up" type of film.

3. Within the unit certain activities, like the first reading of textbooks, helped to locate the experience and comprehension level of the children on a concrete-to-abstract continuum. Beginning then at the level of abstractness at which the children were known to be able to handle the essential concepts, the activities were organized to proceed from the more concrete to the more abstract.
4. When it was found that the pupils lacked the perceptual experience required to understand such an abstraction as, "The earth is 93 million miles from the sun and eight thousand miles in diameter," perceptual experience was provided in the field trip and other activities. Emphasis was placed upon understanding and comprehension, not upon memorizing or repeating the abstraction.
5. The characteristics of the concept to be taught influenced the choice of learning activities. It is obviously impossible to make a drawing in which both the size of the planets and their distances from the sun are to scale. The field trip on which the model of the solar system was built was the only way to hold the scale constant for both size and distance.
6. By using a variety of activities, it was more likely that every pupil, regardless of his peculiar abilities and interests, would find one thing he could do, understand, and enjoy. Some pupils mastered the concepts of size and distance by drawing. Others did not comprehend them until they had actually covered the three miles between the big ball that represented the sun and the small pea that represented Pluto.

It is apparent from the preceding paragraphs that the integration of audio-visual instructional materials and methods with the organized curriculum depends on a number of things: (a) a penetrating understanding on the part of the teacher of both subject matter and children, (b) freedom for the teacher to plan and conduct learning experiences without too much interference from time schedules and course-of-study outlines, (c) a variety of readily available teaching materials, and (d) flexibility and adaptability of physical conditions in the schoolroom. The teacher could not have taken the field trip on which the pupils built the scale model of the solar system if he had had to confine his teaching solely to single class periods. He probably could have forced the majority of students to memorize the sizes and distances from the sun of the planets in half the time required by the field trip and the subsequent chart-making. Teaching as he did, however, using a variety of materials to achieve real understanding, made it practically impossible to "cover the textbook." There was not enough time.

The chairs in the classroom had to be moved for the dramatization of the planet's revolutions. (It was still too crowded.) Two motion pictures and the equipment to show them had to be ready when needed. Beyond all this, the teacher had to know what films existed and which one should be used first. He also had to have the imagination to think of all the teaching-learning activities that could be used, and the interest and energy to employ those that were finally selected.

Present Practices in the Use of Audio-Visual Instructional Materials and Methods in the Schools

Use at Different Educational Levels

Use of audio-visual instructional materials and methods is not limited to any one level of education, although differences may be observed in both types and quantities available for use at different levels. Analysis of 3,758 sound and silent films contained in Part II of the Educational Film Guide (6), for example, reveals the following percentages for films according to the grade level for which they are rated as "useful":

Educational Level	Percentage of Usable Films
Primary grades and higher	4.15
Elementary grades and higher	20.45
Junior high school and higher	62.90
Senior high school and higher	86.40
College and adult	81.50
Adult only	77.10

Respondents to questionnaires in the National Education Association study of audio-visual education programs in city school systems (2) were asked to report the grade level at which the audio-visual program appeared to be strongest.[3] In larger cities (populations of 30,000 and over) from which 161 replies were received, and in all cities (regardless of size) in which audio-visual departments were maintained, ratings indicated that elementary teachers made more extensive use of motion pictures, radio broadcasts, recordings, models, charts, maps, pictures, exhibits, slides, filmstrips, and other audio-visual materials than did teachers at junior and senior high school levels. Ratings regarding the percentage of teachers who made use of films frequently,

---

[3] The N.E.A. study referred to may be criticized on at least two bases: (a) It dealt only with a survey of projected instructional materials and did not give attention to the vast use of nonprojected materials of instruction, and (b) it probably presents an unduly optimistic picture of school utilization of projected audio-visual materials since those systems with low utilization practices were undoubtedly in the majority among the nonrespondents.

occasionally, or never, showed that the median percentage of teachers using films "frequently" was somewhat higher at the secondary than at the elementary level. However, there appeared to be approximately the same percentage of teachers at all grade levels who "never" used films. We may infer from these data that elementary-grade teachers made use of more audio-visual materials of a "nonfilm" nature, since their over-all use of audio-visual materials was rated higher than that of junior or senior high school teachers.

Kindergarten-, primary-, and elementary-grade instructional materials and methods are influenced particularly by the nature of learners at these levels. Here emphasis is placed upon the use of realia (objects, specimens, sandtable models, models constructed by students), charts (word charts, flash cards), field trips (in the immediate environment), dramatic participation (enacting stories), teacher telling ("the story hours"), and listening to recordings (stories, music). An increasing production of sound motion pictures suitable for use with young children (such as "Adventures of Bunny Rabbit," "Safety to and from School," "Farm Animals," "The Fireman") offers opportunity for providing them with further realistic vicarious experiences. The frequent use of audio-visual instructional materials with young children is based on a belief that they should be introduced to verbal abstractions only when their experiential background is such as to make the words meaningful.

At the *junior and senior high school levels* departmentalization begins, and there often is more emphasis upon "academic instruction" and the learning of "essential facts." Here dependence upon the textbook is usually excessive. There tends to be less reliance upon learning experiences derived from the local environment—the "familiar" to the student—and more upon vicarious experiences remote from actualities. The study of national politics may be interlaced with examples obtained from the local political scene; but an extension of the local scene must be made through reading, accumulating national and international statistics, viewing motion pictures, filmstrips, slides, listening to dramatizations, or other activities. All of these activities are aimed primarily at enabling the student to build meaningful, accurate concepts. Instruction at the junior-senior high school level is more highly specialized than at lower levels. Audio-visual instructional materials have potentially great contributions to make here in extending the vicarious experiential base for all students, in providing perceptual experience as a basis for language development, and in enabling the less verbally facile students to "experience" in ways other than through printed or spoken words.

Junior college and college instruction, up to the present, has not been characterized by as widespread use of audio-visual materials as the two levels of instruction previously discussed. The 3¼" x 4" standard lantern slide has probably been used more frequently in colleges than any other type of audio-visual instructional material. One survey recently completed (1) in forty-eight midwestern colleges and universities engaged in training Navy students during the last war reported that:

1. Sound motion pictures, models, and slides (in that order) were of greatest *potential* usefulness in college instruction, and particularly in science classes.
2. The greatest values of films for college classes were that they showed motion, clarified difficult concepts, and added realism and concreteness to instruction.
3. Difficulties standing in the way of extended utilization of motion pictures for college classes (aside from lack of projection equipment and adequate physical facilities) were chiefly: inability to obtain films at times they fitted into the course of study, lack of suitably mature films for college use, and lack of films which deal in detail with small teaching areas and which do not attempt to "cover half the course."

This survey supported the need for centralized services at the college level to produce audio-visual materials for college classes. Such a comprehensive service would also facilitate projection, improve physical facilities, procure and distribute audio-visual materials for various college departments, and provide opportunities for in-service training in the utilization of audio-visual instructional materials in teacher-training courses.

The University of Wisconsin, University of Minnesota, Syracuse University, Ohio State University, Indiana University, College of the City of New York, University of North Carolina, Cornell University, Pennsylvania State College, and many other large colleges and universities in the United States now maintain such comprehensive services in audio-visual instructional materials for use by instructional staff members. Facilities are provided for planning and producing instructional charts, slides, filmstrips, exhibits, flat pictures, and, in some instances, motion pictures—all of which are adapted to specific local instructional needs.

Adult educational activities in which audio-visual instructional materials and equipment play a prominent part have been stimulated in the years since World War II by activities of several adult-education groups. The American Library Association, the American Association for Adult Education, the National University Extension Association, and the Film Council of America—to name only four—carry on activities aimed at increasing and improving the use of audio-visual materials for adult informational and general educational purposes. One result has been an increased production of "discussion-type" or "forum" films concerned with current social problems of interest to responsible citizens. Public libraries in Cleveland, Detroit, Rochester, and other localities have recently begun local distribution of motion pictures and other audio-visual materials to organized formal and informal adult study groups.

Audio-visual materials are also used for adult-education purposes by government agencies, churches, and units of business and industry. An outstanding example of visualized adult-education activity by government is the U. S. Department of Agriculture (28) which, through its motion-picture and filmstrip production departments and network of distribution facilities, reaches a vast rural audience with up-to-date information on problems ranging from "conservation" and "contour plowing" to "raising chickens" and "preventing botulism." The interest of church-workers in the visualization of religious and social ideals and problems is indicated by productions such as those of the Protestant Film Commission. This interest is further indicated in special columns appearing in the *Educational Screen, Film World, Audio-Visual Guide,* and *See and Hear* magazines as well as in journals in the religious field. Business and industry, in many instances, have pushed ahead of schools in capitalizing upon the educational and indoctrinational values of audio-visual materials. Personnel-training programs which include planned production and utilization of motion pictures, filmstrips, exhibits, illustrated manuals, models, dramatizations, slides, and charts in conjunction with lectures and reading are common in department stores, automobile agencies, factories, and sales organizations. General Motors, the Ford Motor Company, the Standard Oil Company, Libbey-Owens-Ford Glass Company, and the Bell Telephone Company are five of many hundreds of business organizations which make wide use of company-planned and company-produced audio-visual instructional materials in personnel-training and public relations.

Use in Different Subject-Matter Areas

The use of audio-visual instructional materials and methods is not limited to any area of the curriculum, although there appear to be differences in the quantities of such materials available for the various curriculum areas. Ten large film libraries [4] in the United States, for example, report the following median percentages of stocked 16-mm. sound and silent motion pictures for the subject-matter areas indicated, rated according to their "primary usefulness":

Subject Area	Per Cent of Films
Social Studies	30.0
Science	25.0
Industrial Arts and Vocational Education	15.0
Health and Physical Education	10.0
Guidance	4.0
Language Arts	3.5
Art	3.0
Music	2.0
Mathematics	1.0
Foreign Language	1.0

A similar classification resulting from analysis of 3,758 films contained in the *Educational Film Guide* (6) yielded these percentages:

Subject Area	Per Cent of 3,758 Films
Social Studies	27.2
Science	16.2
Industrial Arts and Vocational Education	20.1
Health and Physical Education	14.1
Art	2.5
Music	2.4
Mathematics	0.6
Other (including Language Arts, Foreign Language, and Guidance)	16.9

The National Education Association questionnaire (2) asked respondents to indicate areas in which teachers were making "most effective" use of teaching films. Of 816 replies for elementary schools, 730 mentioned "social studies" and 487 mentioned "science." The next most frequently mentioned area, "health," was checked 139 times, and "mathematics" only three times. At the junior-senior high school level, science and social studies headed the list. "Science" was checked 803 times, and "social studies" 714.

Some indication of the curriculum areas and grade levels in which audio-visual instructional materials are *needed* was provided by this

---

[4] Reports were received from the University of Colorado, University of Wisconsin, New York University, Oregon State College, Washington State College, University of Michigan, University of North Carolina, Syracuse University, University of Tennessee, and University of Texas.

same questionnaire. "Social studies," "English," and "science" were most frequently mentioned. The order of frequency of mention of these areas for elementary, junior high school, and senior high school levels was essentially the same.

Science instruction which depends largely upon reading assignments, workbook "experimentation," and lecture-demonstrations leaves much to be desired (20). The potentially rich perceptual elements of life in and out of school, however, may form an effective basis for expanding and developing the child's meaningful understanding of and interest in the many varied details it contains. Direct experience gained from planting seeds and watching growing plants develop, from designing and building a balanced aquarium, from watching and giving demonstrations of scientific phenomena, or from making field trips to observe, to feel, to smell, to taste, and to hear elements as they exist in nature may stimulate interest in science or encourage the statement of science problems concerning which hypotheses may be advanced and later studies made. The science museum in the school, too, becomes a potential means of clarifying in concrete terms what might otherwise be little understood scientific concepts.

Science teachers, as a rule, make frequent use of educational motion pictures. With such pictures they are able to arouse interest, to dramatize, to slow down, to speed up, or to magnify natural phenomena, to "see the insides in operation," and to demonstrate in such a way that every person in the class has a "front seat." Motion pictures are particularly helpful in demonstrating and explaining the nature of many phenomena which cannot be seen, as illustrated in such films as "Atomic Energy" and "Molecular Theory of Matter." Here the animated diagram creates a simplified concretion which even the most powerful miscroscope is unable to reach. Still pictures, projected and unprojected, provide means of expanding the "experience area" of the child and of studying phenomena in unhurried detail. Radio and recordings dramatize events in science and history, thus humanizing them. The wide use of charts and other graphic materials in science suggests their particular applicability to the understandable presentation of large bodies of data for meaningful interpretation by students.

Social-studies instruction (18) can be improved at all levels by the use of a variety of audio-visual instructional materials. Boys and girls can learn vicariously about foreign countries by studying motion pictures. Experiences gained through constructing model foreign villages on sandtables, planning and painting murals, taking part in plays or pantomimes written by students about persons and events in foreign countries, visiting portions of a city in which persons of foreign origin live and work, or collecting and arranging an exhibit of articles from the country studied help to develop understanding of social concepts.

The teaching of history and civics, particularly, can be improved if a variety of instructional materials and methods is used. Student research into the history of the local community is a firsthand and highly educative experience for children. Study of social, political, and economic aspects of the community—its population, its agriculture, its government, its social welfare activities, its occupations, and its opportunities—may require field trips, library research, or interviews. By dramatic participation, students may re-create ways in which peoples of the past have solved common problems. Motion pictures become media for dramatically re-creating the past and for making characters and events of the past live convincingly in the present to provide perspective for the future. Recordings and transcriptions, together with certain radio dramatizations, are similarly used. Still pictures and graphic materials (including maps, globes, charts, time lines, and other devices) simplify, co-ordinate, and add meaning to a study of historical trends and developments. All of these materials add to the fund of possible learning experiences. They provide different study approaches from which the student draws his own broader, better-founded conclusions.

Industrial arts and vocational education, like science education, has made extensive use of audio-visual instructional materials. "Direct" learning in the shop involves, among other activities, performance of jobs, following job-sheet outlines, and appraising finished products. Demonstrations by instructors and by students are used as learning experiences. Models and mock-ups, exhibits, and specimens simplify processes and orient students with regard to difficult procedures and steps. Field trips to factories and to places of business enable instructors to "bring to life" and to anchor in reality aspects of industrial arts and vocational education. The numerous motion pictures and filmstrips produced during the war by the U. S. Office of Education, together with those produced before and since the war by other agencies, provide valuable guides for studying shop operations. Further, they permit direction of student attention to specific aspects of the equipment or practice studied, they allow for repetition without loss of efficiency, and, in some instances, they provide experience which otherwise would be unavailable because of restrictions of time, space, or cost.

Health, safety, and physical-education instructors find frequent use for a variety of instructional materials and methods to provide essential learning experiences for children. *Doing* comprises much of the learning activity in these areas—*practicing* foul shots, *applying* tourniquets, *diving* from the high board. Models and mock-ups of body organs, basketball courts and football fields, street plans with safety zones and traffic signals, and other devices bring to the classroom for detailed study some aspects of life in and out of school. Demonstrations of proper and improper posture; field trips to health agencies, dairies, or water-filtering plants; exhibits; and a variety of charts, diagrams, and posters are used for different instructional purposes. Motion pictures reach beyond some of the other teaching tools by animating "unseeable" body functions; by introducing slow-motion sequences of fast actions in sprinting, jumping, or football plays; or by dramatizing certain health or safety problems to stimulate desirable action by the observer.

The use of audio-visual instructional materials in the *language arts* is considerable, despite the present scarcity of appropriate projected teaching materials. Here the aim is to improve and to increase the learner's use of language. The enrichment of the learner's experience, together with *practice* in the use of the words in meaningful ways, rank high on the list of desirable activities. Primary teachers who bring to the classroom *things* (rabbits, chickens, specimens) about which stories are told and word charts developed are aware of the need for relating reality to word-building. Similarly, the use of dramatic participation and observation provide realistic bases for vocabulary extension. Field trips involve functional uses of language in listening to the guide's explanations, in reading signs and booklets, in asking questions, in taking notes, or in writing summaries. Motion pictures, too, stimulate interest in reading and stress the importance of clear writing, of proper punctuation, or of good diction. School-made wire, tape, or disc recordings are used frequently to "mirror" speech habits of students. Hearing themselves as they are heard by others provides strong motivation for remediation.

Some Encouraging Trends

There are several encouraging trends with regard to audio-visual instructional materials which have to do with their planning and production, their use by classroom teachers and others for general and specialized purposes, and their distribution.

Simultaneous planning and production of different types of instructional materials is a relatively recent innovation. Co-operation between textbook publishers and authors and the writers and producers of educational motion pictures, filmstrips, recordings, charts, and other audio-visual materials gives promise of well-integrated series of instructional materials, each portion of which strengthens and supplements the others (37). Prerequisite to such production is careful analysis of specific learning contributions best provided by each instructional medium. While research designed to measure various aspects of the instructional efficiency of such co-ordinated instructional units has not yet been done, the present background of experience and observation indicates that it is a logical plan which offers promise.

Increased attention to teacher-training in the use of audio-visual instructional materials is covered in greater detail in chapters v and vi. When more than 750 school systems throughout the country were recently asked to name major barriers to wider and more effective use of audio-visual materials in their schools, the statement most frequently made was: "Teachers not interested—not prepared to make effective use of audio-visual aids" (2). The report concluded:

If this is true—and the conclusion finds support in most of the recent literature on the subject—a tremendous program of teacher education is indicated which will include both specialized instruction in the colleges of teacher-training and locally arranged programs for on-the-job training. The latter cannot be ignored, since the professional education of the great majority of teachers now working in the public schools included virtually no instruction on the use of the newer multi-sensory aids. . . . . Probably the initial step toward a more effective program in many communities should be a well-planned program of in-service education for teachers which would awaken their interest in audio-visual procedures and create on their part a genuine and insistent demand for suitable multi-sensory materials. (2).

The present literature indicates that a serious attack is being made on these problems at the in-service level by state departments of education (12), by teacher-education institutions at the preservice and in-service level (7, 15), by national educational organizations (18, 31, 32, 35), and by research and writings aimed at determining basic skills and knowledges needed by teachers to make adequate use of audio-visual instructional materials (9, 19, 26). At least two states (California and Pennsylvania) require teachers to take courses in audio-visual instruction before they may receive teaching credentials.

Increased understanding of the contributions of and conditions necessary for the use of audio-visual instructional materials was gained through wartime experiences of the armed forces (30). Such understanding has led many school administrators and teachers to agree upon the need for enriching teaching by making greater use of audio-visual instructional materials. Another aspect of this interest is shown in the appointment of specialists to administer audio-visual instructional-materials programs in schools, school systems, institutions of higher education, and state departments of education (2, 3). It is further evidenced in increased appropriations by many state departments of education and county and city school systems for the purchase of audio-visual materials and equipment and for the supervision and administration of their utilization. It is reflected, finally, in architectural features of some new school buildings to provide efficient classroom facilities in which projected and recorded audio-visual instructional materials may be used (39).

Research in audio-visual instructional materials shows recent tendencies toward increasing both in range of problems attacked and in the depth to which studies are carried. Earlier research frequently attempted to prove the "superiority" of the visual as opposed to the verbal method of instruction. More recently, researchers have tried to identify specific purposes for which audio-visual materials are best suited and to establish principles to guide producers, distributors, and users. One compilation of doctoral dissertations under way in 1947-48 (17) lists thirty-four studies in the field of audio-visual instruction. These studies involve identification and appraisal of administrative practices in audio-visual instruction, evaluations of different specific techniques in film and filmstrip production, investigations of children's abilities to "read" visual materials, and evaluations of contributions of selected audio-visual instructional materials to the over-all effectiveness of school programs.

Corollary developments in research in this field are the promising trends toward the concentration of research projects in large blocs and the co-operative participation of many qualified individuals who have adequate financial support throughout an extended period of time. Examples of such concentrations are activities of the Motion Picture Project of the American Council on Education (21), the Commission on Motion Pictures in Education (10), the Nebraska study of educational enrichment through the use of motion pictures (29), the instructional film research project at Pennsylvania State College (5), the activities of the Center for the Study of Audio-Visual Instructional Materials, University of Chicago, and the Evaluation of School Broadcasts project, Ohio State University (45).

Use of audio-visual materials in helping to solve international problems and improving understanding between countries has occupied the attention of many educators and representatives of government and industry (46). The 1946 conference sponsored jointly by the American Council on Education and the Film Council of America (33) resulted in a series of recommendations to UNESCO related to information about and the production, evaluation, certification, distribution, and utilization of audio-visual instructional materials on an international basis (11). A summary report of the United Nations film unit (36) suggests its present concern with production and international distribution of films, filmstrips, and similar materials under such titles as "The Fight against Illiteracy" (Mexico), "In Every Port" (medical care for seamen), "The Eternal Fight" (on epidemics), and "What Is the United Nations?" The unit also produces English-, Spanish-, French-, Russian-, and Chinese-language versions of filmstrips and attempts to facilitate their distribution to schools and other educational agencies within the boundaries of member nations. Attention to the problems of utilizing audio-visual materials in the development of intercultural co-operation is given attention in the literature of the field (14).

Increased production of improved audio-visual instructional materials and equipment is another encouraging sign. Increased experience with the media, broader insight into their strengths and weaknesses, and improved technological processes have resulted in the production of better audio-visual instructional materials and equipment. The introduction of natural color and of sound-on-film, for example, has extended the range of accuracy with which the sound motion picture records or re-creates world realities for classroom study. Likewise, improved processes make possible the production of superior animated film sequences. Again, new developments in radio, (frequency modulation, television) and in recording processes (tape, wire, disc, and film) have extended the range of usefulness and reproduction fidelity of many audio-visual devices. The general photographic quality and teaching effectiveness of educational motion pictures produced since the last war are generally regarded as being superior in many ways to those produced earlier. While techniques introduced into some of the new films have, in most instances, been subjected as yet to no scientific tests, the consensus of users is that the protagonist device, the employment of recognized authority, the use of participation techniques, and the inclusion of motivational and summary sequences have resulted in more useful instructional products.

Investment by schools and school systems in audio-visual instructional materials and equipment is increasing. Tabler's study (38) of one hundred public school systems in the United States revealed that by 1957 the anticipated use of audio-visual instructional materials would exceed by 600 per cent their use in 1947. This same study included reports of audio-visual expenditures from school superintendents in Mason City, Iowa; Freeport, Illinois; Wilmette, Illinois; Glencoe, Illinois; Oak Ridge, Tennessee; St. Louis, Missouri; and Fond du Lac, Wisconsin. Per-pupil expenditures in these cities for audio-visual materials and equipment in 1947 ranged from 52 cents to $4.00. The trend of expenditures over the past ten years or more was, in each case, decidedly upward. Ownership by school systems of the audio-visual materials required for teaching purposes appears to be replacing an earlier practice of renting or borrowing from outside sources. As professionally trained audio-visual personnel are placed in charge of instructional-materials centers which house such materials, and as efforts are made to stock many audio-visual materials within individual schools, their day-to-day classroom application promises to become more feasible and useful.

Production of lighter weight sound motion picture projectors promises to increase the use of films for instructional purposes. Introduction of revolutionary sound-film forms may result in radical cost reductions and serve to place films and projectors within reach of more schools. Increased markets for such materials may invite additional competition and continued improvement of the product.

A final encouraging trend in audio-visual instruction is that toward *decentralization of distribution facilities*. The purchase by individual schools of greater quantities of filmstrips, recordings, slide sets, transcriptions, models, charts, and similar materials, more nearly insures their being available when teachers need them. Establishment of educational motion-picture collections within school units on regional, county, and city levels is also recommended (21, 22) and practiced (3, 4) in several states in which state appropriations have been provided for this purpose.

Some Deterring Factors

While there are many trends which justify optimism regarding the status of audio-visual materials in education, a realistic view demands recognition of several deterring factors. These obstacles to the wider use of audio-visual instructional materials are the subject of the next chapter.

References

1. Abbott, Robert B. "Study of V-12 Colleges Relative to Equipment, Program, and Plans for the Utilization of Audio-Visual Aids to Instruction" (unpublished manuscript). Washington: Bureau of Naval Personnel, 1945.

2. *Audio-Visual Education in City School Systems.* Washington: Educational Research Service, Research Division, National Education Association, December, 1946.
3. "Audio-Visual Staff and Organization in State Departments of Education." Washington: Research Division, National Education Association, 1948 (mimeographed).
4. BROWN, JAMES W. *The Virginia Plan for Audio-Visual Education.* Chicago: Center for the Study of Audio-Visual Instructional Materials, University of Chicago, 1947.
5. CARPENTER, C. R. "A Challenge for Research," *Educational Screen,* XXVII (March, 1948), 119-21.
6. COOK, DOROTHY E., and BORDEN, BARBARA. *Educational Film Guide.* New York: H. W. Wilson Co., 1947.
7. COREY, STEPHEN M. "Audio-Visual Aids and Teacher-Training Institutions," *Educational Screen,* XXIV (June, 1945), 226.
8. DALE, EDGAR. *Audio-Visual Methods in Teaching,* New York: Dryden Press, 1946.
9. DEBERNARDIS, AMO, and BROWN, JAMES W. "A Study of Skills and Knowledges Necessary for Use of Audio-Visual Aids," *Elementary School Journal,* XLVI (June, 1946), 550-56.
10. "Do Motivation and Participation Questions Increase Learning?" *Educational Screen,* XXVI (May, 1947), 256-59.
11. "Draft for a Convention for Facilitating the International Circulation of Visual and Auditory Materials of an Educational, Scientific, and Cultural Character," pp. 1-9. Unpublished report of the State Department, Washington, D. C., 1948.
12. DURR, W. H. *The School Division Film Library.* Richmond, Virginia: Bureau of Teaching Materials, State Department of Education, 1946.
13. FEDERAL RADIO EDUCATION COMMITTEE. *Catalog of Recordings and Transcriptions for Schools.* Washington: U. S. Office of Education, 1947.
14. FLORY, ELIZABETH H. (Editor). *Films for International Understanding.* New York: Curriculum Service Bureau for International Studies, Inc., 1947.
15. *Functions of an Audio-Visual Department in a Teacher-Education Institution.* Macomb, Illinois: Western Illinois State Teachers College, 1946.
16. GOOD, CARTER V. (Editor). *Dictionary of Education.* New York: McGraw-Hill Book Co., 1945.
17. ―――. "Doctor's Dissertations under Way in 1947-48," *Phi Delta Kappan,* XXIX (March, 1948), 305-25.
18. HARTLEY, WILLIAM H. (Editor). *Audio-Visual Materials and Methods in the Social Studies.* Eighteenth Yearbook of the National Council for the Social Studies. Washington: National Education Association, 1947.
19. *Handbook of the Audio-Visual Program.* Bloomington, Indiana: Audio-Visual Center, University of Indiana, 1948.

20. HEISS, ELWOOD D.; OBOURN, ELLSWORTH S.; and HOFFMAN, C. WESLEY. *Modern Methods and Materials for Teaching Science.* New York: Macmillan Co., 1940.
21. HOBAN, CHARLES F., JR. *Focus on Learning.* Washington: American Council on Education, 1942.
22. ———. *Movies That Teach.* New York: Dryden Press, 1946.
23. HOBAN, CHARLES F.; HOBAN, CHARLES F., JR.; and ZISMAN, SAMUEL. *Visualizing the Curriculum.* New York: Dryden Press, 1937.
24. HUTCHINSON, THOMAS H. *Here Is Television.* New York: Hastings House, 1946.
25. KOON, CLINE M. *School Use of Visual Aids.* U. S. Office of Education Bulletin, 1938, No. 4. Washington: Government Printing Office, 1938.
26. LEMLER, FORD. "What Is Teacher Competency in Audio-Visual Methods?" *University of Michigan, School of Education Bulletin,* XIX (February, 1948), 70-74.
27. LEVENSON, WILLIAM. *Teaching through Radio.* New York: Farrar & Rinehart, 1945.
28. LINDSTROM, CHESTER. "To 24,000,000 Americans," *See and Hear,* II (April, 1947), 20-21, 44.
29. MEIERHENRY, WESLEY. "Classroom Movies Are Here To Stay," *Research Report,* II (Summer, 1948), 5-7 (University of Nebraska).
30. MILES, JOHN R., and SPAIN, CHARLES R. *Audio-Visual Aids in the Armed Services: Implications for American Education.* Washington: American Council on Education, 1947.
31. *Multisensory Aids in the Teaching of Mathematics.* Eighteenth Yearbook, National Council of Teachers of Mathematics. New York: Bureau of Publications, Teachers College, Columbia University, 1945.
32. NOEL, ELIZABETH G., and LEONARD, J. PAUL. *Foundations for Teacher Education in Audio-Visual Instruction.* Washington: American Council on Education, 1947.
33. PRESTON, HELEN S. *Use of Audio-Visual Materials toward International Understanding.* Washington: American Council on Education, 1946.
34. REID, SEERLEY. "Respondents and Nonrespondents to Mail Questionnaires," *Educational Research Bulletin,* XXI, (April, 1942), 87-96.
35. SEATON, HELEN HARDT. *A Measure for Audio-Visual Programs in Schools.* Washington: American Council on Education, 1944.
36. "Summary Report on UN Film Activities," *Educational Screen,* XXVII (March, 1948), 126, 144-45.
37. "A Symposium: The Correlation of Films with Textbooks," *Educational Screen,* XXVI (December, 1947), 543-49, 565.
38. TABLER, C. H. "The Next Decade of Audio-Visual Use in One Hundred School Systems," *See and Hear,* II (February, 1947).
39. TERLOUW, ADRIAN L. "Planning for Audio-Visual Education," *Architectural Record,* XCVIII (September, 1945), 76-81.

40. *Time,* LI (March 29, 1948), 28.
41. VANDERMEER, ABRAM W. "Textbook to Movie to Television," *Elementary School Journal,* XLVIII (January, 1948), 276-79.
42. ——————. "The Status of Audio-Visual Materials in Fourth-class Districts in Pennsylvania." State College, Pennsylvania: Pennsylvania State College (unpublished mimeograph study), 1948.
43. WHITE, THURMAN. "Audio-Visual Materials in Adult Education," *Educational Screen,* XXVI (November, 1947), 489-91.
44. ——————. *Speaking of Films.* Chicago: Film Council of America (6 West Ontario Street), 1947.
45. WOELFEL, NORMAN, and TYLER, I. KEITH. *Radio and the School.* Yonkers-on-Hudson, New York: World Book Co., 1945.
46. "World Film Report," *See and Hear,* II (May, 1947), 19-35.

CHAPTER III

OBSTACLES TO THE USE OF AUDIO-VISUAL MATERIALS

CHARLES F. HOBAN, JR.
State Teachers College
West Chester, Pennsylvania

INTRODUCTION

It is the purpose of this chapter to examine reasons why audio-visual materials are not more widely used in schools and colleges and to point out what must and can be done if wider and more effective use of these materials is to be developed.

There are two major types of obstacles to the use of audio-visual materials. The one type results from the nature of the materials themselves in their present stage of development and use. The other type is more deeply rooted in some of the basic problems of education that confront the nation at this time, such as inadequate concepts of teaching and learning and an overcrowded curriculum.

Major attention is given in this chapter to the problems that are characteristic of audio-visual materials per se. Those problems which are chiefly concerned with theories of learning and curriculum organization are more elaborately treated in chapter iv.

CHARACTERISTICS OF AUDIO-VISUAL MATERIALS

There are these five major characteristics of audio-visual materials which act as deterrents to the more rapid extension of their use in the curriculum: (1) Many of these materials are expensive. (2) They are difficult to obtain when they can be used to best advantage; sometimes they are nearly impossible to obtain at all. (3) Expensive equipment is required for their projection. (4) This equipment requires manual skill for operation and technical skill for maintenance. (5) Some form of building modification is often necessary for the effective use of this equipment.

Before examining each of these deterrents, it is advisable to point out that none is impossible to overcome, all of them have been overcome to some degree in a substantial number of schools and colleges, and the introduction of technological devices normally requires changes in traditional ways of thinking, acting, and constructing in many aspects of modern life. It makes little sense that educational institutions pioneer in technological discovery and development, yet lag in the employment of these very discoveries in achieving their own intrinsic goals.

Audio-visual Materials Are Expensive

Audio-visual materials cost money. Some cost a great deal more than others. Motion pictures are the most expensive of all.

The relatively high retail price of audio-visual materials is partly due to the cost of their production and partly due to the small market for these materials after they have been produced. The irony of this situation is that the expense of audio-visual materials acts as a deterrent to their expanded use in schools and colleges, and the small market tends to keep the price of these materials excessively high.

The production cost of an educational motion picture, for instance, varies from approximately $2,500 to approximately $10,000 per ten-minute reel, depending on many factors. A conservative estimate of the production cost of a twenty-minute educational film is $15,000. At the current market price for the latter of approximately $80 a print, it is necessary that over 175 prints of this film be sold in order to pay initial production costs. Adding such incidental costs as those of reel and can, and such overhead costs as those involved in advertising, promotion, sales, and accounting, at least 250 and probably 300 prints must be sold before the producing agency recovers the costs of production and distribution.

Yet, the ready market for the average educational motion picture seldom exceeds 200 prints. Even by intensified and expensive promotion, this market seldom expands beyond 300 prints. It is the extraordinary educational film that sells in excess of 300 prints.

The cost of educational motion pictures used in schools and colleges today has seldom been borne in full, or even in fair proportion, by the schools and colleges which use these materials. Most of the educational films currently available have been subsidized in production one way or another. Sometimes this subsidy has taken the form of capital investment in companies organized for the sole purpose of making films for educational use. In such cases, the amount of invested capital has usually been increased from time to time if the company continued production.

In other cases, the cost of producing educational film has been subsidized by some parent company which stands to profit in the long-range future by the development of a market for film, related equipment, or other educational materials produced by the parent company. In still other cases, the cost of producing educational film is charged off to advertising and promotion of a particular product, and schools and colleges are offered "free" films for such promotional or public-relations values as may accrue to the "sponsor" of the film from its exhibition in schools or colleges.

Some of the most inspirational films in current educational use were produced by major Hollywood studios for showing in public theaters, and later released in 16-mm. reels for use in schools and colleges. The cost of production of these films was borne either by the producer, if the film failed to pay off at the box office, or by the general public, if the film was a box-office success. After their theatrical tour, these films have been leased to schools and colleges at prices which pay merely for the production and distribution of the prints themselves and for the informational materials describing their contents and the terms of their availability.

Other educational films widely used in educational institutions have been produced by federal or state governmental agencies. Still others have been financed by foundations. In the former case, the cost of production was paid out of tax monies. In the latter, the cost was borne by an endowment which was probably established for some more general social purpose.

The situation is similar in the production of filmstrips, slides, educational recordings and related materials. It is perhaps less desperate in that producers of these materials have remained in business by subsidizing their educational productions in part from their industrial and public-relations activities; but basically the production structure for these materials remains unstable. This instability is largely the result, on the one hand, of the uncertainty of the market for any particular film, filmstrip, recording, or set of pictures; and, on the other, of the relatively few educational institutions which comprise the predictable market today for these materials.

Filmstrips which are now priced between $2.50 and $4.00 or $5.00 could conceivably be sold for a dollar or so if the market were to triple in size. Motion pictures selling for fifty dollars a reel could be sold for less than thirty dollars if the market were to expand to one thousand prints. Recordings costing several dollars could be priced at a dollar or less under similar circumstances.

Once schools and colleges in appreciable numbers begin to purchase audio-visual materials for their own use, rather than depending on occasional rental from a regional source or doing without, the price of motion pictures, filmstrips, and recordings will normally decline as much as one-third or one-half their present cost. To the contrary, if schools and colleges do not purchase audio-visual materials, the cost of these materials to the purchaser will remain at least as high as the present level and may actually increase because of rising production costs.

One fact, however, cannot be altered by expanded markets. The truth about audio-visual materials is that their use involves an increase in the cost of instructional services. The purchase of audio-visual materials cannot be financed by reducing expenditures for books and other printed materials, or by increasing class size and reducing the size of the teaching or administrative staff.

Furthermore, the use of audio-visual materials requires the addition of administrative personnel for cataloguing, circulation, maintenance, and projection. The idea that administrative and instructional problems related to the extensive use of audio-visual materials can be solved by adding them to those of the librarian, simultaneously renaming the library a "materials supply center," is no solution to the problem. It simply serves to increase the duties and responsibilities of the already overburdened librarian. The fact is that an effective program of audio-visual materials requires additional trained personnel for the distribution of these materials, the maintenance of equipment, and, frequently, for supervision of the use of such materials.

Audio-visual Materials Are Difficult To Obtain When Needed

It is frequently impossible for classroom teachers to obtain films, filmstrips, recordings, slides, and other analogous materials at the time they can be used to best advantage. It is precisely this breakdown of the audio-visual distribution system which, on the one hand, is so depressing to the producer who cannot sell the materials he has produced and, on the other hand, is so frustrating to the teacher who needs these materials but cannot obtain them.

In the development of an adequate and efficient system of distribution of audio-visual materials lies the key both to their more effective use and to their more abundant production. The mere availability of the materials does not, of itself, result in their effective use in teaching. Effective use is physically impossible when these materials cannot be obtained when they can be most effectively used. Consequently the use of such materials cannot be satisfactorily developed without a substantial improvement in the distribution system.

An adequate system for the distribution of educational materials to classroom teachers and other educational users requires that those materials frequently used by classroom teachers be available from a local source, and those materials which are more specialized in nature be available at least from a more remote source. A third factor, that of cost, also enters into the program of distribution. Less expensive materials should be available from a source close to teachers; more expensive materials, of economic necessity, must be made available from a more remote central source, serving a larger geographic area or population group.

In most states the audio-visual distribution system has developed along either exclusively local or exclusively centralized lines, and, unfortunately, in some states very little of either type of distribution exists. There is scarcely a state or region of the nation in which the distribution program has been worked out so that (a) local distribution units are widely established throughout the state to serve local schools with basic materials, and (b) state distribution facilities are established both to reinforce the local units with more expensive and more specialized materials and to serve those audiences not ordinarily served by local distribution facilities.

In some instances, state agencies which distribute these materials have developed and expanded to the extent that they now actually tend to discourage the development of local distribution facilities. In almost all cases, these state agencies—state universities or state departments of education—have pioneered in the development of audio-visual aids to instruction and have assumed a much needed leadership both in distributing and in promoting effective use of the requisite materials.

However, it is increasingly apparent that the role of the state agency is changing. As demand for specific films, slides, recordings, and other similar materials expands, there is need for decentralized distribution centers close to the localities where the materials will be used. Perpetuation of centralized supply tends, at least psychologically, to maintain a sense of inaccessibility to these basic materials for instruction. The feeling exists among teachers that, since the source is remote, the supply is uncertain.

The new role of state agencies in the audio-visual field is seen to embrace four activities:

1. Organization of audio-visual programs for new audiences, such as parent- and adult-education groups, service clubs, labor organizations, professional groups, and the like. This involves promotion, program-planning, supply of materials suited to these audiences, and assistance on their effective use.
2. Reinforcement of local school and college distribution facilities with supplementary, rare, expensive, and specialized materials, the use of which in local situations is not frequent enough to justify local ownership and distribution.
3. The supply of basic classroom materials, such as motion pictures and other relatively expensive materials, to local schools and colleges in those areas or those situations in which the development of local distribution facilities is impractical because of lack of financial resources or wide geographic dispersal.
4. The co-ordination of audio-visual activities throughout the state, and the development of state-wide leadership through conferences, institutes, and publications.

It follows from this concept of the role of state or regional agencies, that the local school systems and institutions of higher learning have an obligation to establish their own facilities for the supply of frequently used audio-visual materials. Some of these should be supplied to the individual classroom, others should be centralized in the individual school for the use of the faculty of the school, and still others must be made available from a central agency of the city or county school system or university. Certain maps, globes, recordings, permanent pictures, exhibit materials, manipulative and raw materials, filmstrips, and slides are used recurringly in any school and are frequently interchangeable among different grades and subjects. Hence, they belong in the individual school. However, motion pictures are expensive and, because of this fact, their supply on a city or county basis is likely to be necessary at this stage of development.

Even throughout entire areas of the country, both the local and the regional distribution of audio-visual materials is wholly inadequate. In the southeastern states, for instance, there are thousands of square miles of territory which have no adequate local supply of these materials, and such state or regional sources as are available are far from adequate either in variety of required materials or in duplicate copies of the materials available.

The task of developing wide and effective use of audio-visual materials is an impossible one when the supply of these materials available to classroom teachers is inadequate. The tragedy of this situation is that inadequate supply of educational materials is a common characteristic of those regions in which the need for richness of educational experience is the more acute because of the barrenness of the physical and spiritual environment in which the people live.

It is significant that a new and vigorous leadership is developing in some of these depressed areas, and that there is a firm resolve from within the regions to improve their status, their opportunities, and their resources. It is equally significant that this new leadership attaches a high degree of importance to the role of audio-visual materials in the process of intellectual, spiritual, and economic uplift.

The development of networks of local and state distribution facilities in every state of the country would not only make possible the wide use of audio-visual materials by teachers on all levels of education but would automatically provide the necessary broadening of the commercial market for audio-visual materials, which, in turn, would result in increased production of needed materials, and substantial reduction of the unit price of the materials.

Expensive Equipment

The majority of audio-visual materials require expensive projection equipment for their use. Not only is this equipment expensive but a considerable variety of equipment is needed. An adequate audio-visual program cannot be developed without a sufficient number of 16-mm. sound motion picture projectors, opaque projectors, slide projectors (3¼" x 4" and/or 2" x 2" slides), filmstrip projectors, playbacks for recordings and transcriptions, radios, screens, and projector stands. Some of these projectors are obtainable in combination, but each of them can be used for only one purpose at a time, and a wide use of a variety of materials means that separate projectors for each purpose is economical in the long run.

The most expensive equipment is the 16-mm. sound projector. Up to recently, only large and heavy general-purpose sound projectors, varying in price from $475 to $575, were available for educational use. Within the past year, however, new lightweight projectors weighing 35 pounds or under, and retailing for under $400 (several of them retailing for less than $300) have been placed in quantity production.

These projectors are adequate for the projection of 16-mm. sound motion pictures to audiences of approximately 200 and are more than adequate for use in the normal-size classroom. New lightweight projectors, costing less than $300, are adequate for classroom use not only with black-and-white film but also with color film. In general, color film requires greater sound amplification than does black-and-white film.

The development of lightweight, less-expensive, 16-mm. sound motion picture projectors has several implications for wider and better use of educational films.

1. Their reduced weight increases their mobility, and hence their flexibility in the educational program. They can be moved without extraordinary effort from room to room and from floor to floor, a feat which has taxed the sheer physical ability of faculty and students when applied to the general-purpose projector weighing in the neighborhood of eighty pounds.
2. The reduced cost of lightweight projectors makes possible the purchase of this equipment by many schools which could not afford the more expensive models. Among the more affluent schools and colleges, and those with indulgent parent organizations or patrons upon whom has fallen the burden of purchasing audio-visual equipment, the reduced cost of lightweight projectors makes possible the acquisition of several projectors by a single school. This, in turn, creates a greater demand for more audio-visual materials for school and college use. This demand, in turn, builds a larger market for audio-visual materials.
3. The lightweight projector promises to open the home market for educational films. The surprisingly large segment of the public which seldom goes to the movies, as well as the majority of the population which does, constitutes a potential market for nontheatrical films. Up to the present, this home market is relatively unexploited because of the few sound projectors in American homes. The lightweight projector may change this situation. It is conceivable that libraries of educational films may ultimately be as common in the home as are sets of encyclopedias today. Furthermore, the rental market for educational films in the home is likely to expand. Both possibilities lead to interesting speculation about Junior's homework and the family circle.

Other projection and playback equipment, while not particularly heavy, is still priced above the level that would be necessary were the market to increase. Lack of standardization has also acted as a deterrent. Producers of radio receivers, for instance, have not standardized a classroom model, largely because of the absence of a sizeable market. The standardization of classroom radio-receivers is further complicated by the prevalence of both AM and FM educational broadcasting. Another factor which complicates the situation of audio-visual equipment is the diversity of equipments within a single audio-visual function. For instance, there are three types of recording machines: disc, wire, and tape. The latter two are relatively new, whereas the former, the disc recorder, is older but relatively little used in schools. Wire and tape recorders are available in inexpensive models for school purchase and are enjoying comparative popularity. Nonetheless, the fact that three types of recording machines are now available introduces momentary confusion into the field and, with it, a tendency to withhold development of this field pending standardization. The problem of expensive equipment is being overcome by the application of engineering, assembly, and mass production. Prices of the most expensive items of equipment have been reduced approximately 50 per cent by the production of projectors especially designed for the school market. Whether or not this step forward is to be permanent depends largely on the schools and colleges themselves and their willingness and ability to create a market for this equipment large enough to justify the continued production of low-cost projectors. Prices of other audio-visual equipment are subject to proportionate reduction in an expanded market.

Manual Operation and Maintenance

The fourth deterrent to wider and better use of audio-visual materials is the fact that projectors and sound reproducers and recorders require manual skill in their operation and technical skill in their maintenance. Despite the growing popularity of courses in audio-visual education in which, among other things, instruction is provided in the operation of projectors and reproducers, the fact is that the great majority of teachers do not know how to operate these teaching devices. This lack of operational competency acts as a deterrent to the use of such equipment as is available, and tends to prevent a strongly vocal demand on the part of teachers for increased quantities of this equipment in the schools. The great popularity of courses in audio-visual education among teachers in service is indicative of the interest of teachers in acquiring the skills demanded in the use of the new materials.

Several facts about the operation of audio-visual equipment seem evident.

1. Teachers must learn to operate the technological devices of their profession.
2. The prevalence of audio-visual equipment in the home, the movie theater, and the church calls for a high degree of performance skill by teachers in the operation of this equipment if the teaching profession is to escape odious comparison with other occupational groups.
3. However desirable it may be to use the services of students for operation of audio-visual equipment, this fact does not relieve teachers of the obligation of competence in the operation of the equipment.

4. Thorough training in manual operation of audio-visual equipment is essential in the preservice education of all new teachers, and the in-service education of all teachers in service.

Another deterring characteristic of audio-visual equipment is that it requires competent maintenance and repair for continued operation. Some types of equipment require more technical maintenance than others, but all equipment requires some kind of maintenance, if nothing more complicated than replacing a lamp, cleaning the lens system, or replacing a fuse. This maintenance problem implies two things. (1) A supply of replaceable parts must be maintained for all such equipment. This may mean a supply of lamps for all projection equipment, a supply of needles for phonographs, or a supply of tubes for radios, playbacks, or sound projectors. This supply must be readily available to the user of the equipment, so that the audio-visual program will not be interrupted by normal wearing out or breakdown of replaceable parts. (2) Beyond the replacing of a lamp or a phonograph needle, maintenance of electronic equipment and projectors with complicated operating parts and lens systems requires the services of a trained technician. This may be supplied commercially by the agency which sells the equipment, or it may be supplied by the audio-visual department or center, if sufficient equipment is serviced by this center to justify institutional maintenance. Irrespective of the agency employed, a technical maintenance service is indispensable, and its indispensability increases as the equipment increases in age and quantity of use.

This fact leads to the consideration of a new type of educational personnel, the need for which is increasingly evident. In addition to highly trained professional personnel—often untrained and not particularly talented in the field of applied mechanics and electronics—there is a growing need in schools and colleges for technicians who can perform efficiently and economically many of the mechanical operations presently performed by professional personnel. The need for subprofessional personnel is particularly evident in the audio-visual field; but there is recognition of similar need in the library field and in the field of educational testing.

Building Modifications for Use of Audio-visual Aids

A fifth deterrent to the wider and more effective use of audio-visual materials is the fact that school and college plants are not suitably designed for the use of these materials. For effective use of the new materials, modifications are required both in older school and college buildings and in plans for newer structures.

In theory, the use of audio-visual materials introduces no new problems in design of school and college buildings. The old problems are simply intensified—lighting, ventilation, acoustics, and adequate electrical outlets. However, in practice, the introduction of audio-visual materials involving projection, power outlets, ventilation, screens, room-darkening, and electrical amplification of sound often taxes the ingenuity of the teacher and school administrator. Consequently, it is no small or insignificant task to make the most simple provisions for the use of audio-visual materials in a school plant in which these needs were not anticipated in the planning and construction stages.

Modern architects who design new schools in the glassy modern style, the while neglecting problems of sound amplification, room-darkening for projection, and ventilation during projection, are adding to the woes of education in the future in so far as the use of audio-visual materials is concerned.

In the prevalent school and college buildings, there is very little provision for darkening classrooms, nor is there satisfactory provision for room ventilation when rooms are darkened by the use of shades which also exclude fresh air. Electrical outlets in the front and rear of classrooms were apparently regarded as unnecessary accessories by the school architects who designed these buildings, and perhaps they were unnecessary in the long-ago when most of the school and college buildings in use today were designed and constructed. Whatever the origin of the deficiency, it exists and, as such, constitutes a serious obstacle to the use of educational equipment requiring alternating current for operation.

More important is the lack of even the most elementary provision for good acoustics in most school and college classrooms. Hard-surfaced walls, ceilings, floors, and furniture tax the fidelity and audibility of sound under the best of circumstances and do a great injustice to the students when this sound is amplified electrically, as it is in phonographs, radio receivers, and sound motion picture projectors.

Three simple and relatively inexpensive measures may be taken to recondition old buildings and to improve the efficiency of new school and college buildings for audio-visual education.

1. Soft draperies may be used instead of window shades, thereby improving the appearance of the classrooms, their acoustical qualities, and the ventilation.
2. Acoustical tile may be added to walls and ceiling for additional improvement of acoustical qualities and to reduce nervous fatigue.
3. Electrical outlets may be installed in front and back of classrooms, thereby

providing for the classroom use of projectors, radios, playbacks, and other electrical equipment.

The introduction of these improvements will bring school and college classrooms into a position of favorable comparison with the livingroom of the ordinary home. With the exception of acoustical tile, unnecessary because of the prevalence of upholstered furniture and rugs, all of these devices are standard in the home.

While all these deterrents are serious in the sense that they are realities and that they have slowed down the development of audio-visual education, each of them is yielding to improvement. Commercial improvements in equipment and materials are being made more rapidly than has the school's use of this equipment and material.

More General Educational Deterrents

There is more to the problem of wider and better use of audio-visual materials than their cost, their availability, and the operation and maintenance of equipment required in their use. These are essentially problems of finance, administration, and training. There are, however, deeper causes of much of the abuse or the lack of effective use of audio-visual materials in education. They are sometimes related to the financial difficulties of schools and colleges, the lack of effective administration, or the lack of trained personnel. They are the basic causes of widespread uncertainty of teachers as to how they should use audio-visual materials, how they will find the time to use them, and why they cannot continue to "teach" without these materials.

Teachers are sensitive to the pressures which have been exerted on them in educational literature and in professional meetings to use more audio-visual materials. They have also received reports of the extensive use of these materials in the war-training program, and these reports tend to increase the pressure for audio-visual education in schools and colleges. Teachers are, for the most part, interested in audio-visual education and sincere in their desire to employ any and all materials which will produce better educational results.

It is, however, doubtful that most teachers are aware of the sources of their confusion in this field. They believe they can be led from darkness to light by training in the operation of projectors and by demonstrations of effective classroom methods of using films, recordings, science experiments, industrial arts materials, filmstrips, radio programs, and the like. It is here submitted that while these two measures will be of some help, they will not be of much help in the development of a really effective audio-visual program. Substantial progress in the effective and extensive use of audio-visual materials is severely handicapped by inadequate concepts of the purposes and processes of learning in school and college and by a curriculum which becomes increasingly crowded.

Inadequate Concepts of Learning

In a subsequent chapter, the process of learning and the decisions teachers must make in order to facilitate this process will be discussed in detail. It is intended here merely to indicate that inadequate concepts of what students should learn and how they learn what they do learn are prevalent from kindergarten to graduate school.

It is almost superfluous to point out that much formal learning-experience in school and college is predominantly verbal, that such desirable learnings as result from this experience are frequently a knowledge about things and theories rather than a familiarity with them. It is also superfluous to point out that those learnings tested and measured by teachers may be and usually are only a small fraction of the actual and total learnings that have taken place in, around, and because of the school or college environment. Were the actual and total learnings tested and measured, the results might indeed be horrifying to the teachers.

The goals and the processes of learning that have been characteristic of this type of school and college curriculum have been identified by a tolerant public as "book learning." The term itself connotes a certain remoteness from the complexities and practicalities of everyday living and further implies that the individual, so schooled, has seldom established in his own mind the relationship between what he learned from books and what he thinks and does in the world about which the books are written.

If, as set forth in a later chapter, it is accepted that people learn what they practice, and if it is true that in school the learning experiences are largely those of reading and listening, with some intermixture of talking and writing, it follows that schools teach people to read, listen, talk, and write about the kind of subject matter that is presented in class and assigned for out-of-class study. The fallacy in this type of learning-experience is that all four of these verbal activities are dependent for real meaning on the degree to which people have had more direct experience with the things symbolized in print or in spoken words. It is only recently that we have begun to understand that people get out of any medium of communication—verbal or pictorial—proportionately what they bring to it.

For some time past, it has been assumed that audio-visual materials were best for the dullard, that it was a waste of time to use them with the brighter or more advanced students. Research in the use of films in the war-training program has supported the opposite theory, i.e., that brighter and better-educated persons get more out of films than do the duller and less well-educated.

This evidence indicates that it is in a richness of experience, rather than in the intense use of a single medium of learning or teaching, that the process of education thrives. Audio-visual materials, selected and used with care, contribute to this richness of experience, and, hence, to the process of education.

The Overcrowded Curriculum

Apart from the mechanical difficulties of using audio-visual materials previously discussed, many teachers have invited attention to the fact that they simply do not have time to use films, filmstrips, recordings, manipulative materials, radio, and the like, and still cover the course of study. There has been a tendency to dismiss this complaint by peering down the nose at the teachers who voice such educational heresy.

The fact remains that there is a great deal of truth to what these teachers say, granting their assumption that there is a course of study which must be covered. This assumption is based on the idea that there is a certain body of subject matter—sanctified by time or by contemporary pressures—which must be transmitted in its entirety or in fractionated sequences to all students who enrol in a given class. This assumption becomes a ghostly specter that assumes pencil-and-paper form late each spring when standard achievement tests are administered on a city- or county-wide basis and early in the fall when placement examinations are administered to entering students. These achievement tests constitute a measure of a given teacher's success in covering the course of study.

The course of study specter takes another form when students enter junior high school from elementary school, high school from junior high school, college from high school, and graduate school from college. Teachers on each higher level blame teachers on the preceding level for having failed to meet course-of-study requirements in the preparation of their students.

Whether a course of study is simply an idea which has a universal substance but a different form in the mind of each teacher or whether it is hammered out in black and white in an endless stream of bulletins mailed at teachers from administrative headquarters, its existence, its precision, and its requirements are part of a cultural pattern that most teachers accept as a reality. Furthermore, if the course of study does not exist in print, teachers ask that it be printed.

By an additive process, this omnipresent course of study has become increasingly complex, increasingly varied, and increasingly difficult for the teacher. The extension of human knowledge during the past century has added enormously to the content of the course of study. Teachers are admonished to give adequate time and attention to education for the air age, education for the atomic age, education for world peace, education for UNESCO, education for home-and-family living, education for intercultural relations, education for safety, education of the emotions, education for proper diet, education for health, education for citizenship, general education, and the like.

At the same time, teachers are cautioned against lowering standards in the more historically established subjects and skills of reading, arithmetic, spelling, composition, handwriting, and literature. They are also expected to teach some rudiments of expression in art, music, and the dance. And, with all this, there is strong pressure for an "activity program" in which "units" crossing all disciplinary boundaries are introduced in order to reconcile "scope" and "sequence."

On the college level, where general education is introduced as a compulsory sequence of orientation and integrated courses in the Freshman and Sophomore years, the situation is even worse. The world of science (physical and biological), the humanities, (art, literature, music, and the dance), and problems of health and personal adjustment are hurled at students who suffer through the impossible assignment of integrating what they have not learned and being oriented in a culture they have insufficient time or experience to learn to know.

Under these circumstances it is understandable that teachers ask when and where they will find time to use enriching materials.

To their relief and amazement, more and more teachers are discovering that the crowded curriculum can be made meaningful in many of these areas only through the use of films, slides, and recordings, and that the crowded curriculum remains relatively meaningless to many students without these materials.

Audio-visual materials are not the whole answer. There is no answer to some of the problems of the crowded curriculum except through the elimination of many superficial or unessential elements that are causing the crowding or through the better distribution of time allowed the different elements. But audio-visual materials are indispensable in many areas of education in elementary and high school, in college and university, if education is to meet its obligation to prepare students for living in this complex, turbulent, explosive twentieth century.

Implications for Teaching

The crowded curriculum accentuates the need for reconsidering the role of the teacher and the role of teaching materials in the educational process. In practice, the teacher frequently thinks of himself as the paramount source of the learning experiences of his students rather than as a guide to the student in his development and an administrator of the learning environment which stimulates this development. The steady increase in the amount of subject matter to be transmitted, the extension of the curriculum into areas of human knowledge and behavior hitherto avoided or neglected in school and college, and a re-emphasis on broad educational objectives of mental and emotional maturity and discipline make the concept of the teacher as the primary source of learning experiences an increasingly difficult one to apply. Traditional methods of teaching, traditional motivation, and traditional teaching materials are not adequate. Teachers who have faced classes with the "new look" in high school and college, including many so-called "nonacademic" students who were formerly eliminated before reaching high school and college, are well aware of the limitations of the old teaching methods and the old teaching materials.

For one thing, the increase in school and college enrolment has brought to these institutions new types of students whose patterns of behavior and sense of values do not conform to the academic requirements of the teacher-textbook-lecture curriculum. These new students do not regard the cultural heritage of western civilization either as an obligation to accept and transmit or as of practical value in the competitive business of earning a living in an industrial, technological civilization. The burden of proof of such values is placed on the teacher and the school administrator by these postwar students. Unaccustomed to justifying a pattern of values which is economically as real to teachers as it is unreal to students, the teacher is often hard put to establish such proof. Instead, he tends to intensify traditional methods and traditional attitudes toward "learning for its own sake" in a somewhat desperate struggle for economic and professional self-preservation. However, the solution to this problem is not retrogression, but progression. Values can be preserved and disseminated by more effective methods of presenting these values, not by lofty insistence on the sacred nature of these values or by methods of presentation which actually serve to reinforce students' attitudes of rejection.

For another thing, the teacher himself has difficulty in keeping abreast of the expanding frontiers of knowledge, even in his own field of specialization. Also, he may have had little training in some of the subjects he is assigned to teach. This situation is increasingly prevalent with the teacher shortage in elementary and high school and in college and university. Finally, just lecturing and assigning reading are inadequate methods of communication, even when there is ample time for communication and a relatively small body of concepts to be communicated.

The use of audio-visual materials has two important implications for the crowded curriculum. First, many concepts in the curriculum and many of its objectives can be presented and attained more effectively with audio-visual materials than through verbal methods only. It is regrettable that so little analysis has yet been made of the curriculum to determine the kinds of experiences and the kinds of instructional materials that are most efficient for various learning objectives. It is only recently that the need for such analysis has received wide recognition. This recognition is an important step in the improvement of education, provided it is followed by further analysis and experimentation.

Second, audio-visual materials are essentially media of mass communication that can be used with large audiences as effectively as with small audiences, often more so. The recent interest in group dynamics has served to re-emphasize the fact that audience reaction and subject-matter presentation are inseparable in the learning situation. A hostile audience makes the best presentation ineffective. A receptive, alert, and responsive audience improves even the worst presentation. With audio-visual materials, particularly with motion pictures, the size of the audience has a stimulating, tonic effect on the individual. There are in the motion-picture learning-situation certain elements of what may be called "mob psychology." The response to a given film varies greatly with audience size. A few people looking at a film, even in a small room, react quite differently than does a large group looking at the same film. This same phenomenon is probably true in almost any situation involving visual presentation. The group itself seems to influence the reactions of individual members of the group.

It is the writer's belief that one of the fundamental mistakes in the production and promotion of educational motion pictures has been the tendency to conceive and produce them for exhibition to small groups, much in the pattern of the textbook, which is essentially a medium of individual instruction. The natural tendency of the teacher and school administrator is to exhibit educational motion pictures to large audiences, just as they are exhibited in the theater. From their own experience, teachers and pupils, like other human beings, have learned that motion pictures are highly effective provokers of audience reaction when shown to large groups in theaters. The factor overlooked in this "transfer of training" is that the very psychological elements which make motion pictures effective educational experiences in the theater have been omitted in the films produced for the school. As a result, these films lose much of their potential power with any kind of an audience except that in which a rich background has been developed for the understanding receptivity demanded by the kinds of films produced for classroom use. This is not to contend that no films, filmstrips, recordings, or other audio-visual materials should be made to fit the small-class teaching situation but, rather, that the almost exclusive production of audio-visual materials to fit this pattern of use has unnecessarily and almost inexcusably limited the development of the field and restricted the teaching potentials of these media.

Very little analysis has been made of the curriculum in terms of the kinds of activities and the kinds of materials that are effective with large groups and those which demand individual, teacher-student attention, or small-group instruction. It is highly probable that much of the teacher's time and energy could be saved for those teaching situations requiring individualized instruction through the use of appropriate audio-visual materials with large class sections or groups of classes studying the same subject.

A re-examination of audio-visual materials in the light of their potential values in large-group instruction, and in the light of the subject matter and objectives of education, brings to the fore the question of the degree to which the factors of learning should be incorporated into the materials themselves: motivation, intrinsic interest, identification, dramatic emphasis, a sense and touch of humor, suspense, repetition, continued motivation, pacing, etc. These are psychological factors which facilitate learning. Lack of them impedes learning.

It is not maintained that all these factors be prefabricated in all teaching materials any more than it is maintained that they should be omitted from all of them. Under present circumstances, it would seem better to err by incorporating the known factors of learning in instructional materials than by omitting them entirely.

The problems that lie ahead are those of discovering the concepts and objectives of the curriculum that lend themselves best to audio-visual presentation, those that can be met with large-group instruction using audio-visual materials, those techniques of teaching which should be incorporated into the materials, and those which should be left to the teacher himself. Perhaps the crowded curriculum is a blessing in disguise.

REFERENCES

BROWN, JAMES W. *Virginia Plan for Audio-Visual Education.* Chicago: University of Chicago, 1947.

BROWNELL, WILLIAM A. "Place of Meaning in the Teaching of Arithmetic," *Elementary School Journal,* XLVII (January, 1947), 256-65.

COREY, STEPHEN M. Review of Grierson's *On Documentary, Library Quarterly,* XVIII (April, 1948), 124-26.

―――. "The Unique Contribution of Audio-Visual Instructional Materials to the Curriculum," *California Schools,* XIX (January, 1948), 3-12.

DALE, EDGAR. "Seeing the Meaning," *Educational Screen,* XXVII (January, 1948), 11-12.

FLORIDA STATE DEPARTMENT OF EDUCATION. *The Audio-Visual Way.* Tallahassee: State Department of Education, 1947.

GRIERSON, JOHN. *On Documentary,* pp. 191-226. Edited by Forsyth Hardy. London: Collins, 1946.

HARTLEY, WILLIAM H. (Editor). *Audio-Visual Materials and Methods in the Social Studies.* Washington: National Council for the Social Studies, 1947.

HOBAN, CHARLES F. *Movies That Teach.* New York: Dryden Press, 1946.

KELLEY, EARL C. *Education for What Is Real.* New York: Harper & Bros., 1947.

LARSON, LAWRENCE C. "Basic Criteria of an Audio-Visual Education Program," *Bulletin of the School of Education, Indiana University,* XXII (July, 1946), 7-10.

MAYO, ELTON. *The Social Problems of an Industrial Civilization,* chap. vi, pp. 113-23. Boston: Graduate School of Business Research, Harvard University, 1945.

NOEL, FRANCIS W. "Providing Facilities for Use of Audio-Visual Materials," *California Schools,* XVI (1945), 181-82.

SEATON, HELEN H. *A Measure for Audio-Visual Programs in Schools.* Washington: American Council on Education, 1944.

TABLER, C. H. "The Next Decade of Audio-Visual Use in One Hundred School Systems: Equipment and Supply Needs, and Financing the Optimum Program," *See and Hear,* III (January, 1948), 13-16.

Use of Training Aids in the Armed Services: Some Implications for Civilian Education. U. S. Office of Education Bulletin, 1945, No. 9. Washington: Government Printing Office, 1945.

WITTICH, WALTER A. "Curricular Aspects of Audio-Visual Materials," *High School Journal,* XXX (March, 1947), 62.

CHAPTER IV
THE TEACHERS' DECISIONS

Stephen M. Corey
Teachers College, Columbia University
New York, New York

and

Edgar Dale
Ohio State University
Columbus, Ohio

Introduction

A ninth-grade teacher in Chicago is talking to his class. He says, "Friday I want you to be able to name the major industries in Illinois. You should be interested in these industries because Illinois is your home state. Read pages 168 to 184 in your text. We will have a test on this Monday."

All of the major areas in which a teacher makes decisions are represented in this "assignment." The teacher first stated his objective: "I want you to be able to name the major industries in Illinois." Second, he tried to make this instructional aim seem important to his pupils: "You should be interested in these industries because Illinois is your home state." Next, he suggested an activity in which the pupils should engage in order to learn: "Read pages 168 to 184 in your text." Finally, the boys and girls were told that a test would be given to enable everyone concerned to find out whether or not any learning resulted from reading the text.

This teacher—as is the case with all teachers—was trying to bring about a change in the behavior of his pupils. At the time the assignment was made, the boys and girls probably would have answered, "I don't know," if they had been asked, "What are the major industries in Illinois?" Their teacher wanted a different response to this question. He wanted the boys and girls to change so that, instead of saying, "I don't know," they would correctly name the major industries in Illinois.

Much of the time of most teachers is spent trying to get pupils to change their *verbal* responses to specific questions.[1] Every type of teaching means some modification in the behavior of the learners. The specific kinds of behavior that are changed vary. A kindergarten teacher may want her pupils to learn part of the meaning symbolized by the word "hen." If they are city children and see a real hen for the first time, their response probably will be the question, "What is that?" Later they may look at a hen and say, "Hen." Their verbal behavior has changed. If the change persists, they have learned what they practiced—verbal behavior.

How can this learning be explained? What "causes" it? A complete answer, if one could be given, would take several hundred pages.[2] For the purpose of this chapter it is enough to say that the child changed his response to the hen situation because of certain experiences he had had. These experiences came between the time he looked at the hen and said, "What is that?" and the time he looked at the hen and said, "Hen." Maybe the experience was a very simple one involving no more than the child hearing the teacher say, "Hen," while she pointed. He then said, "Hen" himself, and the teacher smiled and nodded, or said, "That's right." If the child felt rewarded or pleased, he would be disposed to repeat his response the next time he was faced with the hen-question situation.

The second-grade child's improvement in handling a hammer illustrates a somewhat different type of learning. At first he is awkward. Several months later the hammer is grasped correctly, and the child frequently hits what he aims at. His behavior has changed as a consequence of at least two factors. One is his increase in physical maturity, which brings better muscular control. The second factor is the experience with hammers and hammer-nail situations in which the

---

[1] One study revealed that, during the course of a year, six teachers asked their pupils more than 35,000 oral questions. All of these pupils in turn asked their six teachers less than 4,000 questions. This was a rate of about 6,000 queries per year for each teacher and 33 for each pupil. See Stephen M. Corey, "Teachers' Questioning Activity," *Research in the Foundations of American Education,* pp. 143-46. American Educational Research Association Proceedings, 1939.

[2] Learning is difficult to define. For a summary of points of view about learning see Ernest R. Hilgard, *Theories of Learning.* New York: Appleton-Century-Crofts, 1948. Hilgard says, "Learning is the process by which an activity originates or is changed through training procedures (whether in the laboratory or in the natural environment) as distinguished from changes by factors not attributable to training." The author admits this definition is evasive and tautological (p. 4).

child felt rewarded when he hit the nail on the head. The learning was a consequence of these experiences. Improved muscular co-ordination that results largely from physical growth is one aspect of what is called "maturation."

Learning often involves increased understanding. Again, when this takes place, behavior is different afterward. A simple understanding may mean no more than the realization that things taken from a hot stove may burn the hand. After a small child has reached this understanding, he behaves differently when dealing with the pan-on-the-hot-stove situation. Similarly, an eleventh-grade girl who learns from her study of American history that wars are almost always followed by periods of depression, behaves differently because of this understanding. She improves her prediction of future events and interprets history more realistically.

The change in the reaction of some boys and girls to skin color represents still a different type of learning. The seven-year-old child may be almost completely unaware that one of his playmates has a dark skin. The fact of a dark skin does not influence the way he acts. Seven years later, skin color has become important and may result in well-defined behavior when associating with dark-skinned people. This change results from many experiences the child has had during the seven-year period. His behavior toward dark-skinned people has a complicated history, but it has been learned.

In order to find out whether or not learning has taken place requires observation at two different times. The learner must be watched "before and after," so to speak. The observation is always of behavior —including speech—or of the product of behavior—something that has been written or constructed. The fact that teachers must rely upon observations of behavior in order to find out whether or not children have learned is important. No one has direct access to the "mind" of another person. A teacher may talk about the mental development of his pupils, but the observations are always of the pupils' behavior or some product of their behavior.

The central responsibility of any teacher is to make certain experiences available to his pupils—experiences which the teacher, or preferably the teacher and his pupils, believes will bring about desirable learning. Speaking more precisely, the teacher can do no more than arrange situations which he hopes will result in good learning experiences. He alone can only help set the stage. The child must play his part. The experience a pupil has is a private matter. It is *his* experience, not the objective situation as it is perceived by someone else, that changes him.[3] A teacher may read poetry aloud and assume that his pupils, by listening, will increase their appreciation of good literature and their disposition to read more of it. If a pupil, however, perceives the situation as unpleasant and to be avoided in the future, he changes in ways that the teacher may not anticipate.

The kinds of learning situations teachers create in the classroom vary in many respects. One important respect involves the degree of abstractness or symbolism of the stimuli the children react to. Sometimes an attempt is made to teach by providing pupils with verbal experiences only. The boys and girls are expected to listen, to read, or to express themselves orally or in writing. The teacher assumes that these experiences will bring about desirable changes in behavior.

At other times the learning situation involves more direct experience with objects and relationships. Boys and girls, for example, who are in the last year of high school and studying rural life might spend two or three months actually living and working in a rural community accompanied by a teacher to help them think and generalize from their experiences; or there may be a reforestation project which students carry out under the guidance of their teachers and forestry experts.

Concrete, life-like experiences are not necessarily superior to experiences that involve reaction to words.[4] It is true, though, that some "firsthand" experiences must come either before or simultaneously with the experiencing of the word, if the latter is to be meaningful. A word "stands for" or represents an object, a kind of behavior, or a type of relationship. Unless the learner has had some experience with this object, this behavior, or this relationship the word is meaningless. Only when the word actually represents objects or activities or rela-

---

[3] It is difficult to know what a given classroom situation *means* to a particular child. Certainly the "same" situation means quite different things to different pupils or to the same pupil at different times. The quality of a pupil's experience depends upon many factors such as how he feels, his interest at the time, his previous experiences, his attitude toward the school situation, and his physical condition. For a discussion of learning from the point of view of the learner, see Nathaniel Cantor, *Dynamics of Learning* (Buffalo, New York: Foster & Stewart, 1946); or Earl C. Kelley, *Education for What Is Real* (New York: Harper & Bros., 1947).

[4] If the reader wishes to go more deeply into this subject, he may read Edgar Dale, "Relation of Reading to Other Forms of Learning," in W. S. Gray and Others, *Reading in General Education*, chap. iii (Washington: American Council on Education, 1940); or Ernest Horn "Language and Meaning," (pp. 377-413) in *The Psychology of Learning*, chap. xi (Forty-first Yearbook of the National Society for the Study of Education, Part II, distributed by University of Chicago Press, 1942).

tionships that the child has experienced can he learn from it. A word can be seen or heard. It can be a visual signal or a sound signal. The sign for "stop" may be at the side of the road or it may be a policeman's whistle.

The meaning of *nine* is learned by counting objects, or dots, or by seeing that it is seven objects and two objects more, or by realizing that it is the number that comes just before ten. The figure or the word, "nine," are symbols and represent a generalization from a great deal of varied experience. The concept or understanding of "nine" is continuously extended or tested by using it. The symbol means much more to a mathematician than to a fourth-grader.

This argument that a word is meaningful in the degree that it actually does "stand for" experiences with the object or activity or relationship is clear in the case of the number "nine." It is equally true in the case of the reactions of various boys and girls to the word "dog." To some who have had limited experiences with real dogs, the word stands for little. To other children who have had their own dogs, have played with them, been bitten by them, and have seen them fight, the symbol "dog" is rich in meaning.

This point can be further illustrated by referring to the "assignment" which introduced this chapter. The meaning of the words "major industries in Illinois" can range from the ability to name half a dozen to the much richer meanings that result from actually working in mines or factories or on farms—and thinking about what goes on. For example, the manufacture of steel is a major industry in Illinois. A boy who has spent several summers working in a steel mill gets more from the expression, "the manufacture of steel," than does the girl who has seen a few pictures of a steel mill and has driven by one as the open furnace doors reflected light against the clouds.

The fact that the meaning of a word can be rich or limited raises a difficult problem. Referring to the "major industries of Illinois," what level of meaning should a ninth-grade teacher in Chicago expect these words to have? The answer depends upon the use to which the boys and girls put their "knowledge." If the use will involve no more than naming six or seven industries when the question is asked, all that is necessary is to learn the names so that they can be repeated in answer to the question. If the expectation is that the pupils are learning about the various industries in order to receive some help in making their vocational plans, a much richer experiential background must be symbolized by words like "farming," "commerce," "manufacturing," "factories," and "labor."

The Four Instructional Questions

Whether or not the learning situations arranged for pupils result in experiences which bring about desirable changes in behavior depends upon the quality of the teacher's answers to these four questions:

1. What is the nature of the important changes that should be brought about in pupils? In other words, what are they to learn?
2. How can the importance of these changes be made clear to the learners and the changes be made to seem worth achieving?
3. What kinds of learning experiences will efficiently and permanently establish these changes?
4. How can evidence be obtained which will indicate whether or not the desired learning has taken place?

As teachers, from kindergarten to the graduate school, go about their day-by-day tasks, their answers to these questions—their actions —imply certain convictions about objectives, about pupil motivation, about learning situations, and about evaluation. These convictions are derived from beliefs teachers hold about the world they live in, about the relationship of schools to this world, about the psychology of learning, about the interests and needs of young people, and about themselves.

The rest of this chapter deals with some of the convictions and beliefs which determine the decisions teachers make. The authors have tried particularly to show how the teacher's ideas about instructional materials influence his judgment. The instructional materials a teacher uses have great influence upon the objectives he tries to achieve, the way in which he motivates learning, the kinds of learning situations he devises, and the methods he employs in order to find out whether or not learning has taken place.

The amount of independence a teacher now enjoys in making decisions in these several areas varies from situation to situation. For example, most classroom teachers have relatively little to do with the over-all design of the elementary- or secondary-school curriculum. The major objectives to be reached in a particular grade may be determined without consulting the teacher. It is assumed that he will accept and strive to achieve them. The systematic study of geography may begin in the sixth grade for all of the schools in a school system. The sixth-grade teachers, or other teachers, may have little to do with this decision.

Not only are the major objectives often decided upon by persons other than the teachers who are expected to achieve them, but even the specific "unit" objectives are frequently established in the same fashion. Despite such prescriptions, there is often leeway for teachers to exercise good judgment in their selection of some objectives from a long list or in the emphasis they place upon this or that specific objective.

Even though there may be specific curriculum requirements, the *methods* which teachers use to motivate the learning of their pupils are less likely to be prescribed by others. In this area the teachers' decisions are in a real sense their own. What is done depends upon the teachers' understanding of children, of the behavior that is expected of them by their peers and their parents, of the influence upon their behavior of growth factors, and of certain broad conceptions of desirable human relations.

The freedom of the teacher to make his own decisions about instructional materials would seem to be limited by curriculum requirements and other conditions. This limitation, however, is often more apparent than real. Even with a large amount of prescription of textbooks and other kinds of materials, there is much opportunity for teachers to use their judgment as they make a selection from a variety of materials and choose those which they believe will bring about desirable changes in the least time.

When it comes to day-by-day testing, teachers have much freedom to exercise originality. The extensive use of standardized tests imposes some restrictions on the methods teachers may use to find out whether or not they have taught to good effect. Such tests, however, rarely if ever constitute all of the evaluation program.

A number of curriculum-workers, in reaction against situations where teachers do little more than follow directions and obey orders, have argued for greater teacher participation in the planning of curriculums.[5] The writers believe that this defensible and rational reaction against too much thinking done for the teacher sometimes goes to the other extreme of expecting teachers to make independent decisions about everything. Given the circumstances under which most teachers teach, however, the expectation that they make creative decisions regarding every aspect of their tasks is probably romantic. A distinction must be made between teachers making all of the decisions that must be made in order to teach and teachers accepting and understanding and being willing to carry out some decisions that are made by other people. It is the proper balance that is troublesome—a balance that holds teachers responsible for those decisions that they are in the best position to make.

---

[5] For a statement of this point of view, see Alice Miel, *Changing the Curriculum: A Social Process.* New York: D. Appleton-Century Co., 1946.

In this connection the curriculum-makers who have been working with the problem of reorganizing secondary education have developed one approach which holds promise. This approach is known as the "resource unit" and takes various forms.[6] The primary purpose of the resource unit is to give the teacher the security she formerly had using the textbook-workbook-classroom method and at the same time to allow for flexibility in planning specific learning units.

Resource units normally are concerned with large problem areas of human living such as "science—servant or master," "living in the air age," "problems of inter-cultural relations." The typical resource unit usually has these several identifiable parts: (a) a brief statement of the philosophy of the school or system in which the resource unit will be used; (b) a statement of the scope of the problem area which indicates the major hypotheses and problems to be considered; (c) a listing of a large number of possible activities which teachers and students might carry on in order to have learning experiences related to the problems of the unit; (d) a list of books and pamphlets for teachers and pupils bearing on the general problem and evaluated with respect to reading difficulty; (e) a comprehensive and annotated list of possible audio-visual aids; and (f) a description of possible evaluation procedures that might be used to determine the success of the unit.

The best resource units are usually those prepared by committees of teachers in the school or school system in which they will be used. Such units have, however, been prepared on a state level, as in Michigan, on a county level, as in Maryland, and by certain national groups, such as the National Council for the Social Studies. These latter resource units are somewhat different from the types described above since they usually include an authoritarian statement of the problems and suggestions by a master teacher of possible learning procedures.

The resource unit can probably be regarded as a modern equivalent of older forms of preplanning, such as the Herbartian lesson plans. It differs from these formalized attempts, however, by including an area of human experience and providing a list of resources from which teachers and pupils in planning their learning units may select those which seem most desirable for their objectives.

Teaching Objectives

This brief section on the teachers' objectives deals with only a few of the problems involved in curriculum construction. Determining what should be taught in the elementary or secondary school involves a

---

[6] For a discussion of the resource unit, see Harold Alberty, *Reorganizing the High School Curriculum*. New York: Macmillan Co., 1947.

broad understanding of: (a) the demands made upon children by various American cultural groups, and American culture in general, (b) the interests and needs of children, and (c) the psychology of learning.[7]

In the degree that any one of these areas is slighted, a school program becomes unrealistic and therefore ineffective. When a small group of educators arbitrarily decides what boys and girls of the elementary school or the high school should learn without taking into consideration the expectations of the parents of these boys and girls, conflicts and confusion result. Similarly, when adults decide what boys and girls should learn without considering the interests and needs of these children, school work is likely to be boring and relatively meaningless. When the school fails to take into account the capacity of children for learning at various developmental levels, as well as their previous experiences, learning is inefficient.[8]

The emphasis the authors have chosen for this section has been determined by the subject matter of the present yearbook. There is an intimate relationship between the instructional materials used by a teacher and the curriculum objectives he tries to achieve. Until recently most of the statements about educational objectives were either couched in comprehensive terms or specified as subject-matter content boys and girls were to learn. The former type of statement, while providing a degree of broad orientation, did little to help teachers improve their day-by-day teaching.[9] A helpful description of educational objectives, as inferred from several persistent life situations, appears in a book by Stratemeyer and others.[10] This volume represents the tendency to develop curriculums through identification of

---

[7] Two recent publications describe comprehensively the kind of elementary- and secondary-school curriculums that a large group of educators believe appropriate for American boys and girls. These books are published by the Educational Policies Commission, 1201 Sixteenth St., N.W., Washington, D. C., and are called: *Education for All American Children* (1948) and *Education for All American Youth* (1946).

[8] For a description of the way curriculum-workers bring these various considerations about society and learners into play in curriculum-planning, see Hilda Taba, "General Techniques of Curriculum Planning," in *American Education in the Postwar Period: Curriculum Reconstruction*, pp. 80-115, Forty-fourth yearbook, National Society for the Study of Education, Part I. Chicago: University of Chicago Press, 1945.

[9] Illustrative statements of broad comprehensive educational objectives appear in many sources. A fairly recent pronouncement is entitled *The Purposes of Education in American Democracy* and was prepared by the Educational Policies Commission of the National Education Association, Washington, D. C., in 1938.

[10] Florence B. Stratemeyer, Hamden L. Forkner, Margaret G. McKim, and Others, *Developing a Curriculum for Modern Living*, pp. 106-18. New York: Bureau of Publications, Teachers College, Columbia University, 1947.

tasks at which children must succeed at any developmental level. After these tasks or persistent life situations have been identified, the school provides experiences in them under circumstances that give reasonable assurance that boys and girls will succeed. If the child succeeds at the task and thinks about it, he has acquired whatever knowledge, skills, and attitudes are required for success. This approach to curriculum construction concentrates upon the kind of situations boys and girls must learn to cope with, rather than upon the understandings, skills, and attitudes necessary to cope with these situations.

Teaching objectives that are stated as specific subject-matter content to be learned give direction to classroom activities but rest upon some mistaken notions about learning and the relationship between objectives and learning experiences. Probably the most common type of statement of the day-by-day teaching objectives of most teachers is synonymous with the textbook information that children are expected to learn.[11]

The tendency of curriculum-planners and teachers to describe teaching aims in terms of behavior, both verbal and nonverbal, and to state their objectives specifically and in some detail provides classroom teachers with a great deal of help. Much greater precision and consistency is possible in selecting learning experiences that will enable boys and girls to learn the behavior represented by the objectives if teachers have clearly in mind the specific ways children should act or behave as a result of their school experiences.

A social-studies teacher would not appear to have very clearly in mind just what the outcomes of his instruction should be if he does no more than describe one of his objectives like this: "I want to teach boys and girls to be better citizens." This objective as an over-all, orienting objective, which might differentiate between social studies and mathematics, has some merit. The statement, however, is too vague and general to use as a guide to direct the teacher's practices. If this teacher were to follow this generally stated objective by "spelling out" specific kinds of behavior that mean good citizenship, his decisions as to methods and materials would be wiser.

Teaching for better citizenship at the ninth-grade level, for example, might involve teaching boys and girls to:
1. Take an active part in school elections. This means:
   (a) Developing a concern for school problems subject to attack by the school political organization.

---

[11] Even though subject-matter content to be learned is rarely confused with educational objectives explicitly, the confusion is extensive in actual school practices. See Stephen M. Corey, "Subject Matter: Means or Ends," *School Review*, XLIX (October, 1941), 577-86.

(b) Voting regularly.
(c) Actively supporting good political practices such as:
   (1) Fair and objective reports of issue and candidate competencies.
   (2) Honest balloting practices.
   (3) Open discussion of issues kept as free as possible from bias, etc.

In stating objectives as "ways of behaving," the teacher must steer between two extremes. One is represented by statements of objectives that are very vague and general. At the other extreme the teacher tries to anticipate every possible situation in which a pupil may find himself and in which he should behave in such and such fashion. For example, "Developing a concern for school problems subject to attack by the pupils' political organization" would involve different behaviors depending upon the kind of problems, the kind of school, the maturity of the pupils, and the particular locality in which the school is situated. If one were to attempt to describe specific behavioral objectives that would be appropriate for all of these variables in all possible combinations, the task would be endless. It would also assume a necessity for specific learning for every specific task. So detailed a statement of objectives overlooks the fact that learning is always more or less general, in the sense that some of what is learned in one situation can be used in others.

The learning that the school tries to bring about always involves some degree of generalization. What we try to do first is to teach boys and girls how to behave with a sufficient degree of specificity. We do what we can to cause them to think about and generalize from this behavior so that adaptations can be made to other similar situations. The job is to state objectives in enough detail to clarify what needs to be done, and yet to recognize the undeniable fact that life is complex and the schools cannot teach boys and girls specifically and concretely everything they should be able to do under all conceivable circumstances.

The aims of any teacher are influenced in obvious and subtle ways by his habits of thought regarding teaching materials. If he consistently thinks of instructional materials as being printed, it is natural for him to consider his major aim as developing the ability of pupils to learn and to repeat the verbally stated information they have read.

The influence of this kind of thinking about educational outcomes is well illustrated by the *New York Times'* investigation of history-teaching in our schools. Because of the general notion that learning history means becoming verbally familiar with what is written in history books, the *New York Times* criticized the schools because the boys and girls did not show sufficient familiarity with what appears in the history books. Understanding American history thus meant being able to answer questions about people, dates, and events. Because, in the judgment of the *Times'* writer, children had insufficient knowledge about their country, it was recommended that they get more of the very type of history-teaching that had proved to be unsatisfactory.

A fourth-grade teacher, who thinks of the outcomes of her teaching as relating to textbook information, may state an interest in having her pupils "understand" Colonial America. But her concept of understanding is definitely limited by the teaching materials she employs. If she depends mostly on a text, she may say that she has reached her objective if the boys and girls show that they understand Colonial America by their ability to repeat certain dates like 1492, 1607, 1620, and their ability to answer other questions that are based on the textbook.

A teacher, on the other hand, who had formed the habit of using a variety of teaching-learning situations involving books, films, construction activities, radio, discussions, and school journeys would find it easier to include under "understanding" a sympathetic appreciation of and identification with the kind of life that children might have lived in Colonial America. What did ten-year-old girls do hour by hour during the day at that time? What did they eat for breakfast? What kind of clothing did they wear? Where did they get it? Did they go to school? If so, what was the school like? Did they write letters to their cousins in England? If so, what did they write about? How long did it take the mail to go from Boston to London?

It might be possible for some fourth-grade children to reach an understanding of these activities from reading. More than likely, however, such children would need a number of more concrete experiences before the words they read would be meaningful. Even what appear to be adequate concrete experiences are sometimes insufficient because they conflict with strongly established concepts. For example, a group of Columbus, Ohio, children visited a reconstructed log-cabin in the Ohio State Archeological Museum. They went inside and saw the tools, the utensils, and the furniture. One child asked: "Where is the rest of this home?" The log cabin, of course, was all there was to it, but this girl found it impossible to visualize such a small home from her previous reading.

To consider another illustration, two teachers might say that each was interested in having boys and girls understand about spinning wool. The one who had habitually thought of teaching as helping boys and girls become familiar with textbook materials would probably have them read about spinning and look at some textbook illustrations. The other teacher, whose knowledge of instructional materials was more extensive, would at least consider the possibility of having the boys and girls card and spin wool. If the required equipment were not available for actual carding and spinning, motion pictures of these activities might be used. If there is good reason for learning the meaning of words like "card" and "spin," the activities and apparatus symbolized must be handled and worked with, or at least observed.[12]

Motivation

Probably the most pervasive and troublesome decisions teachers make have to do with motivation. What can be done to give reasonable assurance that the behavior to be taught in school is behavior that boys and girls want to learn? Is it enough to tell pupils: "You should be interested in these industries because Illinois is your home state." One of the reasons that school teaching is so strenuous emotionally is that a great deal of time is spent by teachers trying to get boys and girls to learn "lessons" in which they have little interest and which do not seem to them important.

This situation frequently results from a conflict between the interests of children at any particular time in their development and the demands of society which usually are enforced by adults. Another way of stating this conflict is to differentiate between children's interests and their needs. The former pertain to what boys and girls may want to do at any particular time. Their needs refer to what is good for them. Even those psychologists and educators who place most stress upon the ephemeral quality of children's interests do not deny the fact that one excellent index of what boys and girls need is their interests.

A classical demonstration of this fact was reported several years ago and involved the choice of food by young children.[13] It was found that infants who were allowed freely to choose whatever food they wanted from a "lush" food environment eventually consumed a well-balanced diet. A choice based on their food interests met their needs. The diet was not balanced for each meal, which practice adults have recently made something of a fetish, but, over a period of time, the

---

[12] If you want to discover how meaningless the term "spin" or "spinning" is to the average pupil, or adult, for that matter, ask him how a spinning wheel works.

[13] For a summary of many studies of animals and humans demonstrating the "wisdom of the body" see Curt P. Richter, "Total Self Regulatory Functions in Animals and Human Beings," *Harvey Lectures*, XXXVIII (1942-43), 63-103.

child ate food that adults judged was good for him. It should be remembered that these children were very young and had not yet had their appetites "spoiled."

A rather strong case can be made for the practice of teaching boys and girls at any developmental age how better to do the things these boys and girls are "naturally" trying to do. The argument is that, as children grow older and are subjected to the influence of school and out-of-school experiences, their interests and concerns will mature. As these interests mature, the school curriculum becomes more and more like adult life. When boys and girls are concluding their formal education, their maturity has increased to a point where they are interested in adult activities, and the school provides help in teaching them to behave like adults.[14]

Historically, schooling has usually been thought of as *preparation* for adult life. This notion, coupled with the belief that verbal learning almost inevitably carries over to practice, served to justify a curriculum consisting of "lessons" organized logically in an eight- or twelve-year sequence. Considered in their totality these lessons taught whatever skills, understandings, and attitudes were needed to cope with the problems of a somewhat static adult society. The interests and needs of children as children were considered unimportant unless they could be exploited to motivate the learning of lessons appropriate for adult life.

This conception of school as preparation for adult life poses two curriculum problems. First, how can the behaviors to be taught be determined? And second, when should these behaviors be taught? One decision results in identifying, for example, the words that boys and girls should be able to spell correctly. The second decision involves determining just when particular words should be taught.

Whatever conflict there is between the interests of the child and the demands of society has more to do with the timing of "lessons" than with their nature. This is a broad generalization, but trouble arises, not so much because society requires that children learn certain definite ways of behaving in particular situations, but rather because the school often requires that these ways of behaving must be learned in a chronological sequence that does not take into account the interests of the learners.

This point can be illustrated by reference to arithmetic. Society

---

[14] The reader will recognize this as one of the arguments upon which progressive education has been based. It is impossible to say conclusively whether or not the practice of education in conformity or in partial conformity with this notion has been successful or unsuccessful. Certainly only a very small percentage of American boys and girls have been to schools dominated by this point of view.

does what it can through the schools to teach children how to behave appropriately in situations described by these symbols: $2 \times 2 = ?$ $12 \times 9 = ?$ $73 - 37 = ?$ $116 \div 8 = ?$ $162 + 117 = ?$ $\sqrt{864} = ?$ In due course, children, too, appreciate the importance of appropriate behavior in most of these situations. Because of the vast differences among pupils, however, it would be only by coincidence that all of the boys and girls in a particular grade would have reached an appreciation of the importance of extracting square root at the time that their teacher insists they must learn it.

The problem of motivation has long been appreciated. Teachers have always known that they must do whatever they can to increase the interest of pupils in what they are learning. The various efforts of teachers to motivate their pupils can usually be classified into two types. One may be called "extrinsic" and the other "intrinsic." A pupil is intrinsically motivated if he recognizes the importance of what he is learning in school and believes that he will be better off if he learns his lessons because they represent changes he wants to make in his behavior. When there is this kind of motivation boys and girls learn a great deal on their own. They are likely to be resourceful, persistent, and self-directive because their learning is related to their interests.

When learning is extrinsically motivated, boys and girls do what the teacher asks them to do because they realize that, unless they do, they cannot get *other* things they want or cannot avoid unpleasant consequences. When "extrinsically" motivating their pupils, teachers make use of both positive and negative incentives. Prizes, stars, permission to participate in extra-curriculum activities, and smiles from the teacher are used as rewards when children keep at their work. Negative incentives are represented by many types of actual and threatened punishments inflicted on boys and girls unless they do what the teacher asks them to do.

Extrinsic motivation has a number of interesting consequences. When boys and girls do not view what they are expected to learn in school as being inherently significant, teachers must spend a great deal of their energy keeping pupils at their tasks. A contest develops. The teacher tries to make the pupils do what he believes they should, and the pupils use their ingenuity to keep on doing what they want to do. Energies are wasted.

Furthermore, when learners do not use what they have learned, they soon forget. School pupils who do not see much meaning or importance in what they are expected to learn do not use the new behavior that they have been "taught." The literature on the retention of school learning is disillusioning.[15]

Several things can be and are being done to increase the amount of time children spend in school learning lessons which appear to the pupils themselves to be significant. One practice suggests that teachers spend some time in an in-service teacher-training program learning more about their pupils.[16] At the present time in most school systems there is not much incentive for teachers to become well acquainted with boys and girls in their classes. Doing so takes a great deal of time and leads to few tangible rewards. Major recognition usually goes to those who are able to teach the most subject matter and maintain the best discipline. Public school administrators have not been particularly inventive and ingenious in providing ways for teachers to work together to understand their pupils. When such provisions are not made, teachers probably are correct in inferring that their "superiors" put little premium on such understanding.

There is no single formula which will result immediately in extensive improvement of the school curriculum. However, when large numbers of teachers actually reach a more penetrating understanding of the boys and girls in their classes, the curriculum will improve. The rapidity of this improvement would be greater if teachers could have more help learning how to relate their increased understanding of a child to his school program. So far there has been much emphasis upon helping teachers get better acquainted with their pupils. It seems to be assumed that this will inevitably result in better teaching. This assumption is plausible, but teachers are sometimes frustrated as they learn more about a child because they do not see how necessary curriculum changes could be made to meet the newly discovered needs of pupils.

The existence of this problem does not deny the importance of learning about children. A sixth-grade teacher, for example, could probably not help but be more successful in his attempts to teach a particular boy if he had learned this about him:

Frank recognizes his leadership ability. I think that he feels sure of the

---

[15] Many research investigations have been conducted to find out how permanent school-learning is. For an interesting summary, see Sidney L. Pressey and Francis P. Robinson, "The Permanence of Schooling," *Psychology and the New Education,* pp. 541-70. New York: Harper & Bros., 1944.

[16] A good description of procedures that teachers in service can employ to improve their teaching by learning more about their pupils appears in *Helping Teachers Understand Children.* Washington: American Council on Education, 1945.

group's loyalty and feels secure in the use of his hands. He feels very insecure in academic work—is easily upset about drill work. He realizes his limitations as a leader because of his academic incapabilities. Yet one would not quickly judge that his intelligence rating is as low as it is. He has many special abilities which compensate for his inability to succeed in drill work. In his art, athletics, and dramatics, he is happy and secure.

Experiences at home and in the community have helped him gain a practical knowledge. He has been given much responsibility at home. He has taken care of the younger children, helps keep house, helps with the family washing. He earns money to buy his own clothes, to buy bonds, or to use for school expenses. This experience has taught him the value of money and the integrity of work. Frank's experience background may mean that Frank can feel a sense of security in manual labor regardless of the fact that he can make no progress in reading and other drill subjects. His attitude toward work seems sound to me. Frank wants to be the very things that he excels in now—a great football player and an artist. Yet, for some reason, he accepts the fact that he will in all probability just be a "mill-worker."

Frank's personality is not well knit. He seems to be very changeable. The record shows that he is kind, sympathetic, and helpful. It also reveals that he loses control of himself and finds it hard to readjust himself. Frank is consistent with himself in the things in which he feels his security—athletics, art, dramatics, and manual work. In the things he feels insecure about—drill work, not being able to go out to play—he is inconsistent. He has shown an unreasonable attitude toward these things.

I think that Frank is not a stable person. He is easily upset emotionally. He laughs loudly with a swaying motion, bites his fingernails; he does not gain control of himself quickly and with ease; he cries easily, looks worried at times. Frank is happy over his present-day successes. If he can continue to feel secure and happy in his ability to use his hands, he may become a better adjusted personality as he grows older.[17]

There is another practice that serves to bring more nearly into harmony the interests and needs of boys and girls and the lessons they learn in school. It involves letting boys and girls plan at least some of their school activities with their teachers.[18] This need not mean that the teacher exerts no influence, but rather that he has greater assurance that the school activities in which the boys and girls engage have greater significance to them. Incidentally, teachers who encourage boys and girls to play a part in planning what goes on in school learn more about their pupils. An incidental benefit to the pupils is

---

[17] This is an excerpt from a teacher's report about a particular boy that appears in *Helping Teachers Understand Children*, pp. 225 ff. Washington: American Council on Education, 1945.

[18] Teacher-pupil planning occurs in many degrees and under many different types of circumstances. For a discussion of the problem and practices involved, see H. H. Giles, *Teacher-Pupil Planning*. New York: Harper & Bros., 1941.

that through participating in the planning of their school experiences, they learn something about planning in general which enables them to learn more efficiently after they have left school and are on their own.

Learning Experiences

It is hard to define instructional materials (see chap. ii). Despite this difficulty there is general agreement that such materials are used as one means of controlling the experience of learners so that desired changes in behavior will result. A teacher asks boys and girls to read —that is, to react to—the words in a textbook, because the teacher believes or assumes that this kind of experience will be most likely to bring about important changes in information, attitudes, or other kinds of behavior. The choice of a textbook represents a selection from a variety of other experiences. Presumably the textbook is chosen because all things considered—and this includes economy of time and money—the teacher believes that the textbook will bring about the desired changes most quickly.

A great deal of the time boys and girls spend in school is spent reacting to instructional materials. They read books, encyclopedias, and mimeographed material. They may watch motion pictures or still pictures. They use globes, maps, and charts. They may take field trips or construct things. In some schools boys and girls listen to the radio or to transcriptions. In other words, what children do in school is usually a consequence of the kinds of instructional materials used by the teacher.

Everybody learns whatever he practices and feels rewarded for. In the degree that the activities in which children engage in school are different from those implied by the instructional objectives, learning is inefficient. This point can be made clear by reference to the teaching of "democracy." If boys and girls, when presumably learning "democracy," spend most of their time reading, listening to, speaking, and writing ideas about democracy, they are primarily learning what they are practicing. They are learning better how to read, listen to, speak, and write ideas about democracy.

A teacher rarely says, however, that he is satisfied with his instruction if it results only in increased ability to read, speak, listen to, and write ideas about democracy. The major instructional objective when boys and girls are being taught "democracy" is to make them better able to behave democratically. It is actual democratic conduct that is wanted. Such learning requires specific practice under circumstances that make children feel satisfied when they do the "right" things.

As has been implied, the variety of experiences that teachers or teachers and pupils agree upon as being most likely to result in the kinds of learning described by the instructional objectives is great. Children can read, speak, write, listen to the teacher, look at maps, pictures, or motion pictures, listen to the radio, handle objects, make things, work in a miniature post office, take field trips, or work in the community. Few teachers use the variety of experiences that children might have, and often *must* have, in order to learn whatever lessons the school wants to teach.

An important thing to remember in evaluating instructional materials is the psychological fact stated above, namely "children learn what they practice and feel rewarded for." An excellent way to find out what boys and girls are learning in school is to watch what they are doing. When they feel rewarded for spending their time watching a motion picture and trying to identify the important concepts, and discuss them afterwards, they are learning better how to watch a motion picture, how to identify the important concepts, and how to discuss them afterwards. If this is what the teacher wants to teach, the learning experience is a good one. If such is not the case, the learning experience is ineffective.

Of course it is true that children generalize from any specific experience. One of the big jobs of the teacher is to increase the amount of generalization or carry-over. When children generalize from a specific learning experience, they can apply their learning in different situations. This generalizing, too, requires practice.

Since children learn *what they do*, the instructional materials a teacher uses are crucial because these materials usually determine the activities in which boys and girls engage. If the materials provide boys and girls with the kinds of practice which the teacher's instructional aims require, the materials are good ones. If, on the other hand, they lead boys and girls to engage in activities which are not consistent with the teacher's objectives, the materials are poor ones. Instructional materials are means to an end. They cannot be evaluated apart from a consideration of the behaviors which are being taught.

Regardless of the particular type of instructional material that a teacher uses, the general methodology of utilization is the same. The teacher and whatever resources she can draw upon must arrange for: (*a*) preparation of the boys and girls so that reaction to the particular instructional materials used will provide continuity in their learning, (*b*) the pupils' learning experience to occur under circumstances that are least distracting, (*c*) follow-up activities which will provide further continuity and lead to further experiences that will result in additional learning.

This argument does not mean there is no room for variety in methods of using various kinds of instructional materials. The variety, however, involves what specifically is done to prepare boys and girls, to provide the experience under best circumstances, or to arrange follow-up experiences which give continuity.

No new psychological or methodological principles are needed to explain how to use audio-visual materials effectively. Why then are they used so poorly? They are used poorly in large part because the methods of teaching appropriate to text materials are not easily adapted to field trips, motion pictures, construction activities, and recordings. The reading-memorizing-reciting approach does not work with audio-visual materials. Most of our preservice and in-service training assumes that the instructional materials of basic worth are printed. A textbook, by its very organization, will often determine the verbal responses that are to be made to it. The workbook prescribes the role of the teacher even more completely.

Contrast this textbook situation with a field trip. There may be nothing in the files of the school to indicate what purposes might be served by a visit to a local dairy plant. The range of purposes may be exceedingly broad. What is seen at a dairy is life itself in all of its concreteness. Thus it would be possible for a first-grade group and a college class in dairy technology to benefit from a visit to the same dairy. The difference, of course, lies in the purpose of such visits. While two such diverse groups might well visit a school dairy, they certainly would not be expected to make use of the same textbook.

It must be remembered, too, that entirely new purposes come into use with audio-visual materials. Few textbooks arouse the emotions of the child or the older student, yet a film such as "The River" or "The Plow that Broke the Plains" can be very powerful emotionally. It can make the individual concerned about answering the question: "Why have we wasted our soil and our forests?" The film can build a mood. This is also true of radio and recordings.

Evaluation

In all kinds of schools teachers are interested in finding out whether or not the pupils have learned. In schools where the curriculum is related to the needs and interests of children, the boys and girls also want to find out how much they have improved. Many different methods are used by teachers to answer the question: "What have the children learned?" Tests of varied sorts may be given—most of them involving reading and writing. Interviews or conferences sometimes are held. Children may be asked to react to apparatus or equipment in order to find out if they have learned how to deal with such materials.

Before wise decisions can be made about evaluation of methods or materials of instruction, teachers and pupils must have clearly in mind just what was to have been learned. Most successful efforts to evaluate learning in school result when the teacher:

1. Describes the aim of his instruction in behavioral terms so as to make it possible eventually to observe children and see if they can behave in ways the objectives imply.
2. Devises situations which enable boys and girls to indicate the degree to which they have achieved the learning intended.
3. Works out a method for describing quantitatively the behavior of boys and girls in the testing situation.
4. Interprets the quantitative test scores so as to provide maximum guidance for the pupils involved.[19]

It is easy to overlook the important relationship between the way the teacher evaluates pupil learning and the lessons the pupils learn. Unless school children are intrinsically motivated they will merely try to do well on the tests they take. This is true because by and large boys and girls receive ever so many obvious, subtle rewards for doing well in school, which usually means doing well on the tests the teacher gives. Even though a teacher may say many times that his chief objective is to enable boys and girls to think critically, if his tests require that they do no more than recall facts or items of information from a textbook, they are going to learn whatever they must in order to recall and answer these questions.

The ideas a teacher has about instructional materials have a greater effect than is generally realized upon his testing practices. Teachers who spend most of their time trying to get boys and girls to reproduce materials taken out of a textbook tend to develop verbal tests very much like the textbooks. These tests often consist of questions with important words left out or statements that must be marked true or false. When a variety of teaching materials is used, a teacher is disposed to increase the variety of the testing situations he uses. A motion picture, for example, may be not only a learning experience but a testing situation as well.

Eventually evaluation data must serve the needs of a number of

---

[19] R. W. Tyler has described in greater detail what he considers to be the major steps involved in evaluation. See "Evaluation Must Be Continual and Flexible; It Must Evaluate," *General Education in the American High School*, pp. 290-308. New York: Scott, Foresman & Co., 1942.

groups, the most important of which includes the pupils who are being taught. Of great importance, too, are the needs of the teachers and administrators in the school system. Any curriculum rests on the belief that certain kinds of learning experiences are good because they bring about desirable changes in pupils. A comprehensive program of evaluation should make it possible constantly to test such a belief. If a large number of teachers and administrators are convinced that secondary-school-age boys and girls will think with greater penetration as a result of having studied algebra and geometry, this "hypothesis" should be put to a test. The only reasonable test is to find out how boys and girls think who differ only in that some have studied algebra and geometry and others have not.

A good program of evaluation must meet the needs of parents too. They should learn what is happening to their sons and daughters. In many instances the vigorous criticisms parents make of schools would be eliminated if the schools provided evidence to justify their practices.

Overloading the Teacher

The preceding discussion of the decisions the teacher must make and the extent to which these decisions are affected by concepts of instructional materials is rather forbidding. It describes the job of the teacher in terms that make it seem an impossible one. Teachers are expected to learn about their pupils, to become familiar with a wide variety of instructional materials, to learn how to use all of these materials, to be thoroughly acquainted with their community, to develop ingenious evaluation instruments, and to live a normal life.

Whether or not fine teaching and normal living are possible depends to a large degree on the way the administrator in the school system plays his role. One of his major responsibilities is to remove from the shoulders of the teachers the burden of red tape frequently involved when a variety of instructional materials is used. The administrator must make help available to teachers, so that they will not need to tackle independently the large number of problems whose solutions are already known.

A teacher, for example, who has thirty to forty pupils in her classroom must not have the additional burden of procuring, caring for, using, and evaluating dozens of different types of audio-visual materials. If help is not given, many teachers who do not have the time and may not have the ability to make all of these choices on their own are continuously frustrated.

Just as the able physician has excellent reference volumes at hand to help him in the prescription of drugs, so the teacher should have at hand carefully evaluated lists of films, recordings, filmstrips, and maps. Suppose that a teacher of literature is having her class read *Julius Caesar*. There should be a reference volume for the teacher in which she could discover that the film excerpt available for purchase from the Eastin Company would be especially useful. She might also decide to play the Orson Wells Mercury Theater records of the play. There may be simple directions available on how to construct a model of the old Globe Theatre. A source unit may provide such information.

A great deal remains to be done before it is reasonable to expect that teachers generally will extend the variety of teaching materials they use. In the first place, materials must be accessible. In many places excellent books, texts, or reference volumes are not available to teachers and pupils. When many types of materials other than books are added, the job of the teacher is greatly complicated. Radio offers an excellent example. Suppose the teacher of an American History class meeting at 2:30 wishes to make use of the President's Address to Congress. It is given at 1:30 P.M. How does she arrange it?

If recording equipment is available in the school, and if an operator is standing by to record such material, there is no problem. The teacher asks to have the broadcast recorded. It is delivered to her for use in the class the next day.

But what if she wishes to have her social-studies class listen to the live broadcast. A rearrangement of class schedules must be made. Or the principal might decide that the broadcast is important enough for everyone to hear. Some broadcasting stations may rebroadcast the material in the evening, and the class can be asked to listen to it. The problem of film accessibility has been discussed in other parts of this yearbook. It is no simple problem.

Another difficulty that deters teachers from using a sufficient variety of teaching materials is that, in all too many instances, little guidance is given in the use of these materials by teacher-training institutions or those responsible for in-service training. (See chaps. v and vi.) The situation with respect to preservice training is improving, but hardly more than one teacher in ten is even now receiving a minimum of instruction in this field. Hundreds of thousands of teachers do not have even the simplest understanding of how to operate and use audio-visual equipment, how to conduct field trips, or how to prepare materials for exhibits or bulletin boards.

CHAPTER V

PRESERVICE TEACHER EDUCATION FOR USE OF AUDIO-VISUAL INSTRUCTIONAL MATERIALS

WILLIAM G. GNAEDINGER
Head, Bureau of Visual Teaching
State College of Washington
Pullman, Washington

INTRODUCTION

Schools, as institutions, have grown to be complex. School personnel reflects this complexity in two ways. On the one hand, we find more and more specialties in the program and specialists on the school staff. And on the other hand, classroom teachers, as the practitioners of the curriculum, are faced with the necessity of becoming familiar with even more educational developments and practices in order to take advantage of the services which new specialties afford. As a result, the curriculum for teacher education has become, over the years, extremely crowded.

Few of the additions to teacher-training present the problems and potentialities that lie in the field of audio-visual instructional materials. Let us examine the ways in which beginning teachers are being trained to utilize the newer materials and methods in order to realize that potential.

It is only about thirty years since the first courses were offered to prospective teachers in the use of audio-visual materials. Courses of this type remained few (about ten or a dozen in the United States) until about 1930. During the early years of the ensuing decade a number of additional institutions offered audio-visual training, and by 1940 there were probably five or six times as many courses offered. Since 1940, the course offerings in the audio-visual field have increased so rapidly that there are, at this writing, somewhere near four hundred available, thirty or forty times as many as in 1930.

The increase in courses offered to American teachers is spectacular.

Yet the total number of courses is not sufficient. As late as 1946, superintendents of city school systems reported that one of the chief obstacles to their development of successful audio-visual programs was "disinterest on the part of the classroom teachers or inability on their part to select and use audio-visual materials in an effective way. If this is true—and the conclusion finds support in most of the recent literature on the subject—a tremendous program of teacher education is indicated which will include both specialized instruction in colleges of teacher education and locally arranged programs for on-the-job-training."[1] This obstacle is obviously not going to be completely overcome by adding more college courses. Much will depend on the effective organization of in-service training for teachers now in the field. This matter is treated in chapter vi. The responsibility of teacher-training institutions is to work toward the end that the prospective teacher will not become an in-service liability. That will take more training at the preservice level and training of a high quality.

The Content of Preservice Audio-visual Courses

An investigation by DeKieffer[2] into the present (1947) status of teacher-training in the audio-visual field presents rather complete information as to the content of introductory audio-visual courses. DeKieffer reports the following distribution of units or topics, and the percentage of all courses which included each item:

Unit or Topic	Percentage
1. Utilization of materials	97.0
2. Selection of materials	96.0
3. Operation of equipment	95.0
4. Evaluation of materials	93.0
5. History and philosophy of audio-visual education	87.0
6. Administration of audio-visual programs	78.0
7.* Production of nonphotographic aids	63.0
8.* Production of photographic aids	44.0
9.* Radio script-writing, transcriptions, and recordings	35.0
10.* Other types of production	21.0
11. Other items	12.0

* Production activities were separated into four groups marked * for more precise information on those activities.

---

[1] *Audio-Visual Education in City School Systems*, p. 165. Research Bulletin of the National Education Association, Vol. XXIV, No. 4. Washington: Research Division of the National Education Association, 1946.

[2] Robert E. DeKieffer, "The Status of Teacher-training in Audio-visual Education in the Forty-eight States," pp. 79-81. Unpublished Doctor's Dissertation, State University of Iowa, 1948.

There is evident concentration of emphasis on the first five items reported. The chief reason for this is that all of them pertain to the basic problem—to the fact that teachers need to be able to select and use materials effectively. Item five fortifies that ability with basic understanding.

The remaining units diminish quite rapidly in frequency of inclusion in courses. As a matter of fact, it is rather surprising in some respects to notice that "administration" holds such a high rank in what is basically a teacher's area of study. Perhaps this emphasis on administration is in recognition of the need to develop new leadership for school departments of audio-visual materials. Or it may be fairly general acceptance of the principle stated by Dale in his discussion of the administration of audio-visual materials. He says, in part: "All teachers must participate in administration. As a teacher you must help plan for effective administration of curriculum materials, for, if you do not, a curriculum will be handed down to you from above." [3]

That less emphasis is placed on teacher production-skills is readily understandable. Heavy demands are made on any institution which offers audio-visual training with respect to providing equipment, materials, and personnel. Training for production increases that demand sharply and adds a heavy drain on student and instructor time. All of these factors will have a profound effect on determining the content of the introductory audio-visual course.

DeKieffer's study [4] does not include data on the content of courses in the audio-visual field other than those cited. A separate attempt has been made to find out other ways by which institutions, in general, are meeting the problems incurred by the broad content and special skills inherent in audio-visual practices. A study of the listings in catalogs and announcements of over one hundred colleges and universities known to be offering such training points out certain trends. Next to an introductory or survey course in audio-visual methods and/or materials, a separate course in administration of such programs is most frequently offered. As in the tabulation of topics for introductory courses, there is a wide difference in frequency of appearance of the third course offered, namely, a course in production techniques, either photographic, nonphotographic, or in a combination of those two areas. There is no general grouping of special audio-visual courses outside of those just mentioned, except in the field of radio

---

[3] Edgar Dale, *Audio-Visual Methods in Teaching*. New York: Dryden Press, 1946.

[4] *Op. cit.*

(in education). They are not included here, though their number exceeds the audio-visual administration listings, because it was impossible to ascertain which of them were directed specifically to teacher training.

Along with the units included in audio-visual courses for the prospective teacher, and courses which develop some of these units into specialized areas of study, the methods by which these materials are presented is of considerable significance. The whole substance of the audio-visual field implies the concept of "doing." It is anomalous for instructors in the audio-visual field to fail to "practice what they preach." And yet one course is known to have been offered recently which consisted wholly of a series of lectures covering the audio-visual field. That is, of course, and fortunately, an exception. DeKieffer again offers some data to support that statement. He states:

> The questionnaire returns indicate that from 75 to 100 per cent of the (teacher training) institutions require students to handle and operate all of the following types of material and equipment: slide and filmstrip projectors, 16-mm. sound motion picture projector, opaque projector, flat pictures, maps and globes, objects, specimens, and models. In 50 to 75 per cent of the institutions students operate and handle all of the following: record and transcription players, exhibits, and dioramas. In 25 to 50 per cent of the institutions students are required to handle and operate all of the following: 16-mm. silent motion picture projector, classroom radio, recording equipment, and the still camera. (The) microscope projector, microfilm reader, motion picture camera, and darkroom for developing photographic aids are audio-visual materials and equipment which students in 25 per cent or less of the institutions are required to operate and handle. The percentage of institutions in which instructors only use and demonstrate these tools to learning varies from 6 to 38.[5]

In all of these cases except one—recording equipment—the institutions reported that the percentage of student operation exceeded instructor operation, generally to a very high degree.

To recapitulate the important elements in this discussion of the content of present audio-visual materials courses:

1. Present introductory courses emphasize selection, use, and evaluation of materials. Practice in handling materials and equipment is stressed. Considerable attention is given to the history and philosophy of audio-visual education, and a somewhat surprising amount to the administrative aspects of the program.
2. Production of materials of all kinds receives a secondary emphasis in present introductory courses.

---

[5] *Op. cit.*, p. 77.

3. Special courses in certain aspects of the audio-visual materials field are offered by many institutions. Of these, administration of audio-visual programs appears most frequently. Production of materials is next most frequently offered as a special course. Radio (in education) is widely offered, but its orientation to teacher-training is not plain.
4. In general, the methods stressed in audio-visual training characterize the courses offered to teachers.

Teachers' Needs in Audio-visual Training

Following is a list of the most difficult problems faced by beginning teachers and reported by them:

> Give us guidance in what to do about discipline.
> Help us to know children and provide for their individual and group needs.
> Show us how the teaching-learning situation may be made more effective.
> Help us to locate materials of instruction.
> Give us leads in working with other adults.
> Tell us about routines (school operation mechanics).[6]

One course in audio-visual materials and methods will not meet all of these needs, but there are some rather obvious points of coincidence. Such a course should certainly help in locating materials of instruction. Learning the mechanics of procurement and handling of materials should contribute greatly to acquaintance with school routines. The study of administrative aspects of the materials problem should be even more helpful in this regard. However, the greatest contribution of training in the audio-visual field should come in meeting the second and third of the problems listed above. Corey sets the stage for this contribution in his statement:

> Certainly, instructional materials of any sort . . . have one major function. They tend to control the experiences of children so that their activities will result in desirable learning . . . when boys and girls study a motion picture in the classroom (they) do so because they, or their teacher, or both, are convinced that reacting to this particular motion picture (instructional material) will change attitudes, or increase information, or perfect some skill in a relatively efficient manner.[7]

Instructional materials are the tools, the wise use of which will give the teacher many ways to meet the needs of individuals and groups. And certainly they will make the learning situation more effective. The end is desirable learning, and instructional materials are

---

[6] "These Are Our Concerns," *Educational Leadership*, V (December, 1947), 145-54.

[7] Stephen M. Corey, "Imperatives in Instructional Materials," *Educational Leadership*, V (January, 1948), 211-14.

important means to that end. The teacher must be competent in their utilization, and the lack of such competency is implicit in both the superintendents' and teachers' reports of obstacles and problems.

THE PLACE OF AUDIO-VISUAL TRAINING IN THE TEACHER-TRAINING PROGRAM

Specific, introductory courses in audio-visual materials are becoming more common in American teacher-training institutions. The content of these courses seems to be fairly well adapted to the needs which teachers mention as their reason for seeking such training. One rather consistent characteristic of audio-visual courses has been the inclusion of numerous laboratory experiences. In this respect, the audio-visual course represents a departure from most teacher-training as it has been generally known. Especially interesting in this regard is the fact that many of the teaching materials and techniques which antedate the "audio-visual era" are given more specific attention than formerly. For example, many of the present courses in materials contain sections dealing with theory and practice with such long-known devices as the blackboard and bulletin board. The prospective teacher now often learns by practice how to mount and classify flat pictures, to prepare models, dioramas and exhibits, to take photographs, write radio scripts and other dramatic presentations, and to make lantern slides, charts and maps. Along with these construction skills, attention is given to familiarizing the teacher with the operating skills to enable her to manipulate projectors, players, and other mechanical devices. Thus, audio-visual courses have been designed to encompass newer materials and techniques, and, as they expanded their scope, have given specific training in better uses of many older ones. Such detailed emphasis on practice prior to use has not been a characteristic of similar types of teacher-training in the past.

One trend developing from increasing interest in audio-visual materials is the introduction of more varied materials and techniques into the teacher-training program as a whole. The second trend which is discernible at present is traceable to a considerable extent to the first. This movement appears in the development of more specialized courses. They still appear under "audio-visual" headings but represent more specific approaches. In many cases, of course, they are not designed to fit general teacher-training. Rather, they attempt to present a field for specialized study, to prepare the specialist who will appear in schools as the director, co-ordinator, or supervisor of audio-visual materials services. On the other hand, there is a tendency in some places to encourage all teachers to enrol in a series of courses dealing with the materials field. The offering in most institutions numbers two or three courses. The first of these is designed to give a survey of audio-visual teaching materials and methods. Subsequent courses usually emphasize administrative phases of audio-visual programs or production activities, such as photography, recorded sound, handicraft and design, together with emphasis on manipulation of mechanical equipment and devices.

Generally speaking, the tendency toward multiple courses for teacher-training is found in institutions which consider the problem of instructional materials to merit about the same emphasis as the problems of methods, supervision, or other similar special fields.

In the eyes, then, of many who are responsible for the preservice training of teachers, there is opening another broad area of experience for the prospective teacher. In some instances it is being treated as an aspect of method. Elsewhere, audio-visual materials are included in general curriculum studies or allied only with laboratory-school or cadet-teaching experience. In a few institutions the materials field has been given equal emphasis with other areas of teaching preparation.

In many teacher-training institutions there has been a reluctance to take steps which would tend to isolate teaching materials from the more conventionally accepted areas of study in teacher preparation. Rather than adding courses to the teacher-training program, these institutions have chosen to expand existing course work to include experiences with audio-visual materials. No fixed pattern exists for this approach to the problem. In some cases "audio-visual aids" is only a section of the reading reference list in the general methods course. In others, a topic or unit of the general methods training is given over to consideration of all instructional materials. Expanding this somewhat, the unit is sometimes accompanied by several hours of laboratory experience with the manipulation of various types of equipment and with the examination and handling of several kinds of materials. Still another approach to audio-visual materials is represented in those methods courses which intersperse experiences with various materials and techniques along with the study of various approaches to classroom situations.

A departure from the correlated activity suggested by these different treatments appears in the form of a laboratory which functions separately from, but concurrently with, general- or special-methods instruction. As the laboratories are organized, they are designed to teach prospective teachers specific skills involved in the organizing and handling of audio-visual materials and equipment and to relate the laboratory experiences to the activities of the methods classes.

Closely akin to this arrangement is one by which a series of experiences of a laboratory nature is distributed over an extended period, in some instances, of several years. Under this plan, during one phase of the teacher-training program, a student might spend a few hours learning to manipulate projection equipment. At another time, and in connection with another course, he would be studying a collection of materials to develop skill in selection of items for various classroom needs. Again, a few hours are spent in simple production practice, such as making lantern slides or mounting pictures for study or display. In each case, he undertakes the laboratory experience at a time when it relates to course work underway in some part of his total training program. It might be added that this plan for training in audio-visual practices is possible only where there exists a well-equipped college audio-visual center. It is a type of program which demands considerable flexibility and a resourceful consultant staff, together with large collections of materials and equipment to meet needs on a nearly individual basis.

In nearly all the situations discussed above, the units, topics, or laboratory periods dealing with audio-visual materials are related to methods courses. In some few instances, however, they appear in connection with courses giving a general introduction to education, with curriculum courses, or with courses dealing with the organization of elementary, junior high, or high schools. Other units appear also in plans for training of administrators, general supervisors, and specialists such as guidance counselors, librarians, and subject-matter directors.

Among a great many of those who are at present engaged in the training of teachers in audio-visual methods, there is general agreement on one very important opinion. Their task would be greatly simplified if the well-planned, well-executed use of audio-visual materials were characteristic of the whole teaching program at their respective institutions. Thus, one very important aspect of the preservice training of teachers in the audio-visual field is the in-service training of the college staff. These instructors have had no more opportunity to become acquainted with new materials and methods than have the teaching staffs of our public schools, and yet their practices will, invariably, be reflected in the teaching done by their students. It can probably be agreed that these teaching staffs should represent the highest development of classroom skill, but the effect of class experiences which their prospective students have in other departments should not be minimized.

Many of the teacher-trainers who have been consulted as to their opinions on the need for, and emphasis on, specific training in audio-visual practices agree that there would be no need for course work in the field if student-teachers were accustomed to participating in classes where varied materials and techniques were brought into play to meet the constantly changing learning situation.

These teaching staffs would be content to reserve the specialized training for those who plan to become specialists in audio-visual instructional materials. They view the possibility of achieving such ends as so remote, however, that a very considerable majority not only favor specific course work in audio-visual methods but even favor such a requirement for graduation and/or certification of teachers. The whole problem of just what to require for teacher-training is complex, and no useful purpose can be served by going into it at length here. It might be well to point out that the first "certification" effort to require teachers to be well qualified in audio-visual practices (in Pennsylvania) has not met with spectacular success. It probably remains true that prospective teachers will reflect more desirable outcomes from those courses in which they are most interested, whatever the reason for that interest. A marked reaction to required courses is the development of attitudes which tend to regard requirements as obstacles to personal freedom, and teacher-education programs are notorious already for their lack of elective flexibility. Over against these arguments can be set the feeling of urgency on the part of a great many that teachers must be given an opportunity to become skilled in the use of newer communication tools. The results of the recent adoption in California of audio-visual training requirements for certification will be watched with interest.

A proposal is receiving study in at least one institution which might have very broad implications with reference to the place of audio-visual training in the over-all preservice program. A plan is being considered to combine several education courses into single, larger, more inclusive areas of study. Out of such action, if it were taken, might come a plan by which instructional materials would be dealt with, now as a curriculum problem, again in context with the "unit approach to teaching," and again in terms of their place in the school organization. Such decompartmentalization presents some interesting possibilities if it ever becomes a reality. It is worth noting here that most specialists in audio-visual materials, who were asked to comment on the possibilities of integrating audio-visual training into methods courses only, were not inclined to think it could be satisfactorily done. School administrators who responded to the query were in favor of such a move.

A summary of the above discussion will be helpful in pointing out trends or directions which audio-visual training may take in our teacher-training institutions.

1. Introductory courses in audio-visual materials are being offered in more and more institutions. Laboratory experience, of a highly practical nature, is characteristic of these courses.
2. Some institutions are adding several courses in the audio-visual field, both for teachers and for specialists.
3. Some institutions are handling the matter by including units or topics on instructional materials in existing education courses.
4. Other institutions are setting up audio-visual training as laboratory experience, integrated closely with an existing education course, or supplied at intervals throughout the preprofessional training.
5. The usual orientation of short courses, units, and topics, as well as of laboratory experiences, is with methods classes or cadet-teaching. Some institutions, however, place these experiences within curriculum courses or those dealing with general school organization and function. Special methods courses, and those for the training of administrators, supervisors, counselors, and librarians, sometimes include units on audio-visual materials.
6. Instructors and others interested in training teachers in the audio-visual areas agree that effective use of instructional materials in *all* college classes would facilitate their work. Many say that such a practice would eliminate the need for any specific audio-visual course work.
7. A majority of such teacher-trainers who have been consulted in connection with this paper not only favor requiring audio-visual courses separate from other course work but even favor such a requirement for graduation and/or certification of teachers.
8. One proposal, at least, has been advanced to combine the audio-visual training problem with others and to meet them all by organizing broad, integrated education courses which would combine many experiences in varying situations, without the bias of specific course objectives.

The chief conclusion which can be drawn from this summary is that teacher-training institutions have not yet settled on a uniform standard for the organization of audio-visual training experiences for the prospective teacher. The growth of the number of introductory courses, as previously noted, and the fairly uniform course content, outlined under the "Content of Preservice Audio-visual Courses," shows that the need is recognized. The problem is one of determining the best way to include audio-visual training in an already complex program.

The studies, books, and articles referred to in this paper are guideposts along the way to a solution of the problem. Many others might be mentioned. Quite aside from the audio-visual materials field, the whole problem of teacher education is under scrutiny and study. Perhaps many other aspects of this total problem will need to be adjusted before we arrive at a fairly satisfactory solution of the one dealt with here.

From recently available information, two projects now under way give some promise of help in making audio-visual training more effective. One of these is a doctoral study at Columbia University by Constance Weinman, entitled "A Guide for a Teacher-training Institution in Initiating and Developing an Adequate Audio-visual Program." A second study which promises specific help for teacher-training in the audio-visual field is that of the State College of Washington, under the direction of Herbert Hite. The project title is "An Evaluation of Teacher-training Activities in Audio-visual Education in the State of Washington, 1937-47."

It is safe to say that the use of audio-visual instructional materials is characteristic of good teaching programs in good schools everywhere. It should be equally safe to predict that teacher-training institutions will add what they learn as time passes to what they now know and do; and that adequate preparation of prospective teachers in audio-visual methods will become an integral part of the training of every prospective classroom leader.

The College Audio-visual Center

No treatment of audio-visual training for teachers would be complete without at least the mention of the facilities which give body to the experience. It is safe to say that adequate teacher-training will depend to a great extent on the type of services and materials available for use during the teacher's preservice experience. The whole logic of an audio-visual materials program revolves around the concept that teachers in the field will gain results accordingly as they are able to *do* things *with* things. What, then, more natural than that, in their training, they must be supplied with all possible services in the way of materials, equipment, and guidance in order that the desired competencies can be practiced? Therein lies the function of the college audio-visual center. It is a necessity in the preservice audio-visual training program.

One guide to the functions of such a center is supplied in the report of the results of an investigation carried on in 1945 by Western Illinois State Teachers College. The problems and functions of a college audio-visual center appear in this publication as "Problems To Be Considered by the Institutional Faculty."[8] They are:

1. The need for guidance in setting up an audio-visual program that will function effectively.
2. Misinterpretation or indifference in regard to the functions of the audio-visual department.
3. Recognizing and assuming responsibility in training teachers.
4. Providing an extensive in-service training program for the faculty of the institution.
5. Developing an efficient and systematic method of keeping the faculty informed concerning new materials as they become available.

Pertinent to the above, and listed as special problems in the same discussion, were three means by which the five general problems might be met. They probably apply equally to any institution and to any program of teacher education, particularly in its audio-visual aspects. These three means to the end are: adequate staff, adequate equipment, and adequate materials. A fourth is noted and is worth special mention. It calls for using the means at hand more effectively.

An implication might be drawn from the last statement which would not bypass the importance of developing an adequate college audio-visual center, nor does it mean that nothing need be done. It does suggest that teacher-training in the use of audio-visual materials might be vastly improved, starting where we are. Every college campus represents a collection of resources for resourceful teachers. Perhaps the most immediate gain and, at the same time the most lasting, lies in making the most of what is at hand. Therein may lie the most important mission of the college audio-visual center.

REFERENCES

Audio-visual Education in City School Systems. Research Bulletin of the National Education Association, Vol. XXIV, No. 4. Washington: Research Division of the National Education Association, 1946.

COREY, STEPHEN M. "Audio-visual Aids and Teacher-training Institutions, *Educational Screen,* XXIV (June, 1945), 226-27.

[8] *The Functions of an Audio-visual Department in a Teacher-education Institution.* Western Illinois State Teachers College Bulletin, Vol. XXVI, No. 4. Macomb, Illinois: Western Illinois State Teachers College, 1946.

———. "Imperatives in Instructional Materials," *Educational Leadership*, V (January, 1948), 211-14.
DALE, EDGAR. *Audio-Visual Methods in Teaching*. New York: Dryden Press, 1946.
DEBERNARDIS, AMO, and BROWN, JAMES W. "Study of Teacher Skills and Knowledges Necessary for the Use of Audio-visual Aids," *Elementary School Journal*, XLVI (June, 1946), 550-56.
DEBERNARDIS, AMO, and LANGE, PHIL C. "Teacher-training in the Use of Instructional Materials," *Educational Screen*, XXIV (December, 1945), 447-49.
DEKIEFFER, ROBERT E. "The Status of Teacher-training in Audio-visual Education in the Forty-eight States." Unpublished Doctor's Dissertation, State University of Iowa, 1948.
The Functions of an Audio-visual Department in a Teacher-education Institution. Western Illinois State Teachers College Bulletin, Vol. XXVI, No. 4. Macomb, Illinois: Western Illinois State Teachers College, 1946.
HOBAN, CHARLES FRANCIS; HOBAN, CHARLES FRANCIS, JR.; and ZISMAN, SAMUEL B. *Visualizing the Curriculum*. New York: Cordon Co., 1937.
JAYNE, CLARENCE D. "Standards in Teacher-training in the Use of Visual Aids," *Educational Screen*, XIX (March, 1940), 110-14.
MCCONNELL, R. E. *Audio-visual Education in Teacher Education*. Twenty-sixth Yearbook of the American Association of Teachers Colleges. Washington: National Education Association, 1947.
MCKOWN, HARRY C., and ROBERTS, ALVIN B. *Audio-visual Aids to Instruction.* New York: McGraw-Hill Book Co., 1940.
MILES, JOHN R., and SPAIN, CHARLES R. *Audio-visual Aids in the Armed Services: Implications for American Education*. Report of the Commission on Implications of Armed Services Educational Programs. Washington: American Council on Education, 1947.

CHAPTER VI

IN-SERVICE TEACHER EDUCATION FOR USE OF AUDIO-VISUAL INSTRUCTIONAL MATERIALS

Amo DeBernardis
Director of Instructional Materials
Portland Public Schools
Portland, Oregon

Introduction

Three years ago Mary Smith would have been called by many a "traditional" teacher. She was content to cover the material in the textbook and to follow the course of study to the letter. She had been teaching for fifteen years and had developed a definite pattern for doing things. She had made the "three R's" the center of her educational philosophy. That is the way she sized up teaching until one day three years ago. In a staff meeting she saw a film on the "Constitution." It was a good film, and it happened to be shown at a time when her class was studying the chapter on "The Constitution" in the textbook. That film set off a chain of events which changed Miss Smith's concepts of teaching. This did not happen overnight. It was a slow process and it is still going on.

Miss Smith felt that she must have that film for her class, and the principal arranged to have it shown for her in the auditorium. The class enjoyed it very much and asked many questions about the people in the film. Why did they dress the way they did? How long did it take for letters to go from New York to Philadelphia? Why were people so slow in ratifying the Constitution? In fact, so many questions were asked which were not answered in the textbook that children began to bring in other books and materials to help them find the answers. As a result, Miss Smith found it difficult to limit the discussion and reading to the chapter in the textbook. The children even wanted to make a trip to the museum in a near-by city to see some photostatic copies of the original documents. This she was reluctant to do as the children would miss school for a day, and, besides, there were the problems of transportation and expense. But even Miss Smith felt some of the enthusiasm generated in the class.

Many things have happened since Miss Smith used her first film. The principal, aware of her growing interest in films, encouraged her to use other films and to enrol in an extension course on audio-visual aids. The materials co-ordinator in the building helped her to locate other teaching aids which she found just as useful as the motion-picture film. In time, Miss Smith became an active participant in staff discussions on the use of audio-visual materials. To put it in her own words: "These aids have made my teaching more interesting for me, and I know my children enjoy their classes more. I found, also, that their mastery of the tool subjects progressed at least as rapidly as it had before I introduced these more interesting features into the daily program."

The experience of Miss Smith is not unique. It can be duplicated many times, not in exactly the same way, but with comparable results. It should be observed that Miss Smith's understanding and use of audio-visual materials was not begun through some administrative order. It was initiated by chance, but, after that interest was manifested, sympathetic and understanding leadership helped provide her with many and varied opportunities for growth in the use of these materials.

Through the whole process of in-service education, Miss Smith became a better user of audio-visual materials and, consequently, a better leader of boys and girls. In the first place, she acquired a better understanding of the psychology of learning. She learned the importance of supplementing the verbalism of the usual classroom instruction with such actual or vicarious experiences as she could manage to bring into the classroom. Second, she became acquainted with a variety of audio-visual aids which have helped her to provide worth-while experiences for boys and girls. Third, she became aware of the administrative procedures necessary to carry out such a program and learned how to take advantage of them. Above all, she became a more original person because she threw off the rigid restraints of the textbook and acquired a greater freedom of choice and a greater sense of personal direction. Let us analyze this process of in-service training in order to discover how it operates and how it may be developed to its highest efficiency in the school system.

FACTORS WHICH CONTRIBUTE TO A SUCCESSFUL PROGRAM OF IN-SERVICE TEACHER EDUCATION FOR AUDIO-VISUAL AIDS

Anyone charged with the responsibility of planning audio-visual in-service experiences for teachers would do well to consider some of the general factors which help to make all such programs successful.

Since in-service training is, for the most part, a group activity, the whole problem of group dynamics is crucial. Questions such as these immediately come to mind: How do you get all individuals in a group to participate? What is the responsibility of the leader (instructor, supervisor)? How is progress to be measured? How large a group can be handled effectively? What kinds of facilities are necessary? How should individual, as well as group, problems be treated? No attempt will be made here to answer all the specific questions relating to group work. Perhaps the general principles listed below may be of help.

Provide effective leadership. This is the crux of any program. Without adequate leadership any plan is doomed to failure. An effective leader is one who knows how to obtain and develop co-operation, who recognizes the worth of every member in the group, who allows others to assume roles of leadership when appropriate situations arise, who knows how to delegate responsibility, who recognizes the various roles which must be assumed in a group to make it successful, and who realizes that he doesn't know all the answers but understands that a free exchange of ideas is basic to group action.

Fit the program to the needs of the teachers. No learning situation is quite so successful as one which meets the needs of the individual learner, be that learner a child or an adult. Most teachers have problems on which they need help, but unless the proper rapport exists between the teacher and the leader, the teacher may not ask for the needed help. A co-operative spirit must be an accomplished fact before the teacher will define the areas in which he wants assistance. It is the responsibility of those directing the in-service program to develop this rapport and thus get at the real needs of teachers. Only in this way can the instruction in the classroom be affected.

Proceed slowly. The acquisition of a new skill, idea, or concept is not a rapid process. What seems simple to an experienced person may require a considerable length of time for the inexperienced person to grasp. Anyone who is anxious to get things moving in a certain direction may hasten progress to a point where dissatisfaction is the result. "Frequently a change is adopted 'on paper,' but, in instance after instance, the very rapidity with which the change has been put into effect has brought about a reaction which leaves the school staff more confused and possibly more conservative and reactionary than it has been before the change was initiated."[1] Endeavoring to cover a set amount of ground in a definite time may not lead to maximum teacher understandings and skills. This is especially true when developing skills in the operation of equipment. The acquisition of these skills is important and, though they may take more time than the instructor thinks he should spend on them, sufficient time should be allowed for the necessary practice. It will "pay off" in better teacher attitudes toward audio-visual aids and better use of them in the classroom.

Provide for group planning. Every individual wants to feel he is part of a group. Teachers are no exception. Perhaps there is no better way to develop this feeling of "belongingness" than to have the teacher participate actively in the planning of the program of in-service education. The audio-visual area offers many opportunities for teacher participation in every stage of each activity. Previews, field trips, committee reports, and scheduling of equipment are aspects of an audio-visual program in which those participating can help plan the work for the group. By getting the teachers to help with organizing their own experiences in in-service education, a more active and interested group is sure to be the result.

Keep size of groups small. If groups become too large, it is difficult to break down the reserve of the individual. Large groups have a tendency to make the learning environment more formal so that many teachers are reluctant to express themselves. Also, if groups are too large, finding sufficient opportunity for instruction on the use of equipment becomes a problem. The maximum number of teachers for effective group work in audio-visual aids seems to be about twenty.

Provide adequate time. If the growth of teachers in proper use of audio-visual aids is worth while, then adequate time should be provided in the daily or weekly program for in-service training. Some of the plans tried by various schools to provide more time are: early dismissal of all children one day a week to take care of other activities such as dental appointments; Saturday-morning meetings once a month; one week previous to the beginning of the term, or the week immediately following the end of the term, for workshops, committee work and other planning activities. This time should be included in the salary schedule. Teachers cannot be expected to add the work of

---

[1] Stephen M. Corey, "Co-operative Staff Work," *School Review,* LII (June, 1944), 341.

in-service education to a full schedule of teaching duties without some compensation.

Provide adequate facilities, materials, and equipment. Nothing discourages a teacher more in a program of audio-visual training than lack of materials and equipment with which to work. All types of equipment and a large variety of materials should be available to meet individual needs. Preview room and work laboratory are valuable additions to the audio-visual department. The audio-visual library should include books, periodicals, and pamphlets, in sufficient number to fill the requirements of the group.

Methods and Techniques for Facilitating Teacher Growth in the Use of Audio-visual Aids

Any plan for in-service education of teachers should consider the various methods and techniques which have proven valuable for the implementation of the program. It is unwise to claim that any one of the activities listed below is more successful than any other. What may be effective in one situation may not be of equal value elsewhere.

Space does not permit a detailed discussion of all the types of in-service training that have been employed to improve the use of audio-visual aids. However, some of the more common practices are discussed below.

Extension Courses

Since colleges and universities now accept responsibility for teacher education beyond the formal work taken on the college campus, many institutions are providing opportunity for continued college work "off campus." In recent years, the number of extension courses given in audio-visual aids has increased. Many teachers like this type of in-service education as it allows them to earn college credit toward advanced degrees and at the same time get needed experience in the use of these newer instructional aids.

The following program offered by the University of Connecticut is a good example of the topics covered in the typical audio-visual extension course:

First meeting:	Description of the Course
	The great movement for audio-visual teaching aids in education
Second meeting:	The role of audio-visual aids in the setting for learning
Third meeting:	The school journey
Fourth meeting:	Museum material and museums
Fifth-sixth meeting:	The motion picture

Seventh meeting: Standard, hand-made, and 2 x 2 slides
Eighth meeting: Filmstrips, opaque projection, and the flat picture
Ninth meeting: Radio in education
Tenth meeting: Recordings and dramatizations
Eleventh meeting: Graphics
Twelfth meeting: Teacher competence in the utilization of audio-visual aids
Thirteenth meeting: Administration and supervision of audio-visual aids. The role of the teacher in developing centralized audio-visual aids services
Fourteenth meeting: Physical aspects of audio-visual aids utilization
Fifteenth meeting: Final examination

A somewhat different plan for giving extension work in audio-visual aids has been put into effect by the Oregon state system of higher education. This plan combines the feature of the conferences with laboratory and individual-project method. A one-day institute is held in a given community during which time schools are not in session. Specialists, teachers, administrators, and commercial representatives are first asked to present an overview of the entire field of audio-visual materials. Demonstrations of various types of equipment and materials are then given throughout the day. Provision is also made for teachers to meet later in small discussion groups to consider specific types of aids. A typical institute program is shown below:

8:30	Introductory remarks—objective of the course
8:45— 9:05	The place of instructional aids in the learning process
9:05— 9:35	Community resources as aids to learning
9:35—10:05	The bulletin board as an aid to learning
10:05—10:25	The blackboard as an aid to learning
10:30—12:30	Sectional meetings devoted to various types of aids
12:30— 1:30	Lunch
1:30— 2:30	Planning—key to success in use of audio-visual aids
2:30— 3:00	The place of motion pictures in learning
3:00— 5:00	Sectional meetings

The one-day conference is followed by three evening-laboratory sessions. Here the participants have an opportunity to learn how to operate and use the various types of audio-visual equipment. Enough assistants are provided to give each teacher individual instruction. As a finale to the group phase of the plan, each teacher selects two projects which are of primary concern to him. These projects are worked out on the job and are turned in to the person in charge of the program of audio-visual extension.

Examples of these special "individualized" projects are: the documenting of the use of motion pictures in a study of contemporary American life; or a log of a field trip in conjunction with the study of the dairy industry. Every effort is made to fit this phase of the work to the needs of the teachers and to acquaint them with the types of aids available. Teachers are encouraged to plan the use of audio-visual materials for all the units they teach. The response and approval of teachers and administrators to this type of in-service training has been most favorable.

If the extension, or off-campus, work is to be nothing more than another college course, its effectiveness will be limited. There is no reason why these off-campus services cannot be planned to fit the needs of teachers and have the same air of informality that other in-service techniques have. Colleges planning off-campus work in audio-visual aids should strive to keep the program of courses as flexible as possible and not regard them as subject-matter courses.

Audio-visual Conferences and Institutes

One of the traditional methods of helping teachers grow in service is by means of the conference or institute. Although audio-visual conferences are held each year, the usefulness of this device in promoting teacher growth has been seriously questioned. However, many of the criticisms leveled at the institute can be traced to inadequate planning and poor leadership. One of the faults of audio-visual conferences is that they are too general in nature and too verbal.

Audio-visual meetings should offer good examples of the best usage of the materials the teachers are advised to use. Teachers cannot be expected to develop much enthusiasm for the materials if all they have witnessed is a good example of verbalism. Many people are beginning to realize this and are making the institute more practical and realistic. A good example of this approach is the Tacoma, Washington, Audio-Visual Education Review (conference). The plan holds speech-making to a minimum and allows most of the time for critical observation of audio-visual aids in action. The schedule is so arranged that teachers can see as many as three different types of aids in use. As many specific situations are illustrated as possible. At the March, 1948, conference, approximately thirty-eight different demonstrations were given. The teacher, in the time allowed for the conference, could select any three which appealed to him. A few are listed below to illustrate the variety:

Graphic materials in economics
Opaque projector in physical education
Homemade equipment in science
Flower arrangements for the home
The tape recorder in junior high school music
Miniature slides in junior high school social studies
The tape recorder in junior high school literature
Phonograph records in second-grade spelling
Slidefilm in fifth-grade geography concepts
Motion picture, "Candlemaking," in kindergarten handwork
Museum objects in a sixth-grade social-studies unit on Mexico
Charts in intermediate music

A conference of this kind has the advantage of allowing teachers to select from a large variety of topics those which fit their individual needs and interests. Also, most of the demonstrations were conducted by classroom teachers who are actually using the aids in their instruction. Teachers tend to be more receptive to new techniques when they hear one of their own group relate experiences with them. Planners of audio-visual institutes would do well to include more classroom teachers on the program and base the discussion and demonstrations around actual classroom situations. Audio-visual methods should be used wherever possible. Only in this way can the conference method become a valuable experience for teachers.

The Professional Teachers' Meetings

One of the methods frequently employed for stimulating a greater use of audio-visual aids is the teachers' meetings. Perhaps no other activity offers more opportunity for real teacher growth. However, if much of the time is consumed by announcements or lectures on topics of little interest, not much can be expected in the way of creating teacher enthusiasm for the improvement of instruction. "The teachers must be interested in a program of professional improvement, and, if they are interested, they will be willing to give their time to the consideration of educational problems which pertain to their professional growth." [2]

The principal of the school has the responsibility for developing the teacher's interest in professional improvement. Very little progress in the use of new methods and techniques of audio-visual education can be expected unless the teaching staff has been sufficiently motivated

---

[2] William C. Reavis, Paul R. Pierce, and Edward W. Stullken, *The Elementary School: Its Organization and Administration*, p. 287. Chicago: University of Chicago Press, 1931.

to investigate its possibilities. A great deal can be done in these faculty meetings to broaden the teacher's concepts of instructional materials and to encourage the use of new materials.

Interest in the study of these aids may be generated in a number of ways. Perhaps a new piece of equipment has just come on the market. A demonstration will do much to create discussion as to its values and limitations. Any spirited discussion centered around the problems confronting teachers in the use of audio-visual materials and equipment in the building will create interest. An equipment clinic where teachers can learn to operate machines might be the spark which will set off a great deal of thinking and experimentation. Previews and discussions of new materials have been used with a great deal of success in acquainting the teaching staff with the variety and usefulness of materials relating to different subjects.

An example of how a series of professional meetings might be devoted to the study of audio-visual aids is here given.

First meeting:	General discussion of the program of audio-visual aids and its implications for the school
Second meeting:	Audio-visual director from neighboring school district to discuss audio-visual aids—committee appointed to make survey of local audio-visual situation
Third meeting:	Committee report on local survey of audio-visual situation—selection of audio-visual co-ordinator
Fourth meeting:	Demonstration of audio-visual equipment and materials
Fifth meeting:	Committee report on audio-visual services in the local area: film libraries, equipment, slides, etc.
Sixth meeting:	Group planning and discussion on audio-visual aids to correlate with the curriculum. Committee appointed to investigate materials for various areas of curriculum
Seventh meeting:	Organized program for school—appoint committee on audio-visual aids to set up long-range plan
Eighth meeting:	Plan program of in-service training for teachers
Ninth meeting:	Selection of materials and equipment. Plans for further meetings discussed [3]

The principal is the key person in developing a program of in-service training within a particular school. The audio-visual program is no exception. The kind of educational climate which is created by

---

[3] Amo DeBernardis, "A Program for a School," *The Principal and Audio-Visual Education*, pp. 20-21. Washington: Department of Elementary School Principals of the National Education Association, 1947-48.

the principal for the use of these aids will, in a large measure, determine how effectively they are used. Without his leadership and guidance no program for teacher growth in the use of instructional materials can hope to be successful.

The Audio-visual Workshop

The audio-visual workshop offers a great deal of promise as a technique for in-service education of teachers. It gives teachers an opportunity to work on individual problems; it allows for flexible schedules; it helps to develop a co-operative work spirit; it provides for more individual guidance; and it helps develop a better attitude toward audio-visual materials. The essential requirements are:

1. A group of teachers who have specific problems on which they want help
2. A capable leader to direct the workshop
3. Enough resources (materials, equipment, consultants) to meet the individual and group needs
4. An adequate work space

A successful audio-visual workshop was conducted at the University of Florida during the summer of 1947. Seventy-five principals, teachers, supervisors, salesmen, and curriculum directors participated in the program, which ran for a four-weeks' period. At the initial meeting a steering committee was elected to help co-ordinate and guide the activities of the group. Members discussed their particular interests. Persons with similar problems formed committees if they so desired. Each committee planned its own work schedule. Laboratory facilities for previews, production, and equipment were available. Recreational activities, such as community sings, melon cuttings, swimming parties, and song fests, all had a part in building a co-operative and friendly group spirit. Daily bulletins kept the workshop personnel informed of each day's schedule. A great deal of "cross pollination" took place as various committees presented their reports. There were many manifestations of the effectiveness of such motivating devices while the workshop was in progress. It is, moreover, a reasonable assumption that the workshop technique in in-service training can readily be evaluated in terms of the attitude which is developed toward the use of audio-visual materials and how the teacher uses these materials after the workshop experience.

The Audio-visual Co-ordinator

Efficient use of audio-visual materials in a school or a school system requires a close liaison between the teacher in the classroom and the source of supply (library or audio-visual department). Experience has shown that if instructional aids are to be distributed and utilized without friction or loss of time, some one person in each building must assume the responsibility of co-ordinating the activities related to the supply and demand for needed materials.

Many schools find it advantageous to appoint a teacher to act as co-ordinator of all audio-visual aids and equipment. The duties of this person will vary according to the particular situation. Some co-ordinators are nothing more than clerks concerned with the mechanical and clerical aspects of the job; others are capable of influencing the educational utilization of these materials in the classroom.

In the Portland, Oregon, Public Schools, audio-visual co-ordinators help solve the materials problem in the following ways:

1. Keep teachers informed of new materials and equipment.
2. Assist all teachers in the selection and use of audio-visual materials.
3. Supervise the training and work of student and teacher operators.
4. Co-ordinate the ordering, delivering, use, and return of audio-visual materials.
5. Promote effective utilization of audio-visual materials.
6. Co-ordinate the use of audio-visual facilities, equipment, and materials in the building.
7. Provide a clearinghouse for handbooks, bulletins, and other resource materials.
8. Supervise care and storage of audio-visual equipment and materials.

Assistance in locating the needed aids and equipment encourages a teacher to use new teaching materials. The audio-visual co-ordinator can perform this service and thus become an important stimulus to the teaching staff of any school. It is difficult to overestimate the influence of such a person on in-service growth in the use of teaching aids.

Bulletins and Handbooks

One of the easiest ways to assist teachers in the use of audio-visual aids is to employ printed or mimeographed bulletins to provide information and guidance of value to them in their work. The practice may, however, be abused. If teachers are flooded with bulletins, handbooks, and leaflets from all the various administrative offices in a school system, the net result is a progressively lower rate of teacher growth. However, if carefully planned, the distribution of printed materials can contribute a great deal to the in-service education of teachers. Much depends upon eliminating unnecessary matter and concentrating on quality rather than quantity. In large systems there should be a clearinghouse for all publications to avoid duplication and to raise the standard of usefulness of the materials.

Printed bulletins and handbooks are effective in keeping teachers informed about new equipment and materials. Periodic, concise bulletins listing new aids are read and used by most teachers. There is, of course, a place for a comprehensive handbook, or catalog, which lists all the various aids available. Some catalogs include suggestions on utilization and give instructions for ordering equipment and materials. They should be so organized that the teacher can easily find the type of material needed. Periodic supplements should be issued to keep the catalog up to date.

Digests of research and recent developments in the field of audio-visual aids have proven useful. Reporting good utilization practices and results of film previews makes interesting reading. Nothing has such immediate carry-over as learning what other teachers are doing in a new and practical field.

Entire bulletins devoted to special topics have been used successfully. One issue might be devoted to the procedure of organizing a student operators' club, another to the making of transcriptions and recordings, and another to the use of motion pictures in the social-studies field. The list of titles for special issues is practically unlimited. To be effective they should be addressed to actual teacher needs. These special bulletins should be printed in a form that is easily filed.

Time spent making printed materials attractive as well as usable will insure a better teacher response. The following suggestions for the preparation of bulletins will be found helpful.

1. The format should be attractive. The title page may well have a drawing, a cartoon, or other decorative device. A challenging title is a distinct asset.
2. The general organization should be clear-cut and definite, not buried in long paragraphs or in rambling, nonsequential discourse.
    a) The problem, issue, or purpose should be stated clearly and briefly at the very beginning.
    b) Explanation and background, when necessary, should be brief and follow immediately the statement of the problem.
    c) The sequence should "match," that is, should go along with reasonable rapidity and brevity. Specific illustrative materials, however, should be used freely. Drawings, cartoons, graphs, and pictures should be used to supplement verbal descriptions.
    d) The conclusions or summaries should be concrete and definite, often in numbered outline form.
3. The relation of a given bulletin to a series should be made quite clear.

4. Credit for all quotations and for contributions from local teachers or other staff members should be given without fail in footnote references.
5. Printing is ordinarily superior to stencil-reproduction.[4]

School Visitation

Most teachers seldom have the opportunity of seeing what their fellow-workers are doing. Firsthand observation of audio-visual tools being used in an actual teaching situation can be a stimulating experience for teachers. If Teacher A visits Teacher B to observe how films are used in teaching sixth-grade social studies, careful planning is necessary in order to make the situation as natural as possible. Care should be taken that Teacher A is not made to feel inferior to Teacher B. It is best if the teacher herself asks to make the visit. In this case she has contacted the teacher to be visited and made all the preliminary arrangements. Although it is difficult to set up rigid procedures to be followed in cases of interschool visitation, getting one teacher to visit another for the purpose of observing some specific technique is so valuable that the effort is worth while. The exchange of ideas and discussion of problems on the use of audio-visual material will be beneficial to both parties.

What happens when the teacher returns such a visit is equally important. Sometimes a formal report is required. This usually puts the damper on any future visits. An informal conversation between the principal and the teacher will serve to help the teacher "justify" her visit and make her feel more enthusiastic about the experience. Judiciously used, school visitations can help the teacher to make better use of audio-visual aids in her own teaching.

The Audio-visual Center

Many school systems have organized audio-visual departments, or centers, to assist teachers in obtaining needed audio-visual aids. The easier it is for the teachers to obtain needed materials, the more frequently will they want to employ them. Teachers cannot be expected to use these aids if the "red tape" involved in their procurement is burdensome.

The center can be an important factor in promoting teacher growth in the use of these teaching tools. The central department should be more than a storehouse of materials. It should be a resource center to which teachers look for help in selection, preparation, and utilization

---

[4] A. S. Barr, William H. Burton, Leo J. Brueckner, *Supervision*, pp. 728-29. New York: D. Appleton–Century Co., Inc., 1947.

of audio-visual tools. Materials should be attractively displayed and conveniently arranged. Laboratory facilities for making slides, posters, recordings, or photographs should be provided. Preview and auditioning rooms are a necessary part of a dynamic audio-visual department. If the center is advantageously located and the "welcome mat" is out for teachers, it will become a moving force in improving the use of audio-visual materials.

An important extension of the central department is the individual school resource-center. It is a duplication on a smaller scale of the main department. The school center serves the important function of maintaining a close liaison with the central department and co-ordinating the use of aids and equipment within the building. In planning the school resource-center, attention should be given to adequate work space. All teachers have pictures to mount, slides to make, posters to prepare, and models to construct. If all materials and tools for these purposes are kept in this central room in the building, it will save teachers much time and effort. A school center is a step in the direction of bringing the materials resources closer to the teacher and the classroom.

The methods and techniques listed above for in-service teacher growth in the use of audio-visual materials are not all inclusive. Space does not permit a discussion of all methods. An attempt has been made to describe the techniques most frequently used. In-service growth of teachers in the use of audio-visual materials is not something that just happens. It must be planned and the selection of methods and techniques is only one phase of the total program.

Evaluating the Results of the Program of In-service Education

Without proper evaluation one cannot determine what progress has been made toward the goals set up or determine where the weakness of the program lies. A co-operative evaluation of the in-service training in audio-visual aids will help to focus the attention on the places where improvement is needed and point out features which have been successful.

The following list could well serve as a guide for evaluating programs of in-service education for audio-visual aids:

1. Do teachers have access to professional books and magazines on audio-visual aids?
2. Are audio-visual materials readily accessible to teachers?
3. Are teachers encouraged to use a variety of materials in their instruction?

4. Does the principal provide effective leadership in the use of audio-visual materials?
5. Do pupils look upon the use of motion pictures as a "movie show"?
6. Do teachers know how to operate the more common types of audio-visual equipment?
7. Do teachers know the main sources of audio-visual materials?
8. Do teachers participate in the selection of audio-visual aids and equipment?
9. Do teachers participate in the formulation of policy regarding audio-visual aids?
10. Is the administration providing adequate facilities for use of audio-visual aids?
11. Are audio-visual materials integrated into the instructional process?
12. Are teachers encouraged to make inter- and intra-school visits?
13. Are teachers kept informed of developments in the audio-visual field?
14. Are material resource-centers being maintained in each school?
15. Is proper leadership being provided (director, co-ordinator)?
16. Is there an exchange of ideas, practices, and techniques among the teachers? Is this encouraged?
17. Are facilities provided for preparation of flat pictures, stencils, handmade slides, and other such materials?
18. Do teachers know what safety practices should be observed in handling equipment?
19. Do teachers recognize the values and limitations of different types of audio-visual aids?

It is always important to get teachers' reactions to the program of audio-visual in-service education. In order to find out what some teachers thought of existing programs for providing them with audio-visual in-service experiences, the writer sent questionnaires to one hundred teachers in California, Oregon, Washington, New York, Georgia, and Illinois. Eighty-four questionnaires were returned.

Most of the people taking in-service work in audio-visual aids did so because they wanted to learn more about these aids. Only two people enrolled at the request of the principal. Interestingly enough, sixty-four persons wanted to learn how to operate equipment. This is an important disclosure because administrators frequently minimize the extent of teacher interest in equipment. It should be obvious that teachers will not feel secure in using audio-visual aids until they have competence in the operation of equipment. This experience should be more than a superficial acquaintanceship. It should give the teacher the basic skills that will build up confidence in her ability to use the various types of equipment.

No teacher of the eighty-four felt that the in-service experience was of no help; twenty-seven said it was some help, while fifty-six said it was a great deal of help. Through in-service training, teachers not only learned how to operate equipment but they also gained insight into the how and why of audio-visual methods.

In response to the question concerning co-operative planning, only eighteen persons said the group had no part in the planning of the training program. Most of the teachers felt they had a part in helping to organize the in-service experience. Group planning is a valuable factor in promoting a co-operative attitude, but this is only a preliminary step. How the plan is carried out and what each participant derives from it depends on good organization by the leader and earnest effort on the part of the teacher. Democratic planning can become just as formal as the stereotyped lecture.

To the question, "What did you like about the in-service training work?" teachers pointed out that it broadened their knowledge of instructional aids and gave them better insight into the teaching process. Democratic procedures and usefulness of the work carried on were mentioned often. In answer to the other question, "What things did you dislike about the in-service training work?" teachers protested against crowded conditions, the tendency to cover too much ground, and work that was not definitely geared to the classroom situation.

If the reactions and opinions of these eighty-four teachers are any indication of the value of the audio-visual in-service program, it can be assumed that in-service programs generally are reasonably successful. However, there is a great deal that can be done to improve the quality and usefulness of such work. Every effort should be made to avoid using one technique or device to the exclusion of others. New ideas should be tried and a constant evaluation made of the results. Only in this way can the full values of in-service programs for helping teachers with audio-visual aids be realized.

SUMMARY

In this chapter the author has indicated the need for in-service teacher growth in the use of audio-visual aids and has insisted that this growth is a continuous process which must be integrated into the total education program. Emphasis was placed on the idea of co-operative planning and the principles of group action. Factors which contribute to a successful program of in-service teacher growth in audio-visual aids were pointed out to be (a) fit the program to the needs of the teacher, (b) proceed slowly, (c) provide for group planning, (d) provide for effective leadership, (e) keep size of group small,

(f) provide for adequate time, and (g) provide adequate facilities, materials, and equipment. The following methods and techniques for facilitating teacher growth in audio-visual aids were emphasized: (a) extension courses, (b) audio-visual conferences and institutes, (c) professional teachers' meetings, (d) the audio-visual workshop, (e) the audio-visual co-ordinator, (f) bulletins and handbook, (g) intra-interschool visits, and (h) the audio-visual center.

A need for an adequate evaluation of the audio-visual in-service program was brought out. A detailed list of points which might serve as a guide for evaluation was included.

REFERENCES

"Administration of the Audio-visual Department for Lake and Mendocino Counties of California." Ukiah, California: Office of the Mendocino County Superintendent of Schools (mimeographed).

Audio-visual Education in City School Systems. Research Bulletin of the National Education Association, Vol. XXIV, No. 4. Washington: Research Division of the National Education Association, 1946.

"Audio-visual Program Standards (In-service Training)," *See and Hear,* III (December, 1947), 26-27.

BARR, A. S.; BURTON, WILLIAM H.; and BRUECKNER, LEO J. *Supervision,* pp. 565-750. New York: D. Appleton–Century Co., Inc., 1947.

BAXTER, BERNICE. "In-service Teacher Education," *California Journal of Elementary Education,* XIV (November, 1945), 96-100.

BROOKS, HAROLD B. "Program for Teachers' In-service Education," *California Journal of Secondary Education,* XXI (November 15, 1946), 336-38.

Co-operation: Principles and Practices. Eleventh Yearbook of the Department of Supervisors and Directors of Instruction, National Education Association. Washington: National Education Association, 1939.

COREY, STEPHEN M. "Co-operative Staff Work," *School Review,* LII (June, 1944), 336-45.

DARLINGTON, MEREDITH W. *In-service Education of Teachers and Rural Community Building.* Stillwater, Oklahoma: School of Education, Oklahoma Agricultural and Mechanical College, 1944.

DEBERNARDIS, AMO. "In-service Training for Better Audio-visual Utilization," *See and Hear,* I (April, 1946), 44.

DEBERNARDIS, AMO, and BROWN, JAMES W. "A Study of Teacher Skills and Knowledges Necessary for the Use of Audio-visual Aids," *Elementary School Journal,* XLVI (June, 1946), 550-56.

DIEDERICH, PAUL B., and VAN TIL, WILLIAM. *The Workshop.* New York: Hinds, Hayden & Eldredge, Inc., 1945.

GOSLIN, W. E. "When We Work Together," *Educational Leadership,* XI (January, 1944), 221-29.

HEATON, KENNETH L., and OTHERS. *Professional Education for Experienced Teachers: The Program of the Summer Workshop*. Chicago: University of Chicago Press, 1940.
HELBLE, H. H. "In-service Education of Teachers," *American School Board Journal*, CIX (September, 1944), 35-36.
HERRICK, VIRGIL E. "The Principal Looks at Himself," *Educational Leadership*, IV (April, 1947), 442-48.
HOBAN, CHARLES F., JR. *Movies That Teach*. New York: Dryden Press, 1946.
HOBAN, CHARLES F.; HOBAN, CHARLES F., JR.; and ZISMAN, SAMUEL B. *Visualizing the Curriculum*. New York: Dryden Press, 1937.
In-service Growth of School Personnel. Twenty-first Yearbook of the Department of Elementary School Principals of the National Education Association. Bulletin of the Department of Elementary School Principals, Vol. XXI, No. 6. Washington: Department of Elementary School Principals, National Education Association, 1942.
LANGE, PHIL C. "Five Days with a Group in Action," *Educational Leadership*, V (February, 1948), 313-18.
Leadership at Work. Fifteenth Yearbook of the Department of Supervisors and Directors of Instruction of the National Education Association. Washington: Department of Supervisors and Directors of Instruction, National Education Association, 1943.
MACKENZIE, GORDON N. "Developing and Administering the Curriculum and Pupil Services," *Changing Concepts in Educational Administration*, pp. 20-52. Forty-fifth Yearbook of the National Society for the Study of Education, Part II. Chicago: University of Chicago Press, 1946.
McKOWN, HARRY C., and ROBERTS, ALVIN B. *Audio-visual Aids to Instruction*. New York: McGraw-Hill Book Co., Inc., 1940.
MIEL, ALICE. *Changing the Curriculum*. New York: D. Appleton–Century Co., Inc., 1946.
―――. "Let's Work Together on the Curriculum," *Educational Leadership*, V (February, 1948), 294-300.
MILES, JOHN R., and SPAIN, CHARLES R. *Audio-visual Aids in the Armed Services*. Washington: American Council on Education, 1947.
MISNER, PAUL, and OTHERS. *Group Planning in Education*. 1945 Yearbook of the Department of Supervision and Curriculum Development. Washington: National Education Association, 1945.
NOEL, ELIZABETH GOUDY, and LEONARD, J. PAUL. *Foundations for Teacher Education in Audio-visual Instruction*. Washington: American Council on Education. 1947.
REED, PAUL C. "In-service Training in Visual Education," *Education*, LVIII (April, 1938), 488-92.
"Report of Audio-visual Education Administrative Workshop." Sacramento, California: Division of Audio-visual Education, State Department of Education, 1947 (mimeographed).

SEATON, HELEN HARDT. *A Measure for Audio-visual Programs in Schools.* Washington: American Council on Education, 1944.

"Suggestions for the Organization of a County Audio-visual Education Program," *California Journal of Elementary Education,* XIV (February, 1946), 163-74.

TAYLOR, JOHN W. "County-wide Audio-visual Services," *California Journal of Secondary Education,* XXI (May, 1946), 154-57.

The Functions of an Audio-visual Department in a Teacher-Education Institution. Bulletin of the Western Illinois State Teachers College, Vol. XXVI, No. 4. Macomb, Illinois: Audio-visual Education Committee of the Western Illinois State Teachers College, 1946.

The Improvement of Teacher Education. A Final Report by the Commission on Teacher Education. Washington: American Council on Education, 1946.

The Improvement of Teaching. Based on the group reports of the Oxford Conference. National Commission on Teacher Education and Professional Standards. Washington: National Education Association, 1947.

The Principal and Audio-visual Education. Washington: Department of Elementary School Principals of the National Education Association, 1947-1948.

Training Teachers and Supervisors in Service. Prepared by the Association of Assistant Superintendents. New York: Board of Education, City of New York, 1945.

TROYER, MAURICE E., and PAGE, C. ROBERT. *Evaluation in Teacher Education.* Washington: American Council on Education, 1944.

TYLER, RALPH W. "Trends in the Preparation of Teachers," *School Review,* LI (April, 1943), 207-12.

WEBER, C. A. "Promising Techniques for Education of Teachers in Service," *Educational Administration and Supervision,* XXVIII (December, 1942), 691-95.

―――. "Reactions of Teachers to In-service Education in Their Schools," *School Review,* LI (April, 1943), 234-40.

―――. "The School's Role in the In-service Education of Teachers," *School Executive,* LX (September, 1941), 34-35.

WITT, PAUL W. F. "In-Service Education of Teachers in the Use of Audio-Visual Materials of Instruction. Unpublished Doctor's Dissertation, Teachers College, Columbia University, 1947.

―――. "Toward More Effective Utilization of Audio-Visual Materials and Devices," *Teachers College Record,* XLIX (November, 1947), 108-18.

CHAPTER VII

THE PROGRAM OF AUDIO-VISUAL EDUCATION IN CITY SCHOOL SYSTEMS

ELIZABETH GOLTERMAN

Director, Division of Audio-visual Education
St. Louis Public Schools
St. Louis, Missouri

INTRODUCTION

In order to illustrate the principles that might well characterize the operation of audio-visual programs in city school systems, the author has devoted this chapter primarily to a rather complete description of the organization and administration of the Division of Audio-visual Education in the St. Louis public schools.

THE ROOTS OF VISUAL EDUCATION IN ST. LOUIS

Early in the history of education in St. Louis, it was recognized that children's ability to think and their understanding of the world in which they live could be developed by giving them training in careful observation. Field trips to examine historic landmarks, to study river activities, and to observe natural phenomena are recorded in early descriptions of educational activities in St. Louis. The idea that youngsters could learn from seeing pictures, objects, and exhibits was accepted many years before visual education, as a name, was conceived. In 1876, William Torrey Harris, then Superintendent of Schools of St. Louis, pointed out that children must be trained to think upon what they see. "Every lesson," he wrote in a section of his annual report dealing with natural science, "should be given in such a way as to draw out the perceptive powers of the pupil by leading him to reflect on what he sees or to analyze the object before him. It is at first thought strange—although it is true—that the powers of observation are to be strengthened only by teaching the pupil to *think* upon what he sees."[1]

The philosophy of William T. Harris influenced school procedures in St. Louis long after he left this city to become United States Commissioner of Education. His associates continued to explore the method of instruction then labeled "original investigation." Led by F. Louis Soldan (who became superintendent of schools in St. Louis in 1895), they worked vigorously to put into action this new teaching theory. And in 1905, a generation after Harris' pronouncement, the visual-education program had its formal inception in St. Louis.

That year St. Louis was host to a world's fair, known as the Louisiana Purchase Exposition. During the period of the exposition, classes from all the schools visited the fair grounds, accompanied by their teachers. As children visited one building after another, they were confronted with the representatives of different nations and races, surrounded by a wealth of material from all corners of the world, and, in effect, mentally transported to distant lands. At the close of the exposition, Superintendent Soldan and his assistant, Carl G. Rathmann, appealed to the exhibitors to donate parts of their displays to the public schools. These formed the nucleus of the Division of Audio-visual Education, which carried the name of "Educational Museum" from 1905 until 1943.

The Museum was founded in an endeavor to enrich classroom experiences. Educators were beginning to realize that the meaning of one word was not found in another, that children needed many direct contacts with the world outside the covers of their textbooks. They were becoming more and more aware that ideas are the result of experience.

"Bring the world to the child" was the Museum's early motto. It was based upon a belief that the actual experience a child acquires in his study of objects, pictures, and exhibits assists in bridging the gap between the reading of verbal descriptions and the development of realistic concepts.

In a bulletin published in 1915 by the United States Bureau of Education, Rathmann described the Educational Museum of the St. Louis Public Schools and defined its function as follows:

> To make the child acquainted with the world in which he lives, we must bring him into personal contact with the world. Telling him or having him read about the earth, about the great changes produced on its surface through

---

[1] William T. Harris, *Twenty-first Annual Report of Board of Directors of St. Louis Public Schools*, 1875, Appendix, p. clxiv.

the activity of nature and man, about the people, their life and work, and their adjustment to their environment, will not give the child vivid and lasting impressions, nor arouse in him the desire and develop the power to do his own exploring and discovering. We must, as O'Shea says, "take him into the world or bring the world to him."[2]

The practical realization of the theory that children in the classroom need to have the rich experience of the world brought to them was the achievement of Miss Amelia Meissner, Curator of St. Louis' Educational Museum from 1905 until her retirement in 1943. She assembled collections of food products, materials for clothing and shelter, exhibits showing the lives of other people, mammals, birds, sea life, insects, rocks, minerals, scientific apparatus, photographs, booklets, stereographs, charts, lantern slides, and phonograph records.

As the visual-education program in St. Louis expanded and new materials were developed, educational films, filmstrips, and kodachrome slides were added to the supply of teaching materials. New projection devices became accepted as standard school equipment. Under her leadership, emphasis was placed on the preparation of materials for circulation in the schools and on cataloguing the materials and developing systematic procedures for ordering and distributing them. In explaining the service of the Museum, Miss Meissner said its purpose was "to make possible in the schoolroom the use of just the illustration which is wanted, just when it is wanted."[3]

When radio entered the school program and other new audio devices were designed and adapted to classroom needs, the name "museum" was changed to Division of Audio-visual Education. Since 1943, under the leadership of Superintendent of Instruction Philip J. Hickey, increased emphasis has been placed on the improvement of instruction, including the extension of facilities for the use of sensory materials.

FUNDAMENTAL PRINCIPLES: GUIDE TO DEVELOPMENT OF
AUDIO-VISUAL EDUCATION PATTERNS

Translated into a workable philosophy for the Division of Audio-visual Education are the convictions of the founders of the Educational Museum and the leaders in the development of audio-visual education in St. Louis today. Their beliefs are expressed in the follow-

[2] Carl G. Rathmann, *Educational Museum of St. Louis Public Schools.* U.S. Bureau of Education, Bulletin 48, 1915. Washington: Government Printing Office, 1915.

[3] Amelia Meissner, "Educational Museum of St. Louis Public Schools: Its Origin and Service," *Public School Messenger,* June 30, 1927, p. 5.

ing fundamental principles which serve as a guide in providing visual materials to assist teachers in accomplishing their classroom objectives.

1. Visual materials bring outside experiences into the classroom which can contribute to the development of the child's powers of observation and judgment, to his acquisition of new understanding, and to his ability to think for himself.
2. Recognizing that all experiences are not equally educative, visual materials should be selected which develop the child's thinking, arouse curiosity, stimulate initiative, create constructive desires and purposes, and add to his personal knowledge.
3. A great variety of materials is necessary if a student is to receive training and practice in the examination of many facts to underwrite his own opinions.
4. In a large city school system, it appears more economical and feasible to centralize all visual materials in one distribution storehouse than to supply each school with a complete selection of teaching aids.
5. A successful city-wide visual-education program depends upon a well-organized system for the preparation, cataloguing, and circulation of materials.
6. Effective learning with visual aids depends upon the availability of the materials at the time a student is interested in the subject and has a purpose for seeking additional information.
7. In the utilization of any visual aid, the child must be taught to "think upon what he sees." Only by trained, thoughtful observation can the student bridge the gap between the intangible idea and the specific concept.

ADMINISTRATION AND PERSONNEL OF THE DIVISION OF AUDIO-VISUAL EDUCATION

Responsibilities of Staff

These principles of visual education serve as a guide to the twenty-one members of the staff of the Division of Audio-visual Education who are assigned the responsibility for leadership in visual education. Their responsibilities are outlined briefly in the regulations of the Department of Instruction, which describe the Division of Audio-visual Education as a "service division," the functions of which are as follows:

1. To supervise and be responsible for the quarters assigned to this Division.
2. To recommend to the superintendent of instruction audio-visual materials and equipment for use in the schools.
3. To serve as custodian of, and to deliver to the schools, the audio-visual materials and equipment approved by the Board of Education.

4. To assist the superintendent of instruction in developing the effectiveness of the use of audio-visual materials and equipment.
5. To assist the superintendent of instruction in developing a program of radio education in the St. Louis public schools.

Organization of Staff

The staff of the Division of Audio-visual Education is headed by a director, who is responsible to the assistant superintendent in charge of instruction and research. He, in turn, reports to the superintendent of instruction. The director of the Division of Audio-visual Education works with two assistant directors, one in the field of visual education, the other in radio education. In addition, one teacher is assigned to the staff in visual education and two full-time teachers plan and prepare classroom broadcasts. Twelve staff members are directly responsible for the preparation, maintenance, and distribution of materials. Three others are stenographers. Two drivers are assigned by the Building Department to deliver and pick up visual materials used in the schools. The custodial service is also furnished by the Building Department.

Policy-making Committees

The administration of a successful city-wide visual education program is not limited to the staff of a central agency such as the Division of Audio-visual Education. In St. Louis, for instance, two committees of teachers and principals, representing a cross-section of school interests, have been appointed by the superintendent of instruction to advise on policies guiding the expanding audio-visual education services. These committees are the Visual-Education Committee and the Committee on Radio Education. The activities of the former only are described in this chapter.

Visual-Education Organization within the Individual School

Since each principal is responsible for the improvement of instruction in his school, the use of visual materials in his building is within his jurisdiction. However, general guidance in the utilization of visual aids is provided by staff members of the Division of Audio-visual Education. The principal receives detailed assistance from the visual-education co-ordinator, a teacher who assembles the orders for visual aids for the entire school, distributes in-coming materials, and advises individual teachers in the selection of visual materials. The co-ordinators attend general meetings, usually held at the headquarters of the Division, to become acquainted with new audio-visual materials, to learn proper uses of projection equipment, and to hear speakers who are authorities in these fields.

Co-ordinated Long-Term Planning

A study of the status of visual education in the St. Louis public schools, made during the school year 1943-44, marked the beginning of budgetary rethinking. This was needed to provide audio-visual service consistent with the growing realization of its importance.

A study made by members of the Visual-Education Committee and the staff of the Division of Audio-visual Education revealed the inadequacy of the supply of visual materials to meet the teachers' needs for them. There was dearth of projection equipment and a lack of electric outlets, darkened rooms, and other physical facilities within school buildings necessary for ready use of projectors.

Faced with the fact that only 30 per cent of the city's teachers had been able to get the sound films they needed at the time they wanted them, the superintendent recommended that a four-year plan be adopted, as suggested by the Visual-Education Committee, and that the money needed to put this program into effect be provided. In contrast to the appropriation of approximately $4,300 during the year of the study, the following year's budget for purchase of materials to be loaned was $48,000. Added to this was provision for underwriting 25 per cent of the cost of projectors bought by elementary schools, up to an annual total of $100 per school.

Long-term planning needs frequent reconsideration and revision, especially in a field that changes rapidly. In planning conferences, thought should be given to provision for audio-visual materials and equipment, both in the central loan division and in individual schools. There are also the problems of adjusting old school buildings and providing new schools with increased facilities for audio-visual methods in teaching; of developing improved utilization; and of providing the staff needed to keep all of this in operation.

Selection of Visual Materials

Criteria for Choosing Teaching Aids

These six practical questions provide help in the selection of audio-visual teaching materials:

1. Does this film, slide, or recording help to fill a curriculum need of your school?

2. Will this visual aid assist the teacher in bringing about a desired change in the behavior pattern of students?
3. Does this filmstrip or chart help to develop new concepts of democratic living? Does it bring to school and community a wider understanding of the responsibilities, as well as the rights, that go with world citizenship in a democracy?
4. Will the inclusion of this make a more representative and balanced library of visual aids?
5. In practical terms of the budget, has it been considered how many duplicate prints will be required if this title is recommended?
6. Has a small proportion of the budget been set aside for the purchase of material for experimental use? Has your school system accepted responsibility for pushing forward frontiers in the production of visual materials? Does it produce new materials and support the creative efforts of others?

Importance of Teachers' Recommendations in Selecting Materials

Today, the majority of school systems operate upon the fundamental principle that those teachers who actually use audio-visual materials with children should participate in the process of evaluating and selecting available items and desirable materials. The final selection of materials is sometimes made by committees of teachers appointed by, and acting with, subject-matter experts, consultants, or supervisors. In other systems, this responsibility falls upon the course-of-study committees or upon a standing visual-education committee. Some large school systems prefer to have final choices made by individual teachers who have used such materials with children. Classroom testing of materials is an important factor in evaluation. Pupils' reactions are illuminating.

The St. Louis public school system has sought in a different way to find the most effective method of selecting films, filmstrips, and recordings. For two years, evaluation committees of teachers in specific subject areas have been appointed to serve during a two-week summer period and have been paid for these services. These committees have also performed two additional services. They have evaluated films which have been in the library for some time, making recommendations regarding the withdrawal or retention of titles. They have also written teachers' study guides, when these were not provided with the film purchased.

Variety of Materials

In the belief that a variety of teaching materials will help a student receive training and practice in the examination of many facts to underwrite his own opinions, the St. Louis collection of audio-visual aids includes a wide range of types. They are objective, pictorial, and auditory.

Objective materials, though difficult to obtain, continue in popularity as classroom aids. Objects, however, have limitations. They provide concrete experiences for children but fall short by being isolated from their functional setting. To help children visualize these objects in relation to their sources and uses, other supplementary materials are required. In this connection, motion pictures, filmstrips, lantern slides, and mounted photographs play an essential role.

To maintain an up-to-date visual service demands constant rethinking in terms of types of materials. What materials should be discarded? What aids need improvement? What subjects could be illustrated more effectively through some different media? Are new types of materials given due consideration?

Satisfactory selection of materials requires a competent staff, having the over-all picture of needs and sources and working in harmony with teacher committees who evaluate the film, recording, filmstrip, or other visual aid in terms of its actual contribution to child growth.

Preparation, Inspection, and Repair of Materials

The nature of audio-visual materials, involving a variety of shapes and sizes, requires skill in designing boxes for efficient storage and circulation. Essential to effective distribution are containers which are durable, easy to handle, and clearly marked for identification. Protection against breakage and misplacement is necessary.

In the St. Louis school system, collections of objects are placed in boxes, without protecting glass, so that children may touch or examine the actual object in which they are interested. Marking each separate piece with catalogue number and title is important.

All materials, after return from a weekly loan to schools, are inspected and counted before being returned to the shelf for circulation. During the summer, all material is thoroughly checked and cleaned. Labels and envelopes are replaced and boxes repaired and painted.

Objective Material

Each individual bird, mammal, and amphibian has a tailor-made box. For the box itself, poplar or pine wood is used, the thickness being $\frac{1}{4}''$, $\frac{3}{8}''$, or $\frac{1}{2}''$ depending on the size of the box and weight of the animal. The box is finished with dark oak stain. The opening is on the broad side.

Every specimen is mounted on a wooden board which slips under two cleats, one located on each side of the box. These cleats hold the board firmly in place so that even though the box is turned upside down or to the side, the specimen cannot move and will not be broken.

The lid fits in a groove at the botton of the box so that it will not slip out. A web strap across the lid, fastened with a snap button, holds it in place. A loop of the web strap is on the lid to facilitate opening it. For carrying purposes, a similar strap is placed over the top of the box and fastened to the sides.

A specimen mounted on a board and pulled out from the box makes it more accessible with minimum damage occurring in removing and replacing it in the box. The name of the school to which the specimen is sent is stamped on a dated shipping tag attached to the outside of the box.

Both containers and specimens are refurbished during the summer vacation. The inside of each box is washed with a solution of water and carbolic acid after which it is brushed with oil of cedar leaf (exception: reptiles and amphibians) to prevent moth damage. Each bird and mammal is brushed, the glass eyes, bills, and feet are wiped off with a damp cloth, and all needed repairs are made.

Other objective material, such as sea-life specimens, rocks and minerals, historical collections, and industrial products, are circulated in sturdy cardboard or wooden boxes, depending on the size and weight of each collection.

On the outside of each box is the number and name of the collection and the number of pieces contained therein. Each individual piece of material is labeled with the collection number and title. Any school having several collections of rocks returns them in the correct box by merely checking the collection number on the box with that on the rock. This can be done by a child and need not be an added teacher responsibility. The specimens are cushioned with tissue paper to prevent breaking. This paper is replaced when necessary. During the summer, boxes are repaired and washed, shelves are washed with a mild solution of carbolic acid and water, specimens are cleaned, labels on specimens and boxes are replaced, and fresh tissue paper is used to repack the boxes.

Prevention of moths is an important consideration in many collections such as sugar, cocoanut, wool, insects, and butterflies. These boxes and materials are sprayed with D.D.T. Camphor balls are placed in some boxes. This material needs to be frequently inspected.

Films

New films are prepared for circulation by having a six-foot white leaderstrip and at least a four-foot yellow end strip attached. These strips are essential because they bear the brunt of frequent breaks that often occur in threading or rewinding a film. On the leaderstrip the catalogue number and title of the film are printed with India ink and on the end strip the word "end" is stamped along with the catalog number. This labeling is an aid in returning the material to the correct box.

Schools are asked not to rewind films after their last use in the building. Upon its return to the Division, every film is inspected and small breaks and damages are repaired as it is rewound. After inspection a round gummed seal—red for sound film and blue for silent film—is placed over the hub hole of the reel. If this seal is punched through when the film is returned to the Division, the inspector knows immediately that the film has been on a projector and that it must be inspected.

Each film is in a reel can and is boxed according to size. The 400-foot films are placed in black cloth-covered boxes with cloth-reinforced corners and overlapping lids, with inside dimensions of $7\frac{1}{2}"$ x $7\frac{1}{2}"$ x $1\frac{1}{2}"$. In the box with the film is the study guide (if one accompanies the film) and a card containing suggestions for projecting a film correctly.

On the side of the lid, the catalogue number and title are stamped on a gummed label, together with information as to whether or not a study guide accompanies the film. The film boxes stand upright on the shelf with this information facing out for ready reference.

On the bottom of the box is a gummed label and 4" x 6" card on which the school and date of delivery are stamped. The card is held in place by two picture corner mounts so that it can be easily removed after it has been stamped. On the other side of this card is the catalogue number, title of the film, and date the film was purchased. Notations of a scratched film surface or other damages are made. The card is kept at the office of the Division and filed according to date of delivery. It is returned to the film box after the film has been inspected by matching the school and date stamps. Thus the card with notations about the condition of the film is always kept with the correct film.

On a shelf below the first copy of each film is placed a gummed label with film catalogue number. This helps replace films in their proper place.

The 800-, 1200- and 1600-foot reels are sent out in cans placed in masonite boxes, $12\frac{1}{4}''$ x $12\frac{1}{4}''$ x $1\frac{1}{2}''$, 14" x 14" x $1\frac{1}{2}''$, and 16" x 16" x $1\frac{1}{2}''$, respectively (outside dimensions). A web strap with a snap button fastener across the narrow open top serves as a handle to prevent the film from slipping out. A string shipping tag, slipped through a loop in the handle, is used instead of the gummed label which is time-consuming to remove and replace. These films are shelved separately from the 400-foot films.

The summer care of films is a necessary and important task of maintaining a film library. Before film cleaning, all films are inspected and rewound and put on the shelf. Then in systematic order each film is cleaned with a prepared solution of carbon tetrachloride. The film is run between two felt pads saturated with carbon tetrachloride. These pads must be changed frequently for a great deal of dirt accumulates on the film in a year's use. The film is then rewound between two felt pads saturated with Vitafilm. Vitafilm prevents the film from becoming brittle and prolongs its life. The cleaning and vitafilming are done on a treatizor machine designed especially for that purpose.

Repairing boxes and replacing labels and titles are an important part of summer work. At this time, reshelving to provide for new films is also done.

Filmstrips

Filmstrips have the catalogue number and title printed with white ink on the leaderstrip. Each filmstrip-can has the number written on the lid and, if a study guide or manual accompanies it, an "M" is also placed on the lid. All filmstrips ordered by a school are placed in cardboard filmstrip boxes in either of two sizes. The 5" x $3\frac{1}{2}''$ x $1\frac{3}{4}''$ (inside dimensions) carries six filmstrips, and the 5" x 7" x $1\frac{3}{4}''$ size holds twelve filmstrips. A gummed label on the bottom carries the school and date stamp.

The filmstrips are shelved in steel cases with slanted shelves. Vertical dividers separate the rows of filmstrips according to titles. As the front filmstrip is removed, a duplicate slides forward. The study guides are kept on a near-by shelf with catalogue number on the shelf to facilitate finding the correct one.

During the summer, the filmstrips are cleaned and treated with Vitafilm. The filmstrip ends are held down by a strip of wood and a felt pad saturated with carbon tetrachloride is rubbed over each filmstrip. The surface is then wiped with a pad saturated with Vitafilm. This is done on both sides of the filmstrip.

Kodachrome Slides

Slides in 2" x 2" size are usually purchased without protective glass mounts. Three types of mounting are used for the St. Louis collections: (a) bound slide mounted between glass; (b) Leica mount; and (c) Slic-Slide mount. The bound slides mounted between glass are most practical. Title, catalogue number, and thumb print are under glass. The materials necessary to mount the slides are: glass squares (2" x 2"), masks, ⅜" binding tape, thumb print, gummed labels with typed titles and numbers.

The thumb print is placed on the upper right-hand corner of the white side of the mask to mark the way the slide fits into the projector, thumb print toward lamp. The title typed on a gummed label is placed on the bottom of the mask; on the left side of the mask is placed the collection number and the serial number of that slide in the set. The film itself is brushed with a soft camel's hair brush to eliminate any lint and is then slipped into the mask under the four flaps, upside down in relation to the thumb print. The flaps are then pressed down.

In setting the film in the masks, care is taken that the emulsion side is away from the lamp *i.e.*, the shiny side toward the lamp. Some duplicates may vary. It is well to check. It is important that all are mounted in the same way.

The glass must be washed and polished so that no lint is on the inside which encloses the film. The mask is then placed between the glass and held firmly while a 3½" strip of binding tape is applied around the edges. The tape is pressed flat on the edges, corners are mitred, and then each side is pressed down.

Slides in Leica and Slic-Slide types of mounts are mounted between glass but are not bound with tape. The Leica has a light-weight aluminum frame and the Slic-Slide has a coating of adhesive to hold the two pieces of glass together. They use no masks so the necessary information is placed on gummed labels on the outside. This necessitates a change of the label when torn or soiled.

The slides are circulated in black cloth-covered boxes with cloth reinforced corners and completely overlapping lids. The inside dimensions of the boxes are as follows: 2½" x 2" x 2" for 22 or less slides; 3¼" x 2" x 2" for 30 or less slides; 5⅜" x 2" x 2" for 40 or less slides.

The catalogue number, the title of the set, and the number of slides are listed on a gummed label on the side of the box lid. If a study guide accompanies the slides, that also is noted. Study guides are kept on an open shelf where they are readily accessible to those who fill the orders.

Photographs and Prints

All photographs and prints are mounted on Nat-Mat cardbord, 14-ply, ripple medium brown, and cut to size to allow a margin of at least one inch on top and 1½" to 2" margin on sides and bottom. They are mounted with a dry mounting press.

Titles are printed beneath the photograph to help interpret the picture to the child. If information does not come with the pictures, the necessary research is made and information is written about it, including background material necessary to help interpret the picture. This information is duplicated on a gelatin roll duplicator which enables many gummed paper labels to be made from each typing. One label is glued to the back of each picture. The collection number also is stamped on the back so that pictures may be checked and counted quickly on their return to the Division.

The set of pictures is placed in a brown kraft envelope, made from 40-lb. stock paper, bound with one-inch gummed cloth tape. An envelope allowance of ½" over the thickness of the set of pictures allows sufficient space for getting the pictures in and out of the envelope easily.

Collection number, title, and number of pictures are printed on a gummed label on one side of the envelope and a blank gummed sticker for school and date stamp is on the other side. Envelopes and labels are replaced during the summer.

Booklets

Illustrated booklets ranging from all phases of social studies to natural and physical science are in collections, usually eight booklets in a set. Each booklet is stamped with collection number and the Division stamp and sent out in a brown kraft envelope of the type used for photographs.

Charts

Charts are mounted on muslin and tacked to double half-rounds on top and bottom. A six-inch waterproof protective flap is fastened between the top rounds with a double snap fastener closure.

A gummed label on the protective flap bears school and date stamps. Labels are replaced during the summer. Collection number and title are placed on the chart stick. The rolled charts are filed in a large case, divided into sections for individual charts.

Chart bags made of heavy blue denim hold several charts for delivery. A string shipping tag on the bag is stamped with the school and date.

Framed Pictures

Large colored pictures for primary grades are mounted on Upson board and framed. The picture is given a coat of white shellac so that it may be washed to remove finger prints and smudges. Fiberboard containers with a top opening fastened with cloth webbing carry the pictures.

Phonograph Records and Transcriptions

All records and transcriptions have the catalogue number on the center record seal. Individual records are retained in their paper jackets and are placed in a container made of corrugated cardboard bound with two-inch bookbinding tape. The sizes of these containers are as follows: $11\frac{3}{4}"$ x $10\frac{1}{2}"$ container for a 10-inch record; $13\frac{1}{2}"$ x $12\frac{1}{2}"$ container for a 12-inch record; and $18"$ x $16\frac{1}{2}"$ container for a 16-inch transcription.

It is necessary to break down (spread apart) these containers before records can be taken in and out of them easily. To prevent the record from slipping out, it is important to have a closed side of the jacket toward the open side of the container. Each container has a gummed label on which the school and date are stamped.

To transport the records as safely as possible, carrying cases that have a three-inch spread are provided so that records or albums may be sent together to one school. This carrying case is made of two pieces of heavy cardboard. Riveted in the center of each side are straps of heavy cloth webbing. One strap fastens with a seat-cover button to provide an opening. This also acts as a handle. A shipping tag is attached to the case and carries the school name and date. Sizes for these cases are as follows: 10-inch record in container requires 12-inch square cases; 12-inch record in container requires 14-inch square cases; and 16-inch transcription in container requires 18-inch square cases. On the truck the carrying cases are in a large assembly box divided into individual sections for each school's order. The bottom of the box is lined with sponge rubber to absorb any shock.

When albums of records are bought, the album is retained and is placed in a container, tailor-made of .175 caliper fiber board for ten- and twelve-inch records. Heavy webbing across the top opening prevents the albums from slipping out. The label for the school and date stamp are on the outside of the box.

Radio Scripts

Selected radio-scripts are circulated in brown kraft-paper envelopes bound with one-inch tape. Ten scripts are included in an envelope and are retained in the school three weeks. Each individual script is stamped with the catalogue number.

The envelopes have a gummed label with catalogue number, title, and number of scripts on one side and a gummed label to hold the school and date stamps on the other side.

CATALOGUING, ORDERING, AND DELIVERY

Based on the principle that audio-visual materials should be available to all teachers on the basis of "what they need and when they need it," a system of weekly ordering and distribution has been developed. No film, no object, no recording is sent to a school except on the request of a teacher. Booking of materials far in advance is not necessary as a general practice.

St. Louis provides each of its 3,000 teachers with a 232-page printed catalogue of available materials, kept up-to-date with printed supplements. Each teacher is encouraged to consider the catalogue his personal property, to annotate it in any way that will make it more useful, and to take it with him if he is transferred to another school. Its use is essential if he is to select intelligently the materials that best fit his student group.

As a source-book of information about available teaching materials, an audio-visual catalogue should be easy to use. The St. Louis bulletin includes listings of titles and order numbers of available audio-visual materials, grouped in such a way that they can be found quickly. Descriptions are full enough to indicate the content and concise enough to minimize catalogue size. In addition, particularly with films and recordings, data are included on maturity level, running time, producer, reference to co-ordinated materials, and suggestions for use. A workable index and table of contents are essential. School delivery schedules, information about ordering and distribution, suggestions about care of materials, and other information that will help the teacher are included.

In addition to the one-per-teacher catalogue and supplement, mimeographed announcements of current additions and special listings for subject areas are sent to each school's visual-education co-ordinator from time to time. Course-of-study committees, in developing new curriculum materials, include information about audio-visual teaching aids.

Some indication of the variety of loan material is given by the following list, which shows how the 3,781 catalogue title listings are grouped. The number of duplicates of each title ranges from two to twenty-five, according to need.

Objective Materials (437 listings)

Birds and mammals	197
Other science study collections	127
Industrial products	58
Pioneer, Indian, and foreign dolls	55

Audio Materials (691 listings)

Records, 78 r.p.m.	402
Transcriptions, 33⅓ r.p.m.	210
Radio scripts	**79**

Pictorial Materials (2,653 listings)

Sound films	760
Silent films	191
Filmstrips	571
Slides	154
Photographs	293
Pictorial booklets	496
Charts and framed pictures	175
Equipment	13

How the School Gets Audio-visual Materials

The weekly order, compiled by the school's visual-education co-ordinator from the requests made by the teachers, is mailed in time to be received at the Division forty-eight hours before the school's delivery day. Personal pick-up service is also provided for teachers who have immediate need for a loan item or who, after coming in for consultation and advice, wish to take out material they have examined.

Forms used include printed order blanks, provided in blocks of fifty to each co-ordinator at the opening of the school year, with additions sent as needed; delivery reports, printed in four-color quadruplicate continuous-fold for quick typing. Two copies of the typed report are kept by the school co-ordinator so that he may post one and have one for his desk record; the third is for the driver; the fourth for the department record.

What happens at a particular school? Froebel School receives a delivery each Friday. Every Tuesday the co-ordinator sends a pupil to each room to collect the audio-visual requests for the next delivery. He makes out one school order, arranging in numerical sequence the items requested by his twelve teacher associates, and mails it to the Division in a stamped, addressed envelope sent to him with the previous week's delivery.

As teaching-materials adviser, the co-ordinator tries to keep informed about new audio-visual additions so that he may help other faculty members identify items that they may want to try. He is the liaison person between the Division and his school.

On Friday, when the delivery truck arrives at Froebel School at its usual time (eleven o'clock), student assistants have already collected and checked the audio-visual loans delivered the previous Friday, now ready to be returned after their week's use. These boys help the driver carry the "returns" to the truck and the newly arrived items into the school. The new deliveries are checked with the delivery report and then distributed to the teachers, according to the original request that each had made a few days before. Thus, the school is supplied for another week. Throughout the school year, this continues in regular procession.

In schools that have clerks, the co-ordinator is relieved of much of the routine of ordering and checking. As a materials adviser, however, the co-ordinator is a vital factor in the curriculum-planning of each school.

At eight o'clock each morning at the Division of Audio-visual Education, the two Board of Education trucks load deliveries for the group of schools on that day's route. Elementary schools are reached once each week, high schools and colleges twice. By eight-thirty the trucks have reached the first schools. By mid-afternoon, they are back at the Division, fully loaded this time with the returns from the schools. Unloaded, on wheeled dollies, these audio-visual materials are taken to the sections where they will be checked, inspected, given necessary repairs, and re-shelved, ready for issue again.

In-service Education in Utilization

The value of any audio-visual aid is determined by the skill and purpose with which it is used. Probably the most important way in which skill is developed in using new teaching aids is by individual experimentation by the creative teacher who welcomes up-to-date visual aids which meet the needs and interests of his children. Creativity in the use of any teaching device depends upon a flexible curriculum, an experimental philosophy of education, and an administration which encourages teachers to pioneer in new fields.

As the individual teacher finds better ways of utilizing visual materials, opportunities may be provided in which he shares his findings with others. Professional meetings and college courses may be organized to give training in the use of materials. In St. Louis, as in most other cities, this training for improved utilization is provided. Some of the in-service practices are:

A. Professional meetings and conferences, sometimes with visiting authorities, sometimes with the leadership and help coming from local groups

1. Faculty meetings, for individual schools or for groups of schools
2. Demonstrations
3. Principals' meetings
4. Visual-education co-ordinators' meetings
5. Visual-education committee meetings
6. Conferences with parent groups
7. Open-house showings and try-outs of newly acquired materials

B. Individual conferences at Division of Audio-visual Education between teachers or small groups and members of the staff

C. Help within individual schools, given by teachers to one another, by visual-education co-ordinators and principals, by consultants, supervisors and through the staff of the Division of Audio-visual Education

D. Assistance that "helps a teacher help himself" by means of such material as catalogue write-ups to guide his thinking; handbooks issued with films and other visual materials to serve as a springboard for new ideas; special lists for topics of current interest, with suggestions of helpful materials; and suggestions presented in curriculum bulletins

The teachers' continuous experience and growing skill in the selection and evaluation of new materials help increase the thoughtfulness and perception with which they use materials.

Much of the leadership for the utilization program has come from members of the Visual-Education Committee. The teachers and principals who make up this group have been a constant source of ideas; have shared in all long-term planning; and have contributed generously to the realization of the objectives of the visual-education program. In St. Louis, this combination of ideas, planning, and action, from a group working closely with staff members of the Division, has been one of the most important factors in the developments of recent years.

CHAPTER VIII

THE PROGRAM OF AUDIO-VISUAL EDUCATION IN RURAL SCHOOLS

CHARLES FREMONT MILNER
Associate Director, University Extension Division
University of North Carolina
Chapel Hill, North Carolina

There has been a great deal written about audio-visual programs in city and county school systems. Very little of this material, however, pertains to the small rural school.

In 1941-42 there were 107,692 one-room, one-teacher schools in the United States.[1] There were 456,627 rural teachers instructing 11,387,612 rural pupils. At the same time there were 441,374 city teachers for 13,174,861 urban pupils.[2]

Since more than half our teachers and nearly half our pupils are in rural schools, the audio-visual program must be extended beyond the urban areas and must reach the pupils and teachers in small schools and isolated communities. It is common knowledge that rural schools have not kept up with recent advances in audio-visual education. Adequate equipment, materials, and services have not been provided. The rural teacher's solution has been to adapt what has been available and to make it fit his needs wherever possible. While he has had excellent opportunities for such things as field trips, exhibits, and assembling collections of flat pictures, he has had only limited access to the mechanical aids and program services that are now generally available in urban areas.

---

[1] David T. Blose, "Statistics of Schools in Urban and Rural Areas, 1941-42." Federal Security Agency, U. S. Office of Education Circular No. 231. Washington: Government Printing Office, 1945 (out of print).

[2] As defined by the United States Bureau of the Census, "cities and incorporated places having a population of 2,500 inhabitants or more are considered urban." All smaller localities or communities are designated "rural."

If the rural school is to gain the maximum benefits from the use of these enrichment materials, it is necessary to establish a basic plan which will be applicable to conditions in rural areas. A satisfactory plan requires at least partial answers to these four questions:

1. What are adequate objectives for the rural audio-visual program?
2. What methods have been suggested for achieving these objectives?
3. What is the status of audio-visual programs in rural areas?
4. What improvements are feasible in these programs?

What Are Adequate Objectives for the Rural Audio-visual Program?

Teacher Readiness

Teachers must be trained in the use of audio-visual materials. This training includes the operation of different types of equipment as well as the selection and presentation of materials for most effective use. When the planning and mechanics of operation are mastered, the instructor can strengthen and enrich his teaching through the use of these media.

The teacher must have mastered the fundamentals of good teaching. "But if a teacher has a sound understanding of good teaching she will recognize and use all teaching materials as media—as agencies which help transmit understandings. She will realize that audio-visual materials are usually means and not ends." [3]

Thus, the classroom teacher must have an open mind to the use of auditory and visual aids to learning and must be willing to utilize such teaching materials in the effort to make the pupils' learning experiences more concrete and lasting.

Availability of Materials

The ideal plan is to have a library of audio-visual materials in each school building. The following items are usually school-owned and school-housed: exhibits, graphic materials, microscopic slides, models, recordings, slides, and specimen and flat pictures for opaque projection. These materials should be located in a central place and catalogued in such a manner as to be readily accessible for the teacher.

The audio-visual materials assembled in the school building may

---

[3] Edgar Dale, *Audio-visual Methods in Teaching*, p. 4. New York: Dryden Press, 1946.

be supplemented from other sources by such teaching aids as motion pictures and filmstrips.

In the rural schools the greatest difficulties to be met are those of providing space, darkening facilities, electric current, and the equipment necessary for the use of projected aids. In schools where there is not a teacher for each grade, the problem of screening films or using other projected aids in such a manner as to meet the needs of a wide age range is also troublesome. In the one-room school, for example, the teacher must use the aids in situations involving as many as eight grades and pupils varying in age from six to sixteen.

To overcome these difficulties the individual schools or school systems in rural areas should establish a central audio-visual service which would include a film library, distribution facilities, and repair and maintenance services. Such a service would involve provisions for the distribution of materials and equipment for scheduled use in the schools of the entire area. For example, sound motion picture projectors could be circulated on schedule to one-room schools where outright purchase would not be justified.

Integration of Materials with the Curriculum

The proper integration of audio-visual materials with other materials results in better teaching. Dale emphasizes three points to be observed in promoting the most effective learning: (a) proper motivation—the "way"; (b) clear goals—the "what"; and (c) adequate use —the "how." [4]

If the teacher keeps these three goals in mind when selecting teaching materials for use in the classroom, he will be able to provide the student with learning experiences which are more meaningful and more closely related to his needs.

The objective in every rural-school administrative unit should be the provision of the right aid at the right time. To reach this objective a well-prepared catalogue of materials should be available, together with directions for making the best use of the facilities provided. If audio-visual materials become something apart from the course of study, they tend to foster amusement instead of education. Every effort should be put forth by the administrative unit to see that the auditory and visual materials purchased are functionally valuable and closely tied in with the curriculum. One of the best ways to insure this integration of audio-visual materials with the curriculum is to

[4] *Ibid.*, p. 13.

establish a committee of interested teachers to help select and organize the materials and to plan for their distribution.

Student Participation

Student participation is desirable and necessary in a workable audio-visual program. Students learn by doing and by being held responsible for the results. They should be encouraged to operate and maintain the audio-visual equipment in so far as practicable. This allows the teacher to devote his time to the material being presented.

Appropriate ways in which a pupil learns by doing include preparing exhibits, assemblying graphic materials, assisting in the planning of field trips, and giving demonstrations. Any program which allows for active student participation increases the value of the learning experiences provided.

Students preview films, filmstrips, and slides with the teacher or teachers. Their reactions assist in planning for more effective use of the teaching aid and in the determination of its value.

Utilization of Community Resources

The teachers must know the resources of their communities. The nature of these resources can easily be determined through co-operative study of the community by teachers, pupils, and representatives of citizens' organizations. Field trips, speakers, printed materials, special events, or community-improvement projects can often be utilized to provide desirable learning situations for students with the co-operation of community groups or other local agencies.

An Informed Citizenry Regarding the Educational Values of the Program

The teacher must keep the parents informed about the school. Parents should be welcomed into the school and classroom at all times. When parents are invited, the use of exhibits, models, pictures, and visual equipment enables them to see what is meant by audio-visual education.

Civic, church, or community gatherings offer an opportunity to discuss audio-visual education. Representatives of the school, speaking before these groups, can help to explain the school's educational aims and program to the community. Any written material that goes into the home may carry a reminder of the program or a recent aspect of it.

What Methods Have Been Suggested for Reaching These Objectives?

In-Service and Preservice Teacher-Training

One of the most important problems is teacher education. "Preservice and in-service education in the field of audio-visual-radio education must be provided for teachers, superintendents, principals, supervisors, audio-visual education personnel, and college and university faculties. This will continue to be a major problem for a long period of time."[5]

The preservice training of the classroom teacher is the responsibility of the teacher-training institutions. A teacher cannot be expected to use audio-visual materials if he has not seen them used in the college classroom. In rural areas, particularly, each new teacher must know how to use all types of audio-visual equipment and must understand how to incorporate audio-visual materials into the classroom procedure.

Although the preservice training must be left to the colleges and universities, most of the in-service training must be planned in terms of activities that can be carried on in the locality. The rural classroom teacher who has been out of school and on the job for several years must be brought abreast of progress in the field of audio-visual education and kept up to date.

Any in-service training that is planned for the rural teacher must be available within the radius of a few miles. The center for this work can usually be planned on the basis of county lines.

Financial Support and Distribution of Materials

Adequate funds must be secured to administer an audio-visual program in the rural school. It may sometimes be necessary to organize fund-raising drives, to enlist the aid of parent-teacher associations, or to resort to other means to get the program started. As soon as the value of these materials in the classroom is proven to the community, funds for the operation of the program should be provided annually in the regular school budget. The appropriations should be sufficient to maintain old equipment and materials as well as to purchase new items as needed.

Even though the available funds are very limited at first, the

---

[5] State of California, *Division of Audio-visual Education Reports*, June 19, 1946. Sacramento, California: State Department of Education, 1946.

beginning phases of an audio-visual program for the rural school can be undertaken. An example of such a beginning is reported in a letter from Harry M. Hanson, Superintendent of Schools in Dane County, Wisconsin. At a maximum expenditure of $100 per school, a basic filmstrip kit, a shadow box, and a projector of small wattage is furnished each rural school. Additional filmstrips are available from a county library. The teachers in rural Dane County are becoming aware of the values of the filmstrip as a teaching aid along with the charts, maps, and pictures with which they are familiar.

A survey conducted by a committee of the Educational Film Library Association [6] showed that the small school rents rather than purchases films.

In most rural sections of the United States, the funds available for the operation of an audio-visual program are meager. Careful planning is necessary to utilize the available funds to secure the best educational values from the expenditures. A small library of basic teaching materials should be supplemented by the rental of materials from centralized agencies such as the co-operative film library. Scattered throughout the United States are groups of schools which have united in the purchase and distribution of teaching materials. Under this plan small school systems and isolated rural schools can provide the latest and most effective audio-visual materials at small cost. One such co-operative group is composed of seven rural schools located in central Wisconsin. The services of the co-operative are described as follows:

"Mimeographed material on evaluation, utilization procedure, the care of the films, evaluation sheets, and study guide material have been . . . . sent to each of the schools. . . . . Their recognition of a definitely planned and organized program in visual education . . . . (meets) the needs of the individual and (extends) . . . . the educational opportunities of rural youth . . . . (without excessive expenditure)." [7]

The film library in Pierce County, Washington, was organized in 1940 to provide good visual materials for the co-operating schools when they want them. The films are consigned to the school for a sufficient period to make certain that pupils have an opportunity to acquire the information which classroom films portray. The library

---

[6] Leslie E. Frye, "Financing an Audio-visual Aids Program," *See and Hear*, I (January, 1946), 30-31.

[7] Kenneth F. Bartels, "Seven School Co-op Film Library," *See and Hear*, I (November, 1945), 29-33.

now serves 27 schools with 540 teachers and 12,000 pupils. It has accumulated about $11,000 worth of teaching material and library equipment.[8]

The ordering and distributing of audio-visual materials should be as simple as possible. The best distribution is usually to be obtained through the existing channels of communication between the rural schools of a given area. This may be through the use of a county-owned truck, by scheduling materials to coincide with county-wide meetings of principals and teachers, or by use of the rural mail service.

Continuous Evaluation and Correlation of All Materials

A central county audio-visual library for the distribution of films and other materials to individual schools may be started with a small number of carefully selected materials. Each acquisition to the library must be carefully evaluated and correlated with the instructional program. "Selection has two phases: (a) the preliminary selection of materials for their general educational worth in terms of broad curriculum objectives; and (b) the choice of specific audio-visual materials for a particular instructional situation." [9]

This evaluation and correlation may be made by the teachers with the assistance of supervisors or co-ordinators. The same procedure should be used with each addition to the audio-visual libraries.

Student-Teacher Surveys and Projects

The rural teacher and the students can carry through projects together for the enrichment of the school curriculum and to explain the school program to the community. One method is to show the school's accomplishments and needs through pictures, slides, or filmstrips. This may take the simple form of an exhibit, or may become as elaborate as facilities permit.

Student participation in carrying through a survey of community facilities or any project to be undertaken by the school not only increases the interest of the student but also increases his gains from the work.

---

[8] Sheldon Osborn, "Co-op in Washington," *See and Hear*, I (March, 1946), 65-68.

[9] Elizabeth Goudy Noel and J. Paul Leonard, *Foundations for Teacher Education in Audio-visual Instruction*, p. 26. American Council on Education Studies, Series II, *Motion Pictures in Education*, XI (June, 1947).

Public Relations

The teacher should avail himself of every opportunity to further the understanding of the audio-visual program in the community through well-founded community relationships. If the program of the school—particularly any new method of instruction—is understood by the parents, it receives more support.

The best method is to acquaint the community with what is going on in the classroom. This can be accomplished through talks before parent-teacher groups, civic clubs, church groups, and other community organizations. The school audio-visual equipment should be used in these community meetings to put the message across and to demonstrate the value of these aids.

A community-supported school program will have better sucess and make greater progress.

What Is the Status of Audio-visual Programs in Rural Areas?

To gather data on the use of audio-visual materials in rural schools in the United States, a list of rural schools with good audio-visual programs was obtained from state departments of public instruction, university extension divisions, and colleges in the various states. One hundred ninety-nine questionnaires were sent out. Sixty-nine of the usable forms returned came from individual rural schools. An analysis of these returns gives some indication of what are considered "good" programs in rural areas.

Audio-visual Programs in Individual Rural Schools

The sixty-nine rural schools are distributed through twenty-nine states, with representation of all the major regions of the United States. The number of teachers in the schools reporting varies from 1 to 67; the number of students, from 14 to 1,800. Fifty-seven schools have less than 30 teachers, and 43 have less than 400 students. The school year varies in length from 170 to 190 days.

Only one school reports a full-time director of audio-visual education. This school has the largest student body. There are 26 part-time directors. The persons most generally responsible for the audio-visual program in the school are the classroom teacher and the principal. The science teacher is usually the teacher assigned this duty.

The 69 rural schools reporting have the following audio-visual equipment:

TABLE 1

Kind of Equipment	Number of Schools Reporting Each Item	Range in Number of Equipment Units per School
Filmstrip projector	57	1- 3
Microprojectors	19	1- 8
Motion-picture projectors	68	1- 3
Opaque projectors	34	1- 2
Radios	51	1-16
Intercommunication systems	3	1
Record and transcription players	50	1- 8
Recorders	23	1-12
Screens	57	1- 4
Slide projectors	37	1- 3
Three-dimension projectors	3	1- 3

Most of the equipment is owned by the individual schools and is operated by the students and teachers. The visual aids are used in the classroom and auditorium. Some schools use the equipment constantly; others, infrequently. In general, the motion-picture projectors and filmstrip projectors are most used. The 69 schools reported the use of audio-visual materials as follows:

TABLE 2

Kind of Material	Number of Schools Reporting Use	Number of Times Used per Year
Exhibits	26	1- 15
Filmstrips	41	1-250
Graphic materials	45	10-280
Microscopic slides	22	24-206
Models	25	1- 48
Motion pictures	55	15-350
Recordings	32	25-250
Slides, 3¼" x 4"	18	12-250
Slides, 2" x 2"	19	24-300
Slides, 3-dimensional	1	300
Specimen and flat pictures for opaque projection	28	12-3,000

In a few cases exhibits, graphic materials, microscopic slides, models, recordings, and slides are rented; however, most of these materials are owned by the individual schools. About three-fifths of the filmstrips are school-owned; the rest come from rental sources. Approximately one-third of the 16-mm. films used are owned by the individual schools or school system. The sources for rental materials are commercial companies and state film libraries.

The amount spent on the audio-visual program is between $25 and $1,500 a school year. Forty-three schools spend between $25 and $400. The chief source of funds for 47 schools is tax money. Other sources mentioned are school functions, student fees, parent-teacher associations, supply sales, and library fees. Only four schools are responsible for raising all the funds needed; one, for three-fourths; four, for one-half; three, for one-third.

Thirty-four schools report that no audio-visual materials have been produced by the school. Fourteen have made graphic materials; ten, specimen and flat pictures for opaque projection; ten, slides; seven, recordings. Others report the production of screens, exhibits, filmstrips, models, motion pictures, window darkeners, bulletin boards, sand tables, and dioramas.

In 27 schools, the teachers select the audio-visual materials they use; in 18, the teachers and principal are jointly responsible for the selection. In other schools the choice is by the principal or by a teacher committee working with students.

Sixteen of the 69 schools report that one teacher has had a course in audio-visual education; 13 report two teachers who have attended courses; in 23 schools, from 3 to 25 teachers have had such training. Seventeen schools have no teacher who has had a course in audio-visual education.

In fourteen schools there has been no in-service training. Thirty-three schools have held a total of 41 lectures with a teacher attendance ranging from 2 to 45. Committee meetings on audio-visual education were held by 26 schools, with from 2 to 36 teachers present. Twenty-one schools have had workshops with from one to five meetings, from 1 to 44 teachers having attended these workshops. Other types of in-service training reported include equipment demonstrations, county conferences, institutes, extension courses, and demonstration lessons. From 1 to 3 schools reported these different activities, with a small attendance in most cases.

From the reports received, there appears to be little co-ordination of the rural school audio-visual program with the county audio-visual program. Each school apparently operates independently. Forty-seven of the schools reported that there was no connection between their local program and the county program. Seven schools receive materials from the county organization; three follow county courses of study; seven are part of a county-wide program.

In 35 schools there is no relationship between the local program and the state audio-visual program. Thirteen schools use the state unit for audio-visual education as a source of materials; nine follow the suggestions offered by the state audio-visual agency.

All 69 of the schools have at least one room equipped for the use of audio-visual aids. One school reports an audio-visual room for each department. Two schools have special rooms for audio-visual instruction.

In 34 schools no feature pictures are shown. In 31 schools the use of feature pictures varies from once a year to one showing each week. Only eleven schools report the showing of feature pictures monthly or oftener. The attendance varies from 40 to 1,200 students. Usually the entire student body attends.

In 37 schools no community resources are utilized in the audio-visual program. In 21 schools, field trips and excursions are taken. Other community co-operation includes local speakers, films, radio programs, pictures, slides, music, and forums.

The reports from 62 schools indicate that community reaction is favorable and interested. In six instances, the public is characterized as unconcerned; and one school reports that the public is unaware of the audio-visual program.

There is a preference for motion pictures by the students in 47 of the rural schools. The second choice is for filmstrips. In 15 schools no preference is expressed. When a preference is expressed by the teachers, it is in agreement with that of the pupils.

In 61 schools the audio-visual program is considered inadequate. In three schools it is considered adequate; in three, it is characterized as fair.

In consideration of the money involved and the time expended, the 16-mm. sound film is regarded as most valuable educationally for the students in 42 schools. In 13 schools, filmstrips are adjudged most valuable.

The schools used in this study were selected as representative of schools having good audio-visual programs. In most cases, these programs have been in progress long enough to become definitely established as part of the school operation.

To summarize these questionnaire returns, the typical rural school with a superior program does not have a full-time director of audio-visual education. A classroom teacher or the principal supervises the program. The school has purchased a filmstrip projector, a motion-picture projector, a radio, a record and transcription player, and a screen. This equipment is operated by the students and teachers in the classroom and auditorium. The teaching materials are school-owned, except for a few filmstrips and films. Schools that own some films and filmstrips usually supplement their libraries from rental sources. The school spends annually between $25 and $400 for materials and upkeep of the audio-visual program. The school produces no teaching aids except a few graphic materials, specimen and flat pictures, slides, and recordings. The selection of the teaching materials is by the teachers and principal. One teacher has had a course in audio-visual education. Most of the teachers have attended a lecture or committee meeting dealing with problems in this field. This is the only training received. The county and state have assisted very little in the program as it functions in the school. The school may show no feature pictures or may show one once or twice a year to the entire student body. Community resources are used for an occasional field trip or excursion, if at all. Public reaction is favorable to the audio-visual program. Students and teachers prefer films and filmstrips for use in the classroom. The program is inadequate. The greatest value in time and money is received from classroom films.

The reader will keep in mind that the 69 usable returns from this survey, although constituting a very small sample of schools in rural areas, are supposedly from the best rural audio-visual school programs operating in 29 states. If this survey reflects conditions in the best situations in the rural schools in the 29 states represented, it is reasonable to assume the audio-visual program in the rural schools throughout the United States is most inadequate.

Audio-visual Programs in County Systems and Other Rural School Systems

In addition to the 69 questionnaires returned by individual rural schools, 51 usable reports were received from rural school systems in 20 states. The reports showed that excellent audio-visual programs were in operation in a few places. These programs seem to have sprung up spontaneously over the United States.

Two audio-visual county programs have been organized in Alabama. These are in Jefferson and Tuscaloosa Counties. They are in their first year of operation under full-time directors.

The parishes in Louisiana have libraries of audio-visual materials, and the schools within these areas are uniting in an organized program. Such a program is found in the St. James Parish System at Vacherie.

Many of the townships in Connecticut (there are no county divisions in New England) have programs under the supervision of part-time and full-time directors of audio-visual education. Westport, Fairfield, West Hartford, East Haven, and Enfield Public Schools have established such programs.

Florida is branching out from county programs organized for the utilization of films to include all teaching materials. Programs operate in Broward, Pinellas, Alachus, and Dade Counties.

For some years the number of programs in counties in North Carolina has been increasing. Approximately one-third of the county school systems now own at least a small library of films and filmstrips. Supplementary materials are secured from rental sources. Guidance in the organization of these programs has come from the State Department of Public Instruction and the Extension Division of the University of North Carolina. Workshops, demonstrations, and university extension courses have assisted in achieving a better understanding of the correct use of these teaching materials. A better utilization program has been facilitated through a direct delivery service, making projectors as well as films and other audio-visual materials available to counties.

The state of Washington has some well-organized county programs. Two outstanding ones were reported in Spokane County and King County.

The Virginia program has received much impetus since state funds have been appropriated for its development. The various school administrative divisions receive state funds for equipment as well as for teaching materials.

Other county programs were reported in Indiana, Kentucky, Michigan, Minnesota, Utah, and New Jersey.

A few representative county audio-visual programs are described briefly in the following pages.

King County, Washington. In November, 1940, the King County Commissioners appropriated $4,500 to establish an educational film library for the King County Schools. "It is the policy of the department to confine the aids distributed from its library to educational films and such other aids too costly for purchase by individual school districts. The department will encourage the development of school and district centers of audio-visual aids that will care for the teachers' needs in so far as all types of audio-visual aids are concerned. The department will keep the Instructional Aids Co-ordinators in the schools through the county currently advised regarding the availability of slides, strip films, museum materials, models, flat pictures, transcriptions and other aids that will contribute to the local school or district instructional aids center."[10]

New Hanover County, North Carolina. Since 1939, New Hanover County has had a full-time director of audio-visual education. The library of 16-mm. films, filmstrips, and recordings is supplemented with additional rented materials. Preview committees select the teaching materials used in the schools. A helpful manual [11] is available to aid the 364 teachers in more effective use of these media. Workshops are held throughout the year to assist teachers in solving their problems. This county program is well-organized and is moving forward according to good practices in the utilization of audio-visual materials.

Dade County, Florida. The county co-operative audio-visual association serves practically all schools in the county. Any school having projection equipment can become a member. There are four film-selection committees: primary, intermediate, junior high, and senior high. A full-time director is now in charge of the program. Demonstration meetings are held throughout the year. The association is now aiming at instructional materials and overcoming the limitations of the audio-visual program: lack of funds, inefficient committee members, limited library personnel.

California County Programs. County libraries have been in existence in California for some years. These include Santa Clara, Los Angeles, Kern, Alameda, Ventura, and San Diego. The Division of Audio-visual Education of the State Department of Education is guiding more counties in the organization of county programs. The following are fundamental objectives in the program:

1. Development among teachers of ability and willingness to make effective use of audio-visual materials.
2. Provision of an adequate supply of readily available audio-visual materials which have been chosen to enable teachers to develop and interpret the subject matter of the curriculum in the clearest possible manner.
3. Provision of a guide to available audio-visual materials, services, and equip-

---

[10] Donald L. Kruzner, "Development of the King County Instructional Aids Department." Seattle, Washington: King County Schools (mimeographed).

[11] John L. Glisson, "Audio-visual Aids and How To Use Them." Wilmington, North Carolina: Board of Education, 1946-47.

ment so that each teacher can locate immediately materials which can be used in teaching.

4. Provision of equipment and building facilities to enable teachers to make convenient and effective use of available audio-visual materials.

5. Provision of consultant service on curricular selection, utilization in terms of acceptable instructional practices, and evaluation of audio-visual materials.[12]

Other states will be watching this development with interest, especially as it operates in the smaller, rural counties in California.

The above descriptions give a small picture of the progress of the county-wide organization of audio-visual programs in the United States. Although many of the county-wide programs are not mentioned, the sampling shows the type of work being done in different sections of the United States.

The Nebraska Experimental Project

Nebraska is largely an agricultural state with some sparsely settled sections. This results in numerous high schools with small enrolments (fewer than a hundred students) and small faculties (three to five teachers). These few teachers are responsible for offering all of the subjects of the standard curriculum.

The College of Education of the University of Nebraska and the State Department of Public Instruction became interested in this situation, raising the question, "Can motion pictures be used to enrich the standard courses in these high schools and can motion pictures offer supplementary enrichment material which provides information and education in enrichment areas beyond the subjects of the standard curriculum?"

These two state-wide agencies enlisted the co-operation of the four state-supported teacher-training colleges and the University of Omaha. Under the leadership of a joint administrative committee representing all of these institutions and agencies, a plan of experimental operation was developed. Faculty and staff members were assigned to organize and supervise the project.

From four to six schools in areas adjacent to each of the educational institutions have been selected as experimental centers. The teachers in these experimental centers meet for in-service training for

---

[12] "Suggestions for the Organization of a County Audio-visual Education Program." Sacramento, California: California State Department, Division of Audio-visual Education, October 23, 1946.

the project and are also assembled at the state universities each summer to participate in an eight-weeks' workshop and to lay out their plans of operation for the ensuing year.

Two semesters of a total six-semester experimental period have been completed. No results from the tests are available for appraisal at this time. The program has developed strong elements of teacher education. The use of the motion picture in the classroom requires thoughtful preparation. The institutions in Nebraska are emphasizing the adequate preparation of the teacher for a better instructional job. The result is reported to be teacher improvement with a consequential improvement in pupil motivation. This project includes only 16-mm. educational films.

What Improvements Are Feasible in These Programs?

In order for the small rural school to participate in a program which will provide audio-visual opportunities on a basis comparable to efficient programs in urban or consolidated schools, the following improvements seem necessary:

1. *Teacher training.* The preservice training offered the college student should include courses in audio-visual education. These courses should combine both theory and practice.

    In-service training should be available to the teacher. Courses should be offered at conveniently located centers. Teachers should receive special instruction in the use of all types of audio-visual aids and in the proper integration of such teaching materials with classroom instruction. Workshops should be held in the rural and county schools to bring the teachers the newest information on audio-visual methods of instruction and to help them solve their problems. Demonstration lessons should be conducted in all schools. Conferences should be held in the schools to help the teachers organize and utilize teaching materials.

2. *Financial support.* The small rural school will probably always be handicapped in financing a program which includes a wide variety of audio-visual materials comparable to programs already developed in many urban schools. The future of this program in the rural school points in the direction of consolidation of these schools or in a more carefully planned program of active co-operation among schools.

    State financial support should be provided for the audio-visual program in the schools. This allotment of funds should be made on a per-pupil or per-teacher basis as are allotments for other materials and supplies. However, a per-pupil or per-teacher allocation of funds will not provide an adequate program in the small rural school. Several rural schools within a geographical area can combine their allotted funds for use collectively. This is especially true for the inauguration of an audio-visual program. In this way, the initial expenditure can be justified in terms of the total school budget.

3. *Leadership.* State departments of public instruction and state universities and teachers colleges must assume the leadership in this program. They should have staff and resources sufficient for the guidance and co-ordination of selection, utilization, and production of audio-visual materials for rural and county schools.

4. *Administration.* In the small rural school, the administration of this program will be by the principal, a teacher, or a committee of interested teachers. Where a large number of rural schools have combined in the operation of an audio-visual program, a full-time director is needed. Trained personnel should be available to direct this program. The duties of this full-time director should include:

   (a) The determination, in co-operation with the teachers and administrators, of the audio-visual needs of the individual schools.
   (b) The wise expenditure of funds in terms of these needs.
   (c) The development of a program for effective cataloguing, circulation, and utilization of these materials.
   (d) The promotion of a continuous in-service training program.
   (e) The stimulation of teachers to make an optimal use of local resource material in teaching.
   (f) The dissemination of up-to-date information on the developments in this field.

5. *Physical facilities.* Adequate space must be provided for the storage, maintenance, display, and utilization of all audio-visual equipment and materials. For the projected aids, provisions must be made for electrical current outlets at the front and back of each room, adequate darkening of rooms for good projection, sufficient ventilation for physical comfort and well-being during projection, and satisfactory acoustics.

6. *Research program.* There should be a continuous evaluation program in each school to determine the worth of teaching materials and to correlate them with the curriculum. Much of the research should take place in the rural classroom under conditions facing the typical rural teacher and pupil. Such study would reveal the existing difficulties and would be a means of finding suitable ways of overcoming them. Discovery of better ways of selecting materials and of distributing and using them for the enrichment of teaching in rural schools will do much to improve the program. The results of such research should be made available to other schools and school systems through publications and a continuous sharing of experiences for the enrichment of all audio-visual programs.

CHAPTER IX
STATE PROGRAMS OF AUDIO-VISUAL EDUCATION

Francis W. Noel

Chief, Bureau of Audio-visual Education
California State Department of Education
Sacramento, California

Principles Directing the Operation of a State Audio-visual Unit

The organization and operation of a state program of audio-visual education must be consistent with broad policies established by the existing state educational authority, usually referred to as the state department of education. This department is usually developed in harmony with certain fundamental concepts of education in a democratic society.[1] An examination of those concepts indicates several which have implications for the establishment and development of audio-visual education activities at the state level. Most important of these are the following:

1. The basic function of the school is the maintenance and improvement of the instructional process, and the teacher is the most important agent in the instructional process. The state and local education authorities must be regarded as facilitating agents to make the teacher's work more effective.
2. Citizenship in today's world is more demanding than ever before, and the problems of living in a technological society are more complex and more exacting. Government and society have increased in complexity. Solutions to problems are no longer simple. These facts imply that:
   a) The educational needs of both children and adults are greater than ever before.
   b) Education must be a continuous process throughout life.
   c) Education must be related to life and sensitive to change.
3. Democratic objectives are best achieved through democratic processes. The basic method of democracy (voluntary co-operation) is the operation of group intelligence which has been defined as "the ability and disposi-

---
[1] Adapted from Arthur B. Moehlman's *School Administration*, chaps. ii and v. Boston: Houghton Mifflin Co., 1940.

tion of a social group to come to agreement on common goals and to direct concerted, effective action to their attainment."[2] Plans and procedures in school administration should follow democratic methods and be developed through group planning, participation, and evaluation.

4. The use of community, state, and national wealth to educate the children regardless of where wealth comes from or where the child lives has been established as a legal principle. This affects the financial structure of the school system and hence the distribution and allocation of state moneys for education by the state education authority.
5. Equality of educational opportunity is the right of every child. This means that every child should be given a fair chance to obtain a complete, well-rounded education by the methods and with the materials best suited to his inborn capacity. A highly differentiated and diversified program of instruction is required to achieve this objective. The state education authority can provide important leadership in activating this concept.
6. Public education in the United States is decentralized. It is not dictated by a federal or a state government. The system has grown out of the needs of the people as recognized and expressed in their own communities through local boards of education. Attempts to control or coerce schools at the local level either by a state education authority or the federal government have been resisted. The state education authority must depend upon creative leadership to fulfil its functions.
7. A major factor determining specialization of educational activities is size. Such specialization is essential with the increase in scope and complexity of educational services. The larger the educational activity, the greater the need for specialization. Specialization at the city, county, or state level then depends on the size and scope of the educational activities involved.

A State Program of Audio-visual Education

Establishment of a state audio-visual division (department, unit, or bureau) as a specialized activity of the state education authority is today logical and necessary; and it is educationally sound if based upon the educational concepts just discussed and upon the state's responsibilities implied by them.

Since the state education authority is the agency responsible for the maintenance and improvement of instruction, it should meet this responsibility by the initiation of appropriate activities and by the appointment of personnel who are directly or indirectly concerned with improving the instructional process. Because both research and the training experiences of World War II have proved that the use of audio-visual materials and methods can help meet modern educational

---

[2] *Group Planning in Education,* 1945 Yearbook, Department of Supervision and Curriculum Development. Washington: National Education Association, 1945.

objectives and thus improve the quality of instruction, *the state education authority, as a facilitating agent, should employ its resources and leadership to encourage the use of these materials at all educational levels and to assure continuity of use; to improve the quantity and quality of utilization in all phases of the instructional process; and to give advice on setting up local departments or services.* The establishment of an audio-visual education division (department or bureau) not only constitutes recognition by the state education authority of the importance of this activity but also establishes a type of prestige which is of value in the development and improvement of existing services and the creation of new departments on local levels.

Democracy as a way of life has always presupposed an informed and enlightened citizenry, but requirements for an informed citizenry in today's world are constantly increasing in number and complexity. Education must be not only universal but also a lifelong process. The educational needs of both children and adults are more numerous, more varied, and more difficult to satisfy than those of a simpler society. Consequently, the size and scope of the school activities have been greatly expanded, and the educational system has become more complex. This is notably true of the audio-visual education activity. Use of these materials requires an efficient and well-planned service; it also demands higher quality and better trained teaching personnel. There are attendant problems of physical facilities, equipment, materials, and matters of finance. *Because these problems are state-wide in scope, their solution requires specialization at the state level as well as at the local level.*

Removal of educational inequalities is a responsibility of the state education authority. The right of every individual to a complete and well-rounded education by methods and materials best suited to his needs and capacities calls for a highly differentiated and diversified program of instruction. Psychologists and researchers have provided evidence that the use of audio-visual materials is one way of effectively achieving differentiation and diversification in the instructional program.[3] A specialized audio-visual education division (department or bureau) at the state level can contribute to this goal by: (a) promoting the effective use of audio-visual materials throughout the program of instruction so that all children within the state may have equal opportunity to learn according to their abilities and needs; (b) working with curriculum specialists toward revisions, the need for

---

[3] Elizabeth Goudy Noel and J. Paul Leonard, *Foundations for Teacher Education in Audio-visual Instruction*, pp. 5, 6. Washington: American Council on Education, 1947.

which will become apparent with the extensive utilization of audio-visual materials; (c) assisting local schools in setting up adequate and efficient services so that teachers will be assured of having the right materials at the right time; and (d) developing an adequate preservice and in-service teacher-education program to improve the quality of instruction.

Educational opportunities may also be equalized by providing the financial resources to assure an adequate instructional program. The principle that the wealth of the community or state may be used to educate the child regardless of where the wealth comes from or where the child lives makes it necessary for the state education authority to play an important part in the administration and allocation of state funds for school purposes. Adequate funds are necessary to carry out an audio-visual education program and it is important that a specialist who understands the problems of developing local services be available at the state level to interpret the needs to the legislature and to the people. He will also be able to assist local departments in making the best and most efficient use of these funds.

PRESENT STATUS AND TRENDS OF STATE PROGRAMS

The status of existing programs of audio-visual education at the state level cannot be discussed without considering certain factors which include: (a) the comparatively inadequate general programs of education in certain states; (b) the comparatively recent arrival of audio-visual education on the educational scene and the subsequent dearth of experienced personnel to help guide states that are initiating programs; and (c) most important of all, a traditional concept that the program of audio-visual education should revolve around a film-distribution service. The last concept has arisen, in part, from the financial success of many large university film-rental libraries. Then, too, there is a temptation to develop a film service and to be able to point with pride to an imposing array of films, racks, service equipment, and related paraphernalia. Sometimes the situation is further complicated by legislative pressures originating with business concerns, which have assisted in gaining passage of appropriation bills that provide state funds for such services. However, as will be shown later in this chapter, there are indications that broader concepts of the functions of a state audio-visual education service are being recognized.

In the fall of 1947, the National Education Association undertook a survey of state programs of audio-visual education.[4]

---

[4] "Report of the Audio-visual Staff and Organization in the State Departments of Education." Washington: Research Division of the National Education Association, February, 1948 (mimeographed).

About the same time, Robert E. deKieffer conducted an investigation of teacher education in audio-visual education,[5] the report of which included a chapter on state programs.

In order to supplement the information contained in the N.E.A. survey and the DeKieffer study, and to have a report on later developments, the Bureau of Audio-visual Education of the California State Department of Education on May 28, 1948, directed letters to the chief state school officer in each state requesting further information.

From these three investigations, it was found that thirty-five chief state educational authorities recognize audio-visual education in some way in the administrative structure of the education department. Fifteen of them have a separate unit, designated as such, in charge of audio-visual education activities. This is an increase of four units since the N.E.A. survey was made in the autumn of 1947. Twenty states include audio-visual education work with other activities, such as a state library or a division of instructional materials or of instructional services, but do not list this activity as a separate unit in the organization of the education department.

The following excerpts from the summary of the report of the N.E.A. survey [6] indicate the resources and activities of state departments that were employed at that time to promote audio-visual education.

In the late fall of 1947 thirty-five states and six outlying areas of the United States reported the status of audio-visual staff and organization within the state or area department of education. Two (West Virginia and Guam) reported that no work is done in the central office. Twenty-three states and four outlying areas assign audio-visual work as part of the task of an individual or unit within the department. One of this group, the Canal Zone, has a separate budget for the audio-visual program, mostly for the purchase of equipment and materials.

Eleven states and one outlying area have a special unit for audio-visual work. The work of these eleven only is summarized here. Mississippi did not indicate what workers were assigned to the unit nor whether they worked full time or part time, but the report has been included in the summary. New Mexico reported a budget intended both for textbooks and the audio-visual program (most of the money at present goes for textbooks) but, in view of the assignment of three full-time workers to the unit, it also has been included in the summary.

---

[5] Robert E. deKieffer, "The Status of Teacher Training in Audio-visual Education in the Forty-eight States." Unpublished Doctor's Dissertation, University of Iowa, 1948.

[6] "Audio-visual Staff and Organization in State Departments of Education," op. cit.

Nine states and Hawaii reported having a budget allotment entirely for the audio-visual program, and one reported that the unit was so new that its budget was still indefinite. The largest amount appropriated to the central office was $120,000 in Ohio. However, in California, where the program is decentralized, over $800,000 of state funds is allocated to the counties for audio-visual work in addition to the amounts appropriated for the central office.

The staffs of most of the state department units range from two to eight full-time workers, but Virginia has fourteen full-time employees, and Ohio, thirty-two. The largest number of professional employees is four; the others are in clerical, stenographic, or other classifications.

Nine states and Hawaii distribute audio-visual materials to local school systems.

Eleven states and Hawaii attempt to promote interest in audio-visual instruction among educators of the area.

Ten states and Hawaii advise individual teachers on the use of audio-visual aids. California qualifies this somewhat by pointing out that because of the size of the state, most efforts to reach the teachers must be indirect, through workshops or conferences intended primarily for administrators or publications.

Seven states and Hawaii report that they review motion pictures and list those suitable for use by schools.

Four states and Hawaii inspect audio-visual equipment and list the items suitable for purchase by school systems.

Two states prepare and broadcast radio programs to the schools.

Among the other functions mentioned in the reports on the status of audio-visual education were the following: development of teacher-training programs; teacher education in service; development of balanced audio-visual programs in local districts; co-ordination of state-wide programs; advice to school officers on efficient administrative procedures; assistance in planning school-building facilities and in selecting equipment; distributing information on the state; selection, purchase, and care of audio-visual materials; development of local schools-of-the-air; research; and publishing pamphlet materials on audio-visual education.

Various states indicated in the N.E.A. survey[7] that their future plans include the following: expansion of state library of audio-visual aids; development of regional or local libraries of audio-visual aids; increased funds to allow for matching local funds with state moneys; preparation and broadcasting of radio programs; reviewing of motion-picture films; increased funds to permit development and expansion of existing services; and addition of new staff members.

The three most significant trends to be noted from these studies are: (a) the rapid growth of state programs of audio-visual education since the war; (b) the trend toward decentralization of services;

---

[7] *Ibid.*, p. 7.

and (c) the emphasis placed on both preservice and in-service teacher education.

Of those reporting the date of their initiation, New York was the first, being established in 1904. The development of other state programs was slow up to 1945. The Virginia and California programs were started in 1945, to be followed in rapid succession by Mississippi, Arkansas, Minnesota, Tennessee, and Washington. From these facts it appears that state chief school authorities are increasingly recognizing the need for such units. The states replying to the California letter of inquiry indicate that a majority are seeking to develop services and leadership on local or regional levels rather than attempting to centralize authority and matériel at the state level.

Increasing emphasis is being placed on teacher preparation in most states. Courses in audio-visual education are a function of teacher-education institutions. The DeKieffer study[8] reports that 128 teacher-education institutions in 1947 offered 186 audio-visual education courses in their summer session, and 119 offered 168 courses during the academic year. Many of these courses resulted from efforts on the part of the state audio-visual units to encourage teacher-education institutions to present such courses. Also, many *in-service* teacher-education programs are being initiated by the state units either directly or through local city or county audio-visual departments.

An important characteristic of both old and new state audio-visual units is the tendency to broaden services and expand staffs to meet increasing demands from local districts. New units are generally being placed within the administrative structure of the state office having responsibility for instruction.

Description of the Initiation and Operation of a State Program of Audio-visual Education

There are few published descriptions of state programs of audio-visual education. However, an important document describing the Virginia audio-visual education unit has been published for the University of Chicago.[9] This report describes that program in considerable detail and warrants careful study. The California program, the principal features of which will be described here, suggests another approach to the functions of a unit at the state level. The writer has

---

[8] *Op. cit.*, p. 8.

[9] *The Virginia Plan for Audio-visual Education.* Prepared by James W. Brown, Former State Supervisor, Bureau of Teaching Materials, State Department of Education, Richmond, Virginia. Published for the Center for the Study of Audio-visual Instructional Materials, Department of Education, University of Chicago, 1947.

chosen to describe the California program because he has been associated with its development. Although the formulation of this plan has been influenced by other state-wide programs, several factors originating within the state have influenced the growth of the unit and the direction it has taken. First, there has been a readiness on the part of the lay public and educators to initiate such a program; second, the sound economic position of the state makes it possible to support public education more adequately than is possible in many other states; and, last, state leadership in education is dynamic and is established on a professional, rather than a political, basis.

The idea of a division of audio-visual education in the California State Department of Education had its inception years ago. Vigorous and effective local audio-visual education departments had been operating for some time before World War II in San Diego City and County, in Los Angeles City and County, in Pasadena, Long Beach, Santa Barbara, Oakland, and in a few other localities. Many educators and interested lay groups began to see the need for state-wide leadership and direction. They also saw the advantages of official recognition by the state and the possibilities of increased financial support from state funds. In short, it was felt that the movement, in order to have an opportunity to make its full contribution to the improvement of instruction, needed representation in the department of education at the state level.

The State Board of Education recognized these needs by approving the recommendations of the state superintendent of public instruction and, on April 17, 1944, authorized the creation of such a unit which was established a year later by the appointment of a chief.

Originally, the unit was established as a division, administratively parallel to the divisions of elementary education, secondary education, adult education, health and physical education, and others. Later in a reorganization of the department of education, the divisions became bureaus, and those bureaus concerned with instruction were all placed within a new division of instruction headed by an associate superintendent in charge of instruction. In terms of relationships and operations, the audio-visual education unit, as a bureau within the Division of Instruction, is finding itself in a stronger position and its operations more effective than before the reorganization.

Prior to developing a program for the California Bureau of Audio-visual Education, a series of three regional meetings covering the entire state was called by the superintendent of public instruction. These meetings were held to provide an opportunity for representative school superintendents, heads of departments or schools of education, curriculum directors, audio-visual education personnel, and teachers to help plan the program of the new unit. Each conference was attended by approximately one hundred persons. Ample opportunity was given for individuals to discuss their problems and what the new unit should do to help solve them. The officer of the division acted as chairman and in each meeting posed one basic problem: "Should the state establish a number of matériel depositories under direct state control or should such depositories be developed under the cognizance of the county school superintendents and/or local district superintendents, with the state providing, if possible, some financial support and professional direction in the operation of the services?" In each case a majority of the conferees felt that a decentralized program was desirable, with the state furnishing financial help and professional assistance in the direction and operation of the local units. This has become a basic policy of the state's program of audio-visual education and has influenced the development of local audio-visual centers thoughout the state. The groups also felt that the state office should provide leadership in the development of the movement by directing its attention to such problems as:

1. Achieving teacher competency in the proper selection, utilization, and evaluation of audio-visual devices and materials in terms of good instructional practices.
2. Obtaining greater financial support for the procurement of materials and equipment by local audio-visual units.
3. Influencing commercial companies to produce materials more nearly meeting educational needs and securing state funds for model and diorama materials which are not available on a commercial basis.
4. Achieving a better selection and use of materials in terms of curricular needs at all educational levels.
5. Improving local programs of audio-visual education and developing more effective services.
6. Disseminating pertinent information about audio-visual education to school personnel.
7. Developing a better understanding of audio-visual education by promoting interest in a professional organization, such as a state audio-visual education association.
8. Obtaining better facilities for using these materials in classrooms, both in old school buildings and in new ones.
9. Developing a state-wide radio-education program.

These were state-wide problems and the state superintendent of public instruction approved a program centered upon them. He also directed the division to provide audio-visual materials and equipment, as well as professional counseling in their use for the members of the department staff, which includes more than nine hundred people. It was expected that this service would be similar in character to that of a local audio-visual education department.

Four years have elapsed since the three regional committees suggested the problems they felt were most in need of solution. The first recommendation concerned teacher competency in audio-visual education. In December, 1945, officials of the various teacher-education institutions recommended to the State Board of Education that two units in audio-visual-radio education be required of new teachers. The State Board of Education agreed, and the following regulation was adopted:

> Institutions to be considered for approval to offer the training and to make the recommendation for the kindergarten-primary, general elementary, junior high school, general secondary, and junior college credentials must, effective July 1, 1947, maintain a course, or the equivalent, of at least two semester-units in value in audio-visual-radio education and require that such course be successfully completed by each applicant for one or another of the credentials listed above. (California Administrative Code, Title 5, Section 818).

Some of the teacher-education institutions have been slow to develop adequate programs of preservice teacher education to comply with the regulation. This delay is the result of many factors: (a) a lack of readiness by the faculty to use these materials; (b) insufficient funds to procure competent personnel especially qualified in audio-visual education; (c) a lack of building facilities; and (d) a lack of equipment and materials.

The Bureau conducted an equipment and materials survey of the colleges in the state. Recommendations have been made regarding personnel, equipment, and materials needed to develop their programs. Curiously, the greatest lag is to be observed in some of the institutions supported by state funds. Officials of all the institutions, however, have evidenced a sincere desire to develop adequate programs which comply with the state board of education regulation. One of the universities of the state has developed a comprehensive program which includes a wide offering of teacher-education courses and a university service in audio-visual education for all the instructors of the institution.

The problem of what should be taught to meet the state requirements was defined by a committee appointed by the state superintendent. This committee was composed of twenty-six educators including college presidents, deans of education, superintendents, directors of curriculum and audio-visual education, and teachers. The group did not attempt to write a course of study. Rather, they defined the competency which teachers of audio-visual education should have. Their report[10] also emphasized the necessity for using audio-visual materials throughout all courses.

Teacher-education institutions have offered numerous extension courses for the in-service instruction of teachers. Such courses have usually been taught by local directors of audio-visual education and have been instrumental in improving utilization of audio-visual materials.

County and city superintendents, seeing the need for in-service teacher education, have encouraged their institute committees to include numerous section meetings dealing with various phases of audio-visual education. Demonstrations of good utilization practices, film and record previews, auditions, discussion meetings, and short workshops are featured in most institutes throughout the state. In fact, there are few institute programs at present which do not include one or more meetings dealing with audio-visual education. In this connection, the Bureau initiated efforts to bring national leaders in audio-visual education to California for institute programs and other professional meetings.

The State Department of Education, co-operating with the San Diego State College in the summer of 1947, presented an administrative audio-visual education workshop. This group of fifty-six directors of audio-visual education worked for two weeks on administrative problems. Their final report[11] has proved to be a valuable document in suggesting ways of operating local departments and in generally improving those operations. In studying their problems, the audio-visual educators recognized their own need for a better understanding of the curriculum and felt that curriculum-workers should understand better how audio-visual materials can implement and improve the curriculum. Accordingly, they recommended that a workshop in curriculum audio-visual education be held during the following summer (1948). As this chapter is being written, such a workshop, sponsored jointly by the State Department of Education and the San Francisco State College, is in session. Sixty educators are meeting for two weeks in a Sierra mountain lodge.

A unique aspect of the workshop was the stipulation that the

---

[10] "Developing Standards of Teacher Competency in Audio-visual Education," reprinted from *California Schools*, XVIII (January, 1947).

[11] *Report of Audio-visual Education Administrative Workshop*, held at San Diego State College by the California State Department of Education in co-operation with San Diego State College, August 4-15, 1947.

selection of participants would depend upon each school system sending its directors of both curriculum and audio-visual education to work as a team on common problems. The workshop personnel will compile a report which will be published.

A second problem dealt with the need for greater financial support for audio-visual education throughout the state. Exact figures covering such support are not available. However, local budgets are consistently larger each year for such activities. On the state level, from general funds, the amount has increased from approximately $200,000 before the Bureau was established to $814,000 in the school year of 1947-48. The 1948-49 state appropriation, despite the increased demands upon state funds for other educational activities, will be at least equal and probably greater than that of 1947-48. It is expected that the state will continue to provide such funds to develop county programs. The appropriation of $814,000 was for programs in audio-visual education operated by county superintendents only and does not include sums allocated to city school districts such as Los Angeles, San Diego, Oakland, San Francisco, and others. The state aid to county school systems was expended largely for materials and for salaries of noncertificated (clerical and technical) personnel. Salaries of certificated (professional) personnel are generally paid from state supervision funds not included in the $814,000.

In general, funds for audio-visual equipment used by schools is paid for by each school from local tax revenues, while equipment for use by the county staff is purchased from the funds received through the apportionment of the $814,000 provided by the state. In some instances, where a county superintendent feels that a certain school district is financially impoverished, the state funds are used to assist that particular district in procuring equipment.

Funds for operating the State Bureau of Audio-visual Education (approximately $60,000 in 1947-48) are not drawn from the $814,000 allotted to the county service fund but are provided for in the governor's budget as a part of the operating expenses of the State Department of Education. Although there has been a substantial increase in funds for audio-visual education since the initiation of the Bureau's services, the increases have not been sufficient to meet the needs of all teachers for audio-visual education services.

The third problem concerned the need to interest commercial companies in producing materials and equipment which would more nearly meet educational requirements and to obtain models and dioramas not commercially available.

The Bureau has had the full co-operation of commercial companies in its efforts to obtain equipment and materials which better meet educational needs. Conferences have been held with producers to outline needed changes and improvements. But the Bureau has not been alone in this effort. Many individuals and groups, both in California and in other states, have been working with like purpose. Marked changes have characterized some of the new equipment recently presented for school use. An example is the light-weight, sound motion picture projector.

Currently, discussions are being carried on regarding the possibility of using prison labor to produce models and dioramas for school use. Such production would be confined to the construction of articles which require so many man hours of work that it is not profitable to produce them commercially. At the time of the writing of this chapter, the idea of prison production of such materials is still in the discussion and exploratory stage.

The fourth problem, that of obtaining better selection, utilization, and evaluation of audio-visual materials, is finding at least partial solution in the program of preservice and in-service teacher education. Experience has, however, convinced many audio-visual education personnel that considerable research in this area is needed for a better understanding of the process of learning by seeing and hearing. Improved methods of utilization must be discovered and validated by extensive research. Discussions of this problem with appropriate authorities in a number of the state universities have been held. To date, very little research has been initiated by higher institutions. However, some improvement in the selection of materials has resulted in the Bureau's recommendation that no material be purchased to add to local departments except as it is previewed and recommended for purchase by teacher, supervisor, and student committees.

Numerous conferences with local educational authorities have been conducted in an effort to initiate or improve local programs and services of audio-visual education. The two workshops previously described were designed in part to serve this end. Greater financial support from state funds has made possible better services. The Bureau has assisted local superintendents in procuring personnel to direct local programs of audio-visual education.

Furthermore, the Bureau has consistently encouraged and helped school administrators to initiate audio-visual services. State-wide and regional administrative conferences have included sessions dealing with audio-visual education. County superintendents who have audio-visual departments have met with other county superintendents and boards of education in an effort to help them establish such services.

Members of the Bureau staff have been invited to speak at county school trustees' institutes. The institutes are held annually in each county and are composed of principals, administrators, and members of local school boards. These meetings have been influential in gaining the support of county superintendents in establishing audio-visual services. In each instance the Bureau has recommended that broad services be provided to include films, slides, recordings, use of radio programs, and a variety of other activities. An important aspect of the Bureau's recommendation has been that the county audio-visual education service include professional assistance to teachers on the proper selection, good utilization, and continuous evaluation of materials in terms of curriculum needs and approved instructional practices. This requires a competent director who knows and understands the curriculum as well as audio-visual education. In general, audio-visual departments are staffed by such personnel.

The Bureau is now planning a series of meetings of directors of audio-visual education to develop standards for judging services in audio-visual education.

The basic policy of encouraging decentralization has led to a rapid increase of local departments of audio-visual education from sixteen city and ten county departments in 1944 to twenty-two city and forty-seven county departments in 1948. (There are fifty-eight counties in the state.)[12] The implementation of this policy through support from state funds is resulting in a comprehensive state-wide audio-visual service administered on the local level by local leadership.

Numerous reports and articles have been released by the Bureau dealing with important developments in audio-visual education. Many of these articles have been prepared by professional committees and, occasionally, by individuals. It is the policy of the Bureau to encourage and to lend assistance to individuals and groups preparing such materials. The Bureau publishes reprints and distributes them, usually without charge.

The Bureau has encouraged and has been instrumental in the development of a vigorous state audio-visual education association with regional units. The California State Audio-visual Education Association has approximately five hundred members. Its annual conferences are well attended by personnel from all levels of education, especially by classroom teachers. Each of the five regional sections holds at least two meetings a year which are also well attended. The various units of the organization have been influential in developing

---

[12] Lelia Taggart Ormsby, "Audio Education in the Public Schools of California," pp. 42-43. Unpublished Doctor's Dissertation, Stanford University, 1948.

greater public support for the movement and in achieving understanding among lay and professional groups of the place and purposes of audio-visual education. No member of the Bureau staff accepts office in the organization. The Bureau's policy is to assist in making the organization as effective as possible.

The eighth problem, providing facilities for using projected materials in old or new buildings, has been approached in many ways. The State Department of Education has a Division of Schoolhouse Planning, which has co-operated in making pertinent recommendations to architects and school boards. The University of California and the State Department of Education call an annual schoolhouse planning conference. Since the formation of the Bureau, these conferences have had general sessions dealing with the problems of light control. Architects have shown great interest in making appropriate provisions for darkening rooms and installing adequate electrical outlets in new structures. It should be noted, however, that the Division of Schoolhouse Planning and the architects "propose" and the local boards of education "dispose." Whether or not provisions are made in new structures for room-darkening is decided by the local school board. In general, superintendents have been apprised of the need and are working toward solving the problem. However, progress has been slow.

The darkening of rooms in existing structures has received much attention on the part of the Bureau and regional units of the California State Audio-visual Education Association. Preparation of a bulletin showing different ways of controling light, types of materials used, their cost and availability has been undertaken.

Solving this problem *economically* is very difficult and should be the concern of both educators and equipment manufacturers throughout the nation. At present, scientific answers are not available to questions like, "How dark should the room be for adequate projection?" "How large should the screen be?" "How bright should the image be?" "How adequate are translucent viewing devices?" Until we have more accurate objective information on these questions satisfactory progress toward the solution of this problem cannot be expected.

Considerable attention has been directed toward the development of a state-owned F-M educational network in answer to the ninth problem proposed. Committees from numerous lay and professional organizations have studied the problem, made favorable recommendations, and worked toward establishing a useful system. Details of the network were developed by a joint radio education committee, appointed by the state superintendent of public instruction and the president of the University of California. Although the plan has not been approved by the legislature, the recommendations of these committees are worthy of note. The plan provided for an educational radio system to be jointly operated by the State Department of Education and the University of California. In general, schooltime broadcasting was to be the responsibility of the State Department of Education and non-schooltime broadcasting the responsibility of the University of California.

By the use of a relay system, according to the plan outlined, each station would broadcast programs originating from any one of four studios located in four centers in the state; or, by the use of transcriptions, it could delay the program to meet the scheduling needs of schools in a particular area. Also, a method of repeating programs as many times as needed was suggested.

The University of California and the State Department of Education were each to maintain separate but co-ordinated programming activities; the Department of Education was to be responsible for programs to be used in the public schools. An adequate professional staff comprised of curriculum personnel, research workers, script writers, and others was to be provided in addition to field personnel who were to assist schools in utilizing the programs. Professional actors were not to be employed since school and student personnel were to be used for that purpose. This plan failed to gain legislative approval and financial support. Although the estimated cost of the system was $265,000 for capital outlay and approximately $100,000 for annual maintenance and staff, these were not the reasons for its defeat. Opposition from commercial broadcasters appears to be the primary factor in failure to secure approval.

Failure to gain legislative approval for the broadcasting system has not discouraged plans for developing a greater classroom use of commercial radio programs of value to the curriculum. These plans were implemented in 1947 when the Standard Oil Company of California made a grant of $2,500 to conduct a radio survey in the schools of the state. The recommendations and the writing of a report based on this survey were undertaken as a doctoral dissertation problem by a Leland Stanford University student.[13] This report will be used as a guide for future activities in promoting radio education.

A project of the Bureau in 1948-49 is to promote more extensive classroom use of radio programs having application to the curriculum. This project is an extension of activities already being carried on in

[13] *Ibid.*, p. 24.

a few of the larger school districts such as Long Beach, Los Angeles City, Alameda, Sacramento, and San Diego. The state will be divided into five broadcasting areas. A separate radio log listing selected programs broadcast in each area will be prepared by the Bureau and sent to schools and newspapers. The Radio Committee of the California Congress of Parents and Teachers and various professional organizations have signified their willingness to promote school use of the programs which will be listed. Consultants from the Bureau will advise and work with school personnel in helping them develop good radio utilization programs. These utilization programs will follow the lines of the program developed in Los Angeles County before the war.

As school buildings are equipped with radios and as classroom use increases, local school production of radio programs will be encouraged. Bureau personnel will work largely through local education and lay committees to encourage commercial stations to provide more programs adapted to school needs. The establishing of school-owned F-M stations such as those which are operating in Santa Monica and San Francisco will be encouraged. It is hoped that, as intensive school use of radio programs develops, a state-owned network will receive legislative support.

Since the Bureau was established, a number of activities have been carried on which were not at first anticipated. For instance, the Bureau was asked to provide instructional-film previews for members of the legislature during the 1948 session. These preview sessions and the discussions which followed have produced a favorable reaction, and, since that body must authorize the expenditure of state funds for the program, such relationships are important.

All departments of the state government have training problems. Early in the Bureau's operation, a policy was established whereby its resources of equipment, materials, and personnel were made available to state departments. As a result, the facilities of the Bureau have been used extensively by other departments. In return, their good will has been of great assistance in carrying forward the school program. This service is considered so vital that it is expected a bill will be introduced in the next session of the legislature authorizing the service and providing additional funds to enable the Bureau to give additional services to the other departments of the state government.

The Bureau has also developed a centralized audio-visual education service for the use of staff members of the State Department of Education. All equipment and material needs for each division of the Department and the various bureaus are reflected in the budget of the Bureau of Audio-visual Education. When other bureaus need to use certain equipment, it is assigned on a long-term basis if needed continuously; otherwise, it is checked out to them as needed and returned immediately when they are through using it. The same procedure holds true of films and other materials. No equipment or material is loaned to schools for student work. However, when county or city superintendents conduct meetings where departmental personnel participate, equipment and materials are made available for such use. Personnel from the Bureau give professional assistance to the entire staff of the Department in the selection, use, and evaluation of all kinds of audio-visual materials and equipment. This service has resulted in extensive use of such materials and equipment by some members of the Department staff in meetings and conferences in which they participate. It has been found that the use of such equipment and materials by staff members, and especially by the state superintendent of public instruction, has had significant influence in promoting state-wide development of audio-visual education.

In reading this report, an impression may have been gained that the Bureau performs many of its functions by working with and especially through other people and organizations. This is true. The Bureau's staff, like other state units, is small. It is composed of three professional workers—a chief and two consultants—a photographic technician, and four secretaries. There is a real problem of making a small staff's work effective throughout a large state. This can be done only by gaining the active co-operation and assistance of other individuals, agencies of government, and professional and lay organizations. It is not difficult to gain this co-operation when persons or groups understand that such action on their part will improve the effectiveness of their own work. The state office is trying to provide leadership, not to dictate.

The foregoing description of the operation of the California State Department of Education's Bureau of Audio-visual Education has attempted to show how, as a facilitating agent, it has employed its resources and leadership "to encourage the use of these materials at all educational levels and to assure continuity of use; to improve the quantity and quality of utilization in all phases of the instructional process; and to give advice on setting up local departments or services." [14]

---

[14] *Supra,* p. 164.

CHAPTER X

PRINCIPLES OF ADMINISTERING AUDIO-VISUAL PROGRAMS

FRANCIS W. NOEL

Chief, Bureau of Audio-visual Education
California State Department of Education
Sacramento, California

The purposes of this chapter are threefold: (1) to describe for school administrators the scope of activities necessary for the administration of an effective audio-visual education program and the functions they may expect an administrative unit charged with that responsibility to fulfil; (2) to suggest to prospective audio-visual directors a guide for planning and setting up a department; and (3) to provide directors of departments now in operation a basis for analyzing and evaluating the organization and operation of their activity in terms of its functions.

To achieve these purposes, the major part of this chapter is devoted to a discussion of: (1) Why should a department of audio-visual education be established? (2) What should be the functions of a department of audio-visual education? (3) What general principles and procedures underlie the administration of a department of audio-visual education?

Present-day "answers" to those questions would not constitute a final word on the subject. This is one of the first attempts to consider the various aspects of the audio-visual program in relation to the administrative and supervisory problems involved in operating the program. To do this, the writer has drawn from the experiences of a number of persons now holding positions as audio-visual directors in city or county school systems as well as from his own experience in both state and local departments of education. Additional assistance has been provided by three reports which reflect the thinking and experience of some sixty-one county and city directors in California:

(a) an unpublished report of the Audio-visual Education Administrative Workshop held at the University of California at Berkeley during the summer of 1947; (b) a report [1] of a subcommittee of the Committee on Audio-visual Education of the California State Supervisors Association; and (c) an unpublished report of the Audio-visual Education Administrative Workshop held at San Diego by the California State Department of Education and the San Diego State College in August, 1947.

The term "Department of Audio-visual Education" refers to that unit in the school organization especially charged with administering the services and supervising the use of audio-visual materials by teachers and other school personnel. It may be called a "division," a "section," a "bureau," or by a similar designation. One term (department) is used here to avoid confusion. The department may serve a city, a district, a township, a county, or a region; this chapter does not deal with audio-visual procedures in a single school [2] except as it functions in co-operation with a central department servicing a group of schools.

WHY SHOULD A DEPARTMENT OF AUDIO-VISUAL EDUCATION
BE ESTABLISHED?

Audio-visual materials are being used increasingly by business and industry. Extensively employed by the armed forces during World War II, they are still basic to the training programs of those services. The impact of this use has accentuated the pressures that were already being exerted to stimulate schools to expand their utilization of such materials. True, schools made a limited use of these materials before the war, but, now, general recognition is given to the fact that audio-visual materials of instruction are essential to the attainment of modern educational objectives. Instructional materials play a dominant role in determining the classroom learning experiences, and films, filmstrips, slides, radio, transcriptions, television, study prints, and other audio-visual materials should become an integral part of the learning environment.

As a result of these and other factors, schools are using more audio-

[1] Audio-visual Aids Committee of California School Supervisors Association, "Suggestions for the Organization of a County Audio-visual Educational Program," *California Journal of Elementary Education*, XIV (February, 1943), 163-75.

[2] For a discussion of the responsibilities of an audio-visual co-ordinator in a single school, see chapter iii, *Audio-visual Materials and Methods in the Social Studies*, pp. 25-32. Eighteenth Yearbook of the National Council for the Social Studies. Washington: National Education Association, 1947.

visual instructional materials, but too often in a haphazard, undirected way. At some point in the increasing use of these materials, every superintendent will need to study his situation to determine whether he will: (a) adopt a laissez-faire attitude, (b) give the program order, direction, and leadership, or (c) stop further use and development.

If he chooses to adopt a laissez-faire attitude, the superintendent probably will find use continuing from year to year but accompanied by confusion, waste, and poor classroom utilization. He will find equipment out of circulation because minor repairs are needed; there will be unnecessary duplication of materials; and equipment will be restricted to special departments when it should be available to the entire school system. One city school system faced such problems prior to establishing a department of audio-visual education in 1936. For example, the night-school principal wanted the film, "Servant of the People," for the graduation exercises of the classes in citizenship. Efforts were made to rent the motion picture from a university extension film library. The principal was informed that it had been scheduled by another school. Believing the film essential for the exercises, he wired the university asking whether the school in question might, if requested, change the date of use. Upon checking, the university discovered that a high school under the jurisdiction of the same city school system had booked the film for that date. The university authorities wired, suggesting that the school officials get together locally rather than through the university's facilities. This matter came to the attention of the superintendent who decided to check on the entire situation. His professional and lay investigating committee found many similar problems in the rental of films. They found projection equipment limited to an occasional use by a single department when other departments in the same school needed it. Confusion regarding the physical aspects of use was paralleled by poor utilization and improper selection of materials.

The report of the committee led the board of education to establish a department of audio-visual education, which gave order and direction to the procurement of audio-visual materials and accelerated and improved their use. Some years later, the president of the board publicly declared that the department, *aside from the value of its services in improving instruction, was economically sound, having eliminated duplication of effort, reduced waste, and procured equipment and materials more economically than was otherwise possible.* This is a basic reason for establishing such an administrative unit.

Another reason for establishing a department is that the procurement, distribution, and maintenance of materials is a *complex* operation. It requires handling special materials and equipment such as motion pictures, filmstrips, opaque projectors, and transcription players. Materials and equipment may have to be obtained from a variety of sources. Films, transcriptions, models, exhibits, and other aids must be distributed dependably and promptly. They require inspection and servicing. Operators must be trained in their care and use. All of this points to the need for centralizing the administrative responsibility for such activities and providing the proper facilities.

A superintendent in analyzing these factors may consider the possibility of placing the department of audio-visual education within the library service. To the inexperienced and uninitiated there seem to be many logical reasons in favor of such a decision. However, there are sound reasons why successful audio-visual services have, in general, developed apart from school libraries. These include the need for educational leadership on the part of the director. The conventional training of library personnel, which emphasizes all types of printed materials, is not adequate for the specialized characteristics of audio-visual education. The varied administrative details involved in operating such a service, the knowledge, skills, and insight required to co-ordinate the services with the curriculum, and the technical aspects of the work require more specialized training.

But the job is only half done when the physical and operational aspects are cared for. The problem of continuously educating teachers and other school personnel in the effective use of audio-visual materials is a major one and basic to the improvement of the instructional process. *Someone must be given this responsibility because of its size and scope and because it requires specialization in the fields of administration, curriculum, and supervision.* The problem of interpreting the school's educational program to the professional personnel and to the community is likewise a difficult but important one. It is natural for administrators to seek the best ways of doing this. Audio-visual materials and techniques have been very effectively used to communicate ideas about the schools to the public.

Administrators will recognize the importance of the functions just described and will realize too that careful planning, ample time, and expert leadership are required. If order and direction are to be given to the educational uses of audio-visual materials, there should be established a department of audio-visual education with adequate personnel and facilities. The over-all purpose of such a department then should be to facilitate the instructional process by providing those materials and professional services (a) which will enable teachers, pupils, and supervisors to get and use audio-visual educational materials and equipment in accordance with good instructional practices; (b) which will enable administrators and other members of the professional staff to use audio-visual material for interpreting the total educational program to appropriate groups.

What Should Be the Functions of an Audio-visual Department?

Before discussing the functions of an audio-visual department, it may be well to point out that the degree to which the audio-visual department is organized and set apart from other phases of the school's activity depends upon the scope of the program and the size of the school system which it serves. Obviously, small school systems will have a department with limited services and, perhaps, a director on a part-time basis. In larger systems, the size and scope of the department's activities will be greater. However, in each instance, there should be a director who has been given full responsibility for the operation.

Systems which establish a central department should also work toward the appointment of an audio-visual co-ordinator in each individual school of more than four teachers. The audio-visual co-ordinator should usually be a teacher who has been relieved of extra-school responsibilities and, in larger schools, part of his teaching load. This is necessary if he is to have time to serve his fellow teachers and to act as liaison between his school and the central department. The size and scope of the activity determines the amount of time an audio-visual co-ordinator will need. The co-ordinator should work closely with the director of the central department and members of his staff.

Whether the audio-visual education activity or central department is large or small, it should perform the functions enumerated below. These functions may not be undertaken all at once, but, to carry them out, an audio-visual department will need to establish various policies and procedures.

1. The department should provide those matériel and professional services which will make it possible for teachers to use audio-visual education materials in their own classrooms under the best possible conditions. This implies that:
    a) The department should be able to suggest the best means of darkening classrooms or controlling light, ventilating the room, placing electrical outlets, and improving acoustics. The department should be able to

refer school administrators to reliable and competent technicians or firms who can provide the needed materials or facilities.

b) The department should give guidance and counsel on the proper room conditioning when new school construction is being planned. Experience seems to indicate that the total cost of building or setting aside special audio-visual rooms for the use of projected materials is usually greater than equipping the majority or all classrooms for projection. Furthermore, the latter plan is educationally sounder because these materials should be used in the classroom as an integral part of the learning environment.

c) The department should procure sufficient copies of various materials to be able to meet the additional requests that arise from use by *individual* teachers.

d) The department should urge schools to procure enough portable equipment to meet teacher demand. In general, the equipment for a school should be purchased from its appropriations for capital expenditures rather than from the department's budget.

e) The department should be responsible for the periodic servicing of school-owned as well as centralized equipment. It should provide stand-by equipment for emergency use by schools while their equipment is being repaired, or for extraordinary needs such as the presentation of programs for "Public Schools Week."

f) The department should be responsible for training students, teachers, and supervisors in the operation and care of equipment and the proper handling of materials. If there are audio-visual co-ordinators in individual schools, they can assume this responsibility. If not, a few teachers should be selected and trained who, in turn, can train groups of students and other teachers.

In general, student operators should be used, but the teacher must assume the final responsibility for this activity as well as for others carried on in his classroom. Boys and girls as young as fifth graders, when properly trained, can operate even the most complicated equipment (16-mm. sound projector) satisfactorily. Reports indicate that student operation results in a minimum of film damage and that the attention required to operate equipment does not detract from what pupils learn.

Aside from unnecessary expense, the use of paid operators, such as building cutodians or professional projectionists, assigned exclusively to such work, may lead to labor difficulties. If the projector is considered a mechanical device necessary for using a certain type of instructional material as a regular part of the teaching-learning situation, then arguments for paid operators have no validity. The argument for paid operators is probably associated with the concept of motion pictures as entertainment.

2. The department should provide those services which will make it possible

for teachers to have materials and equipment when they need them. This implies that:

a) The department should issue catalogues, bibliographies, and special bulletins so that school personnel will have accurate, up-to-date information on available materials. These may be master catalogues of all the materials, listings in the courses of study and resource units, and special bulletins about new materials and/or those valuable for special curricula areas such as safety or health education.

b) The department should work out a cataloguing and filing system which is capable of expansion and one that will make materials readily accessible to teachers, pupils, and clerical help.

c) The department should establish a distribution system that will make it easy for teachers to obtain materials. Convenience to the teacher should be considered above convenience to the department. Simple requisitioning procedures and a reliable delivery system are essential elements of the distribution service. The scheduling of equipment in the individual school by the school's audio-visual co-ordinator must conform to the scheduling of materials. Such materials as films, filmstrips, and transcriptions must be available for more than one day so that teachers will have time to preview them and use them as often as necessary.

A delivery service is essential. In rural areas (counties, districts, or townships) delivery by mail or express, by bus, or by other already established means of transportation can often be utilized to advantage. A special delivery service is expensive; it requires purchasing a truck, providing for its operation and maintenance, and hiring a driver. In rural areas, the audio-visual director should compare this cost and the efficiency of such a service with that of increasing the number of prints of various materials to give a comparable service. He will probably find the latter more economical. A delivery system must be frequent, regular, and thoroughly reliable.

d) The department should make every effort to see that the equipment is kept as close to the point of use as possible. In general, equipment should be *owned* by the individual school, having been purchased from its funds for capital outlay. When this is impossible, equipment should be assigned to schools on a long-term basis as transporting it causes more rapid deterioration, thereby increasing the cost of maintenance and replacement.

e) The audio-visual department should be responsible for periodic servicing of all equipment belonging to the school or the department. This does not mean that the department must actually repair equipment or that the director, even in small departments, should regularly perform such work. He should, however, be held responsible for seeing that the equipment is regularly inspected and serviced. Whether a department offers repair service within its organization will depend upon its size and the availability of quick, economical, and satisfactory commercial maintenance service. Minor maintenance operations, such as oiling, replacing lamps or tubes, repair of electrical cords, etc., should be the responsibility of the school owning the equipment and should be performed under the direction of the school's audio-visual coordinator, if one has been appointed.

f) The department should strive for continuous decentralization of materials, that is, the allocation of certain materials to individual schools. The extent to which this can be done depends on several factors, such as unit cost, size of the school system, duration of use, type of delivery service available, and the nature of the materials. Certain items having a low unit cost, such as filmstrips, study prints, and records, will be used more frequently if left in a school on a long-term loan. It is usually more economical to deposit them in the school than to keep the records and provide the delivery service needed to assure frequent use. All such materials should be returned to the central depository periodically for inspection, repair, replacement, and reassignment.

3. The department should provide the materials and services which will make it possible for teachers to select and use audio-visual materials appropriate to the teaching-learning situation. This implies that:

a) The department's director and professional staff should co-operate with supervisors and curriculum-workers in selecting appropriate materials and in guiding teachers in the selection and use of such materials. The director should be responsible for the preliminary screening and elimination of undesirable materials, but the final selection of materials should be by preview committees or other experienced teachers. In general, the director should not procure materials except as they are recommended by those who will use them.

b) The department should plan to acquire materials on the basis of curriculum needs as determined by teachers, supervisors, and curriculum-directors. This avoids haphazard choices and the purchase of materials just for one subject or group or for one or two grade levels.

c) The department should assist supervisors, teachers, and pupils in their choice and use of materials that meet their needs. This can be achieved through an in-service education program which provides teachers and others many opportunities to become familiar with a wide range of materials and to develop standards of judgment.

Preview committees, together with other school personnel, should employ the *same critical bases* and apply the *same standards of judgment* to materials prepared especially for school use and to those prepared for other than educational purposes but which have significant content and provide valuable learning experiences for boys and girls. Materials used for non-educational purposes include, especially, entertainment films or commercially prepared (sponsored) posters, models, and filmstrips, motion pictures, and radio broadcasts.

d) The department should help plan the production of, and, in certain instances, produce simple audio-visual materials to meet special curriculum needs. This type of production should be limited to those materials which are not available from commercial sources or are not of a nature to be generally used if produced professionally. For example, if pictures of historical landmarks are important to a community study, the sequence of pictures should be planned with teachers, pupils, and supervisors, and, if the department does not have a photographic technician, the audio-visual director should arrange to have the pictures taken. In general, the head of the audio-visual department should not make a regular practice of "taking pictures" even if he is a "camera fan."

4. The department should provide the facilities and professional services which will assure that the audio-visual materials will be used as an integral part of the total instructional program. This implies that:

   a) The department should procure materials which will meet the needs of pupils from kindergarten through college, including adult education.

   b) The department should co-operate in working with other school personnel on continuous curriculum-revision programs. Many audio-visual materials have a wide range of use. The contents of a single film may cut across a number of grade levels or subject areas. The same film may appeal in different ways to different pupils; the same pupils may learn different things as the purposes of use vary and the pupils' interests and needs mature and change. Use of such films may affect the choice of other instructional materials or the types of experiences which boys and girls need at a given time. The use of certain audio-visual materials may shorten the time required to complete a unit. Some can clarify and simplify difficult concepts. Some can provide experiences not otherwise available. These and other facts may well lead to a reconsideration of the length of time spent on certain units and their placement in the curriculum or may lead to the introduction of new units. Audio-visual directors, because of their special knowledge of the field and of the learning potentials inherent in the use of audio-visual materials, should give able assistance in this area.

   c) The department should plan for a continuous evaluation of the materials in terms of achieving curriculum objectives and, if possible, for experiments and research which may contribute to curriculum revision.

   d) The department should supervise classroom utilization of these materials at all levels of instruction. This may be done by working (1) directly with individual teachers, (2) indirectly through in-service teacher-education activities, and (3) through supervisors and administrators.

5. The department should provide those matériel and professional services which will enable teachers to make full use of community resources. This implies that:

a) The department should assist in locating materials, places of local interest, and people in the community who can contribute information and rich experiences to the educational program, and it should make information about these resources available to teachers. Such resources include individuals who are authorities in various occupational fields or on certain subjects, as well as factories, mills, museums, parks, historical landmarks, municipal buildings, and airports.

b) The department should work with teachers, supervisors, and administrators to survey and appraise community resources preliminary to the development of a list of those which are suitable for school use. It should work out the essential details for utilizing and evaluating them.

6. The department should provide those professional services which will assure teacher competency in the use of audio-visual instructional materials as well as competency at the supervisory and administrative levels. This implies that:

a) The department will be concerned with a continuous program of in-service growth which will help teachers and other professional personnel gain the knowledge and understanding as well as the skills and abilities that are essential to effective use of audio-visual materials. Such requirements were recently enumerated by a California committee of educators:

1) Knowledge and understanding:
   (*a*) Philosophical and psychological factors underlying the use of audio-visual materials and equipment in the classroom.
   (*b*) Results of research studies, past and present, in the field and their implications for instruction.
   (*c*) Types of audio-visual materials available in the specific area of the teacher's interest and their potential educational worth and uses.
   (*d*) Sources of materials and equipment—local, national, and international.
   (*e*) Nature of the common types of audio-visual materials and equipment, including the educational values and limitations of each.
   (*f*) Methods of procuring, storing, filing, and maintaining the various kinds of materials and equipment.
   (*g*) Principles of good teaching that affect the selection and use of these materials.
   (*h*) Processes involved in the production of some of the simpler materials, such as mounted prints, handmade slides, filmstrips, and photographs.
   (*i*) Services of an audio-visual education department and its personnel, the best ways of using that service, and the teachers' responsibility for co-operating with the department.

(j) Principles and procedures for setting up an audio-visual education service in a single school or in a school district.

(k) Background and development of audio-visual education that have a relation to current trends and practices in the field.

2) Skills and abilities:
    (a) To appraise the educational worth, technical quality, photographic characteristics, and commercial aspects of audio-visual materials.
    (b) To select audio-visual materials to meet pupils' needs and the purposes of instruction.
    (c) To use each audio-visual tool effectively in a classroom situation.
    (d) To evaluate the effectiveness of the use of these materials in teaching situations and to modify and improve future instructional practices on the basis of such evaluation.
    (e) To assemble and operate various kinds of equipment and to perform simple servicing operations such as lubrication and the placement of lamps.
    (f) To provide and arrange the best physical conditions possible for using these materials.
    (g) To plan and successfully execute a field trip or excursion.
    (h) To produce simple materials such as mounted prints, slides, posters, charts, graphs, models, collections of natural science materials, and to prepare exhibits and displays.
    (i) To display materials effectively on the bulletin board, in the classroom, and in other appropriate locations.[3]

b) The department should provide professional leadership which will help attain teacher (supervisory and administrative) competency in the use of these materials through activities such as:
   1) The preparation of teachers' manuals, guides, or handbooks for using certain films, filmstrips, transcriptions, and so on.
   2) The development of curriculum resource units which include a list of specific materials in a possible sequence of use, suggestions for using them, and annotated bibliographies of related materials.
   3) The maintenance of a library of audio-visual publications for teachers, supervisors, and administrators. These may be used as recommended reading materials for extension courses or workshops, placed in the hands of teachers to help solve a particular problem, reviewed and discussed by study groups, and reprinted in part or quoted in handbooks and bulletins.

c) The department should provide professional leadership in the appoint-

---

[3] "Developing Standards of Teacher Competency in Audio-visual Education," *California Schools*, XVIII (January, 1947), 5-6. (A report prepared in co-operation with the American Council on Education's Committee on Content in Audio-visual Education.)

ment of preview and selection committees. Such committees should consist largely of teachers but should also include personnel from among supervisors, administrators, and curriculum directors. It is sometimes advisable to include P.T.A. members, members of the board of education, and a representative of the press. Committees for junior and senior high schools should include some students. The audio-visual director should be an ex-officio member of all committees.

d) The department should provide professional leadership in planning and conducting meetings with faculty groups, teachers from several schools having the same grades, or teachers of the same subjects. The meetings may be planned to achieve such purposes as giving demonstrations of basic techniques of using audio-visual materials, acquainting groups with community resources that can be used to extend the learning experiences of pupils, explaining techniques of producing teacher-made or pupil-made audio-visual materials, and preparing study guides for use with audio-visual materials.

e) The department should provide professional leadership in conducting individual conferences with teachers. The chief purposes of such conferences should be to obtain information about the teacher's needs, to arrange opportunities for him to observe the methods of other teachers, to help him develop simple standards of evaluation of materials and procedures, and to encourage individual research.

f) The department should provide leadership in the conducting of teachers' institutes or workshops based on the needs of teachers, supervisors, and administrators. The director should make arrangements for extension courses in accordance with the demand for them. Such courses should not be presented merely on a verbal level. They should involve direct experience and should grow out of the immediate needs of teachers. There should be multiple opportunities for practice, for demonstration, and for the use of audio-visual materials in specific situations. Instructors should actually use these materials throughout the course so that teachers will learn about audio-visual education from audio-visual materials.[4]

7. The department should provide those matériel and professional services which will help the administrative staff and other school personnel interpret the school's program to both professional and lay groups. This implies that:

a) The department should be able to produce audio-visual materials which will help administrators, supervisors, and others to explain the school's program to its personnel and to the public. This, at times, may involve the production of charts, posters, glass slides, illustrated bulletins or pamphlets, exhibits, and radio broadcasts.

---

[4] For further discussion of this point, see Elizabeth Goudy Noel and J. Paul Leonard, *Foundations for Teacher Education in Audio-visual Instruction*, pp. 41-47. American Council on Education Studies, Series II, No. 9, *Motion Pictures in Education*. Washington: American Council on Education, June, 1947.

b) The department should provide equipment and materials to quasi-educational groups when their use is related to an interpretation of the school's program and should formulate appropriate regulations governing the use of the school's property by lay groups. In the attempt to comply with state laws or local rulings concerning the loan of school property there are always borderline cases involving the judgment of the director of the audio-visual education program. Sometimes the application of these laws is made doubly difficult because the organization wishing materials may have donated a piece of equipment to the school. Although the school may hold clear title to the equipment, certain persons or organizations may feel that they should be favored. Inconsistent decisions or those based upon expediency or favoritism lead to trouble. Guiding policies should be established before problems arise. In general, such policies should be in line with those which apply to the lending of other types of school equipment. Some schools have adopted the policy that no equipment should be loaned unless a qualified and responsible member of the school staff accompanies it. It is important to adopt policies which will maintain those healthy relations with lay groups necessary for the continued public support of the audio-visual program. These policies should be established by the school board and administrative staff upon the recommendation of the director.

What General Principles and Procedures Underlie the Administration of a Department of Audio-visual Education?

Although local conditions will dictate actual procedures for the organization and operation of a particular department, certain general principles of administration deserve consideration. These are discussed below under the following headings:

1. Place of the audio-visual department in the administrative organization
2. Personnel and their qualifications
3. Housing and operational facilities
4. Financial support

The Place of the Audio-visual Department in the Administrative Organization

Since an audio-visual department serves the needs of instruction throughout an entire school system, it should be placed in the administrative organization where it can do this most effectively. Usually, this is within the administrative segment having responsibility for the instructional program. However, administrators should avoid placing the department where it might become involved in the differences and disputes which frequently revolve around curriculum revision. This may happen if it is subordinated to such departments as elementary or secondary education, guidance, or research. On the other hand, the department should not be so placed as to become isolated from the curriculum activity, thereby lessening its opportunities for improving instruction.

Experience seems to indicate that the department can function best in a co-ordinate relationship with other parts of the curriculum division or the division of instruction. If there is no over-all division of instruction, the audio-visual director should be responsible to the superintendent or to his assistant in charge of instruction. His status should be co-ordinate with supervisors or directors responsible for other aspects of curriculum supervision and development.

Although practices vary, the title "director" seems to be more appropriate than supervisor or co-ordinator, since the head of an audio-visual department must perform administrative as well as supervisory functions. He must be in a position to work directly with the city or county school administrative heads in matters of policy and budget-making. He must be able to advise heads of other departments and supervisors concerning the use of audio-visual materials in their respective fields.

It is believed that the director should be an administrator in his department only and that his relation to others, either above him or below him in a line and staff organization should be of a consultive nature. He should be regarded by the line and staff groups as an advisor and an expert observer in the field. Such a person must be free to go directly to the individual in charge of instruction. He must be directly accessible to the principals and teachers as well as to other directors or supervisors and to the chairmen of curriculum groups.

Some administrators favor the establishment of a unified division of instructional materials [5] which would include text and reference books as well as audio-visual materials. In this case, the same general principle of placement within the administrative organization would apply.

Personnel and Their Qualifications

The personnel of an audio-visual department should include the professional (certificated) and noncertificated persons necessary to

---

[5] See Helen Hardt Seaton, *Measure for Audio-visual Education Programs in Schools*, p. 36. American Council on Education Studies, Series II, No. 9. Prepared for the Committee on Visual Aids in Education. Washington: American Council on Education, October, 1944.

carry out the functions discussed in the section dealing with functions. In general, it is not economical to assign duties to certificated personnel which can be performed just as efficiently by noncertificated persons. In other words, the audio-visual director should not book materials, although he is responsible for setting up the procedures and supervising the employees who perform this administrative service.

Certificated personnel include the director and his professional assistants. They should be responsible for or share leadership in the following areas:

1. Evaluation and selection of materials and equipment.
2. Supervision of all aspects of utilization within the schools.
3. Consultation services to teachers, principals, supervisors, audio-visual coordinators, architects, and outside agencies on problems and activities in audio-visual education.
4. In-service education programs for school personnel.
5. Experimentation and research on evaluation, uses of materials, and needs for future production.
6. Interpretation of the school's program, including audio-visual education, to the school personnel and to the public.
7. Production of special curriculum materials.

Nonprofessional personnel include the necessary technicians for the maintenance of equipment, the technical phases of the production of audio-visual aids, and photographic work.

Since the establishment of audio-visual departments is a relatively new development, few school systems have set up definite requirements, either professional or personal, which an individual must meet before assuming the position of director. In most cases, a regular teaching certificate is the only legal requirement; however, because of the need for special training, school systems should adopt technical standards of qualifications for directors. Below are listed the professional qualifications which at present seem desirable for the director of a department of audio-visual education.

1. At least two years of successful teaching experience at either the secondary or elementary level, with subsequent experience in supervision or administration.
2. An understanding of curriculum objectives, of the methods of curriculum construction, and of acceptable instructional practices.
3. A well-balanced and dynamic personality and a wholesome philosophy of life such as are commonly expected of others in comparable positions of educational leadership.
4. Expert knowledge of audio-visual materials and how to use them as an integral part of the instructional program.

5. Skill in the operation and simple maintenance of audio-visual equipment and an understanding of the theory and practices related thereto.
6. A working knowledge of basic fields, such as photography, radio production, recording, slide-making, and so on. Although it is not required that he be an expert in any one of these fields, he should be familiar with the processes involved.
7. Skill in organizing and directing the activities of a department.

The director and his assistants, in co-operation with other school administrative officers, should set up the qualifications for noncertificated personnel on the basis of job-analyses. These requirements will, of course, vary with the size and scope of the activity.

Operation and Maintenance of an Audio-visual Department

Again, local conditions and local policies will determine the exact procedures for the operation of a department, but several administrative problems which are common to most departments will be noted.

Selecting New Materials and Equipment. The director should be qualified to evaluate and select all types of audio-visual equipment for his department and to give assistance to individual schools in their purchases of equipment. It has already been pointed out that committees of teachers and administrators with the help of the director should set appropriate standards for selecting equipment for their own purposes. The director should keep an up-to-date file on developments in the audio-visual equipment field and the sources from which equipment may be procured.

The evaluation and selection of materials should be done by preview committees comprised of persons who will actually use them. The audio-visual director or a member of his professional staff should screen out obviously undesirable materials before they reach a committee. When it is difficult to get teachers together for previewing, the director should send materials to teachers, requesting an appraisal after they use them in a classroom situation. Some directors have asked existing organizations such as principals' and supervisors' associations, health- and physical-education, agriculture, and foreign-language groups, and school nurses to preview materials. The director has the final responsibility for procurement and must decide whether the material should be bought, borrowed, or rented. In regard to motion pictures, if a particular film is used four or five times a year it should be purchased rather than rented. Answers to questions like the following will affect his decision about purchasing materials:

1. Is the relation of these materials to the curriculum basic or supplementary?
2. How often will they be used during a school year?

3. Will they be used continuously from year to year?
4. How many teachers will probably use them?
5. Will they soon be outdated?
6. Can they be as easily and economically obtained from other sources *when* needed?

Cataloguing and Processing New Acquisitions. New materials should be classified and catalogued upon receipt. While variations exist in classification systems now used, it is to be noted that most of the large departments employ a modified (large numbers only) Dewey decimal system. It is used especially for films, filmstrips, and slides because it not only gives a file number but also serves to identify the subject area of the material and relates the item to library references. Directors have often found it advisable to add letters or other symbols to the Dewey decimal number to distinguish between study prints, films, slides, and other types of materials carrying the same accession number.

It is difficult to assign accession numbers to recordings or transcriptions because both sides of the record are seldom on the same subject. Hence, they are often given a number in the sequence of purchase, filed in that order, and then cross-indexed alphabetically by title.

Smaller departments sometimes number the materials in order of acquisition and then distinguish between types of materials with one or two letters of the alphabet. For instance, "F" might stand for films and "FS" for filmstrips. "F-10" might be the number of the tenth film acquired, and "FS-10" might be the tenth filmstrip purchased.

Whatever the classification system chosen, it should be easy to learn, easy to use, and capable of expansion.

Filing and Storing Materials. A system for filing or storing materials should be orderly, easily expanded, flexible, and simple of operation. Most departments using the Dewey classification shelve materials by the Dewey number. Some directors want the materials grouped according to curriculum area, and others prefer grouping by the *type* of material, as for example, films or slides, or study prints. Just how materials are stored or housed depends upon factors such as: (a) how much space is available; (b) whether or not teachers browse in the department; (c) whether materials are distributed in packets; and (d) personal preference.

Servicing and Distributing Materials and Equipment. Distribution and servicing have been partially discussed in previous sections of this chapter. It should be emphasized here that adequate equipment and space should be provided for housing, inspecting, and cleaning film, filmstrips, slides, transcriptions, and equipment as well as for preparing them for distribution. Simple clerical forms will be needed for the servicing and distributing operations. These include request forms for materials, charge-out cards, confirmation forms, shipping lists, and delivery schedules.

Keeping the records, booking materials, and performing routine operations should be kept to a minimum and reduced to their simplest form. Routine operations should be constantly re-examined to see if they can be eliminated or improved. For instance, a large audio-visual department formerly maintained a policy of fining teachers for overdue materials. An analysis of their records showed the department spent $1.00 for every 10 cents collected. Elimination of the fines, together with a program of educating teachers to return materials on time, solved the problem and reduced record-keeping to a minimum.

Preparing Catalogues, Bulletins, etc. Catalogues should be easy to use. Some directors have found that it helps teachers if the master catalogue of all the materials is organized into three parts. If this is done, the first part gives miscellaneous information about the services of the department, such as rules for withdrawing and returning items, the work-, conference-, and visitation-hours of the staff, the organization and operating procedures of the department, and suggestions for using the catalogue.

A second part of the catalogue includes the listing of all materials in alphabetical order or according to the Dewey decimal system, identifying them as films, filmstrips, records, models, study prints, etc. Many larger departments use a modified (large numbers only) Dewey decimal system, while smaller departments use an alphabetical and numerical designation.

A third part of the catalogue involves a grouping of materials according to subject-matter areas, i.e., social studies, science, English, etc., for secondary schools, and according to grade levels for elementary schools. Inasmuch as most of the items have a wide range of application, grade-level groupings should be broad, such as primary, middle, and upper grades. Carefully prepared, but brief, descriptions or annotations of films, filmstrips, recordings, models, and dioramas are essential. Where units of study are common, the catalogue should also include recommendations of material suitable for them in lieu of or in addition to the grade-level groupings.

It is not necessary to publish a complete catalogue for each teacher. A master catalogue, however, should be in the school library and in the co-ordinator's office. If there is no audio-visual co-ordinator, then there should be a catalogue in the principal's office. Each teacher should have a catalogue covering the services which the department offers and the materials which are applicable to the subjects or grade levels he teaches. Since departments are continually adding or withdrawing items, supplementary lists are necessary from time to time. This suggests the catalogue should be so put together that new sheets can be added for easy identification of new materials. For instance, colored supplementary sheets are often used. Suppose the master catalog is issued in 1949. The new materials for circulation in 1950 are printed on orange insert sheets. In 1951, such releases are on blue paper. By 1952 probably a new catalogue will need to be issued and the process repeated.

Housing a department. There are two aspects to this problem, both of which come under the cognizance of the director. One is the housing of the central department and the other is providing proper facilities in school buildings for housing and using audio-visual education materials. A few guides are suggested here to help in planning for the housing of a central department. Facilities at the school level follow the same general considerations.

1. Adequate facilities and space should be provided for carrying out the various functions of the department. The use and arrangement of the space will depend upon the scope of the department's activities and which ones receive a major emphasis. If classroom use is the major emphasis, there will be adequate space for teachers to browse and preview facilities and space for exhibits and conferences. If production is the major emphasis, then space and facilities for a photographic laboratory will receive first consideration. (The latter as a major emphasis is undesirable.)
2. In general, space should be provided for four areas of operation:
   a) Office—for administrative functions.
   b) Library—for storage and circulation of materials and equipment and for display.
   c) Preview room—for selection and evaluation of materials, for certain phases of in-service education, and for teacher conferences.
   d) Workrooms—for processing of materials (such as mounting pictures); for maintenance and distribution of materials and equipment; for local production of materials; and for experimentation.
3. Flexibility in arrangement of space is desirable to provide for expansion and changes of emphasis in the activities of the department.
4. For storing materials, special-purpose fixtures are necessary, such as steel film racks or improvised racks for motion pictures, files for mounted pictures, drawers for filmstrips, etc.
5. In a small department, a preview room may also be used as a conference room or as a studio for recordings or photography.

6. Special-purpose workrooms may include darkrooms, shops, and special production rooms for art work, three-dimensional construction, and so forth.

Financial Support

No business can plan for present and future needs without a financial blueprint. A department of audio-visual education is no exception. Like other school activities, it should receive its funds from public school moneys. Although many factors affect the extent of its financial support, unless an adequate amount is allocated, the functions outlined in this chapter will be impossible of fulfilment. Continued financial support of the department must be based on its contribution to the total instructional program.

Although there is no uniformity in budgetary practices, it seems clear that the preparation of the budget should be the responsibility of the director, in consultation with administrative and business leaders in the school system. The director should also have the major responsibility for administration of the budget. Adequate provisions should be made in the budget for staff travel and on-the-job transportation.

Statements justifying the proposed budget should give the status of the department, the extent of its matériel and professional services, and the size of its staff. Budgetary requests should include a breakdown of the cost of the services rendered. These would include:

1. Salaries and wages
    a) Certificated personnel—director and professional assistants
    b) Noncertificated personnel—clerical, technical, and operational
2. Operating expenses
    a) Office administration
    b) Publication of catalogues, bulletins, etc.
    c) Distribution of materials and equipment
    d) Transportation of personnel (field excursions, school visitations by staff members)
    e) Maintenance of equipment and materials
    f) Fixed charges for space, utilities, insurance, etc.
    g) Procurement of audio-visual materials—new and replacements (rentals, purchases)
    h) Production of simpler materials—photographs, slides, posters, etc.
3. Capital outlay
    a) Facilities—office, photographic, shop, transportation, storage, etc.
    b) Equipment for the department.

No attempt has been made to apply these principles and procedures to the operation of a single department. They must be applied and modified by the director according to the needs of his situation. Doubtless their application will lead to the discovery of new needs with implications for new principles and new procedures.

Although this chapter has emphasized the administration of a department of audio-visual education, the director should constantly remind himself that this activity, as part of the school's administrative organization, exists primarily to facilitate the instructional process. It is only a means to an end, and the final evaluation of its matériel and professional services must be the extent to which they make the work of the teacher more efficient and the degree to which they improve the quality of the learning experiences of boys and girls.

CHAPTER XI

SUGGESTED ANSWERS TO SOME PERTINENT QUESTIONS IN THE AUDIO-VISUAL FIELD

L. C. LARSON

Associate Professor of Education
Director of Audio-visual Center
Indiana University
Bloomington, Indiana

INTRODUCTION

Because the field of audio-visual instructional materials is rather new, teachers, administrators, and audio-visual directors who are working with these materials are raising many questions. It is the purpose of this chapter to suggest answers for some of these questions which are based on a study of the literature and a survey of experiences.

A tentative list of questions was first compiled based upon an analysis of the literature. This list was submitted to graduate classes of experienced teachers and school administrators, who suggested many additional questions related to difficulties they had encountered in administering and using audio-visual materials. It was possible by rephrasing and combining to reduce the initial total of over 200 questions to 117 dealing with functions and purposes, administrative principles and practices, audio-visual staff needs, physical plant requirements, budgeting and finance, bases for selection of materials, preparation of materials, organization of materials for use, circulation procedures, and conditions of use. This list was then sent in the form of a questionnaire to selected leaders in the field with a request for suggestions on further combinations of questions and the addition of questions on important problems and issues not covered.

These questions and suggestions were presented to a graduate seminar in audio-visual materials conducted during the second semester of 1947-48. Participants in the seminar included the professional staff members of the University of Indiana's Audio-visual Center and graduate students with previous training and experience in the field of audio-visual materials. The twenty members undertook as a major project of the seminar the refinement of questions and preparation of suggested answers.

An analysis of the original questions revealed that a number of them dealt with symptomatic rather than the causal factors that are impeding progress in the audio-visual field. These questions were dropped. By combining and rephrasing the remaining questions to minimize overlap and duplication, it was possible to encompass within sixty-six general questions most of the more important problems and issues that had been raised.

Each member of the seminar undertook the preparation of answers to three or four questions. First, outlines were prepared on each question which included a breakdown of the general question into subquestions, a statement of basic assumptions, and a list of ideas that ought to be incorporated in an answer. These outlines were studied by the members of the co-operating group, and the original questions were revised in order to provide a direct and specific answer to that aspect of the problem which was probably the source of most difficulty—"the key log in the jam."

Following the revision of each outline which evolved from group discussion, each member drafted answers to his questions that would present basic principles involved and possible alternatives that seemed most desirable to the group.[1]

The final questions and answers were edited by a committee, consisting of the writer with the assistance of three members of the seminar. Some of the questions and answers, because of overlap and space limitations, were combined and rewritten. Questions and the suggested answers included in the chapter are presented under the following sections: "Role in Education," "Materials," "Utilization," "School Preparation of Materials," "Physical Facilities," "Administration and Finance," and "Responsibilities of State Agencies and Higher Institutions."

---

[1] These statements are presented in the ensuing pages. The following members of the seminar contributed statements pertaining to the specific problems designated: Beryl Blain, Donald Brumbaugh, Edwin Foster, Warren French, Harvey Frye, Carolyn Guss, Fred E. Harris, Otto Hughes, Ann Hyer, Rolland Meiser, Harold Otwell, K. C. Rugg, Charity Runden, George Siddons, Luella Snyder, Betty Stoops, Ernest Tiemann, Charles W. Tyrrell, and Don G. Williams.

Role in Education

What Should Be the Educational Purposes of the
Audio-visual Program?

Audio-visual instructional materials and an audio-visual program are means to an end. The end is to help teachers do better the job of communicating information and ideas, of stimulating desirable attitudes and appreciations, of expanding interests, and of developing potentialities into skills and competencies. To achieve this broad goal, programs will follow various and sundry patterns. All programs will have in common, however, the improvement of instruction through the use of the most appropriate instructional materials.

These audio-visual instructional programs, with their pervasive implications for education, must be directed by capable leadership with a mature educational philosophy, with specialized training and experience, and with such personal traits as enthusiasm and self-confidence. A further requirement for the implementation of the audio-visual program is that every classroom must become a teaching-learning laboratory sufficiently complete with equipment, materials, and facilities to assure a wide variety of learning experiences. Constant evaluation of the effectiveness of the audio-visual program should be made by administrators, supervisors, teachers, and pupils, in order to determine its adequacy and the modifications needed to return the greatest possible dividends.

The specific and immediate educational objectives of any local audio-visual instructional materials program will be determined by the needs of the particular school system under consideration, and the director must extend the scope of the program to meet the demands of the situation.

On What Bases Should Schools Move Ahead in the Use of
Audio-visual Materials?

Whenever possible, decisions about the audio-visual program should be based upon the findings of educational research.

Although some types of audio-visual materials are relatively new, objective studies have already supplied evidence of their educational values. The evidence has been briefly summarized as follows in the *Encyclopedia of Educational Research:*

The following claims for visual materials used adequately in the teaching situation are supported by research evidence:

1. They supply a concrete basis for conceptual thinking and hence reduce verbalistic response of students.

2. They have a high degree of interest for students.
3. They supply the necessary basis for developmental learning and hence make learning more permanent.
4. They offer a reality of experience which stimulates self activity on the part of pupils.
5. They develop a continuity of thought; this is especially true of motion pictures.
6. They contribute to growth of meaning and hence to vocabulary development.
7. They provide experiences not easily secured in other materials, and hence they contribute to the depth and variety of learning.[2]

In addition to the basis supplied by research, many schools are rightfully expanding their audio-visual programs on the basis of practices in institutions generally recognized to be superior. This is commented upon in a recent publication by the State Department of Education in Florida.

Our immediate task as school teachers and administrators is not to justify the use of audio-visual materials in schools, but to catch up with the progress of other social institutions in the use of materials which have long since been justified by experiment and experience. Audio-visual materials such as movies, pictures, recordings, maps, radio, and field trips are widely used in educational programs of industry, military training, adult education, and religious education. They require no elaborate *apologia* to justify their wide use in schools.[3]

How Will Utilization of the Potentialities of Motion Pictures Affect Productions?

Many of the motion pictures which are now available for educational purposes do not make their maximum contribution because they fail to take advantage of the potentialities of the medium. Some of the more common shortcomings include ineffective illustrated-lecture technique; lack of proper type of production technique to develop the concept; inappropriate treatment of content; poor organization; failure to deviate from the pedagogical and academic method of introducing, presenting, and reviewing material; omission of flashbacks to present background material; and lack of indigenous sound. Whereas the academic and scientific treatment dominated the production of materials before the war, one now finds that imagination, abstraction, dramatics, emotional appeal, and the like are being experimented with

---

[2] Edgar Dale and Charles F. Hoban, Jr., "Visual Education," *Encyclopedia of Educational Research*, p. 1323. Edited by Walter S. Monroe. New York: Macmillan Co., 1941.

[3] Florida State University, *The Audio-visual Way*, p. 8. Tallahassee, Florida: State Department of Education, 1948.

and used effectively.[4] Whereas only one or a very limited number of materials was produced for a broad area of instruction, now materials are being produced for specific purposes with specifically intended audiences. Whereas controversial questions were avoided or the answers were included in the material, one now finds that productions deal with timely topics on controversial subjects and frequently do little more than present the problem for group discussion. Whereas the production of educational motion pictures was predetermined by the curriculum, one now finds productions dealing with units of work not prescribed by the curriculum, and which may in themselves become the curriculum. Whereas inferior and unsatisfactory production techniques were often employed because of inexperienced technicians, inadequate resources, and limited market, one is now impressed by the technical excellence of productions. More effective use is now being made of time-lapse photography, slow-motion photography, and various types of animation. Such production techniques enable the material to present effectively concepts which are difficult to present verbally. All these more recent developments stem from utilization of the potentialities inherent in the medium and, it is hoped, presage a greater and more daring use in future productions.

How Will the Use of Audio-visual Materials Affect the Role of the Teacher in the Classroom?

When audio-visual materials are used in the classroom, a broader curriculum is established. This is due to additional experiences being offered and to the increased meaning brought to current experiences. The teacher must be able to utilize this broadened curriculum successfully.[5] The teacher, in order to utilize this broad curriculum, needs a knowledge of the unique contributions of different types of materials, of fundamental principles and techniques of utilization, and of reliable methods of evaluation.

The teacher becomes a designer of experience and a moderator of ideas. He is no longer solely a dispenser of facts. Because of the increased availability of learning experiences, the teacher must assign values and make choices. He deals with a new medium. This medium offers communication which is more lasting, more potent, and more immediate. The teacher has additional time for the individual learner, and more learners participate because communication between the

---

[4] Charles F. Hoban, Jr., *Movies That Teach,* pp. 56-83. New York: Dryden Press, 1946.

[5] Boyd Henry Bode, *How We Learn,* pp. 233-53. Boston: D. C. Heath & Co., 1940.

pupil and teacher is increasingly successful. Meanings are quickly established. This increase in the variety and power of offered experiences gives the teacher a greater opportunity to deal adequately with individual interests. The teacher is able to use a variety of audio-visual materials in diagnostic and remedial teaching, thus providing for individual differences.

This new role of the teacher in the classroom requires added competencies on the part of the teacher. He must know what audio-visual materials are available, and he must be able to select the most appropriate for his needs and to make optimum utilization.

Are There Any Subject-matter Fields or Maturity Levels Which Seem To Benefit More Than Others from the Use of Audio-visual Materials?

The development of meaning is one of the basic problems in learning. Audio-visual materials contribute to the development of meaning by extending the child's experience. It is, therefore, vitally important that these materials be used to the full extent of their potentiality in all subject fields and at all maturity levels.

The more novel a learning situation and the less the learner is equipped with a background of related experience, the more necessary it becomes to utilize a variety of teaching materials. Although this principle suggests the extreme importance of audio-visual materials on the elementary level, it does not follow that these materials should be used only infrequently on the high-school, college, or adult level. The concepts of geometry, chemistry, or anatomy may be as vague and abstract to a beginner in those fields as the discovery of America, long division, or a mountain range is to an elementary pupil.

At one time the idea was accepted that audio-visual materials were best adapted to use with "slow" learners. This is a false belief based on the assumption that all audio-visual materials are simple. These materials exist in all degrees of abstraction and difficulty. The mistake frequently made is that of using materials not adapted to the maturity level of the child. Teaching materials should be neither too simple nor too complex.

Audio-visual materials were prepared first for subject fields dealing principally with well-established facts. This is understandable since these were more easily produced and more acceptable to teachers in general. Recently materials have appeared treating attitudes, values, and controversial issues. This indicates a recognition of the contribution of audio-visual materials to highly emotionalized learning and a broader concept of desired educational outcomes.

What Proportion of Classroom Time Should Be Devoted to the Use of Audio-visual Materials?

There is no quantitative answer to this question, although it is frequently asked. The following "quotation" presents the point of view of the author and his associates.

Each individual teacher must make his own decision concerning the proportion of classroom time that is to be devoted to the use of audio-visual materials. In reaching these decisions, he must take into consideration his students—their intellectual and maturity needs and interests—and the subject matter being studied.

The amount of effective use of each type of audio-visual material will vary for the various subjects and on the different grade levels. For example, in some subjects a teacher could use effectively a ten- to twenty-minute motion picture during every other period. If all subjects and levels are considered, some schools will have the equipment, materials, and staff assistance to make it possible for teachers to use films on the average of one out of five periods; whereas, in other schools the program may provide for the use of motion pictures during one out of each ten periods or during one period of each month or each semester. Probably some types of materials will be used every period, such as flat pictures; or two types may be used in combination, as for example a motion picture and a model, or a phonograph record and lantern slide.

In any event, it is the teacher who, in consultation with the school administrators, the supervisors, and the director of audio-visual materials, must make the decision on the desired frequency of use. These decisions are most important, for the frequency of use will determine the equipment, material and staff assistance needs. Contrariwise, the frequency of use will be limited by the availability of materials, equipment, and staff assistance in the school system. Consequently, teachers will need to assume considerable responsibility in the planning and achieving of the amount and quality of classroom use of audio-visual materials needed for effective instruction.[6]

Why Should Schools Plan for Individual Classroom Use of Audio-visual Materials?

Trends in production, equipment design, curriculum, method, and building construction point to the conclusion that schools should plan for individual classroom use of audio-visual materials.[7]

In the modern school the classroom group is a unit organized for learning experiences. It is essential that this group be provided with

---

[6] AVID of Indiana, *Handbook for the Audio-visual Program*, pp. 11-12. Bloomington, Indiana: Audio-Visual Center, Indiana University, 1948.

[7] Francis W. Noel, "Providing Facilities for Use of Audio-visual Materials," *California Schools*, XVI (October, 1945), 181-82.

the proper materials at a time and place which will best facilitate learning. Materials are now being produced for classroom use which have specific teaching values and which are free from the earlier over-general design. This means that such materials fit more readily into the classroom learning situation. Equipment, too, is now of lighter weight and is more easily portable. Very little audio-visual equipment is designed for permanent installation. This newer equipment helps to solve the transportation problem and reduces difficulties of classroom utilization.

Construction or remodeling costs are actually lower when the learning unit remains in the classroom rather than using special "audio-visual" rooms. Space is economized and the over-all cost of equipping several individual classrooms adequately is less than is required for constructing and equipping a special room.[8]

To What Extent Should the Audio-visual Resources of the School Be Made Available for Community Use?

In many communities the question is being raised as to whether the school's audio-visual resources, such as professional personnel, equipment, materials, and production facilities, as well as auditorium and classroom space, should be offered to adult organizations for the purpose of extending and enriching their educational program. For instance, a local service club might be interested in sponsoring a community safety campaign. To interest their membership, as well as the community, in this project, the club may wish to show a series of safety films to a selected number of community organizations. They may also wish to produce and record several radio programs for broadcast over the local station. To carry out these two projects the club would be very much interested in obtaining assistance from the school's audio-visual staff in selecting the motion pictures as well as in producing and recording the radio programs. Also, projection equipment would be needed to show the films to the various community organizations.

What policy should the local school board pursue in making it possible for community groups to share personnel, equipment, materials, and physical facilities? Since most projection equipment, materials, and physical-plant facilities will probably become obsolete before they are physically worn out, schools should be willing to share them with nonprofit and noncommercial community groups without

---

[8] L. C. Larson, "Basic Criteria of an Audio-visual Program in School Building Planning and Related Problems," *Bulletin of the School of Education,* Indiana University, XXII (July, 1946), 7-10.

making a service charge. Some schools may wish to follow a policy of making a nominal service charge to cover some of the additional expenses incurred in providing this particular service. The authors believe that the schools have much to gain and very little to lose by offering, free of charge or at a very nominal service fee, the use of their audio-visual personnel, equipment, and materials to community organizations. The changing role of the school in extending educational opportunities to the adult population of the community is well illustrated in the following statement:

> To serve these vital needs of adults for continuous educational opportunity is a major responsibility of local school administration. No school system is meeting its full responsibility if it neglects the educational needs of all its citizens. Adult education in a time of rapid change takes on emergency importance since it is the principal method by which citizens can achieve civic competency.[9]

MATERIALS

How Will Educational Purposes Affect Selection?

Educational purposes are the real basis for the selection of instructional materials. The materials that are utilized enable the teacher to give direction to the learning experiences the students will have. These experiences must contribute to the education of the whole child for his present life in a democratic society in which he is called upon to make choices, to act, to co-operate, to appreciate, to understand, and to contribute. Since the teacher recognizes that he cannot accomplish one of these purposes independently of others, he will select materials in terms of both their primary and secondary educational purposes.

On this premise, selection becomes precise and analytical. Teachers will evaluate and select instructional materials by applying certain criteria. Both Corey[10] and Hoban[11] agree that selection on such a basis as this must be participated in by the teacher and involves an analysis of content; a definition of teaching purposes in terms of attitudes, understandings, skills, and abilities; and critical appraisal of the audio-visual materials in terms of strengths, weaknesses, and rela-

---

[9] *The Expanding Role of Education*, p. 82. Twenty-sixth Yearbook of the American Association of School Administrators. Washington: American Association of School Administrators, 1948.

[10] Stephen M. Corey, "Teacher Evaluation of Classroom Motion Pictures," *Elementary School Journal*, XLV (February, 1945), 324-27.

[11] Charles F. Hoban, Jr., "Selecting Films for School Use," *News Letter*, Vol. IV, No. 5. Columbus, Ohio: Ohio State University, 1939.

tive values. Appraisals of materials will often vary from teacher to teacher. This is wholesome because it usually means that teachers are evaluating materials in terms of their own teaching purposes, their own experience with similar types of materials, and their acquaintance with the particular children being taught. Such an approach will eliminate arbitrary grade and subject placement of materials and will permit use wherever the content makes a contribution to the objectives.

What Types of Aids Are Available To Provide Information on Audio-visual Materials?

Sources of information on audio-visual materials can be classified according to the origin of the information, the scope of subject matter presented in the materials, the purpose for which the information is given, the degree of availability of the information, and the form in which the information is disseminated.

General aids published by impartial groups are a basic source of information for both the persons who select materials and those who are to use them. The *Educational Film Guide* is an outstanding example of a general film catalogue which includes important "bibliographic" data, a description, and very often an evaluation of each film. Arrangement is both alphabetical by title and subject headings and according to the Dewey Decimal Classification. The information is kept up to date with monthly and cumulative supplements. *Educators Guide to Free Films* and the EFLA evaluations are other good examples.

Magazines devoted entirely to the field of audio-visual education and professional magazines which include audio-visual departments present valuable information, although their services vary in completeness, reliability, and usefulness. *Educational Screen* and *Social Studies* represent desirable types of magazine sources.

Books, pamphlets and bulletins are available which include descriptions and evaluations of audio-visual materials appropriate to various subject matter or problem areas. These are most often compiled by special-interest groups, educational institutions, or individuals specializing in the area. Examples are William Hartley's *Selected Films for American History and Problems* and the Eighteenth Yearbook of the National Council for the Social Studies, *Audio-visual Materials and Methods in the Social Studies*.

Catalogues of educational films and other teaching materials available from rental libraries frequently provide useful descriptions, as well as rental information.

Advertisements from producers and distributors of audio-visual materials vary greatly in reliability and usefulness. Some are presented for the sole purpose of increasing the sale or rental of particular titles; whereas others, which often include scenes or passages, actually reveal something of the content and purposes of the material.

The teachers' guides published by producers are frequently available to individual schools at a nominal sum. Some of these include complete narrations and other helpful information to aid in selection and utilization.[12]

What Are Desirable Ratios of Teachers to Number of Different Subjects of Each Type of Materials and to Number of Copies of Each Subject?

The library of materials should be planned to meet the instructional needs of all teachers. The desired number of titles of each type of material and the number of duplicate copies will depend on the planned frequency of use in subject areas at the different grade levels and on the number of teachers in the system.[13]

In planning for instructional materials to be obtained either by purchase or on a rental basis, it is first necessary to ascertain the needs of the teachers. In the case of films, for example, a committee of intermediate-grade teachers who are charged with the responsibility of planning a science curriculum should analyze the suggestions of other teachers and discuss their needs with school officials. If they decide that there is a sufficient number of motion pictures appropriate for intermediate science instruction to involve using a film once every five periods, then, in an average school year, films will be used a total of 36 periods per grade, or 108 periods for the three grades.

The number of different film titles will be further determined by the multiple-use factor. If one film can be used in two different units or grade levels, then 108 divided by two, or 54, different film subjects will need to be rented or purchased. If a multiple-factor of three is assumed, then 36 titles would be needed.

Most schools with less than three teachers per grade will probably obtain the more expensive materials on a rental basis. Larger schools will expect to purchase the more widely used films. It is suggested, however, that the number of teacher bookings per print should not exceed 20 per year. In a school system of ten teachers per grade or subject that is planning on a multiple-use factor of two, the average number of teacher bookings per print would be approximately 20. In

---

[12] Charles F. Hoban, Jr., *Focus on Learning*, pp. 162-64. Washington: American Council on Education, 1942.

[13] AVID of Indiana, *op. cit.*, p. 5.

a system of more than 10 teachers per grade or subject, either additional prints of each subject would need to be purchased or the average multiple factor would need to be reduced. When the number of teachers per grade or subject exceeds 20, it would be necessary even with a planned multiple-use factor of one to purchase duplicate prints of some subjects in order to keep the ratio of teacher bookings per print below 20.

Although motion pictures are used to illustrate an approach to determining the number of different titles of each type of material and the number of copies of each title needed, the same approach can be used successfully in planning the needed library of audio-visual materials for all subjects and grade levels.

What Points Should Be Considered in Deciding Whether To Rent or To Purchase Audio-visual Materials for a County or City School System?

Local libraries of audio-visual materials are becoming increasingly common. They are usually built up by purchasing some of the less expensive materials each year while a portion of the budget is reserved for rentals. A few films and the less expensive items such as filmstrips, slides, graphic aids, and picture collections can be purchased each year, while the less frequently used and more costly items are obtained on a rental basis. This provides a means for using a variety of materials in all stages of the acquisition program.

An important factor in establishing a basis for the purchase of materials is the rate of obsolescence due to technological advances or the more effective treatment of subject matter. In the case of materials with a useful life of seven years, a copy should be purchased when the rental per year exceeds one-seventh to one-fifth of the purchase value. For material with a useful life of ten years, copies would be purchased when rentals approach one-tenth of the original cost. Materials of current interest only would be rented when the rental costs reach one-half to one-third of the purchase price.[14]

In all cases the usability of the material, its availability from other sources, and the necessity for adequate storage and housing are additional factors in determining the desirability of purchase or rental of the material.

What Factors Will Determine the Choice of a Classification System for Audio-visual Materials?

The success of any system of classification of audio-visual materials

---

[14] AVID of Indiana, *op. cit.*, p. 5.

depends upon its adaptability to the needs of a specific situation.[15] No one classification system is completely satisfactory for all purposes. The general principles of classification of materials apply equally to the small and the large audio-visual library.

If audio-visual materials are housed with the book collection and are directly accessible to the users, then the same classification system should be used for both in order to avoid confusion. The Dewey Decimal System, often used for books, can be adapted to the audio-visual materials, although it does not provide for any distinction between types of materials.

If audio-visual materials are analyzed for content in a catalogue and are circulated by trained personnel, then the system which provides the most convenient booking and storage should be used. This might involve classification numbers made up of a symbol for the type of material plus an accession number, or a symbol for the subject of the material plus an accession number. A third possibility is a number adapted from the Cutter Expansive Table which represents the author, composer, or subject of the material.

How Can Audio-visual Materials Be Catalogued To Facilitate Use?

Since a complete and accurate catalogue is the only means by which information about all materials on a subject can be brought together, the audio-visual materials library, whether large or very small, must be catalogued carefully and systematically if it is to be used effectively.[16]

Subject headings for the catalogue should be based on a well-established system such as is presented in Sears' *List of Subject Headings for Small Libraries*. New subject headings can be taken from *Educational Film Guide* or the *Reader's Guide to Periodical Literature*. In all cases where the audio-visual materials are listed in the general catalogue, the system used should be the same as for books.

The most readily expandable catalogue form is the regular 3" x 5" library card file. The cards for each title should include a title entry with the content description, subject entries, necessary cross-references, and a shelf-list card. Several complete sets should be available so that

---

[15] Grace O. Kelley, *The Classification of Books*, chap. vii. New York: H. W. Wilson Co., 1937.

[16] Hoyt R. Galvin, *Films in Public Libraries*, pp. 20-21. Chicago: American Library Association, n.d.

one (on colored stock) can be interfiled with the book catalogue, another can be filed separately in the audio-visual materials center, and others can be filed as needed in branch libraries or co-ordinators' offices.

If it seems more desirable to have the catalogue information readily available in a large number of places, the pamphlet form may be more suitable. It should consist of both alphabetical and analytical listings with descriptions given in one or the other. In most cases, confusion can best be avoided by including descriptions in the alphabetical listings of titles, with all appropriate subject headings and grade levels indicated. The subject listings will then include the title, call number, and grade levels.

What Information Should Be Available from Circulation Records?

Circulation records have performed only one part of their role in the total audio-visual program when the materials themselves have been returned to the library and made ready for use again. For the audio-visual director, these records are a rich source of data on which to base a future course of action.[17] The director can also judge the effectiveness of his program partially on the basis of circulation records.

Specific items of information which should be available from circulation records include the following:

1. The relative demand for various titles
2. The relationship between number of prints available and demand
3. The number of requests for a specific title which cannot be met
4. The number of times which a specific title is re-booked by a specific user
5. The subject areas in which the most materials are available for use
6. The age of the materials in the library
7. The number of repairs which are made on various materials
8. The cost of maintenance of various materials
9. The average life of various types of materials
10. The average number of bookings on the various materials
11. The size and type of audience to which the materials are shown
12. Data needed for interpreting the program to the school administrators and the public.

How Can Teachers Contribute to the Improvement of Future Educational Audio-visual Productions?

Teachers have a responsibility in influencing producers to provide audio-visual materials that will best meet their classroom needs. Dur-

---

[17] Frances Henne, "Evaluation of School Libraries," *The Library in General Education,* pp. 342-47. Forty-second Yearbook of the National Society for the Study of Education, Part II. Chicago: University of Chicago Press, 1943.

ing World War II, production techniques in audio-visual materials were considerably improved. Producers have recently been using several different approaches in the production of materials for schools. Whether they continue this practice depends almost entirely on teachers, for the main factor influencing production will be the kinds of materials that are purchased or rented.

Charles F. Hoban, Jr., writes, "From a careful study of the Army's film program, no single fact is more evident than the importance of teamwork between professional educators and professional motion-picture talent—in the production of educational motion pictures."[18] Therefore, teachers should feel a responsibility for communicating with producers about their materials. By pointing out what is good about a production, what changes would have improved the quality, or why the material is considered poor, on the basis of their experiences in using materials, teachers can give producers an idea of the types of materials needed by the schools. It must be granted that, at present, a direct channel of communication from teachers to producers has not been very clearly established.

What Procedures Are Effective for Evaluation of Audio-visual Materials?

The most dependable evaluation of any type of instructional materials follows actual use with a group. The materials are good if reacting to them results in rapid and permanent student growth in the direction of the instructional objectives.[19] Teaching materials, to be effective, should serve one or more of the following purposes: develop new interests; stimulate further activity; provide information; serve as an introduction or a review; and develop attitudes, appreciations, and understandings.

Teacher evaluation of student learning may be made through direct observation of behavior, interviewing, or testing. In addition to evaluation of the effectiveness of materials in his own classroom situation, the teacher is, of course, influenced by reports of strengths and weaknesses made by other teachers, committees, and associations. Demonstrations in workshops or conference situations likewise provide data on the effectiveness of actual use of materials. The teacher will be aided in selecting materials for repeated use by referring to organized files in his own classroom and in the central office of the director or

---

[18] Charles F. Hoban, Jr., *Movies That Teach*, op. cit., p. 81.

[19] "Selecting Audio-visual Materials," *Proceedings of Fifth Annual Visual Education Institute*, pp. 28-41. Madison, Wisconsin: University of Wisconsin, 1947.

librarian. It is highly important that teacher and student reactions to materials be accumulated for reference purposes. The effectiveness of evaluations developed in local situations will be increased if they are supplemented by evaluative data published by such professional organizations and companies as the Educational Film Library Association, the H. W. Wilson Company, and the Motion Picture Association of America.

Utilization

How Can Teachers Become Familiar with Materials?

Teacher acquaintance with instructional materials depends upon alert, intelligent, aggressive utilization of all possible sources of information and experiences. The teacher himself should do a great amount of examination and review of materials; supervisors and directors of audio-visual education should provide teachers the greatest possible amount of assistance through school planning, co-ordination, and training; universities, state departments of education, and other educational agencies charged with the responsibility of increasing the effectiveness of the instructional program should provide leadership, guidance, and assistance.[20]

Sources of information which the teacher might find helpful include professional bulletins in his own teaching field; specialized journals and indexes in the field of motion pictures, radio, etc.; selected bibliographies of audio-visual materials prepared by professional groups; observation and visitation; personal experimentation in selection, utilization, and production of a wide variety of materials within regular classes; enrolment in summer courses and workshops; and participation in committee, departmental, and school projects during the school year.

Supervisors and the director of audio-visual education can reasonably be expected to assist teachers in this area. They should, through regular bulletins or other means, inform teachers about new instructional materials and interpret the materials for the teacher. They should facilitate and encourage teacher preview and evaluation of materials. They should develop committees and projects within the school which will encourage teacher experimentation with materials. They should provide a card catalog and/or bulletin of materials which

---

[20] Elizabeth Goudy Noel and J. Paul Leonard. *Foundations for Teacher Education in Audio-visual Instruction,* pp. 41-44. Washington: American Council on Education, 1947.

the school owns. In a centrally located and convenient place they should maintain a file of data on teacher reactions and appraisals of materials. They should provide within the library service an adequate collection of professional books, indexes, and catalogues. Through the in-service training program and faculty meetings they should provide information on and actual experiences with the newer and more effective teaching tools. School evaluation, criticism, and careful selection will foster and require an acquaintance with materials.[21]

Through co-operative and co-ordinated efforts, universities, teacher-training colleges, and state departments of education need to provide libraries of the best and newest audio-visual materials for the use of teachers and directors. The higher institutions should develop pre-service and in-service training on both the undergraduate and graduate levels, giving special consideration to the opportunity for sharing and pooling resources and research on common problems and necessary assistance in implementing the teachers' and supervisors' programs.

What Factors Determine the Extent to Which Audio-visual Materials Will Be Used?

The general philosophy of the teaching staff of a particular school determines to a great extent the nature of the instructional materials that will be used. Their beliefs about learning and its relation to the curriculum cause some teachers to emphasize the textbook and give little attention to other materials. Other teachers, convinced of the necessity of providing children with a wide range of experience, will use many types of instructional materials. They will employ motion pictures, recordings, field trips, and other materials in addition to textbooks and references.

The child's level of experience and his ability are also determining factors. Primary children and lower elementary-school children need a rich variety of concrete experiences to help them understand and interpret the words they hear and read. For example the modern child finds it difficult to understand the home life, transportation, and communication problems of colonial days. Furthermore, children with low degrees of ability are considerably more dependent upon situations of a concrete nature and benefit greatly from the use of audio-visual materials.

Some subjects, such as social studies and science, lend themselves to motion pictures; literature and music, to recordings; and art and geom-

---

[21] E. J. Zeiler, "Meeting Teacher Problems," *See and Hear*, III (November, 1947), 24-25.

etry, to still pictures. Materials in areas dealing with skills in arithmetic and language arts are now in experimental stages of development. With an increased use of materials, adequate school funds for their purchase, changes in instructional methods, and increased teacher demand for audio-visual materials, commercial companies will be encouraged to produce a variety of materials dealing with many aspects of any given subject matter.

What Procedures for Selection and Utilization May the Teacher Follow When It Is Impossible To Preview Materials before Using Them?

Actual preview of materials is highly desirable since it gives the teacher full knowledge of subject matter and treatment.[22] However, if preview is inconvenient, there are several effective procedures the teacher can follow that will give him enough information to plan for utilization intelligently.[23]

He can consult catalogues of reliable educational institutions. If the institution has thought the material good enough to add to its collection, he has some assurance that it is acceptable, provided the subject-matter content described is applicable to his particular teaching situation. Publications which give annotated bibliographies of materials suitable for certain subject-matter areas are also helpful. Descriptive literature from commercial producers provides useful information, as do the teachers' guides and manuals that accompany many materials.

If the materials being considered are owned by the school or have been used in it, he can refer to the permanent evaluation file of his own audio-visual center or building. Notes from preview or from previous use by other teachers will give him ideas about content, approach, purposes for which the material might be used, grade placement, technical quality, and general educational value.

Talking with others who have used the material will give him more direct information and suggest utilization techniques.

On the basis of his purposes in using the material and the descriptions and evaluations available, the teacher can tentatively plan his utilization procedures and present the material to the class. This initial class-showing serves as the teacher's preview. During the show-

---

[22] Edgar Dale, *Audio-visual Methods in Teaching*, pp. 492-94. New York: Dryden Press, Inc., 1947.

[23] AVID of Indiana, *op. cit.*, pp. 9-11.

ing, the teacher decides upon changes to be made in the discussion and follow-up activities that he has planned.

If the teacher wishes, he may follow another procedure in using material that has not been previewed. He may tell the students that he has not seen it. Teacher and students then plan together for utilization, deciding what purposes the material may have and how they hope it will help them with the unit they are studying. During the showing they watch critically to see if the material meets their needs. After the showing they evaluate its effectiveness and decide whether or not it is worth using again in a similar situation. The evaluation is a result of co-operation between teacher and pupils.

How Can the Teacher Determine What Audio-visual Material To Use and When To Use It in a Teaching Situation?

The kind of learning experience the teacher wants his pupils to have will determine the type of material to use. In situations where a study of objects or processes *in situ* is necessary, field trips will be highly desirable. The motion picture will be selected to bring into the classroom remote places, historical incidents, otherwise unobservable action, mores of people, demonstrations, and dramatic presentations. Listening experiences call for radio, recordings, and transcriptions. A detailed study of visual content can be provided for by the use of slides, filmstrips, or still pictures.

The teacher, after determining the type of audio-visual material to be used, needs to select the precise unit of material. Selection, here, becomes a process of considering the relation of the content of the material to other instructional materials to be used in the unit, the treatment of content, the accuracy of the material, and how it is to be used within the unit. If it is to initiate a unit, the material should give a broad general treatment of the topic. If it is to extend the unit, it should suggest related interest areas. If it is to present specific facts or skills, it should be a lucid, concentrated, and closely organized presentation of the material. For review or summary, material useful for introduction may serve the purpose.

In order to select intelligently, the teacher will need to know the greatest possible number of materials and their potential contribution to the total learning situation. Materials which he has used successfully in the past will always be worth trying again.

What Approaches Can the Teacher Use in Utilizing Audio-visual Materials?

Our concept of the teacher as a purveyor of information and a complement to the textbook has almost faded. Our newer concept depicts the teacher as the architect of pupils' learning experiences. He plans the type of learning environment in which pupils have the kinds of experience they need, as realistic and meaningful as is feasible or possible. To design such experiences, he uses a wide variety of materials and methods. Unless the teacher feels the obligation and the inspiration to select, experiment, originate, create, and invent, he will not be able continuously to frame such experiences.

The teacher must plan carefully the approaches to utilization of all instructional materials. A student committee may be asked to preview the material and handle its use with the class; such a procedure is shown in the University of Oregon film, "Human Growth." The teacher may approach the utilization of materials as an answer to questions which have arisen in the group, or in response to apparent interests of the group, or he may stimulate the group interest in the material he plans to use. The teacher may approach the use of one type of material through the use of another; for example, a visit to the roundhouse might permit the pupils to see only a few types of trains and a film would then be brought in to show other and newer types.

What Techniques May the Teacher Use To Insure Effective Utilization of Audio-visual Materials?

Effective utilization of audio-visual materials follows basically the same procedures essential to the use of any other type of material. These procedures may be considered under four main steps: (*a*) teacher preparation; (*b*) pupil preparation; (*c*) presentation and follow-up activities; and (*d*) evaluation.[24]

Becoming acquainted with a wide variety of materials and the many purposes for which they may be used is essential in teacher preparation. This will facilitate selecting materials that will help achieve the teacher's instructional aims. Study guides or instructional manuals, when available, are helpful in choosing materials or in planning for their use. If possible, a preview is highly desirable for it affords the opportunity to make careful note of the contents, the organization and presentation techniques, and the main points stressed.

The students may be prepared and motivated by acquainting them with the purpose for which the material is to be used, by providing additional information or background, and by asking them to look for specific facts and special interests. In situations where the teacher

---

[24] Edgar Dale, *op. cit.*, pp. 488-98; Charles F. Hoban, Jr., *Focus on Learning*, *op. cit.*, chap. v; "Using the Classroom Film" (16-mm. film, 22 minutes, sound, black and white, produced by Encyclopedia Britannica Films, Inc., 1945).

and students plan together the use of the material, motivation and interest are natural outcomes.

The presentation should be made under the best physical conditions available and should, if possible, be followed immediately by a discussion or review period. At this time any concepts or relationships not understood may be clarified and questions may be answered. The discovery of special interests will provide opportunities for making additional assignments or for planning related activities. In some instances re-using the material may be necessary to achieve fully the purpose.

An observation of the students' responses will provide the teacher with a basis for judging the effectiveness of the material. Change in attitude and conduct, acquisition of skills, or increased information may be further noted. At times tests will assist the teacher in determining the need for further instruction or for more concentrated study on specific subject matter.

What Should Be the Policy of Schools on the Use of Audio-visual Materials Dealing with Controversial Issues?

So far as possible, instructional materials should be selected which represent fairly and adequately all sides of questions on which differences of opinion exist.[25] In many areas the only materials available present a biased point of view. Where this is true, thorough preparation of the group should precede use of the material. Pupils need to be sufficiently informed in order to discern the bias of the presentation. In other areas there are only materials which give fragmentary information. The true picture will be distorted because of insufficient facts. Here the necessary compensations must be made through other means, such as outside reading and discussion. Controversial materials should be used in such a way that pupils arrive at a fair conclusion in the light of the best available information.

It is essential that pupils learn how to evaluate propaganda intelligently. There is the possibility that the school will use films in such a way that pupils become skeptical and reject all types of propaganda. This is not the result desired. Rather, every effort must be made to help the pupils see both sides of a question.[26] The members of the

---

[25] John H. Haefner, "Historical Approach to Controversial Issues," *Social Education*, VI (October, 1942), 267-69.

[26] "The Library's Bill of Rights," *American Library Association Bulletin*, XXXVIII (November, 1944), 449; Ralph W. Tyler, "Implications of Communications Research for the Public Schools," *Print, Radio, and Film in a Democracy*, pp. 154-56 (Edited by Douglas Waples. Chicago: University of Chicago Press, 1942).

group should be guided to arrive at their own conclusions in the light of all phases of the issue. If the pupils reject the point of view of special interest groups as "propaganda," their thinking will not be modified; and they will continue to believe as they previously did even though the ideas espoused need to be considered in arriving at a conclusion. Further, they must be guided to do more than compile evidence about an issue. Being open-minded does not remove the necessity for reaching a decision which will determine further action. Thus, materials dealing with controversial issues have their place in the public school because they are instruments which, when rightly used, will promote the democratic purpose of appraising the issues in such a way that the end result is an improved society.

How Can Audio-visual Materials Be Used in Various School Situations?

Audio-visual materials may be used in a number of school situations: (*a*) classroom, (*b*) auditorium, (*c*) audio-visual center, (*d*) extra-classroom, and (*e*) adult groups.

Ordinarily the use of audio-visual materials is most effective as a regular part of the classroom activity—as a learning experience for a class group. Occasionally audio-visual materials may also be used in the classroom as assigned references for smaller groups within the class or for class committees. The kind and size of group with which the materials should be used depend upon the instructional purposes to be achieved and the appropriateness of the material to these purposes and to the developmental level and experiential background of the children.

The auditorium program may be set up for either heterogeneous or homogeneous groups. Such a film as "Realm of the Wild," which describes the necessity for keeping wild life population in balance with the land's productive capacity, is of such general interest that an entire school might profitably meet as a group to see it. Most audio-visual materials, however, are of particular value when used with a homogeneous group of pupils. All of the fifth-grade children might assemble to see such a film as "Adventures of Chico," or all of the literature classes might meet to see "Romeo and Juliet."

The audio-visual center should consider providing facilities for reference use of materials at the center, as well as in the classroom. Under such a plan students would come to the center to use audio-visual materials just as they now go to the library in most schools to use books. In some instances audio-visual materials may actually be used in the library.

Special interest and hobby groups within the school will find that audio-visual materials will add to their programs. The philatelists might use a film on stamp collecting which would never be brought in as a part of the classroom program.

Adult-education and service groups within the community should be encouraged to use the school instructional materials and resources when they contribute to their objectives.

What Can Be Done To Encourage Utilization by Community Groups of the Facilities and Resources of the Audio-visual Program?

Only when school administrators and audio-visual directors extend attitudes of welcome, express the wish to co-operate, and evince a warmth of interest to the hesitant can they help make patrons and other members of the community eager to use new materials and methods of learning, willing to accept responsibility, and co-operative in the development of harmonious school-community relations.

Ordinary publicity devices—letters, mimeographed bulletins, newspaper articles, radio announcements, talks and film showings before school and community groups, discussions, and demonstrations on use of materials and equipment—may make known the schools' resources. A good audio-visual program in the school may be its own best interpreter and promoter.

Schools may provide materials and equipment either free or at handling cost. They may offer projection service, projection rooms for meetings, assistance in production, and consultant service. The school patrons may be invited to participate in the preview and selection of materials which are being added to the audio-visual department.

The school will best facilitate utilization by community groups of the facilities and resources of the audio-visual program when the school considers itself a service organization of the community.[27] As such an organization, the school is a member organization of the local community council, county council, or council of social agencies. The school superintendent and the director of the audio-visual program will certainly be council representatives from the school.

A local film council—unit of the Film Council of America—may develop as another member organization of the Council of Social Agencies and provide an even more specific center around which the community audio-visual program may function. This must be a

---

[27] Paul C. Reed, "A New Look at a Community," *Educational Screen*, XXVII (May, 1948), 218.

local program evolving from local needs and not handed down from "above."[28]

If a community library or other public service organization also has films for community distribution, the schools' attitude should be co-operative and complementary rather than dictatorial or disinterested. Representatives from each organization can arrange a co-operative plan of service which will best benefit everyone.

In What Ways Can Teachers Direct and Utilize the Out-of-School Radio and Motion Picture Experiences of Children?

Since the school has a great responsibility for guiding and directing the character and personality development of its students, the out-of-school activities with which they come into daily contact must be taken into consideration. Studies indicate that boys and girls spend between two and three hours each day listening to the radio [29] and frequently attend commercial movies.[30] Most teachers recognize the tremendous force of these media on children.

The teacher who is acquainted with the offerings of Hollywood productions and commercial radio programs is better prepared to influence the habits of his pupils. Information concerning radio programs may be obtained from local newspapers and trade magazines such as *Variety, Radio Daily, Broadcasting,* and *Sponsor*. The national networks issue up-to-date bulletins of program schedules, and local or regional radio councils also supply program information.[31] Articles and ratings of current motion-picture productions are featured in magazines such as *Consumers' Research Bulletin, New Movies, National Board of Review,* and some weekly news magazines. Local theaters will furnish on request schedules of their motion-picture programs for several months in advance. By sampling all types of radio programs and Hollywood motion pictures, the teacher provides himself with a basis for making critical evaluations and for choosing those which will be wholesome out-of-school activities.

Teachers of all subjects should include activities in their instruction which will contribute to student development of critical judgments,

---

[28] Paul C. Reed, "Speaking of Film Councils," *Educational Screen,* XXVI (May, 1947), 250.

[29] Roy DeVerl Willey and Helen Ann Young, *Radio in Elementary Education,* p. 10. Boston: D. C. Heath & Co., 1948.

[30] Charles Hoban, Charles Hoban, Jr., and Samuel B. Zisman, *Visualizing the Curriculum,* pp. 93-94. New York: Dryden Press, Inc., 1937.

[31] Norman Woelfel and I. Keith Tyler, *Radio and the School,* chap. ix, x, and xi. New York: World Book Co., 1945.

discriminating tastes, and better selection. Such activities may include discussions of favorite radio and motion-picture personalities, comparisons of various broadcasts and theatrical productions, investigations into the accuracy of the presented information, and the study of production techniques.[32] Subject matter which lends itself to dramatization or simulated broadcasts and special projects initiated through photo-play appreciation clubs or film and radio councils offer additional opportunities. When students know what constitutes a good radio program or motion picture, they are better equipped to judge and evaluate what they see and hear.

What Are the Chief Uses of Teacher-Pupil Evaluations of Audio-visual Materials?

Teacher-pupil evaluations of audio-visual materials can benefit others who have access to the evaluations as well as those who do the evaluating.

The teacher who uses a number of motion pictures, for example, can develop in his pupils an ability to analyze and criticize films which will fulfil their own needs as individual consumers. At the same time, he clarifies his thinking concerning the effectiveness of both the film materials and the utilization techniques used.

The alert teacher bases future choices of materials and utilization techniques partly upon his past evaluations. He should also have access to evaluations made by others for the purpose of choosing new materials or comparing others' reactions with his own.

The audio-visual director can use teacher-pupil evaluations as a basis for the acquisition of materials, the analysis of in-service training needs, the exchange of opinion among teachers, the guidance of individual teachers, the maintenance of balance in the program, the planning of local production, and the evaluation of the effectiveness of the total audio-visual program.[33]

SCHOOL PREPARATION OF MATERIALS

What Are Some of the Purposes for Which the School Might Produce Materials for General School and Community Use?

School-produced materials supplement commercially produced materials. When there is a school or community need for audio-visual materials with subject matter and treatment appropriate to a specific situation, the school as a local institution can produce to meet the

---

[32] William Lewin, *Photoplay Appreciation in American High Schools*, pp. 67-93. New York: D. Appleton-Century Co., 1934.

[33] Charles F. Hoban, Jr., *Focus on Learning, op. cit.*, pp. 146-51.

need. Adaptation to the locality is an advantage most readily achieved by local productions.[34]

Materials which show teacher and pupil activities are effective in interpreting the school to the community and have value in public relations and promotion. School productions can also interpret the community to the students and the community to its citizens. Both students and adults become aware of community problems and realize more fully their responsibility in solving them. Development of mutual interest and understanding helps both school and community.[35]

School production makes possible the recording of outstanding events such as recitals, speeches, sports, graduation exercises, and special programs. Important documents and papers can be preserved through microfilming. Records can be kept of school personnel, and special projects, such as student orientation, can be facilitated by using school-made materials.

What Factors Should Be Considered in Deciding Whether Some Topic or Event Should Be Treated in a Local Production?

Increasing numbers of schools are beginning to produce audio-visual materials to meet local needs. Before any production is initiated, consideration must be given to the specific nature of the need; the money, facilities, and personnel available; and the particular type of audio-visual material that will be most effective.

Locally produced materials can meet the specialized needs of the school, promote public relations of the school, or depict some topic or event that will be of interest to the community. It is seldom the function of a local school to prepare materials of national interest, as these can most economically be provided by commercial concerns.[36]

Good materials require the expenditure of an adequate amount of money. To produce below this figure is to make materials of inferior quality. In analyzing costs, the materials should be justified in terms of the benefits the school or community will derive from them.

The available facilities and personnel are also important factors. The kind of equipment and the competencies of those who are responsible for the production are essential considerations. High quality materials can be made only by a staff that has attained skill through training and experience.

---

[34] AVID of Indiana, *op cit.*, pp. 13-14.

[35] Floyde E. Brooker and Eugene H. Herrington, *Students Make Motion Pictures*, chaps. i-ii. Washington: American Council on Education, 1941.

[36] *Ibid.*, p. 17.

Although the material is produced particularly for a local situation, it should be of acceptable quality. A professional standard has been set for audio-visual materials, especially the motion picture. Since school productions will lack dramatic appeal, they must maintain a high standard of technical quality.[37]

After considering cost, facilities, production personnel, and the need, the type of material to be produced must be determined. The proposed production should seldom duplicate what is already available unless it will be an improvement over the previous production. Each type of material can make its peculiar contribution to the educational or cultural experience of a group. For instance, a single photograph may be an effective medium if it is carefully planned for the purpose intended and well made.

What Are the Major Functions of the Director and the Co-ordinator with Respect to the Local Production Program?

In a local production program the functions of a director and a co-ordinator will usually be similar in type and vary principally in scope. These leaders perform a three-fold production function, i.e., encouragement, co-ordination, and supervision of the local program. The production program should include photographic, audio, graphic art, and exhibit materials.

A director who appreciates production possibilities and limitations will be able to locate areas of need which can be adapted to local production. He will encourage proficient teachers and pupils to produce in their areas and see that materials are provided for approved production projects. Much can be accomplished through an in-service training program.

Co-ordinators and directors can further encourage local production by furnishing technical assistance where needed. In smaller school units, the director himself should possess some general production skills. In large school units he may merely refer those needing assistance to staff members who possess the required skills and knowledge.

The director should serve as co-ordinator in those productions extending in scope beyond a single classroom or for which the school furnishes the raw materials. Co-operation should be stimulated between groups undertaking similar projects. Locally produced materials should be catalogued if they are to be of use to a number of teachers, and all teachers should be informed of their availability.

---

[37] David Schneider (editor), "School-made Motion Pictures," *Educational Screen*, XXV (February, 1946), 90.

The director or co-ordinator should approve and supervise major production projects, such as those of general school or community interest.

What Could Be the Role of Teachers in the Preparation of Center-sponsored Materials for School and Community Use?

In a small or new audio-visual program, the production staff may consist entirely of teachers. In larger or well-established programs, there will be some regular employees with technical training in production. However, the staff is likely to be too small to be adequate, making the assistance of teachers necessary.

In every school system, there are teachers with high competencies and abilities that can be used to advantage. Some instruct in subjects such as arts and crafts which are useful in production. Many have hobbies that can be used to advantage; for instance, the teacher who is an enthusiastic amateur movie-maker. Still others have radio experience or understand the operation of various types of audio equipment. Some will be especially well-equipped to assist in planning and to advise on content and treatment to insure that the finished material will have educational value.

Teachers will be able to assist in all types of production planned.[38] If a film is to be made, teachers can help in the planning, carry out research, serve in an advisory capacity, write, and evaluate.[39] If production is to take the form of school broadcasting, teachers can select and organize content, find talent, handle sound effects, and participate in the actual broadcast. They can take pictures and organize them into sets or series for teaching, or prepare filmstrips. They can plan and prepare graphic materials, build models, make slides,[40] and assemble co-ordinated teaching kits.

The degree to which teachers participate in preparation of center-sponsored materials and the nature of their participation will vary. In a production program just getting started, they will probably be volunteers, working in their spare time on the basis of interest. However, as the program becomes more firmly established and teachers become more experienced and confident, they should be relieved of some of their teaching load and formally assigned to an educational project

---

[38] Kenneth B. Haas and Harry Q. Packer, *Preparation and Use of Visual Aids*. New York: Prentice-Hall, Inc., 1946.

[39] Mrs. C. Delaney, "School Film and Fiesta," *Educational Screen*, XXIV (January, 1945), 17-19.

[40] How to Make Handmade Lantern Slides" (16-mm. film, 21 minutes, sound, color, produced by Audio-visual Center, Indiana University, 1947).

on a part-time basis. In this way, they will be able to put their best efforts into preparation of materials.

How Can Schools Give Students Opportunities for for Experiences in Production?

Production experiences are offered through extra-curriculum activities and clubs sponsored by the school. Students take part in school broadcasts or help with visual productions without receiving academic credit. They engage in such activities as conducting research on subject-matter content, acting in the production, and collecting props.[41] Groups with special interests prepare instructional materials. For example, a photography club assembles a series of pictures on a particular topic. A crafts club makes puppets or miniature sets for props and designs and constructs costumes. A physics club undertakes a project of making glass slides and preparing radio scripts for physics classes.

Some courses offered for credit have units on radio and film production as part of the development of appreciation. This has been done most often in English and social studies. However, art, vocational, and other courses could logically offer experiences which would be valuable to an audio-visual program. Some schools have gone beyond the teaching of separate units and offer entire courses and workshops for credit. These usually deal with radio [42] but point the way to similar activities in photography, graphics, and model construction.

Students who show a high degree of interest and ability in curriculum and extra-curriculum production activities are potential technical assistants for the audio-visual program. An organized plan of pupil activities would be a step forward in solving the problem of finding people with enough experience and training to work in the production of audio-visual materials for schools.

What Audio Materials Can Be Easily Produced?

Because many of the present-day recording devices are low in cost, easy to operate, and portable, the school can and should utilize school-produced recordings more fully.

A wide variety of audio experiences can be recorded and advantageously played back later for instruction or entertainment. The radio offers many educational, documentary, musical, and entertain-

---

[41] Brooker and Herrington, *op. cit.*
[42] Van Rensselaer Brokhahne, "The Story of the All-City High-School Radio Workshop," *High Points*, XXVII (May, 1945), 33-40.

ment features that may be recorded and used in the classroom. Student-produced programs may be recorded and broadcast at a future date. In individual speech, music, and language analysis, the recorder is a valuable tool. It can be used in group analysis of speech, music, and dramatic selections. The school can use this device to make historical records of interviews, athletic contests, and many school activities and events. If the school is producing motion pictures and filmstrips, a running commentary may be recorded to be used with them.

There are three types of standard recording devices: magnetic tape, wire, and the conventional disc. Each has its limitations and its advantages. The magnetic devices are cheaper, and virtually no operator competency is required to operate them. The disc method of recording when used on high-priced equipment gives the greatest fidelity of tone and can be played back on the regular 78 r.p.m. phonograph, or material can be recorded at a speed of 33⅓ r.p.m. and played on a transcription player accommodating 16-inch discs. Minimum equipment in this area will depend on the limitations of the school's budget and its planned audio program.[43]

What Nonphotographic Visual Materials Can Be Produced by the School?

Local productions of nonphotographic visual materials include flat pictures, handmade lantern slides, graphic materials, models, objects, and exhibits.

The primary step in producing nonphotographic materials is the establishment of a pictorial file drawn from all available sources including the school, home, community, government, and industry. When all sources have been thoroughly explored, the materials they have to offer should be collected, evaluated, classified, indexed, and finally used for instructional purposes.[44] From the pictorial file, many types of both projected and nonprojected materials can be developed.

Handmade lantern slides can be made from pictures in the file. They may be made by using the silhouette; the ceramic pencil on clear glass; pencil, ink, or crayon on etched glass; pencil or ink on translucent paper; and copy typed on cellophane.[45]

Copy can also be prepared for use in the opaque projector or visual

---

[43] *School Sound-Recording and Playback Equipment.* Washington: U. S. Office of Education and Radio Manufacturers Association, October, 1947.

[44] Dale, *op. cit.*, pp. 82-100.

[45] "How To Make Handmade Lantern Slides" (16-mm. film), *op. cit.*

cast. Tracings, clippings, drawings, and actual objects make good copy. Material may be adapted for the visual cast by free-hand drawing, tracing, and use of the silhouette. Possibilities for future development in this area are many.

Graphic materials include maps, charts, diagrams, cartoons, and graphs. They may be teacher- or pupil-produced and used in a variety of ways, including opaque projection, bulletin board exhibit, and individual study.

Many different kinds of exhibits, including dioramas, models, mock-ups, specimens, and objects are valuable because of their close relation to reality. They should be made or collected, classified and arranged, and properly exhibited. Students who manipulate three-dimensional objects develop an understanding of relationships through actual experience. Because of their usefulness, schools should produce and use a wide variety of these important teaching aids.

Which Photographic Materials Can Be Produced with Minimum Equipment and Average Competencies?

There are many types of photographic materials that a school can produce using only a minimum of equipment and employing average photographic competencies.[46]

Photographic materials can be conveniently broken into "still" and "motion" pictures. Included in the "still" category are the $3\frac{1}{4}$" x 4" and the 2" x 2" lantern slides which may be produced either in black and white or in color. Photographs of all kinds—varying from flash news shots to routine copy work—are within the reach of the school. Instructional filmstrips are easily produced in black and white. These filmstrips may be simply a photographic record of a field trip, or they may be detailed strips using graphic frames as well as photographs. Another still medium employs microfilms of books, documents, and papers.

Minimum equipment for the above still materials should include a 4" x 5" or $3\frac{1}{4}$" x $4\frac{1}{4}$" press-type camera with a flash gun, a 35-mm. camera, tripod, light meter, microfilm camera (also used is making filmstrips), two or more reflectors, and darkroom equipment including an enlarger, trays, chemicals, and supplies.

---

[46] Thomas H. Miller and Wyatt Brummitt, *This Is Photography* (Garden City, New York: Garden City Publishing Co., Inc., 1945); Willard D. Morban and Henry M. Lester, *Graphic Graflex Photography*, pp. 109-28 (New York: Morgan & Lester, 1944).

Where May a School Staff Go To Obtain Assistance in Planning More Ambitious Productions?

There are several sources of assistance that a school should consider if an ambitious program of production in either the audio or the visual field seems advisable. First, of course, would probably be those people on the instructional staff who have developed outstanding competencies in photography, radio, or the production of materials for exhibits or museums.

The second source may be those people in the local community who are either outstanding hobbyists or, from professional experience, have developed exceptional knowledge in the field. These include photographers, local radio station employees, taxidermists, and cabinetmakers.

Schools and universities with ongoing production programs also are a source of assistance. Most state colleges and universities now have some type of radio and visual center which does production work. Agricultural colleges also make wide use of exhibits. Schools should contact the nearest college or university and take advantage of any assistance that is available.

The school staff might also consult the various commercial companies that are in a position to give assistance to schools and universities in all phases of production. Some of the companies that manufacture supplies and/or equipment have educational departments whose prime function is giving service to schools and universities and assisting in the use of their products. Other companies furnish materials and service in the production of radio programs and motion pictures on a commercial basis. These are scattered throughout the United States and usually provide any type of assistance desired.

Physical Facilities

What Are the Space Requirements for the Audio-visual Center in the School System?

To be effective, an audio-visual materials program requires some space, centrally located if possible, from which its services will emanate. Such a work area or laboratory is commonly called the "audio-visual center" and may range from one room in a smaller school to a suite of rooms or an entire building in a large school system or university. Physical facilities needed for a center will depend upon functions to be administered, the number of teachers and pupils to be served by the center, scope of service to the community, and the local situation.

Adequate office space should be allocated to the director and others of the professional, technical, and clerical staff as may be needed. Storage space for materials should be such that materials can be readily located and circulated. They must be protected from dust and, in the case of films, from extreme variation of temperature and humidity. Work space for circulation should be carefully planned so that the system of distribution can operate effectively.

To make proper selection and utilization possible, a preview room adaptable to all types of projected materials is necessary. Facilities should also be provided for the reviewing of other types of audio-visual materials. Within the center there should be a library containing magazines, books, catalogues, and evaluations in the field of audio-visual materials. Space for servicing equipment and materials is important.

Housing for the preparation of audio-visual materials should be given consideration. In the case of larger schools and colleges, there should be facilities for producing still and motion pictures, radio programs, graphic materials, and exhibits.

What Physical Characteristics of a Classroom Are Required for Effective Utilization of Projected Audio-visual Materials?

The attention and alertness of pupils are related to the physical environment in which projected materials are used. Conditions most directly related are the control of light, the control of sound, and the control of air.

For the use of most projected materials, the classroom should be darkened to the extent that it is difficult but not impossible to read newspaper print.[47] When colored materials are projected, the room should be darker. It is important that no direct beams of light cast high lights on ceilings or walls, and it is particularly important that none fall on the screen. Many feel that the opaque projector, since it operates on the principle of reflected light, requires a very dark room. Light control also includes artificial light and the power used for projection. Outlets should be provided at the front and the rear of the room with more than one circuit, so that a combination of different kinds of equipment may be used simultaneously if desired.

Control of sound has several aspects. Excessive sounds and noises from outside the classroom should be excluded to prevent distractions. The noise level within the room should be low enough that it does not cause interference with activities in adjoining rooms. Within the

[47] "Recommended Procedure and Equipment Specifications for Educational 16-mm. Projection," *Journal for Society of Motion Picture Engineers*, XXXVII (July, 1941).

room, acoustical conditions should be such that each pupil can hear easily and distinctly. Technical assistance should be obtained in the control of sound reverberation.

In a room darkened for projection, window ventilation is reduced. If the room is darkened for an extended period, the air becomes vitiated, and pupils become listless and inattentive. To maintain good classroom conditions, adequate provision must be made for the control of temperature, humidity, and the movement of air.[48]

How May Equipment Needs Be Determined?

Equipment needs will be determined by the anticipated average frequency of use of the different types of audio-visual material.[49] If, for example, teachers on any grade level plan to use motion pictures, on the average, during one of each ten periods, then one motion-picture projector would be required for each ten teachers. In the case of desired use of motion pictures during one of each five periods, then the projector-teacher ratio would be one to five; if one in each twenty periods, then the ratio would be one to twenty.

The following schedule illustrates the application of frequency of average use in determining needs for the more commonly used projection equipment in a school of thirty teachers:

Type of Equipment	Frequency of Average Use	Ratio of Equipment to Teachers	Equipment Required for 30 Teachers
Motion-Picture Projector.	During 1 of each 10 class periods	1:10	3
Slidefilm Projector.......	During 1 of each 10 class periods	1:10	3
2" x 2" Slide Projector....	During 1 of each 10 class periods	1:10	3
3¼" x 4" Slide Projector..	During 1 of each 15 class periods	1:15	2
Opaque Projector	During 1 of each 15 class periods	1:15	2
Screens	One wall screen in each classroom		30

Following a conference with teachers and the administrative and supervisory staff on the frequency of average use desired for each type of equipment, similar tables may be prepared by the director of audio-visual materials.[50]

How May the Various Types of Equipment Be Selected?

Selection of the various types of equipment is influenced by the

---

[48] Vera M. Falconer, *Filmstrips*, pp. 78-81. New York: McGraw-Hill Book Co., 1948.
[49] AVID of Indiana, *op. cit.*, pp. 18-19.
[50] "Audio-visual Program Standards," *See and Hear*, III (January, 1948), 17-19.

needs which the equipment will have to meet. These needs are determined by several factors, including size of the groups with which equipment will be used, number of teachers and students in the school, funds available, simplicity and portability of equipment, and the average frequency of use of the various types.[51] The person who is responsible for purchase of equipment should know what is needed, as determined by such factors, in order to select equipment that will be used and will meet the demand.

When he knows the needs that must be met, he is ready to plan for purchase. From the descriptive materials of reliable manufacturers, he can learn a great deal about equipment—relative costs of various types, special features, and variations in possible use. At equipment exhibits or at conferences and workshops, he can see the equipment for himself and find out from demonstrations whether it is portable and easy to set up and operate.

He will find it helpful to talk with others who have had experience in using the equipment he is considering, especially if they have used it in situations similar to his own. If they have found a certain type satisfactory, he will probably give it more serious consideration. Educational institutions or agencies in the locality which have used various types and makes of equipment will be able to give him helpful information on reliability and service of equipment and also on reliability of the services rendered by near-by equipment dealers.

On the basis of what he learns in these ways, he can narrow his choice of types and makes to one or two. He can then consult dealers he feels will be able to give suitable service and, on the basis of their demonstrations, will be able to make his final selection.

Who Should Operate Audio-visual Equipment?

Equipment should be operated in an efficient and inconspicuous manner. Both pupils and teachers can learn to operate audio-visual equipment efficiently, as it usually takes only two or three one-hour instruction periods to master the fundamentals. Several manuals are available that will facilitate the learning or teaching of operation of audio-visual equipment.[52]

Every teacher should know how to operate the equipment used in his classroom, if for no other reason than the satisfaction that is de-

---

[51] Paul Wendt, Leland Bauck, and James F. Nickerson, "How To Buy Equipment for Visual Aids," *Nation's Schools*, XXXIX (March, 1947), 55-58.

[52] *1946 Audio-visual Projectionist's Handbook* (Chicago: Business Screen Magazine, 1946); Philip Mannino, *ABC'S of Visual Aids and Projectionist's Manual* (New York: Educational Film Library Association, Inc., 1946).

rived from this knowledge. Also, it adds to a teacher's prestige and security to know how to operate equipment or to be able to help an operator in an emergency. There are times when the teacher will want to utilize the equipment in carrying forward class instruction in such a manner that it would be impractical to have another operator.

Even though teachers know how to operate equipment, there are many who prefer in most instances to have the equipment operated by another person, so that uninterrupted attention can be given to the problems of the class. A recent survey shows that 80 per cent of the schools responding found student operators the answer to equipment operation.[53] Student operators may be formed into clubs, which, with proper organization and training, provide worth-while experiences for the members.[54]

In the final analysis, the school policy determines who operates equipment. At the same time provision should be made so that the final decision is left to the discretion of each individual teacher as to whether he or someone else does the operating. In any event, provision should be made to have the heavier equipment moved from one location to another by a man or by older, stronger boys.

What Records Should Be Kept on Equipment?

The audio-visual director supervises the keeping of records and is responsible to the school administration for their accuracy and completeness. Only those records should be kept that will provide useful information. The number and type of records required will vary with the amount of equipment available and the circumstances under which it is used.[55]

Closely related reasons for keeping records are: (a) to determine the kind and amount of service each machine gives, (b) to figure depreciation and the time when new equipment is necessary, (c) to develop a basis for the purchase of new equipment, and (d) to determine the amount of budget allowance for replacement, maintenance, and repair. A record card which can be used to meet these needs may include the following classifications:

Inventory information giving (a) name, (b) type, (c) model, (d) serial number of each piece of equipment, (e) when purchased, (f)

---

[53] Robert E. Schreiber, "Survey Review of 16-mm. Sound Equipment—Present Use and Future Needs," *Educational Screen*, XXV (June, 1946), 322.

[54] H. A. Link, "Student Projectionists," *See and Hear*, III (May-June, 1948), 20.

[55] "Recommended Procedure and Equipment Specifications for Educational 16-mm. Projection." *Journal for Society of Motion-Picture Engineers*, XXXVII (July, 1941).

price, (g) from whom purchased, (h) guaranty period or special provisions of purchase, and (i) insurance.

Maintenance information giving (a) running time of machine, (b) oiling and cleaning schedule, (c) replacement of expendable parts, (d) record of major repair, including labor and replaced parts, and (e) possible cause of breakdown, if determinable.

Operational information giving (a) the location of each piece of equipment, (b) failures or breakdown during operation, (c) temporary records signifying the person using the equipment, and (d) any noticed need for attention.

ADMINISTRATION AND FINANCE

What Are the Advantages of an Organized Program of Audio-visual Materials in the School or School System?

An organized program provides for specialized leadership and for technical and clerical staff necessary to insure the greatest return for the money expended.

Personnel are allocated to duties which they can most efficiently perform, and teachers are freed from routine and technical duties in order that they can more effectively guide the learning activities of children.

Organization further provides for full utilization of equipment and materials. Equipment must be purchased, housed, allocated, circulated, and kept in good running order. Materials must be obtained, evaluated, classified, and catalogued, and information regarding them must be disseminated to all users. These processes cannot be successfully carried on without a delegation of responsibilities and planned co-ordination.

What Professional Staff Is Needed To Carry Forward a Desirable Program of Audio-visual Materials?

A desirable program of audio-visual materials includes the assistance and services necessary to take full advantage of the contributions of audio-visual materials to the improvement of instruction. Professional staff is needed for planning and general administration of the audio-visual program, for the selection and utilization of materials, and for the local production of radio programs, filmstrips, graphic materials, and exhibits. Analysis of such proposed programs in terms of professional staff requirements indicates a need of the equivalent of one staff member of professional status, plus the necessary technical, secretarial, and clerical assistance, for each 50 teachers.[56]

---
[56] AVID of Indiana, op. cit., pp. 23-24.

In a smaller school, the professional staff would include a part-time or full-time director of audio-visual materials, part-time audio-visual building co-ordinators, and teachers with competencies and interests in specialized areas of the audio-visual program who would be assigned specific responsibilities on a released-time basis. For example, a staff member of the science department might be assigned to preview films in the science area and prepare annotations and teacher utilization material; or a teacher with high ability in either still or motion-picture photography might be assigned to undertake problems of school production. Similarly in the area of the production of radio programs, graphic arts, and exhibits, there are many opportunities for using the skills and abilities of faculty members.

In expanded audio-visual programs in larger schools, a full-time director of audio-visual materials will need on his staff other full-time professional members with experience and training in the areas of selection, circulation, utilization, and production. He will also need teachers with high interests and special competencies from the different educational levels and subject fields who would be attached to the staff of the audio-visual center on a part-time basis.

What Should Be the Qualifications of the Director and the Building Co-ordinator?

The competencies of the director of the audio-visual program include the ability to direct an audio-visual program; to stimulate and assist those using materials; to provide leadership in administration, utilization, selection, and production of audio-visual materials; and an understanding of the role of these materials in the educative process.

The director should have had at least five years of successful teaching experience and have demonstrated the ability to make effective use of a wide range of audio-visual materials in his own field. His professional training should include a masters' degree from an accredited institution with a license in at least one major teaching field and in administration and/or supervision. He should have specialized training in audio-visual education, including a working knowledge of audio-visual materials and equipment, their selection, circulation, use, and maintenance. He should be familiar with the preparation of audio-visual materials, including photographic, audio, and graphic aids and exhibits. The ability to organize, administer, and supervise an audio-visual program is also an important qualification, as are such qualities of leadership that will command the co-operation and respect of the administration and staff. He should have a thorough knowledge of the role of audio-visual materials in curriculum development and in the learning processes.

The director should assume the role of administrator in his own department only, and his relation to others either above him or below him in a line and staff organization should be of a consultant nature.[57] Also within his department he should evaluate the adequacy of the program and the work being done and should develop plans for an effective program.

The building co-ordinator should hold a license in one or more subject fields or grade levels and have had at least two years of successful teaching experience. He should have a knowledge of the selection, utilization, preparation, and maintenance of audio-visual materials, with the ability to co-ordinate the audio-visual program with all other phases of the educational program within the building. His personal qualities should command the respect and co-operation of the building principal and the other staff members. He should be willing to maintain at all times a professional attitude toward the building principal and the other building co-ordinators.

What Should Be the Function of the Advisory Audio-visual Education Committee?

An expanding audio-visual program requires the advice and counsel of a representative committee composed of administrative, supervisory, instructional, and lay personnel. They may serve as an advisory body to the director in formulating major over-all policies and in discovering ways and means to implement that policy in the most effective fashion.

The membership of this committee should include the director of audio-visual materials; the superintendent or director of instruction; the general supervisor or curriculum co-ordinator; at least two principals, one from the elementary and one from the secondary level; one member of the board of education or board of supervisors; two or three teachers from each level; and one lay member of the community interested in adult education.

The committee may be interested in becoming more familiar with the aims and objectives of the audio-visual program in order to bring into focus curriculum problems that audio-visual services can facilitate; to formulate policies as to methods for distribution of equipment and materials; to support the director in carrying out the program,

---

[57] *Report of Audio-visual Education Administration Workshop*, pp. 68-76. Sacramento: California State Department of Education, 1947.

including such responsibilities as obtaining adequate equipment and materials and providing the best physical facilities possible for using these materials; to generate interest throughout the school system in the audio-visual program; to formulate maintenance policies and procedures; and to aid the director in organizing and promoting an in-service teacher-education program.

What Should Be the Relationship of a Center of Audio-visual Materials and Its Director to the Administrative Organization of an Institution or Agency and Its Chief Executive?

Since the audio-visual center is primarily concerned with ways and means of enriching the curriculum, it should base its organization and operations on that important function. To that end, the director's basic contribution should be to the improvement of instruction. His administrative duties should be limited to his own department only. His relation to others outside his own departmental staff members should be of a consultant nature. To all line and staff groups, he should be an advisor, a source of information, and an expert observer in his field.[58]

As the administrative officer of the center, the director should be responsible to the chief executive of the institution or agency. In this capacity, the director should be in a position to present his documented financial and personnel needs directly to the superintendent or president.

What Procedures of the Audio-visual Program Should Be Routinized?

To facilitate the administration of the numerous aspects of the audio-visual program, the director should make a careful analytical study of the various operations that are involved. Such an analysis will indicate that many activities involving selecting, ordering, booking, confirming, preparing shipping notices, transporting equipment and materials, inspecting equipment and materials, preparing reports, and cataloguing can be systematized. By preparing a handbook of operations, these routine steps can be spelled out in detail. By following the outlined procedures, much time can be saved by the members of the staff in processing requests.[59]

The director should understand that any systematization must contribute to the ease of processing and to more efficient use of equip-

---

[58] *Ibid.*, pp. 71-72.
[59] Charles F. Hoban, Jr., *Movies That Teach, op. cit.*, pp. 110-34.

ment and materials. Only those procedures which are repetitive, non-creative, mechanical, and/or routine should follow a definitely outlined step-by-step process. At no time should the introduction of routine procedures interfere with the flexibility of the service and become the dictator of the program.

What Services Expected of the School's Audio-visual Center Can Be Decentralized?

To render the most effective service, policies must be formulated which will determine what services should be handled directly from the school system's center, from the co-ordinator's office in each individual building, and by the teacher himself.

Certain services should remain centralized at the center. The execution of the policies governing the service and the general supervision of the distribution and use of the materials rests with the director. At the center should be housed and stored most of the motion-picture films for use by the schools and the community, selected recordings, slides and filmstrips on special subjects, special purpose pictures of unusual value, special maps, record players, and recording and photographic equipment. The extent to which materials and equipment can be deposited in the individual schools depends upon a number of factors which vary in different communities. These include the initial unit cost of materials and equipment, size of schools, amount of use, efficiency of distribution, the type of materials and equipment, and the availability of the items when needed.

A central department can more efficiently produce, catalogue, maintain, and assemble into units the various audio-visual materials necessary to an adequate teaching program and can make them readily available. The smaller units lack special equipment, storage space, personnel, and time.

In order to make it possible for teachers to have materials and equipment available as close as possible to the point of use, long-term loans should be made to individual schools. The more frequently used films, filmstrips, slides, and recordings should be placed in the hands of building co-ordinators on long-term or permanent loan. Exhibit materials, basic maps, and a vertical file of "permanent" pictures should be organized by each co-ordinator.

No hard and fast rules can be laid down in outlining decentralization plans. However, it might be stated that less expensive equipment and materials should be decentralized and located in the individual schools; the more expensive types of materials and equipment should be centralized and distributed as needed.

What Can Be Done To Lessen the Problems Involved in Ordering from a Central Library?

At present it is not practical to provide each classroom with its own supply of materials and equipment. The less-used and more expensive materials will necessarily be shared. This sharing, with its advantages and problems, is similar whether the school secures its materials from its own school library or from a lending library. The major problems fall into two categories: (a) reducing the time and effort of the classroom teacher in scheduling and (b) obtaining materials for the classroom when needed.

Building co-ordinators, with professional training and with time freed for the purpose, can do much to relieve the individual teacher by standardizing the booking and ordering procedure, informing teachers of new materials, training projectionists, and in other ways coordinating and supplementing teachers' efforts. Red tape involved in ordering should be reduced to a minimum.

If there are too many teachers for the amount of available materials, the professional teacher who wants a specific material on a certain date finds it necessary to order a semester or so in advance of that date. This situation discourages the use of audio-visual materials. Sufficient prints or copies of materials should be added to the central library to enable teachers to order ten days or less before the use date with a reasonable degree of assurance that materials will be available. Storage should be decentralized as much as possible, with the inexpensive and frequently used materials being housed, or on long-time loan, in individual classrooms.

If materials libraries are adequately staffed by trained personnel, business-like procedures will be installed, thus reducing errors. This will tend to insure that materials once booked will arrive for use as scheduled.

What Are the Responsibilities of the Local School System in Providing an In-service Training Program in the Field of Audio-visual Materials?

The field of audio-visual materials is growing so rapidly that all teachers and administrators need to have opportunities to take part in an in-service training program that is well-planned and continuous.[60] The audio-visual director is responsible for the success of the program. However, if it is to be successful, the program must evolve out of the

---

[60] "Audio-visual Program Standards: In-service Training," *See and Hear*, III (December, 1947), 26.

teachers' conscious needs and operate on an administrator-teacher-pupil-layman co-operative basis and be an integral part of the overall in-service training program.

The director's responsibility for in-service training includes keeping teachers and community leaders aware of all developments in materials, equipment, publications, and utilization and selection techniques through regular announcements. He will also be available for individual conferences and demonstrations. Committees operating on a revolving and voluntary membership basis will function continually on problems pertinent to the needs of the system as a whole and of individual groups within the organization. On some of these the director will serve as the leader; on others, for example, a curriculum committee, he will serve only as a consultant. Out of the work of the committees should come bulletins, handbooks, study guides, curriculum resource units, selected bibliographies, and other important information.

Due to the fact that all the answers in utilization and selection are not known, teachers should be encouraged to do work of an experimental nature. Worth-while results and ideas from their experimentation should be given to other teachers. Opportunities should be provided for teacher visitation to observe techniques employed by others in the school or school system.

Workshops, institutes, conferences, and professional courses brought to the community can be invaluable in the in-service program. Workshops should be organized on a co-operative basis and should be flexible enough to meet the individual and group needs of the participants. Demonstration-teaching involving the use of audio-visual materials should emphasize not only the techniques in utilization but also the relationship between utilization and the entire teaching process. Recognized leaders in the field can contribute to the worth-whileness of a program, provided preplanning directs utilization of their talents toward the purposes of the program.

Whatever the nature of the in-service program, it should employ all possible audio-visual materials to accomplish its aims. The participants must experience in their learning the kinds of materials or methods they are learning about.

What Are Some of the Better Ways of Interpreting the Values of an Audio-visual Program?

To obtain a general understanding of what audio-visual materials are, their contribution to the learning process, and the relation of audio-visual materials to the curriculum, interpretation is both helpful and necessary. A part of the interpretation will be unaided and unplanned by the school; another and more significant part will be planned and deliberate.

Without any promotion or assistance, to a certain extent, the effective program itself becomes a vital, interpretative medium.[61] The students who learn more quickly and who achieve broader experience backgrounds become adherents of the program. The teachers who find their objectives more completely accomplished become advocates of the use of these materials. The parents who see the growing abilities of their children to cope with the problems which confront them are convinced of the value of the audio-visual method.

To increase public awareness of the values of the audio-visual program, photographic media, pictures in papers and magazines, filmstrips of activities, and motion pictures can be used. Exhibits in school, posters, bulletin boards, special displays, use of school open-house and of demonstrations, local radio programs, and recordings of individual and group accomplishments also provide an opportunity to bring these materials to the attention of the public.

What Basis Should Be Used in Planning the Budget for an Audio-visual Program?

The audio-visual budget is justified by the contribution of audio-visual materials to more effective learning experiences. The problem of budget resolves itself into one of determining the desired goals of service. Teachers working with supervisors and administrators will determine the amount of different types of materials needed to achieve the objectives. The frequency of use desired for each type of material determines the staff, equipment, and materials. The state organization of audio-visual instruction directors of Indiana advocates, for a minimum audio-visual program, an annual expenditure of $50 per teacher for materials and equipment only. A desirable program should have at least $150 for materials and equipment.[62]

To secure the services desired, the audio-visual program must have a qualified director. It will be his responsibility to prepare the budget after consultation with teachers or their representatives and the business leaders of the school system. To make the budget meaningful, the director will set it up so that the objectives of the program, size of

---

[61] "The P.T.A. and a Visual Program," *The Principal and Audio-Visual Education*, pp. 21-23. Washington: Department of Elementary School Principals of the National Education Association, 1948.

[62] AVID of Indiana, *op. cit.*, p. 26.

staff, and extent of services will be indicated. Budget categories such as the following are suggested.[63]

I. Salaries
   A. Professional staff
   B. Technical and clerical staff

II. Operating expenses
   A. Office
   B. Cataloguing
   C. Transportation
      1. Supplies and equipment
      2. Personnel
   D. Maintenance
      1. Equipment
      2. Supplies
   E. Fixed charges
      1. Utilities
      2. Insurance
   F. Instructional supplies
      1. Consumable
      2. Replacements

III. Capital outlay
   A. Equipment (permanent-general)
      1. Office
      2. Production
      3. Inspection and repair
      4. Transportation
      5. Storage facilities
   B. Audio-visual equipment and materials
      1. New materials—slides, filmstrips, maps, models, etc.
      2. New equipment—projectors, radios, recorders, etc.

This breakdown will of necessity be adapted to conditions in different localities. In all cases, however, expenditure should come from the same tax source as comparable items in other departments of the school system.

How Should the Desired Audio-visual Program Be Financed?

Support of the audio-visual program should be an integral part of a well-planned school budget based on a sound educational plan, a careful estimate of receipts, and an intelligent spending program. Budget-builders usually draw on local, state, and federal funds for

[63] *Report of Audio-visual Education Administrative Workshop, op. cit.*, pp. 6-7.

their over-all budget requirements and also for the progressive audio-visual program. A wise administrator will, however, keep an open mind toward the necessity of using gifts from school and community organizations and money earned by pupils and patrons.

Tax sources are chiefly of local origin but may be derived from state and federal equalization plans. An audio-visual program financed through taxation is more apt to be considered a vital and essential part of the curriculum. A program so financed is also assured of a more continuous and constant source of income. State distributive and equalization funds, as well as federal aid that may become available for either general or special educational purposes, should be allocated directly to the local school corporation on a per-unit basis. This gives local school officials an opportunity to use funds derived from all sources for the planning and financing of audio-visual and other essential programs which will meet local needs.[64]

It is true that many a school audio-visual program has been initiated by gifts from interested adult groups, such as a projector given by the P.-T.A. Such procedure may serve to educate the organization membership in the scope, needs, and advantages of audio-visual methods as well as to implement the school program. Money is sometimes earned to assist in supporting the program. Services such as paid noon-day showings, equipment rental fees to out-of-school groups, and income from pupil entertainments are often utilized.

The use of gift funds for the expansion of some experimental aspect of an audio-visual program is justifiable. Once such a program proves its worth, it is best to expand and carry on the project under tax support. For example, the Lions' Club might present to the school a tape recorder for use in remedial speech work, thus opening the door to experimentation in a new field. If and when it is necessary to depend upon other than tax support for the ongoing program, the funds should be considered a subsidy of an admittedly underfinanced program and only a temporary expedient.

How Can Per-Teacher and Per-Pupil Costs of Materials Be Analyzed?

The quantity and quality of school use of audio-visual materials is closely related to moneys available for the audio-visual program. Since the over-all budget necessary for an adequate program is sub-

---

[64] *Proposals for Public Education in Postwar America*, p. 58. Research Bulletin of the National Education Association, Vol. XXII, No. 2 (April, 1944). Washington: Research Division, National Education Association, 1944.

stantial, it is desirable to break down total expenditures into the cost of providing individual pupils with a learning experience.

A program of film ownership in a system with ten teachers per grade, which provides one film showing per week in each of five subjects, may reasonably cost $54.00 per teacher. This figure is derived by assuming that the average cost of each film is $60.00 and that the program operates on a multiple-use factor of two. By a "multiple factor of two" is meant that the films are used on two different grade levels or are used in two different units on the same grade level. Thus, 90 films, each costing $60.00, are required to provide a teacher with 180 (36 weeks x 5 subjects) bookings a year. The $5,400.00 is amortized over a ten-year period (of film life) and again divided by ten to give the cost per teacher. One hundred and eighty film bookings are provided each teacher at a cost of $54.00 per teacher. One film booking is provided at a cost of 30 cents per teacher and, reducing it further, an educational motion picture of ten to fifteen minutes in length is provided at a cost of approximately one cent per pupil.

The above analysis gives the per-pupil use cost of motion pictures, the most expensive of materials. The same approach may be used in ascertaining per-pupil use costs of all types of audio-visual materials and equipment.

What Are Some of the Advantages of Planning an Audio-visual Program on a Per-Teacher Basis?

The use of audio-visual materials must be thought of primarily in terms of the ways in which they can improve instruction in the classroom. Each classroom should be provided with the more important types of audio-visual materials. Each teacher should have available, at the time when needed, the different types of audio-visual materials which will make the greatest contribution to the learning activity. This is true in the larger schools where classes are of more uniform size as well as in smaller schools where the size of some classes may be small, particularly in elective subjects on the secondary level. Since materials and equipment are planned on a teacher-classroom basis, the school's audio-visual program should be planned and financed on the same basis.

If planning is done on a per-teacher basis, reductions in teaching load and class size will not affect the per-teacher expenditure required to maintain a given classroom program of audio-visual materials. If planning is done on a per-pupil basis, then the per-pupil expenditure must be increased as class size is reduced in order to enable teachers to continue effective classroom use of audio-visual materials.

Responsibilities of State Agencies and Higher Institutions

Why Should Teacher-training Institutions Plan for Audio-visual Centers?

There are three major reasons why teacher-training institutions should plan for audio-visual centers: (a) to provide a laboratory-teaching situation for preservice and in-service training of teachers; (b) to meet utilization needs of college classes; (c) to serve school and community groups within the area of the college with both materials and leadership.

Such centers should enable prospective teachers to become acquainted with audio-visual materials and with all aspects of their successful use. Graduate students should be able to obtain practical assistance and experience in advanced problems of production, circulation, selection, and repair and maintenance of materials.

To provide these laboratory teaching experiences, an audio-visual center should encompass these materials and services: (a) consultation service for faculty, school, and community groups; (b) a representative materials library; (c) circulation, repair, and maintenance services; (d) a representative sampling of equipment; and (e) art, audio- and photographic-production services.[65]

An audio-visual center built around these five areas will be able to meet the utilization needs and promote the use of audio-visual materials in college classes.

Most colleges find it impossible to finance a satisfactory library of elementary- and secondary-level audio-visual materials without the income derived from the rental of these materials. Such a rental service will provide the necessary additional funds to enable the college to maintain a library large enough to be representative and a professional staff for teaching, consultation, and administration. It also provides materials to larger schools to supplement their local programs and to smaller school units and adult groups financially unable to purchase or produce their own materials.

How May a Teacher-training Institution Finance an Adequate Audio-visual Center?

An audio-visual center in any teacher-training institution should have a library that contains an adequate and representative sample

---

[65] Audio-visual Education Committee, "The Functions of an Audio-visual Department in a Teacher Education Institution," *Western Illinois State Teachers College Bulletin*, Vol. XXVI, No. 4. Macomb, Illinois: Western Illinois State Teachers College, 1946.

of all types of audio-visual materials in all subject-matter fields and for all levels, including college and adult. Considering the scope of services to be provided, it is unlikely that most colleges, with the present cost of audio-visual materials, production facilities, and the necessary professional, technical, and clerical staff, could charge the entire amount of the annual operating costs to the training of students. For this reason, a number of colleges are planning to recover a considerable part of the annual operating budget through income derived by making the material, production, and staff resources available to schools and community groups on a service-charge basis.[66]

A library of approximately 3,000 prints of motion pictures and proportionate amounts of other types of material and equipment is needed to serve adequately college classes and near-by school and community groups. With an average cost of $60 per print, a motion-picture library of the size suggested requires an investment of $180,000. Other materials and equipment could be expected to cost approximately $70,000. With an annual capital expenditure of $25,000 to $40,000, the center could acquire, over a period of seven to ten years, instructional materials and equipment with a value of $250,000 before comparable annual expenditures would be required for replacement because of wear and tear or obsolescence. Some colleges would be able to obtain sufficient funds to purchase basic materials and equipment within a period of one to three years. Funds required for the initial purchases of materials and equipment by state institutions are logically a part of state support. Private institutions may encourage gifts or grants for such a program.

If all services of a college audio-visual center are provided on a fee basis, at prevailing rates, it is possible to recover each year the annual depreciation of materials and equipment and the total expenditures for staff and supplies. Assuming a maximum useful life of ten years, the annual depreciation charge for replacement of a library of materials and equipment with a value of $250,000 would be $25,000. With a 50:50 ratio between replacement costs and expenditures for staff and supplies, an annual operating budget of $50,000 is required. This budget could be recovered in full through nominal charges for services which the center would be in a position to render. The smaller public and private institutions could probably afford to use the equivalent of less than $10,000 of service for instructional and public relations purposes through a partial subsidization of the annual operating

[66] L. C. Larson, "Functions of a Center of Audio-visual Aids," *Proceedings of the Thirty-first Annual Meeting of the National University Extension Association*, pp. 91-96. Bloomington, Indiana: Indiana University.

costs. The balance of the operating budget can be covered through income from services rendered to school and community groups. Larger colleges and universities need a more comprehensive center and could recover a proportionate amount of the annual operating budget through charges on services to school and community groups.

What Should Be the Contribution of a State Department of Education to the School's Audio-visual Program?

The rapid development of the audio-visual movement in the schools has brought about an increasing need for the state department of public instruction to direct, guide, and advise on evaluation, selection, utilization, and circulation of audio-visual materials.[67]

As teachers use more and more materials as an integral part of classroom instruction, it becomes more important to correlate these instructional materials with state-adopted curriculums.

State department leadership is needed to set up criteria to determine the adequacy of school programs and to encourage the strengthening of the audio-visual activities.

The state department can be instrumental in encouraging the state building commission to require that sufficient electrical outlets, bulletin boards, and other needed facilities be incorporated into all new school building construction.

In evaluating teacher-training institutions, the state department should include an appraisal of the adequacy of their audio-visual training programs to determine whether they meet minimum requirements.

Increased funds are needed on the local level for equipment, materials, and leadership. The state department could be instrumental in making additional funds available to local school corporations in order to support a desirable program of audio-visual materials.

The state department of education should prescribe a certificate for the position of director of audio-visual materials and should set up standards of competency for all teachers, administrators, and supervisors in the selection, use, and administration of audio-visual materials.

The state department could be of assistance in setting up professional training programs for audio-visual personnel in all licensed teacher-training institutions, suggesting necessary staff, material, and equipment resources.

Initiation of research projects by individual teachers and adminis-

---

[67] AVID of Indiana, *op. cit.*, chap. vii.

trators, as well as by professional organizations and teacher-training institutions within the state, should be encouraged by the state department.

What Competencies in the Use of Audio-visual Materials Should Be Considered by State Departments of Education for Certification of Teachers?

The ultimate aim in audio-visual education is that adequate materials shall be properly used to facilitate learning. This requires that the teachers have adequate professional preparation in general teaching procedures. In addition, many skills and understandings related to selection, utilization, administration, and production are required.[68]

The proper selection of materials requires a knowledge of: (a) sources, methods of securing, and methods of evaluating materials; (b) the relation of materials to the curriculum and to method; (c) successful use of the potentialities of the various audio-visual media; and (d) the different materials available, especially in the field of the teacher's interest.

The proper utilization of materials requires, in addition to some of the items listed above, knowledges and skills related to: (a) optimum conditions for the presentation of materials; (b) the operation and routine maintenance of different types of equipment; (c) the psychology of learning and the philosophical concepts underlying the use of audio-visual materials; (d) the use of the proper audio-visual material at the proper time; and (e) techniques of communication through media other than print and oral language.

With respect to administration, the teacher should know: (a) the more common practices in the administration of audio-visual materials; (b) the commonly accepted role of the audio-visual director with respect to the curriculum; and (c) the factors of organization which facilitate the selection, use, and production of needed materials.

The teacher should be able to produce simple materials, such as slides, charts, graphs, models, exhibits, and displays.

These competencies are not only necessary to good teaching with respect to audio-visual materials but are characteristic of all good teaching. They represent a repertoire of abilities, skills, and understandings which are a mark of teaching competency.

---

[68] Elizabeth Goudy Noel and J. Paul Leonard, *Foundations for Teacher Education in Audio-visual Instruction,* pp. 2-3 (Washington: American Council on Education, 1947); "Developing Standards of Teacher Competency in Audio-visual Education: A Committee Report," *California Schools,* XVIII (January, 1947), 5-6.

Who Should Assume the Responsibility for In-service Training of Teachers in the Area of Audio-visual Materials?

The pattern of leadership for in-service training varies considerably from state to state and community to community so that practices are often difficult to define. However, two or three points are becoming clear with reference to the in-service training programs.

First, most programs in this area are originating with the expressed needs of the teachers. This is a "demand" area. Much of this is due to lack of professional training in the past. Recent technological advances have contributed to the demand. Also, certain changes in method which call for teaching for and with meaning instead of by memorization have caused the demand for in-service training in the audio-visual field. When such programs are initiated, the continuous in-service evaluation of method and technique usually remains the responsibility of the teacher.

Second, most in-service training programs in audio-visual education are designed to utilize the leadership of the state department of education and of teacher-training institutions in addition to that of the local community. This is in part due to the fact that much of the professional leadership is concentrated at these two levels.

Third, considerable effort is being made to achieve co-ordination of educational efforts at the local level.[69] Because of the recognition of the fact that audio-visual materials and methods enrich experiences and facilitate the learning process, the in-service training programs are closely co-ordinated with problems of curriculum and method. This makes the program a distinct educational venture.

The further importance of in-service training at the administrative and supervisory levels needs to be stressed. In addition to this, some local directors of audio-visual education still have inadequate training and insufficient experience. These two facts have led to a functional leadership in in-service training by state departments of education and educational institutions.

---

[69] *Report of Audio-visual Education Administrative Workshop, op. cit.,* pp. 20-25.

CHAPTER XII

RESEARCH ON AUDIO-VISUAL MATERIALS[1]

EDGAR DALE
Ohio State University
Columbus, Ohio

JAMES D. FINN
Colorado State College of Education
Greeley, Colorado

CHARLES F. HOBAN, JR.
State Teachers College
West Chester, Pennsylvania

This chapter is not an account of research in "eye learning" or "ear learning." It is an account of research in modern educational methods. Audio-visual materials and devices should not be classified exclusively as "eye" or "ear" sense stimuli. They are modern technological means of providing rich, concrete experiences for students. Wheeler and Perkins say on this point, "The ear alone does not determine what the nature of an auditory experience will be. The meaning of an object will not be apprehended until it is perceived in the light of a total situation with the aid of other senses" (147:140-47). This, of course, in no way denies the significance of the sense of sight or hearing. It does, however, constitute a warning against any breaking down of dynamic mental life into discrete, unrelated elements.

The problem of perception by visual, auditory, or other sensory impressions has been a subject of investigation since the beginning of experimental psychology. The reader who desires information on the

---

[1] The committee is indebted to the Macmillan Company, publisher, and to Walter S. Monroe, editor, of the *Encyclopedia of Educational Research,* for permission to use much of the material contained in this chapter. This material was originally prepared by the authors for publication in the 1949 (revised) edition of the *Encyclopedia of Educational Research* under the headings "Audio-visual Materials" and "Theatrical Motion Pictures, Educational Influence." It has been modified and extended to meet the requirements of this yearbook.

vast literature on perception will find three books (**7, 10, 141**) dealing with general aspects of perception especially useful. Renshaw (**112, 113**) summarizes much of the research done on visual training and cites other research in perception. A summary of studies relating light to vision and seeing will be found in Luckiesh (**78**). Sherman (**123**), MacLatchy (**79**), and Snyder (**127**) present examples of recent research in perception having implications for the audio-visual field.

Little of the work on perception being done by psychologists, artists, lighting scientists, and others has found its way into the journals serving the audio-visual field. There is a great gap between known information on perception and its application in instruction through audio-visual techniques.

The experimental activities of Brownell and Tyler have opened the way for fruitful research on the relation of materials and methods to the development of higher mental processes. Brownell's monographs (**13, 14**) clearly demonstrate that teaching materials and procedures should not be selected initially in terms of the end product of the learning experience but in terms of progressive levels of experience which lead to the end product. Thus, basic, concrete materials are not crutches which impede progress in learning but are materials which provide experience essential to development of higher mental processes. Similarly, Tyler (**139**) has shown that the mere verbal learning of facts and principles does not necessarily lead to their integration and application. By implication, these conclusions point to the necessity of learning in the functional situation, whereby principles are abstracted from and applied to the pertinent data.

General Aspects of Research

The literature from 1940 to 1947 includes at least twenty-seven status surveys of the audio-visual field. These surveys range from the number and types of projectors available in a county, a state, or the nation to the expenditure of funds for audio-visual materials and equipment or the content of film libraries in such areas. The most important of these surveys was the one conducted by the Research Division of the National Education Association (**98**). Other surveys of importance were those of Golden (**51**), Hansen (**55**), Kauffman (**67**), Larson (**71, 72**), McCallum (**80**), McPherson (**85**), Mears, (**89**), Molyneaux (**95**), and Roberts (**115, 116, 117**).

These surveys reveal a wide-spread growth in all phases of the audio-visual field. The amounts of equipment and materials available have sharply increased in the past ten years. Audio-visual mat-terials are much more widely used in public schools, colleges, and universities. However, expenditures for audio-visual materials and services vary greatly from city to city and from institution to institution.

The following claims for properly used audio-visual materials in the teaching situation are supported by research evidence:

1. They supply a concrete basis for conceptual thinking and hence reduce meaningless word responses of students.
2. They have a high degree of interest for students.
3. They supply the necessary basis for developmental learning and hence make learning more permanent.
4. They offer a reality of experience which stimulates self-activity on the part of pupils.
5. They develop a continuity of thought; this is especially true of motion pictures.
6. They contribute to growth of meaning and hence to vocabulary development.
7. They provide experiences not easily secured by other materials and contribute to the efficiency, depth, and variety of learning.

Research in the field of audio-visual education indicates that realistic, objective materials have genuine value in teaching and that their effectiveness depends on the clarity of the purpose for which they are used, the age of the children, the type of children, the type of material being studied, the character of the materials used, the methods of projection or use, place of use, and the influence of the teacher who uses the materials. Significant gains have been reported in informational learning, retention and recall, thinking and reasoning, activity, interest, imagination, better assimilation, and personal growth and expression; and these results have indicated a time-saving, both in preparation of work and in completion of minimum essentials.

The following summary of research dealing with audio-visual instructional materials is presented under eight major headings: (*a*) audio-visual materials in World War II; (*b*) instructional motion pictures; (*c*) theatrical motion pictures; (*d*) field trips; (*e*) still pictures, filmstrips, and lantern slides; (*f*) museum materials; (*g*) graphic materials; and (*h*) radio and recordings.

Audio-visual Materials in World War II

For reader convenience, the research on the use of audio-visual materials in World War II is discussed in two sections: (*a*) in the armed forces and (*b*) in industry.

In the Armed Forces

During World War II (1941-1946) we trained over twelve million men and women for military jobs. Audio-visual materials were widely and intensively used at all stages in the training program, but scientific evaluations of this use are relatively few. Several reasons are given for the paucity of research. Personnel was unavailable for carrying on scientific studies. Another reason given was that most of the audio-visual aids used *were specifically planned for a specific training task.* And when a training technique did not meet this need, it was changed and another tried.

Films. Hoban (59) cites several studies relating to film use undertaken by various branches of the Army. In one study, the Army orientation film, "Prelude to War," was shown to a group of inductees to determine its effect on their information about the war and the effect of this information upon morale.[2] This group was paired with a matched control group which did not see the film. In all cases, the film was effective, but, in addition, the study revealed that while those men with only elementary-school background learned something from the film, those with high-school or college experience learned more.

Similar results were obtained in a study using a film on map reading. The higher intelligence group in this study showed a 20 per cent increase in material learned from the film, while the lower intelligence group showed only a 6 per cent increase. Hoban sums up these findings with the words: "The more the audience brings to the motion picture, the more the audience gets out of the picture" (59:10).

In another study, the use of a film without any additional instruction was compared with the teaching of the same material by a highly competent instructor using a scale model. The subject matter of the experiment involved training in team work. Teams of nine men each were taught to assemble and disassemble a portable radio set. The film-taught groups were able to complete their tasks in a little under 7 per cent less time than the instructor-taught groups. The men who participated were interviewed at the end of the experiment, and the preponderance of opinion was in favor of the film method. Many of the men also pointed out that the instructor used was especially com-

---

[2] The data which Hoban cites on morale films were from sources which were then (1945) restricted. These data are apparently now available as they are quoted extensively by Doob (34) as from a series of studies by Hovland and others (41). The Hovland reference would appear to be an important addition to experimental research in the audio-visual field. At this writing, however, it is not known whether or not the Army has given it general distribution.

petent, suggesting that the film would be greatly superior to a mediocre or poor instructor.

From the results of this experiment and from many observations made during the war period, the motion picture seems especially effective for teaching the teamwork concept, for providing a means for seeing the relationships of jobs to be done, and for setting a standard of achievement.

The Army film on map-reading was shown to a control group and to three experimental groups, one seeing the film without comment, one having a brief introductory period before viewing the film, and one having a short oral quiz following the film. Hoban summarizes the findings as follows:

> In the case of both brighter and duller groups, there was an appreciable increase in learning from a film when the film showing was preceded by the instructor's introductory explanatory remarks.
>
> . . . .
>
> By the use of competent instructional procedures preceding the showing of a film, there is an appreciable increase in audience learning, not only of those parts of the film explained in the introductory exercises but also in other parts of the film as well (59:15-16).

Miles and Spain (91) cite briefly the results of two studies on attitudes developed by films. The films studied were those of the same orientation series as the film, "Prelude to War," mentioned above. A cross-section survey of soldier opinion disclosed that the men who had seen the orientation films were the more likely to believe that they had a clear idea of why we were fighting the war. When compared to those who said they were doubtful, twice as many of those who thought they had a clear idea of why we were fighting the war said they would rather be soldiers than workers in war industry.

Another such survey revealed that 70 per cent of the men who saw the film, "Battle of Britain," believed that the British would have been conquered except for determined resistance, while only 46 per cent of those who did not see the film held this belief. "This study further showed that men who like a film are most influenced by it. For example, answers favorable toward the British changed 16 per cent among those liking the film and only 6 per cent among those not liking the film" (91:63). Finally, a third survey revealed again that attitudes developed by the motion picture are measurable and have remarkable staying power.

Miles and Spain (91) report a study made by the Psychological Test Film Unit of the Army Air Forces. The study compared learnings derived from (a) a training film, (b) studying from a well-illustrated manual, and (c) an organized lecture using nineteen lantern slides. Both the superior and inferior sections of the movie group did significantly better than the other two groups, both immediately and when tested again after two months. There seemed to be no significant differences between the manual- and lecture-trained groups.

Filmstrips. Filmstrips were studied to a lesser degree by the armed services. Miles and Spain report two studies. One was a survey made by the Air Forces to find out the attitudes of training-aids officers and instructors toward filmstrips and to discover more efficient means of using filmstrips. Instructors and training-aids officers reported confidence in filmstrips as a major aid in teaching and a desire to use them although they were making only partial use of available filmstrips. The instructors and training-aids officers seemed to lack experience in using filmstrips in teaching. Some of the reason for non-use and disuse could be laid to the inferior quality of the filmstrips themselves, and an effort was made to produce better strips containing beginning frames offering suggestions to instructors, review and quiz frames at the ends, and the like.

Miles and Spain also report a study made by the Signal Corps using two types of sound filmstrips designed to teach the Signal Corps phonetic alphabet. The only difference between the two was that one required the audience to recite aloud at certain points. The audience-participation group proved superior to the nonparticipation group. Other conclusions were that audience participation is especially valuable in getting across information if "(1) the material is difficult to grasp, (2) the men have little motivation to learn, or (3) if the audience is composed of men in the lower intelligence levels" (91:67).

Hoban (59) made a detailed analysis of the use of filmstrips by the Army, citing several studies in the process. He emphasizes the successful use of filmstrips in the Army's program of training functional illiterates. The filmstrips used were carefully correlated with the Army reader, tied in directly with the military experience of the men, and were eminently successful. (The average illiterate acquired the basic reading and arithmetic skills necessary for modern soldiers in about eight weeks.) In another study, the Army film on map-reading was compared in effectiveness with a filmstrip made up of single frames of key pictures from the motion picture. Using carefully equated groups, the motion picture appeared superior in teaching certain concepts, and the filmstrip superior in others. It might be noted here that the film on map reading itself is more like an animated filmstrip than a true motion picture.

Finally, Hoban indicates that a survey among Army instructors revealed little preference for the filmstrip. Of those surveyed, 48 per cent preferred graphic portfolios (a series of large charts mounted on an easel), while only 20 per cent preferred filmstrips and 18 per cent indicated no preference between the two. A detailed analysis of the reasons why filmstrips were not as popular or effective in Army instruction as films shows no disparagement of the filmstrip itself. The reasons include (a) the abundance of other aids available, (b) the lack of relationship between the production of filmstrips and their rate of use, (c) the additional time and work necessary on the part of an instructor in order to use a filmstrip effectively, and (d) the poor quality of many of the filmstrips as compared to the superior quality of other aids.

Synthetic devices. Special devices, such as mock-ups, gunnery trainers, tracking trainers, etc., were also the object of a small amount of study during the wartime period. Miles and Spain (91) report no significant results. "Some devices were clearly helpful in training, while others had doubtful or negative values" (91:75). Several reasons might be offered for the results reported. In the first place, the research was relatively meager. Second, the devices represented a wide range of inventiveness from simple cards containing a spinning arrow representing a compass to devices like the Waller gunnery trainer using motion-picture projectors, screens, and guns with which to fire at the targets which are projected. No claims can be made for synthetic devices as such. Each device would have to be investigated on its own merits. However, synthetic devices of many kinds were used widely and intensively to teach many things, and their use, which allowed the complete control of the environment of the student at infinitely less cost and danger, probably has much to offer civilian education.

Miles and Spain note several studies made on instructor and trainee attitudes toward training aids. Two major studies of instructors while they were in service were made by the Navy, and one was made by Chambers (19) for the American Council on Education on veterans after demobilization. Miles and Spain summarize the findings as follows:

All studies indicate general approval of extensive employment of training aids; certain studies suggest that trainees desire a balance between use of training aids and operation of equipment; and the majority of instructors prefer movies to filmstrips. Instructors further believe that movies and filmstrips shorten training time, result in greater learning, and stimulate interest and motivation. Finally, returned veterans now in colleges and public schools overwhelmingly indorse a greater use of audio-visual aids than is now characteristic of civilian education (91: 75-76).

In Industrial Training

Audio-visual materials were used in the training of millions of industrial workers during World War II. Most of the industrial-training films and filmstrips were produced by the United States Office of Education. The total figures are impressive: 457 16-mm. sound motion pictures, 432 silent filmstrips, and 457 instructor's manuals.

Brooker (11) and others have critically described the results of the industrial-training film and filmstrip-project program. Brooker lists several unique contributions made by the program, including: (a) the development of a pattern of film production, (b) the promotion of film utilization, (c) the devising of methods for authenticating content, (d) the development of a film series, and (e) the improvement of distribution methods.

Brooker reports three generalizations about the films which were almost unanimous among training directors.

1. Films speeded up training without any loss in effectiveness. Estimates as to the amount of acceleration varied.
2. Films made the classwork more interesting and resulted in less absenteeism.
3. Films made on the university and college level were used successfully on lower grade levels.

A questionnaire was sent out to five hundred purchasers of the Office of Education training films inquiring as to the value and effectiveness of the films. Both industrial and educational users were in agreement that the films increased interest, improved instruction, resulted in greater comprehension, and improved quality of workmanship. However, 73 per cent of the industrial users thought the films shortened training time while only 52 per cent of the educational users thought so. Of significance to future educational use of motion pictures and filmstrips is the fact that 84 per cent of the industrial users and 97 per cent of the educational users stated that the films were correlated with instructional units in classes—a much higher percentage than generally exists in public education where films are very often shown without preview or preparation, or in auditoriums, or in some other situation not connected with instruction.

Finally, Brooker noted certain conclusions resulting from the five years of accumulated experience with the project.

1. Training films will work effectively, and, yet, their present success is based on partial use.
2. We do not yet know very much about the techniques of communication with films, especially for educational purposes.
3. Films are not good in and of themselves. Films are good only if they are well made and well used. Overoptimism is cautioned against.
4. New patterns completely removed from the theatrical tradition of film production must be developed if we are to make films that are truly educational.
5. There is a serious need for professional courses in visual education so that future producers will understand the medium in which they work, the process of education, and the educational system that sets the requirements for their product.
6. Instructional films can be produced in great numbers but not with mass production techniques. Films of any type are a form of artistry.
7. A better understanding of the way students learn from films is needed. There was evidence that students, in viewing films, thought they knew more than they did, and, on the other hand, they had learned some things on a nonverbal level that they could not express. This paradox needs investigation.

INSTRUCTIONAL MOTION PICTURES

One of the first experiments reported was that of David Sumstine published in *School and Society* in 1918. The early studies were subject to a number of limitations: the samplings of students were relatively small, the controls in experimental studies were inadequate, the objectives were often limited, and few films had been produced specifically for school use. In many cases the films used were those produced by industrial or commercial firms for advertising purposes. Since 1929 the experimental studies have tended to be freer from these limitations and to exhibit other desirable characteristics. The instruction periods have been of sufficient length to permit organized use of several films and the accumulation of reliable results. Learning outcomes have been more definitive and more accurately measured. More outcomes, such as greater classroom participation, increased voluntary reading, and permanent as well as immediate results of motion-picture instruction, have been studied.

Value of Films with Respect to Various Purposes

On the basis of various aspects of learning and other pupil activity investigated in the studies, the purposes for which films have been used in instruction may be considered under nine categories.

Learning Factual Information. The value of the film for this purpose is summed up by Wood and Freeman (**157**) in the statement that the film "gives the child clear-cut notions of the objects and actions in the world about him." Results in agreement with this conclusion are found in the experiments of Arnspiger (**4**), Consitt (**26**), Knowlton and Tilton (**68**), Marchant (**97**), Watkins (**144**), Weber (**145**), and others. In most of these studies the film was used as an integral part of the instructional procedure and in comparison with other methods of instruction. The percentage of increase in factual knowledge varied considerably among the studies.

Although the film is found superior in certain aspects to verbal methods of presenting concrete material, its superiority to other visual aids varies with the type of material and the type of learning expected. Freeman, Reeder, and Thomas (**47**) concluded that, in presenting tables, maps, and charts, the film is no better than the actual tables, maps, and charts presented as such. Davis (**31**), in an analysis of the results of certain topical tests used in the Wood and Freeman study (**157**), found visual materials other than the film to be more effective than the film for presenting factual information about objects; but this analysis also showed that there was a tendency for film-taught pupils to make fewer wrong responses than pupils in the control group.

Goodman (**52**) compared the effectiveness of four visual media: the sound motion picture, the silent motion picture, the sound filmstrip, and the silent filmstrip in teaching four units of safety education in the sixth grade. The silent motion picture proved superior to the other three media. The two filmstrips were next and were about equal with each other. The sound film was last. For all media, the learning gains were high, both on immediate and delayed recall.

Retention of Material Learned. Investigations of the effectiveness of films as measured by permanence of learning have been conducted by Arnspiger (**4**), Gatto (**50**), Goodman (**52**), Hansen (**56**), Knowlton and Tilton (**68**), Lacy (**70**), McClusky (**81**), Ramseyer (**109**), Rulon (**120**), Skinner and Rich (**125**), Sumstine (**134**), Weber (**145**), and Young (**161**). Permanence of learning was measured by administering delayed tests from one week to three and a half months after the period of instruction on the experimental material. In general these tests measured factual material on the verbal level.

The experimental procedures of some of these investigations were of such nature that the results cannot be accepted as adequate or reliable. However, these studies consistently show that the use of the film in instruction is superior to the use of verbal material alone or to the unorganized use of other visual aids when retention is measured by delayed tests of the type employed. There is also general agreement among the data of these investigations that the percentage of superiority of retention is higher that the percentage of superiority of immediate learning when superiority is considered in terms of the test results for the nonfilm groups.

The results of the investigations by Gatto and Rulon are particularly significant. Gatto (50) found that the mean score of the film group increased 11 per cent on the delayed test administered five weeks after the instructional period, but the mean score of the nonfilm group decreased 11 per cent in relation to scores on the immediate tests. Gatto, and almost all other experimenters, measured retention by the use of tests which the pupils had taken on some previous occasion during the experimental period—either as a pretest or as a test of immediate learning at the end of the instructional period.

Rulon (120), however, secured results by a method which eliminated the element of practice effect on the tests. To secure measures of immediate learning, Rulon administered a pictorial-verbal test to half of the pupils and a purely verbal test to the other half. On the measurement of retention, the order of the two tests was reversed. He found, as did the other experimenters, that the superiority of the scores of the film group over the nonfilm group was higher than the corresponding superiority in immediate learning. Furthermore, Rulon's tests were designed to measure "thinking" ability as well as a mere knowledge of facts. With practice effects eliminated in the manner described, his results are in harmony with those secured on test scores to which a practice effect might have accrued.

Habits and Skills. Relatively few studies have been made on the influence of the film on learning to perform acts of skill required in certain school subjects or on personal habits which function outside the school. Freeman, Shaw, and Walker (**48**) Hollis (**62**) McClusky and McClusky (**83**), and Rolfe (**118**) investigated the effectiveness of the film in teaching skills required in school subjects. Freeman and Hoefer (**46**) and Hoefer and Keith (**60**) made studies on the influence of the film on health habits in the everyday life of the pupils.

The results of the studies by Hollis, the McCluskys, and Rolfe are in agreement that the demonstration is a method of instruction superior to the use of the film in teaching manipulatory skills in domestic science, in high-school physics laboratory exercises, and in industrial arts. In all three of these experiments oral instruction was given before the pupils were required to perform their tasks, but no instruction was given while the children were engaged in working out their projects. The test of instructional methods was the relative worth of the pupils' completed work as judged by certain established criteria.

Freeman, Shaw, and Walker found that in teaching position in handwriting, the use of a motion picture, shown three times during the course of regular classroom instruction, was a more effective method than either the procedure ordinarily followed in the classroom or the ordinary procedure plus frequent reports to pupils of their scores on handwriting position. On actual improvement in quality of handwriting, however, none of the three methods of instruction was apparently superior to the others.

Two studies (**46, 60**) which were concerned with effectiveness of films in inculcating desirable habits of diet and care of the teeth as compared with other visual aids plus oral instruction did not disclose any superiority adhering to the use of the film. This fact may be explained by a consideration of the possibility that pupils had relatively little control over the factors that were measured, *i.e.*, diet, dental treatment, and the like.

Ruffa (**119**) reported that a film especially prepared for specific purposes provided an excellent medium for teaching elements of track sports.

From these few experiments we conclude tentatively that the demonstration method of instruction is superior to the film and other visual aids in teaching certain complex manipulatory skills required in some of the school subjects. As a method of teaching less complex skills of bodily position, the film was found to be effective, but its value in comparison with objective demonstration of a similar nature was not determined. Conclusions regarding the effectiveness of the film in developing "proper" health habits must be held in abeyance, largely because of the lack of control of pupils over those conditions which make such habits possible. It must be remembered, however, that these conclusions are based on films now outmoded and that, since these data were gathered, greatly improved films have been made available for teaching skills. Further, certain skills, such as those in surgery, are not easily demonstrable to large audiences whereas films of such activities are.

Perception of Relationships. Knowlton and Tilton (**68**) found that historical photoplays tended to interfere with the development of a pupil's sense of time relationships and that groups who saw no films were superior to film groups on verbal tests designed to measure the pupil's understanding of this relationship. On the other hand, the authors found the photoplays to be most effective in teaching a knowledge of interrelationships involving the interaction of events and forces.

Description and Explanation. Wood and Freeman (157) interpreted the results of their essay-type "topical" tests as indicative of the value of the film in developing descriptive ability as this outcome was measured by the tests. On essay-type questions which are even more abstract than those involving description (explanation and comparison), the authors noted that the film and nonfilm groups were approximately equal.

"Thinking" and "Eduction." Clark (22) measured the relative effectiveness of sound and silent pictures on the first-year college level in the development of "ability to think." He found, in so far as short essay tests measured this ability, that the two methods of film presentation were equally effective.

Rulon (120) classified some of his test items under the general head of "eduction." By "eduction" items he meant those which called for more than a mere recall of facts. He was particularly interested in the types of mental activity involving perception of relationship or application of some general principle. In other words, his "eduction" items required intelligent thinking from factual knowledge or generalizations. He found that, in so far as his tests measured "eduction," the film groups were superior to those which had studied only textbook material; the superiority of the film groups was less on purely factual items.

Imagination. Consitt reported on the basis of pupil and teacher opinion that the use of films in teaching history stimulated the imagination of children. "The children realize the past, gain more sympathetic insight into the lives and feelings of the men and women of the past, and get a fuller and clearer picture of the environment; thus, they can the better imaginatively reconstruct for themselves other scenes of the same period as those seen on the films" (26:378). Wise's more recent investigation (151) supports this conclusion.

Development of Interest. Objective measures of some aspects of pupil interest developed through motion-picture presentation have been reported by Clark (22), Dash (30), Freeman and Hoefer (46), Knowlton and Tilton (68), and Westfall (146).

Knowlton and Tilton kept a record of the number of recitations, voluntary and directed, and of the amount of voluntary reading done by seventh-grade history pupils both in class and outside of class.

These investigators found that the "Yale Chronicles of America" photoplays stimulated classroom participation in recitation and discussion and also stimulated pupils to do voluntary reading in the classroom to a far greater extent than did the ordinary classroom methods. No increase in the amount of reading done outside of class was found in the film group, however.

Freeman and Hoefer (46) reported that the use of health films stimulated children to bring in more clippings, pictures, etc. on the topic studied than did the unorganized use of other visual aids. On the other hand, there was no noticeable difference in the amount of voluntary reading outside of class as between the film and nonfilm groups.

Evidence secured from these two experiments indicates that films are effective in developing classroom participation in discussion and recitation, in stimulating interest in other visual and popular reading material on the topic of the film, and in stimulating voluntary reading of materials on the film topics available in the classroom. The apparent ineffectiveness of the film in stimulating a greater degree of reading outside of class may have been due to the lack of available reading material, the press of other classwork, and the unreliability and inadequacy of the pupil reports of this reading.

In the judgment of the teachers in the British inquiry conducted by Consitt (26) and in the elaborate experiment by Wood and Freeman (157), the use of films as an integral part of classroom procedure arouses and maintains pupil interest and increases the amount of voluntary reading and class discussion. Unfortunately neither of these studies inquired into the effectiveness of other visual aids in stimulating pupil interest and activity. The reports in the Wood and Freeman study were confined to the film teachers. Had similar reports been secured from the nonfilm teachers who made wide use of other visual aids, similar values might have been reported for the materials being used.

The data in the American Council study (58) showed that students like classroom motion pictures, that the majority would like more, but that students can rate films critically as to educational values even if they like them. The study showed that certain factors controlling interest determined the response of children to films. Among these factors were age, sex, economic and cultural status, and previous experience. For example, children like films showing characters their own age, are interested in the activities of their own sex in films, respond to familiar things and settings, and interpret film materials in accordance with their sense of values. In considering the film as a means for combating racial prejudice there was evidence that films dealing with minority groups sympathetically break down prejudices but that, if sympathy is not present in the treatment, the film only serves to re-inforce existing prejudices.

Children's responses to films were found to be related to their mental maturity. Older children were found to be more sensitive to the technical qualities of films than younger children. Younger children tended to respond more volubly to film content, and their responses were to specific items in the films. Older children, on the other hand, were not so voluble and were more capable of responding to general ideas. Hoban indicates that the difference between the responses of "dull" and "bright" pupils to films is a difference of degree, not of kind.

Responses to Elements of Films. Despite all the experimentation in the use of films, little attention has been given to the elementary features of films which produce the responses observed in children. Moreover, there has been little study of the specific responses made to these elements. The suggestion has been advanced that the element of "action" is the one important film factor which is not duplicated by other visual aids. While this may be true, the value of "action" in the abstract is neither conclusively proved nor specifically demonstrated.

An elaborate objective analysis of pupil responses to elements of films was made by Terry (**136**). She analyzed the types of children's responses to the "Yale Chronicles of America" photoplays as recorded in the stenographic report of the class proceedings in the Knowlton and Tilton investigation (**68**). From this analysis Terry found that "adolescent children show a decided preference for historical personages" (**136**:133). Sixty per cent of the children's responses in class were classified as responses to persons. Furthermore she concluded that "inasmuch as there were many scenes in the photoplays depicting action, yet so large a percentage of the responses were about persons, it would seem that children are not able to discriminate between people and people as a part of action" (**136**:133).

Sturmthal and Curtis (**132**) used a new technique in the study of films by obtaining audience response to two motion pictures with the Lazarsfeld-Stanton program analyzer, a device used to study audience responses to radio programs. The subjects press two buttons, one for like and one for dislike, as they view the film, and the results are recorded on a moving tape. Thus, a film can be analyzed sequence by sequence in terms of the likes and dislikes of an audience. The investigators also used a self-administering questionnaire and interview technique to supplement and check their findings. About two hundred subjects were studied as they responded to two films, one a documentary on social conditions, the other a film praising conditions in America used by a large manufacturer as a public-relations film.

The investigators found that the visual element was the most important and the one the audience reacted to; that the motion picture to be successful should in fact move; that there was some decrease in liking for certain sequences when shown again, but that the reaction to repetition of sequences or length of sequences depended entirely on how they were done. Transitions and unnecessary or completely familiar material met with indifference. Common things, on the other hand, were liked when the build-up was good or when they had a symbolic value. Close-ups were liked, especially when they reflected the significance of the film content; and mood was found to be very important in determining audience reaction to films.

With reference to content, the audiences liked scenes of well-being and disliked scenes of deprivation but recalled scenes of deprivation more readily; audiences want a story—they like films where "something is going to happen." The grasp of the meaning in a film was found to be proportionate to its clarity. When a film supported beliefs of the viewers it had high appeal. Most people, however, did not recognize the industrial public relations film for what it was.

Finally, Sturmthal and Curtis stated that they could predict with a high degree of accuracy which sex would like a film or any given sequence in a film after studying one-third of the script. People with higher education liked impersonal scenes more than those with lower education, who preferred scenes with people in their homes and the like.

Responses on Nonfilm Items. A few experimenters differentiated the items of tests used to measure results of instruction into (a) the items the answers to which were found directly or indirectly in the films and (b) the items the answers to which were found in material other than the films.

In Rulon's experiment (120) especially written and illustrated textbooks were used in all experimental groups, and films especially constructed to correlate with the material of the textbooks were presented three times on each unit to the film group. His data show that groups to which the films were not shown scored 15 per cent higher on nonfilm items of the immediate tests than did the groups to which the films were shown. On the retention test, however, this difference disappeared.

Arnspiger (4) found that the gains of nonfilm groups tended to be slightly higher in three of the four natural-science units on items not shown in the film but that in all music units the film groups were slightly higher on those items.

Results secured on experiments in which standardized tests were used (25, 50, 68, 96) showed no significant difference between groups using films in instruction and those using other methods including demonstrations, experiments, supplementary reading, and so on. Since standardized tests are not built to measure particular material covered in a film, the results from these four experiments indicate that the mere use of certain films is no guarantee of increase in all types of learning or of increase in learning in all areas of the subject illustrated by a film. Furthermore, these results and those secured by Davis, Rulon, and Arnspiger indicate that, when the learning activities of the control groups are measured to even a slight extent, the control groups are superior to somewhat the same extent in the mental activity in which they engaged and that the experimental groups are superior in the particular activity in which they engaged. These trends are indicated only in so far as the tests actually measure the results of all types of instruction and the objectives of these types of instruction.

Effectiveness of Films with "Dull" and "Bright" Pupils

The relative effectiveness of motion-picture films with "dull" and "bright" children has been studied by Arnspiger (4), Consitt (26), Helen C. Davis (31), Knowlton and Tilton (68), Mason (87), Mock (93), Terry (136), Westfall (146), Wise (150), Wittich and Fowlkes (152), and Wolfe (156). These investigations were carried on in several different subjects, and the effectiveness of the film was compared with that of several different methods.

The effectiveness of films with children of a given level of "intelligence" must be expected to vary with the subject taught and with the learning outcomes measured. Where effectiveness is considered in terms of verbal responses to information tests, films seem to be relatively more effective for "dull" than for "bright" pupils. Where effectiveness is considered in terms of ability to make verbal generalizations, films are not as effective for "dull" as for "bright" pupils. Where effectiveness is considered in terms of number of discriminations, the films are more effective for "bright" pupils. This result is to be expected because "bright" pupils tend to make more discriminations than do "dull" pupils.

Effectiveness of Films on Various Grade Levels

The effectiveness of the film with respect to various grade levels was investigated directly by Consitt (**26**) and R. L. Davis (**32**), and indirectly by Mead (**88**). Many investigations have been made of the values of the film in different school grades, but these three experimenters are the only ones who have given direct attention to the problem as such. Ramseyer (**109**) found much better retention of changed attitudes for senior high school pupils.

Consitt's conclusions were arrived at on the basis of a few teachers' judgments from a few observations; Davis' data were secured from one four-minute presentation of a single film; and Mead's interpretation is based on unequivalent material and tests. Ramseyer's data, however, were fairly extensive. Although the findings from these studies suggest that films are more effective on the higher grade levels, further controlled experimentation is necessary to establish definite generalizations.

Effectiveness of Verbal Commentary on Film Presentation

The effectiveness of verbal commentary on film presentation has been investigated by a large number of experimenters from several points of view. In most studies, however, the measurement has been in terms of verbal responses of pupils on objective tests of factual information. The data from these investigations, consequently, are applicable only to those types of learning which were measured on the verbal level by these tests. Such outcomes as vividness of imagery and variety of visual detail were ignored by the experimenters.

There is general agreement among the results of investigations by Einbecker, (**40**), McClusky (**81**), McClusky and McClusky (**82**), Mead (**88**), Weber (**145**), and Westfall (**146**), that oral commentary on a film is more effective than presentation of a film without oral commentary or with written titles. Hollis (**62**) found evidence that the film followed by verbal discussion was more effective than the presentation of the film following the discussion. Consitt (**26**) reported agreement with this conclusion.

Clark (**22**) found that silent and sound films were equally effective as instructional methods when results were measured in terms of factual information. Sumstine (**134**), on the other hand, found that verbal accompaniment was positively detrimental in film instruction.

Both these investigations, particularly the latter, are considerably handicapped by limitations of technique of measurement. Hansen (57) reported no reliable difference between teacher and film commentary when the verbalization was identical.

When sound films were compared with demonstrations, Clark found neither of the methods significantly superior although the demonstration was slightly superior as measured by tests of factual information. On the other hand, Eads and Stover (36) found a sound film superior to a demonstration in teaching techniques of diagnosis and remedial treatment in arithmetic to teachers on the college level.

Park (102) studied the vocabulary and comprehension difficulties of sound motion pictures by examining the verbal accompaniments to eight films and analyzing the responses of 640 pupils to these films. He found that children learn some difficult words by viewing a film once, especially if the words are illustrated in the film; that the interest of children in sound motion pictures corresponded to the mean vocabulary level of films. Interest in the film and gain in content knowledge are closely related, and there are close relations between sentence length and gain in knowledge, with the greater gain on the side of the shorter sentence. Park concluded that there should be more study and discussion of films in the classroom prior to and after seeing a film in order to clear up vocabulary difficulties and that difficult words in films should be pointed out and defined by the teacher.

Frequency and Distribution of Projection

The problem of frequency and distribution of film projection has not been investigated as such in the experiments reported. Rulon (120) made a short preliminary investigation to determine the optimal number of projections of film materials, and on the basis of pupil opinion he presented three projections in his experiment on values of sound films in general-science teaching. Eads and Stover (36) found that students who saw a film twice made higher scores on a test of factual information than did students who saw it only once. No satisfactory conclusions on the problem of frequency and distribution of projection are justified on the basis of experimental data reported so far.

Auditorium and Classroom Projection of Films

The problem of use of films in relation to the size of the instructional group was investigated by Knowlton and Tilton (68). It was found that the results on factual tests were consistently higher for the groups who had seen the films in the classroom. Krasker (69) found that the use of educational films is not as effective with large groups in the auditorium as it is with small groups in the classroom.

Utilization and Evaluation

While many of the studies reported in other sections include some material on film utilization and evaluation, recent studies are pointing more in these directions. Wittich and Fowlkes (152) studied three methods of using sound films. The first involved little or no class preparation; the second, a limited amount of anticipation of questions to be answered, difficult words to be noted, etc. The third method repeated method 2 and a day later added oral discussion of prearranged questions and a second viewing of the film. The time taken by the various methods is presented below. The percentages are computed with the time required by the first as the base.

Method 1........35 minutes........100 per cent
Method 2........45 minutes........129 per cent
Method 3........90 minutes........257 per cent

However, when we express the accomplishment of the students as percentages of method 1 (based on a 50-item test on the films) they are:

Method 1..........100
Method 2..........123 to 160
Method 3..........157 to 199

Thus, the extra 29 per cent of time spent on method 2 over method 1 gave 23 to 60 per cent increase in information. But the 157 per cent increase in time of method 3 over method 1 yielded only a gain of 57 to 99 per cent over method 1. Method 3 used twice the time of method 2, but gained only about 25 per cent in accomplishment over method 2. Thus we see that method 2 is the most efficient on the basis of the data presented. No study was made of delayed retention.

Krasker (69) in studying various techniques of using educational films in the classroom found that merely showing the film without preparation of the class is an inefficient method. The best technique seemed to be that of using directing questions.

The American Council study (58) re-emphasized the importance of the teacher in the pattern of teaching with films. The teacher must keep in mind the relationship between knowledge of subject matter, development of student abilities, and procedures in the classroom when using films. The purposes should determine film selection, grade placement of film, and teaching technique. Film utilization involves previewing, class preparation, showing, and follow-up activities.

The study furthered understanding of the problems and techniques of film evaluation. Both the expert panel and teacher and student judgments were used in evaluating films. A comparison of these techniques showed that both teachers and students participating in the classroom use of films rate films somewhat higher than a panel of experts. In addition, teacher and student judgments were quite similar. While some differences were found among teachers' ratings of the same film, these differences were due primarily to the different purposes the teachers wanted the film to serve. The results of the thousands of film evaluations were published in the project's descriptive encyclopedia of films (128).

Other publications of the study were those by the staff of the Tower Hill School of Wilmington, Delaware (129), Cochran (24), Noel (101), Bell, Cain, Lamoreaux, et al. (8), and Brooker and Herrington (12). The American Council's Committee on Motion Pictures in Education has, in addition, published later studies, one by Seaton (121), and one by Noel and Leonard (100).

With reference to using films in the curriculum it was found that films must be dealt with rationally in the classroom, i.e., thought about and studied. Films have a wide range of usefulness—on the average a range of nine grades, with some having a range of fifteen grades—but there is a limit to the number of useful showings of any one film. Significantly, interest generated by films can lead to a variety of activities and forms of expression on the part of students. In addition to conveying information, films are useful in building concepts, developing critical thinking, and forming proper attitudes.

The study indicated that films sometimes conveyed misconceptions to children. The sources of these misconceptions were listed as: (a) lack of pictorial or verbal orientation, (b) poor casting and acting, (c) overcondensation, (d) distortion of events, and (e) pictorial omission of elements mentioned in the titles or verbal accompaniment.

The Theatrical Motion Picture

The effect of the theatrical film on the values, information, and character of children and young people has long engaged the attention of parents and teachers. Each week some 85,000,000 attendances are chalked up at the box offices of approximately 15,000 motion-picture theaters.

The Payne-Fund Studies

In 1929, a committee of research workers, supported by the Payne Fund, began a four-year investigation of theatrical motion pictures and their influence. This was the first large-scale study of the effect of mass media upon children and young people. Five areas of effect were studied: information, attitudes, emotions, health, and conduct. The conclusions have been summarized by Charters (21).

Some of the specific findings of the Payne-Fund studies are noteworthy.

1. Dale (29) discovered that, contrary to the data then available from the motion-picture industry, children did form a sizeable part of the total motion-picture audience. He notes that 2 per cent of the audience was under the age of 7; 11.8 per cent were 7-13 years of age; and 22.1 per cent were between the ages of 14 and 20. Boys and girls in the upper grades and high school averaged one movie a week, and children in the primary grades about one movie in every two weeks.

   A study made ten years later by Brother Urban H. Fleege (44), which included 2,000 high-school boys and girls throughout the East and Midwest, duplicated almost exactly the earlier findings reported by Dale.

2. Children acquire considerable information from attending the movies. For children in the second and third grades the average score on an information test was 60 per cent of the average score of adults. For children in the ninth and tenth grades the relative standing was 90 per cent. Retests after six weeks showed a smaller loss for children than for adults. Moreover, "general information presented incorrectly by the pictures is frequently accepted as valid unless the incongruity is quite apparent" (61).

3. Motion pictures have definite, lasting effects on the social attitudes of children: a number of pictures pertaining to the same issue may have a cumulative effect on attitude (105). The influence of a picture is specific for a given child and a given movie. The same picture may influence different children in distinctly opposite directions (124). Data gathered by the American Council study (58) also support this conclusion.

4. With reference to the influence of movies upon conduct, Blumer (9) stated that "they (motion pictures) may challenge what other institutions take for granted. The schemes of conduct which they present may not only fill gaps left by the school, by the home, and by the church, but they may also cut athwart the standards and values which these latter institutions seek to inculcate. What is presented as entertainment, with perhaps no thought of challenging established values, may be accepted as sanctioned conduct and so enter into conflict with certain of these values. This is peculiarly likely in the case of motion pictures because they often

present the extremes as if they were the norm. For the young movie-goer little discrimination is possible. He probably could not *understand* or even *read* a sophisticated book, but he can *see* the thing in the movies and be stirred and possibly misled. This is likely to be true chiefly among those with least education and sophisticated experience" (pp. 196-97).
5. Emotional stimulation as measured by the psychogalvanic technique varies widely for different individuals. "The most extreme stimulation by the motion picture seems to center near the age of sixteen years, where scenes of conflict often gave the maximal response and where love scenes and suggestive incidents quite consistently gave the maximal reaction" (35).
6. Seeing some films "induces a disturbance of relaxed, recuperative sleep in children to a degree which, if indulged with sufficient frequency, can be regarded as detrimental to normal health and growth." Some children should be permitted to attend only carefully selected films (114).

Criticism of Payne-Fund Studies

The Payne-Fund studies have been vigorously criticized by Adler (3), and his criticism has been popularized by Moley (94). Adler produced his criticism at the request of and with funds supplied by "representatives of the motion-picture producers." Using his absolutist Aristotelian and Thomistic philosophy as a base, Adler challenges the Payne-Fund studies on the grounds that (*a*) the research workers were not Thomists, (*b*) the so-called prudent man was not aided by their findings in his life mission of censoring the art the nonprudent will be permitted to see, (*c*) the social sciences cannot be considered scientific, and (*d*) the research workers went beyond their evidence.

An example of the level of the criticism used by Adler may be found in this statement about one of the investigators: "No art, no matter how bad, could be so directly evil in influence as the kind of thinking and . . . teaching which Dr. . . . represents" (3:302). Preceding the criticism of the Payne-Fund studies is a long philosophical discussion of the cinema as viewed through Thomistic philosophy. This discussion establishes to Adler's satisfaction that the prudent man in our society should, while not interfering with the artist, keep the artist's product away from society if he (the prudent man) deems it not acceptable to the masses. Moley interprets the prudent man as the Hays-Johnston office of the motion-picture industry (**94:61**).

Finally, Adler admits that, while motion pictures may not harm mature persons, they are probably harmful to children. He specifically states that, in the case of adults, "there would seem to be a reasonable presumption that the arts are unable to corrupt mature persons" (3:180). With reference to children he says, "There is a reasonable presumption in favor of the proposition that the arts are able to corrupt children and youth because of their instability and susceptibility to influence" (3:180). This latter statement seems to be little different from the findings and interpretations of the Payne-Fund studies about the effect of motion pictures on children and youth which Adler criticizes elsewhere. Adler's criticism is answered by Cressey in an article which challenges his basic philosophical position (27). Cressey attacks Adler on the grounds that (a) his criticism is not guided by objectivity but prejudice; (b) he uses St. Thomas as irrefutable evidence with which to evaluate contemporary research; (c) he has an "amazing ignorance of the social sciences, especially sociology, and a very evident prejudice against them" (27:324); (d) he misrepresents the facts. Cressey's final evaluation of Adler's criticism indicates that five of the Payne-Fund studies were never challenged and that the other five were criticized on the questionable grounds noted above.

Other Studies of Theatrical Motion-Pictures

William Lewin (76) reports the results of his work in a nation-wide study of the teaching of motion-picture discrimination in the schools. Among his significant conclusions are the following: (a) The habits of high-school students in relation to the selection of movies can be significantly improved through the guidance of English teachers. (b) Nearly three-quarters of the students in American high schools have never prepared a theme or talk on a photoplay in connection with their school work, but if given the opportunity students are greatly interested in such assignments. (c) Pupils can learn standards for evaluating current films and can readily follow criteria acceptable to English teachers.

Alice P. Sterner (131) investigated the attractiveness of the medium of communication (radio, magazines, comic strips, movies, etc.) and the interest of the subject matter included. She concluded that, "It is evidently the content of the medium, not the technique of presentation, which leads many young people to spend so much time in these activities" (p. 60). In reference to the motion pictures she says: "Apparently sex, grade, intelligence, and socioeconomic status have little influence upon pupils' choices of specific motion pictures. Generally speaking, a teacher can expect that over 50 per cent of the class will have seen the ten most popular pictures" (p. 41). Miss

Sterner's bibliography includes brief descriptions of studies made by Perry (**104**), Abbott (**1**), Eaton (**37**), Mitchell (**92**), Sullenger (**133**), Dale (**29**), Edman (**38**), Lohmann (**77**), Witty, Garfield, and Brink (**154**), Smith (**126**), and Witty and Coomer (**153**).

FIELD TRIPS

One of the developments in the audio-visual field relates to the community as a resource for teaching materials. Early studies often evaluated a field trip as contrasted with reading materials, a film, etc. Later studies have put much more stress on making available a variety of resource materials for class use. A significant movement for the development of such resource materials has focused around the Committee on Southern Regional Studies and Education which has headquarters at the University of North Carolina. This new approach to resource materials will probably displace the previous concern for discovering the value of one type of resource as contrasted with another. Our experimental concern in the future is likely to lie in studies of integrated use of all resources.

Some of the more recent resource studies are reported by Young (**162**) as those of Edson (**39**), Caplan (**18**), Noe (**99**), Mason (**86**), and Fraser (**45**). The last is especially significant in reporting reliable gains in information, understanding, skills, and attitudes as outcomes from a study excursion undertaken by twelfth-grade pupils.

The scientific study of field trips (school journeys or excursions) is extremely limited. Price (**107**) presented data from 268 elementary schools scattered throughout the United States concerning the number and type of field trips. The rank of frequency of types for 122 of these schools, each of which included the entire eight grades, was (*a*) museums, (*b*) civic buildings, (*c*) libraries, (*d*) urban industries, (*e*) higher schools, (*f*) rural industries, (*g*) newspapers, (*h*) banks, and (*i*) commercial offices. When these schools were asked to indicate whether or not these field trips were of high, medium, low, or no value, more than 75 per cent of all the principals rated these activities as of high value. None of the trips was rated as of low value or no value.

Atyeo (**5**) studied the effect of excursions on an experimental group of twenty-six high-school pupils in ancient-history classes. A control group, matched on the basis of age, intelligence quotient, and performance on standardized history tests, was taught with the same methods excluding only visits to various museums. Atyeo concluded that the excursion technique is superior to class discussion for teaching material requiring comparisons and knowledge of concrete objects which can be more easily visualized with the aid of experiences which the excursion offered and that class discussion yields better results for material for which memory is important—such as dates, dimensions, and items usually presented in list or outline form in notebook or textbook. Although these conclusions may be reasonable, the experimental data presented by Atyeo do not appear to warrant them.

Some other evidence also indicates that the outcomes of field trips include changed or augmented interests, attitudes, points of view, and other controls of conduct not measured by typical achievement tests. Abraham (2) in his analysis of the effectiveness of a visit to Washington, D. C., by a group of high-school students presented certain observations concerning pupil responses. The basic value, he concluded, of this particular journey was represented not so much by a gain in information on political and economic issues as by an enhanced interest in these matters arising from the vividness with which they were presented in direct contact with legislators and other public officials. The total effect of the visit was to increase esteem for the people who make, administer, and interpret the laws of the land.

Atyeo (5) also studied the relative effects of field trips and regular class procedure upon later interests. The experimental group showed an increased desire to visit the countries studied and to visit places in the vicinity which held some relationship to the subject matter covered; the discussion group expressed a stronger interest in reading books relating to the material than in making excursions. On the basis of a many-sided evaluation of a trip which fifteen selected boys and girls of the eleventh grade of Lincoln School made to the coal-mining area of West Virginia, Raths, (110:208) expressed the following conclusion: "What has been collected suggests that carefully planned direct experiences may result in clarifying the beliefs which students hold; it suggests also that greater allegiance to human values, firmer faith in democratic principles, a more flexible outlook which considers solutions to social problems as tentative and not arbitrary are some of the desirable outcomes which may come from educational experiences similar to the West Virginia trip."

Clark (23) identified some of the contributions that the field trip could make to four six-grade units: Egypt, printing, transportation, and communication. Children who went on the field trip recorded for each unit a greater variety of items which especially interested them. They also listed with greater frequency a wider variety of activities in which they stated they would like to engage after the unit was finished.

Still Pictures, Filmstrips, and Lantern Slides

Williams (**148**) studied the preferences of 939 fifth-, sixth-, and seventh-grade children for a collection of portraits on exhibits including thirty-two oil paintings, twenty-eight colored prints, and a number of miniatures, tintypes, and daguerreotypes. The basic conclusions include the following: (*a*) there is a marked tendency for the majority of children to like the same pictures; (*b*) children like pictures of people, places, or incidents with which they are familiar; (*c*) pictures of things unfamiliar to the children but about which they have read and heard are popular; (*d*) pictures which tell a story appeal to children to some extent; (*e*) children like pictures in which there are a few large, easily distinguished objects in the foreground; (*f*) instruction influences only to a small extent a person's liking for certain pictures; (*g*) most children show a tendency to choose pictures which are examples of good painting.

There are several studies of pupil interests and other aspects of their reactions to still pictures. In a study of the effects of repeated showing of reproductions of paintings to pupils in Grades VII and IX, Mendenhall and Mendenhall (**90**) reported that the pupils expressed distinct preferences relative to the pictures shown and that these preferences tended to be intensified as the showings were repeated. The pictures which appealed most were those of a representative type, conventional in content, style, and color; natural scenes were preferred to portraits and figures (**90**:69).

Buswell (**15**) studied the nature of the eye movements of two hundred individuals as they looked at fifty-five pictures of various types. Among his basic conclusions is this statement: "The directions given prior to looking at a picture have a marked influence upon the character of perception." Terman and Merrill (**135**) reported that the reactions of immature and mature persons in viewing still pictures vary from enumeration at the simplest level to description at the second level and interpretation at the highest level. Shaffer (**122**) noted in his study of the cartoon a very sharp increase in the ability to interpret between the ages of twelve and fifteen. Gates (**49**) has shown that children vary greatly in their ability to perceive facial expressions from pictures and that there is a general improvement in this ability with increasing age.

Young (**162**) cites several studies on still pictures used for instruction in social-science courses. Badley (**6**), Park and Stephenson (**103**), and Waddle (**142**) studied picture magazines, stereographs, slides, and flat pictures, respectively. In general, it was found that these materials were effective means of teaching and learning. Stenius (**130**) reports studies by Vauter (**140**) on handmade lantern slides and Halbert (**53**, see also **54**) on illustrations in books that would indicate significant values for these materials. Zyve (**163**) analyzed the relative effectiveness of lantern slides as a device for teaching arithmetic combinations as compared with the use of the blackboard. Under conditions existing in this experiment, she concluded that: "Two days of teaching arithmetic combinations with the lantern slides gave approximately the same results that three days' teaching gave when using blackboard presentations."

Katz (**65**) studied the preferences of elementary-school children for traditional and modern paintings, using about 2,500 subjects from five elementary schools varying in socioeconomic background. He paired sixty-four accepted traditional paintings with the same number of modern paintings which had been accepted by eleven competent judges. The paintings were then made into kodachrome slides (for description of this technique see [**66**]) and shown to the children.

He found that elementary-school children prefer traditional to modern paintings by a ratio of three to two. The high degree of preference for modern paintings as compared with current adult standards indicates a great difference between what children like and what adults think is "good." Katz also found that the children's preferences for traditional paintings increased from the second through the sixth grade where the preferences became more stable. He concluded that adult standards for paintings were gradually enforced on children. There were variations in preferences expressed at the different schools, indicating a relationship between preferences and socioeconomic backgrounds. For subjects of portraiture the traditional was preferred, while for landscape subjects the modern was preferred.

Museum Materials

An experiment by Bloomberg (see **108**) dealt with preparation of children for museum visits. The most successful plan for the brightest group was one in which the museum instructor went to the schoolroom to present the background one week preceding the class visit to the museum. The most effective plan for the medium group, however, was stimulation of children by pertinent questions. The investigator reported that in all the various teaching plans too much material had been presented at a single lesson. She indicated that, if accuracy in observation is an important aim, it is better to attempt less and secure greater clarity. Her further conclusion was the need for less instruction by the teacher and more investigation on the part of the children.

On the basis of experiments carried on in co-operation with the Buffalo Museum of Science, Robinson (see **108**) concluded: (*a*) A silent-reading lesson and a test on the material read, not more than a week prior to the visit, had a marked positive effect on the amount known by the children at the end of the museum visit. (*b*) The test on the silent-reading lesson is a valuable teaching device, and the effect of it is evidenced in the amount the children know at the end of their museum visit. (*c*) The use of pictorial materials and the game-card technique in conjunction with the silent-reading material increases the effectiveness of the preparation for the museum visit. (*d*) The preparation for the museum visit is more effective when it occurs one day before the visit than when it occurs two days, one week, or two weeks before the visit. There is evidence that the preparation has some effect even though it precedes the museum visit by as much as two weeks, but the conservative estimate is that an interval longer than one week reduces the effectiveness of the preparation to the vanishing point.

Studies (see **108**) of the relative effectiveness of a lecture during the museum visit and a discussion led to the conclusion that discussion methods were superior to lecture methods for children of the seventh and eighth grades. Fifth-grade pupils, however, learned more when the museum instructor lectured to them in the museum halls than they did with other methods.

Powel (**106**) reports at length on a co-operative study developed under a grant from the General Education Board in which art museums in five cities participated. The various museums developed experimental programs serving the needs of schools and of school children in out-of-school situations. These programs were evaluated at the end of a three-year period.

The study is descriptive rather than statistical, and several recommendations were made to schools as a result of the experiment. These included: (*a*) Schools must provide better facilities for exhibits and displays. (*b*) The scheduling problem, particularly on the secondary level, must be solved so that much greater use may be made of museum materials not in the school. (*c*) Each school should have some person responsible for the museum program. (*d*) There must be greater emphasis upon teacher education in the use of museum materials, and teachers should make known the needs of the schools to the museums. (*e*) The schools must eventually develop their own visual agencies which will produce materials and work co-operatively with existing museums.

The study also made two recommendations to museums: (a) that museums begin to work up displays and exhibits suitable to school children of all ages tied in with school programs, and (b) that museums begin to develop programs appealing to children on an out-of-school basis to compete with less desirable use of leisure time.

Graphic Materials

Graphs are of two types, conventional and pictorial. The conventional graph uses the bar, the circle, and the line. The pictorial graph presents quantitative data by means of symbols bearing resemblance to the object itself—partly conventionalized, but sometimes an exact pictorial representation of the object itself. Grain may be represented by means of bags, electricity by means of an electric-light bulb, unemployment by means of a conventionalized figure of a man in a dejected, slumping position. Attempts are being made to develop an international set of symbols for pictorial graphs. These international symbols have been called "isotypes" and were developed by Otto Neurath.

Only meager research has been reported upon the use of graphic materials and the abilities required to interpret them. Thomas (**137**) made a study of the ability of fourth-, fifth-, sixth-, and seventh-grade pupils in the reading of circle, two-dimension diagram, horizontal-bar, multiple-picture, and line graphs. She concluded that slow fourth-grade children derive little meaning from graphs, but superior fourth-grade children understand the meaning of simple graphs and can read simple facts from them. She also found that picture graphs, two-dimension diagrams, and circle graphs are the easiest for pupils of all grades to read while line graphs are the hardest. Washburne (**143**) concluded that the bar graph is the form most favorable to the recall of relative amounts (static comparisons) when the comparisons called for involve a fair degree of difficulty.

Wrightstone (**158**) made a study of junior and senior high school pupils to discover the relative effectiveness of pictorial graphs as compared with the more conventional graphs using bars, circles, and lines. Pictorial graphs proved slightly more effective. When individuals were asked their preference for one form versus the other, the attitude of most was favorable to the pictorial type.

More research is needed on the use of graphs to convey quantitative information. There is reason to believe that the effectiveness of pictorial graphs in this relationship is exaggerated.

Young (**162**) reports studies in the use of graphic materials in the social studies by McLeese (**84**), Thompson (**138**), Wise (**150**), and Wrightstone (**159**). With the exception of Wrightstone, all the investigators studied the use of maps only. The results show in general that (*a*) maps are effective means of developing certain concepts, particularly in geography and history, and that (*b*) map-reading must be carefully taught. Wrightstone (**159**) found a gradual growth in the reading of graphs and maps from the seventh through the twelfth grade.

RADIO AND RECORDINGS

There have been several excellent summaries of the results of research on the effectiveness of radio and recordings in education published since 1940. Wrightstone and the staff of the Evaluation of School Broadcasts Project at Ohio State University (**160**) summarized all research done up until 1939. This work was then expanded by Reid and Day (**111**) to include all completed studies of the Project as well as additional research through half of 1942. Woelfel and Tyler (**155**) have combined an analysis of research results with a textbook on radio education which supplies much information on the status of research in radio and recordings up to the present time. If to this list is added the report of the Wisconsin study (**149**) the reader has a list of references which will furnish most of the research information on educational radio and recordings that is available.

It should be noted that research in the use and effectiveness of radio is not limited to educational institutions or problems. The major radio networks and some of the larger stations have their own research departments. Much of their material is unpublished. Advertising agencies and advertisers as well as broadcasters make use of professional research organizations to obtain information about the radio audience, the success of certain broadcast advertising campaigns, and the like. Special organizations like the Bureau of Applied Social Research at Columbia University and the Institute of Public Opinion at Princeton are engaged in radio research. The growing discipline of "communications," or the study of the mass media, is developing its own research criteria, techniques, and results. Education, when considered in its broadest aspects, must take into account the results of these studies as well as the more narrow researches devoted strictly to the problems of the school, the classroom, or the psychology of learning.

References concerning this latter research may be found in two special issues of the *Journal of Applied Psychology* (**63** and **64**), in the two volumes of Lazarsfeld and Stanton (**74** and **75**), in Lazarsfeld and Field (**43**), in Lazarsfeld (**73**), and in Chappell and Hooper (**20**). Almost any issue of the *Public Opinion Quarterly* will contain recent studies made in the general field of radio. Two other studies may be of special interest in that they deal with the psychology of radio: Cantril and Allport (**16**), and Cantril, Gaudet, and Herzog (**17**).

Reid and Day, in their excellent and critical analysis of educational radio research (**111**), made certain generalizations which are as valid today as they were in 1942. At that time they wrote:

> Despite the mediocre quality of some of the studies, despite the insignificance of some of the findings, despite the lack of co-ordination between investigators and between investigations, a synthesis of the field permits four generalizations: (*a*) that there are on the air today many broadcasts highly enjoyable and educationally valuable to pupils and teachers alike; (*b*) that comparatively few teachers use this curriculum resource made available through technological progress; (*c*) that radio broadcasts, like motion pictures, books, magazines, and other teaching aids, can be used effectively in the achievement of educational objectives; and (*d*) that the possibilities of radio—as a medium of communication, as an agency of education, as a form of art and literature—have only been touched as yet in the public schools (p. 316).

It may be questioned that the situation in the general field of radio research can be summarized in Reid and Day's succinct terms. But this much may be said: The American people spend a great deal of time listening to the radio; in many cases their behavior is changed and guided by what they hear. Considering the over-all program balance of American radio as analyzed in the famous "Bluebook" of the Federal Communications Commission (**42**), a great problem has been presented to American educators. This is the problem of developing discriminating, critical listeners—an absolute necessity for the survival of our democracy in the Atomic Age.

References

1. Abbott, Mary A. "A Sampling of High-School Likes and Dislikes in Motion Pictures," *Secondary Education*, VI (March, 1937), 74-76.
2. Abraham, H. J. "Let's Interview the Government," *Educational Method*, XVII (October, 1937), 16-19.
3. Adler, Mortimer J. *Art and Prudence*. New York: Longmans, Green & Co., 1937.

4. ARNSPIGER, V. C. *Measuring the Effectiveness of Sound Pictures as Teaching Aids.* Teachers College Contributions to Education, No. 565. New York: Teachers College, Columbia University, 1933.
5. ATYEO, H. C. *The Excursion as a Teaching Technique.* Teachers College Contributions to Education, No. 761. New York: Teachers College, Columbia University, 1939.
6. BADLEY, T. T. "An Analysis and Evaluation of Picture Magazines as Collateral Material in the Social-Studies Program of the Secondary School." Master's Thesis, Ohio State University, 1938.
7. BARTLETT, F. C. *Remembering.* New York: Macmillan Co., 1932.
8. BELL, REGINALD, and OTHERS. *Motion Pictures in a Modern Curriculum: A Report on the Use of Films in the Santa Barbara Schools.* Washington: American Council on Education, 1941.
9. BLUMER, HERBERT. *Movies and Conduct.* New York: Macmillan Co., 1933.
10. BORING, E. G. *Sensation and Perception in the History of Experimental Psychology.* New York: D. Appleton-Century Co., 1942.
11. BROOKER, F. E. *Training Films in Industry.* U. S. Office of Education, Bulletin, 1946, No. 13. Washington: Government Printing Office, 1946.
12. BROOKER, F. E., and HERRINGTON, EUGENE. *Students Make Motion Pictures: A Report on Film Production in the Denver Schools.* Washington: American Council on Education, 1941.
13. BROWNELL, W. A., and CARPER, DORIS V. *Learning the Multiplication Combinations.* Durham, North Carolina: Duke University Press, 1943.
14. BROWNELL, W. A.; KUEHNER, K. G.; REIN, W. C. *Learning as Reorganization.* Duke University Research Studies in Education, No. 3. Durham, North Carolina: Duke University Press, 1939.
15. BUSWELL, G. T. *How People Look at Pictures.* Chicago: University of Chicago Press, 1935.
16. CANTRIL, HADLEY, and ALLPORT, GORDON W. *The Psychology of Radio.* New York: Harper & Bros., 1935.
17. CANTRIL, HADLEY; GAUDET, HAZEL; and HERZOG, HERTA. *The Invasion from Mars.* Princeton, New Jersey: Princeton University Press, 1940.
18. CAPLAN, R. P. "A Study of Available Excursions in and around Philadelphia for the Teaching of Junior High School Social Studies." Master's Thesis, Temple University, 1937.
19. CHAMBERS, M. M. *Opinions on Gains for American Education from Wartime Armed Forces Training.* Washington: American Council on Education, 1946.
20. CHAPPELL, MATTHEW N., and HOOPER, C. E. *Radio Audience Measurement.* New York: Stephen Daye, 1944.
21. CHARTERS, W. W. *Motion Pictures and Youth.* New York: Macmillan Co., 1933.
22. CLARK, C. C. "Sound Motion Pictures as an Aid in Classroom Teaching." Doctor's Dissertation, New York University, 1932.

23. CLARK, ELLA C. "An Experimental Evaluation of the School Excursion," *Journal of Experimental Education*, XII (September, 1943), 10-19.
24. COCHRAN, BLAKE. *Films on War and American Policy*. Washington: American Council on Education, 1940.
25. COCKRUM, A. E. "An Experimental Study of the Motion Picture Film as an Aid to Teaching General Science." Master's Thesis, University of Illinois, 1932.
26. CONSITT, FRANCIS. *The Value of Films in History Teaching*. London: G. Bell & Sons, Ltd., 1931.
27. CRESSEY, PAUL G. "A Study in Practical Philosophy," *Journal of Higher Education*, IX, (June, 1938), 319-28.
28. DALE, EDGAR. "Analyzing the Movie Market," *Educational Research Bulletin*, XVI (November 10, 1937), 212-16.
29. ————. *Children's Attendance at Motion Pictures*. New York: Macmillan Co., 1935.
30. DASH, A. J. "Effectiveness of Sound Film in Changing Knowledge of and Interest in Chemistry." Master's Thesis, College of the City of New York, 1935.
31. DAVIS, HELEN C. "Specific Values of Educational Films Used as Supplementary Aids." Doctor's Dissertation, University of Chicago, 1932.
32. DAVIS, R. L. "The Application of Motion Pictures to Education." Doctor's Dissertation, New York University, 1935.
33. DE BERNARDIS, AMO, and BROWN, J. W. "Study of Teacher Skills and Knowledge Necessary for the Use of Audio-visual Aids," *Elementary School Journal*, XLVI (June, 1946), 550-56.
34. DOOB, LEONARD W. *Public Opinion and Propaganda*. New York: Henry Holt & Co., 1948.
35. DYSINGER, W. S. and RUCKMICK, C. A. *The Emotional Responses of Children to the Motion-Picture Situation*. New York: Macmillan Co., 1933.
36. EADS, LAURA K., and STOVER, E. M. "Talking Pictures in Teacher Training." Unpublished report of an experiment carried on with the co-operation of Ralph B. Spence, Goodwin Watson, Ina Sartorius, and Margaret Barker of Teachers College, Columbia University, 1932.
37. EATON, REBA E. "Motion Picture Preferences of Passaic High School." On file in English Seminar Room, Teachers College, Columbia University, 1929.
38. EDMAN, MARION. "Attendance of School Pupils and Adults at Moving Pictures," *School Review*, XLVIII (December, 1940), 753-63.
39. EDSON, HAROLD. "The Community Resources of Durand, Wisconsin, for Use in Teaching the Social Studies." Master's Thesis, University of Minnesota, 1939.
40. EINBECKER, W. F. "Comparison of Verbal Accompaniments to Films," *School Review*, XLI (March, 1933), 185-92.

41. EXPERIMENTAL SECTION, RESEARCH BRANCH, INFORMATION AND EDUCATION DIVISION, U. S. WAR DEPARTMENT. *Experimental Studies of Army Education Films*, 1948.
42. FEDERAL COMMUNICATIONS COMMISSION. *Public Service Responsibility of Broadcast Licensees*. Washington: Government Printing Office, 1946.
43. FIELD, HARRY, and LAZARSFELD, PAUL F., *The People Look at Radio*. Chapel Hill, North Carolina: University of North Carolina Press, 1946.
44. FLEEGE, BROTHER URBAN H. "Movies as an Influence in the Life of the Modern Adolescent," *Catholic Educational Review*, XLIII (June, 1945), 336-52.
45. FRASER, J. A. *Outcomes of a Study Excursion*. Teachers College Contributions to Education, No. 778. New York: Teachers College, Columbia University, 1939.
46. FREEMAN, F. N., and HOEFER, CAROLYN. "An Experimental Study of the Influence of Motion-picture Films on Behavior," *Journal of Educational Psychology*, XXII (September, 1931), 411-25.
47. FREEMAN, F. N.; REEDER, E. H.; THOMAS, JEAN A. "An Experimental Study of the Influence of Motion-picture Film Which Consists Largely of Tables, Maps, and Charts, as a Means of Teaching Facts or Giving Abstract Information." In F. N. Freeman (Editor), *Visual Education*, pp. 258-74. Chicago: University of Chicago Press, 1924.
48. FREEMAN, F. N.; SHAW, LENA A.; and WALKER, D. E. "The Use of a Motion-Picture Film To Teach Position and Penholding in Handwriting." In F. N. Freeman (Editor), *Visual Education*, pp. 282-309. Chicago: University of Chicago Press, 1924.
49. GATES, GEORGIANA S. "An Experimental Study of the Growth of Social Perception," *Journal of Educational Psychology*, XIV (November, 1923), 449-61.
50. GATTO, F. M. "Experimental Studies on the Use of Visual Aids in the Teaching of Geography," *Pittsburgh Schools*, VIII (1933), 60-110.
51. GOLDEN, N. D. "The Latest Survey of College and High-School Motion-picture Equipment," *Educational Screen*, XX (March, 1941), 115-17.
52. GOODMAN, D. J. "The Comparative Effectiveness of Pictorial Teaching Materials." Doctor's Dissertation, New York University, 1942.
53. HALBERT, MARIE G. *An Experimental Study of Children's Understanding of Instructional Materials*. University of Kentucky, Bureau of School Service Bulletin, Vol. XV, No. 4, 1943.
54. ———. "The Teaching Value of Illustrated Books," *American School Board Journal*, CXLIII (May, 1944), 43-44.
55. HANSEN, H. R. "Costs of Audio-visual Materials," *Educational Screen*, XXVI (June, 1947), 306-8.
56. HANSEN, JOHN E. "The Effect of Educational Motion Pictures upon the Retention of Informational Learning," *Journal of Experimental Education*, II (September, 1933), 1-4.

57. ———. "The Verbal Accompaniment of the Educational Film: The Recorded Voice versus the Voice of the Classroom Teacher," *Journal of Experimental Education*, V (September, 1936), 1-6.
58. HOBAN, C. F., JR. *Focus on Learning*. Washington: American Council on Education, 1942.
59. ———. *Movies That Teach*. New York: Dryden Press, 1946.
60. HOEFER, CAROLYN, and KEITH, EDNA. "An Experimental Comparison of the Methods of Oral and Film Instruction in the Field of Health Education." In F. N. Freeman (Editor), *Visual Education*, pp. 346-76. Chicago: University of Chicago Press, 1924.
61. HOLADAY, P. W., and STODDARD, G. D. *Getting Ideas from the Movies*. New York: Macmillan Co., 1933.
62. HOLLIS, A. P. "The Effectiveness of the Motion Picture, Demonstration by the Teacher, and Oral Instruction in Teaching Cooking." In F. N. Freeman (Editor), *Visual Education*, pp. 339-41. Chicago: University of Chicago Press, 1924.
63. *Journal of Applied Psychology* (whole issue), "Progress in Radio Research," XXIV (December, 1940), 661-872.
64. *Journal of Applied Psychology* (whole issue), "Radio Research and Applied Psychology," XXIII (February, 1939), 1-206.
65. KATZ, ELIAS. "Children's Preferences for Traditional and Modern Paintings." Doctor's Dissertation, Teachers College, Columbia University, 1942.
66. ———. "Testing Preferences with 2" x 2" Slides," *Educational Screen*, XXI (October, 1942), 301-18.
67. KAUFFMAN, H. M. "Audio-visual Programs in State Universities," *Educational Screen*, XXV (October, 1946), 442.
68. KNOWLTON, D. C., and TILTON, J. W. *Motion Pictures in History Teaching*. New Haven, Connecticut: Yale University Press, 1929.
69. KRASKER, ABRAHAM. "A Critical Analysis of the Use of Educational Motion Pictures by Two Methods." Doctor's Dissertation, Boston University, 1941.
70. LACY, J. V. "The Relative Value of Motion Pictures as an Educational Agency," *Teachers College Record*, XX (November, 1919), 452-65.
71. LARSON, L. C. "Trends in Audio-visual Instruction," *Educational Screen*, XXII (June, 1943), 197-99.
72. LARSON, L. C. "Trends in the Distribution and Use of the 16-mm. Sound Film for Educational Purposes," *Proceedings of the National University Extension Association*, XXVI (1943), 21-24.
73. LAZARSFELD, PAUL F., *Radio and the Printed Page*. New York: Duell, Sloane & Pearce, 1940.
74. LAZARSFELD, PAUL F., and STANTON, FRANK N. *Radio Research, 1941*. New York: Duell, Sloane & Pearce, 1941.
75. ———. *Radio Research, 1942-1943*. New York: Duell, Sloane & Pearce, 1944.

76. LEWIN, WILLIAM. *Photoplay Appreciation in American High Schools.* English Monograph No. 2, National Council of Teachers of English. New York: D. Appleton-Century Co., 1934.
77. LOHMANN, PAULINE. *Moving Pictures.* Washington: Eastern High School, 1941.
78. LUCKIESH, MATTHEW. *Light, Vision, and Seeing.* New York: D. Van Nostrand, 1944.
79. MACLATCHY, JOSEPHINE. "Bexley Reading Study," *Educational Research Bulletin*, XXV (September, 1946), 141-68.
80. McCALLUM, W. J. *Audio-visual Aids in the Secondary Schools of the Southern Association.* Doctor's Dissertation, George Peabody College of Education, 1946.
81. McCLUSKY, F. D. "Comparisons of Different Methods of Visual Instruction." In F. N. Freeman (Editor), *Visual Education*, pp. 83-166. Chicago: University of Chicago Press, 1924.
82. McCLUSKY, F. D., and McCLUSKY, H. Y. "Comparison of Motion Pictures, Slides, Stereographs, and Demonstration as a Means of Teaching How To Make a Reed Mat and a Pasteboard Box." In F. N. Freeman (Editor), *Visual Education*, pp. 310-34. Chicago: University of Chicago Press, 1924.
83. ———. "Comparison of Six Modes of Presentation of the Subject Matter Contained in a Film on the Iron and Steel Industry and One on Lumbering in the North Woods." In F. N. Freeman (Editor), *Visual Education*, pp. 229-57. Chicago: University of Chicago Press, 1924.
84. McLEESE, MARY J. "An Analysis of the Map Concepts Used in a Fifth-Grade Unit in Geography." Master's Thesis, University of Iowa, 1939.
85. McPHERSON, H. M. "The Organization, Administration, and Support of Visual Instruction in California." Doctor's Dissertation, University of California, 1939.
86. MASON, E. W. "The World Outside," *Social Education*, I (March, 1937), 173-76.
87. MASON, W. L. "A Study of the Status of Motion Pictures in Education." Master's Thesis, University of Virginia, 1934.
88. MEAD, C. D. "Visual versus Teaching Methods: An Experiment." *Educational Administration and Supervision*, XIII (1927), 505-18.
89. MEARS, J. W. "The Present Status of Visual Education in Texas." Master's Thesis, University of Texas, 1940.
90. MENDENHALL, J. E., and MENDENHALL, MARCIA E. *The Influence of Familiarity upon Children's Preferences for Pictures and Poems.* Lincoln School Research Studies. New York: Teachers College, Columbia University, 1933.
91. MILES, J. R., and SPAIN, C. R. *Audio-visual Aids in the Armed Services.* Washington: American Council on Education, 1947.
92. MITCHELL, ALICE M. *Children and Movies.* Chicago: University of Chicago Press, 1929.

93. Mock, Alpha A. "The Relative Values of the Use of Motion Pictures with Bright and Dull Children." Master's Thesis, University of Southern California, 1929.
94. Moley, Raymond. *Are We Movie Made?* New York: Macy-Masius, 1938.
95. Molyneaux, Mary L. "Audio-visual Aids: A Survey," *Educational Screen*, XXII (January-February, 1944), 11-15, 65-68.
96. Mount, J. N. "The Learning Value of Motion Pictures in High-school Physics as Compared to the Use of Supplementary Textbooks." Master's Thesis, University of Washington, 1931.
97. National Council of Public Morals, Cinema Commission of Inquiry. *The Cinema in Education.* Edited by James Marchant. London: G. Allen & Unwin, Ltd., 1925.
98. N. E. A., Research Division. *Audio-visual Education in City-School Systems.* Research Bulletin of the National Education Association, Vol. XXIV. Washington: Research Division of the National Education Association, 1946.
99. Noe, Robert. "A Study of Available Excursions in Bucks County for the Teaching of American History and Economic Civics." Master's Thesis, Temple University, 1937.
100. Noel, Elizabeth G., and Leonard, J. P. *Foundations for Teacher Education in Audio-visual Instruction.* Washington: American Council on Education, 1947.
101. Noel, F. W. *Projecting Motion Pictures in the Classroom.* Washington: American Council on Education, 1940.
102. Park, Joe. *A Study of the Vocabulary and Comprehension Difficulties of Sound Motion Pictures.* Doctor's Dissertation, University of Michigan, 1943.
103. Park, Joe, and Stephenson, Ruth. "A Teaching Experiment with Visual Aids," *Education*, LVIII (April, 1938), 498-500.
104. Perry, Clarence A. *The Attitude of High-School Students toward Motion Pictures.* New York: National Board of Review of Motion Pictures, 1923.
105. Peterson, Ruth C., and Thurstone, L. L. *Motion Pictures and the Social Attitudes of Children.* New York: Macmillan Co., 1933.
106. Powel, Lydia. *The Art Museum Comes to the School.* New York: Harper & Bros., 1944.
107. Price, R. H. "A Study of the Values of Field Trips," *National Elementary Principal*, XIII (1934), 502-6.
108. Ramsey, Grace F. *Educational Work in Museums of the United States.* New York: H. W. Wilson Co., 1938.
109. Ramseyer, L. L. "A Study of the Influence of Documentary Films on Social Attitudes." Doctor's Dissertation, Ohio State University, 1938.
110. Raths, L. E. "Some Evaluations of the Trip." *Educational Research Bulletin*, XVII (October, 1938), 189-208.

111. REID, SEERLEY, and DAY, DANIEL. *Radio and Records in Education.* Review of Educational Research, Vol. XII, No. 3, pp. 305-22. Washington: American Educational Research Association, 1942.
112. RENSHAW, SAMUEL. "Tachistoscope in Visual Diagnosis and Training," *Optometrists Weekly,* XXXVI (1945), 1189.
113. RENSHAW, SAMUEL. "The Visual Perception and Reproduction of Forms by Tachistoscopic Methods," *Journal of Psychology,* XX (1945), 217-32.
114. RENSHAW, SAMUEL; MILLER, V. L.; MARQUIS, DOROTHY P. *Children's Sleep.* New York: Macmillan Co., 1933.
115. ROBERTS, A. B. "Audio-visual Education in the Postwar Period," *Educational Screen,* XXIV (September-October, 1945), 283-86, 341-45.
116. ROBERTS, A. B. "Scanning the Nation's Visual Educational Programs," *See and Hear,* I (1945), 30.
117. ———. "Trends in Audio-visual Instruction in Illinois," *Educational Screen,* XXIV (May-June, 1945), 185-87, 228-29.
118. ROLFE, E. C. "A Comparison of the Effectiveness of a Motion-picture Film and of Demonstration in Instruction in High-school Physics." In F. N. Freeman (editor), *Visual Education,* pp. 335-38. Chicago: University of Chicago Press, 1924.
119. RUFFA, E. J. "An Experimental Study of Motion Pictures as Used in the Teaching of Certain Athletic Skills." Master's Thesis, Stanford University, 1935.
120. RULON, P. J. *The Sound Motion Picture in Science Teaching.* Harvard Studies in Education, Vol. XX. Cambridge, Massachusetts: Harvard University Press, 1933.
121. SEATON, HELEN H. *A Measure of Audio-visual Programs in Schools.* Washington: American Council on Education, 1944.
122. SHAFFER, L. C. *Children's Interpretations of Cartoons.* Teachers College Contributions to Education, No. 429. New York: Teachers College, Columbia University, 1930.
123. SHERMAN, H. L.; MOONEY, ROSE L.; FRY, G. A. *Drawing By Seeing.* New York: Hinds, Hayden, & Eldredge, 1947.
124. SHUTTLEWORTH, F. K., and MAY, M. A. *The Social Conduct and Attitudes of Movie Fans.* New York: Macmillan Co., 1933.
125. SKINNER, C. E., and RICH, S. G. *An Experimental Study of the Effects of Visual Aids in Teaching Geography.* Chicago: Society for Visual Education, Inc., 1925.
126. SMITH, DORA V. *Evaluating Instruction in Secondary-School English.* Report of a Division of the New York State Regents' Inquiry into the Character and Cost of Public Education in New York State. English Monograph No. 11. Chicago: National Council of Teachers of English, 1941.
127. SNYDER, H. M. "Report of the Visual Status of Forty-nine Children," *Educational Research Bulletin,* XXV (September, 1946), 168-70.

128. STAFF MOTION-PICTURE PROJECT. *Selected Educational Motion Pictures: A Descriptive Encyclopedia.* Washington: American Council on Education, 1942.
129. STAFF OF TOWER HILL SCHOOL. *A School Uses Motion Pictures.* Washington: American Council on Education, 1940.
130. STENIUS, A. C. "Auditory and Visual Education," *Review of Educational Research,* XV (June, 1945), 243-55.
131. STERNER, ALICE P. *Radio, Motion Picture, and Reading Interests.* New York: Bureau of Publications, Teachers College, Columbia University, 1947.
132. STURMTHAL, ADOLPH, and CURTIS, ALBERTA. "A Study of Audience Reactions to Two Educational Films," *Educational Screen,* XXII (October, 1943), 306, 314-15.
133. SULLENGER, T. EARL. "Modern Youth and the Movies," *School and Society,* XXXII (October 4, 1930), 459-61.
134. SUMSTINE, D. R. "A Comparative Study of Visual Instruction in the High School," *School and Society,* VII (February 23, 1918), 235-38.
135. TERMAN, L. M., and MERRILL, MAUD A. *Measuring Intelligence.* Boston: Houghton Mifflin Co., 1937.
136. TERRY, LAURA G. "Types of Children's Responses to the Yale Chronicles of America Photoplays." Master's Thesis, New York University, 1932.
137. THOMAS, KATHERYNE C. "The Ability of Children To Interpret Graphs," *The Teaching of Geography,* pp. 492-94. Thirty-second Yearbook of the National Society for the Study of Education. Chicago: University of Chicago Press, 1933.
138. THOMPSON, BETTY J. "The Effectiveness of Drill on Basic Study Skills in American History." Master's Thesis, University of Iowa, 1936.
139. TYLER, R. W. "The Relation between Recall and Higher Mental Processes." In C. H. Judd and Others, *Education as Cultivation of the Higher Mental Processes.* New York: Macmillan Co., 1936.
140. VAUTER, SIBYL. "Varied Uses of Slides in Intermediate Grades," *Educational Screen,* XXI (May, 1942), 178-79.
141. VERNON, MAGDALEN D. *Visual Perception.* Cambridge, England: Cambridge University Press, 1937.
142. WADDLE, THELMA I. "The Use of Stereographs in Fifth-grade Geography Instruction." Master's Thesis, University of Pittsburgh, 1937.
143. WASHBURNE, J. N. "An Experimental Study of Various Graphic, Tabular, and Textual Methods of Presenting Quantitative Material," *Journal of Educational Psychology,* XVIII (September, 1927), 361-76.
144. WATKINS, R. K. "The Learning Value of Some Motion Pictures in High-school Physics and General Science as an Illustration of a Simplified Technique in Educational Experimentation," *Educational Screen,* X (May, 1931), 135-37, 156-57.

145. WEBER, J. J. *Comparative Effectiveness of Some Visual Aids in Seventh-Grade Instruction.* Chicago: Educational Screen, Inc., 1922.
146. WESTFALL, L. H. *A Study of Verbal Accompaniments to Educational Motion Pictures.* Teachers College Contributions to Education, No. 617. New York: Teachers College, Columbia University, 1934.
147. WHEELER, R. H., and PERKINS, F. T. *Principles of Mental Development.* New York: Thomas Y. Crowell Co., 1932.
148. WILLIAMS, FLORENCE. "An Investigation of Children's Preferences for Pictures," *Elementary School Journal,* XXV (October, 1924), 119-26.
149. WISCONSIN RESEARCH PROJECT IN SCHOOL BROADCASTING. *Radio in the Classroom.* Madison, Wisconsin: University of Wisconsin Press, 1942.
150. WISE, GERTRUDE E. "Do Formal Instructions in How To Read Maps Result in Improved Ability?" Master's Thesis, Albany, New York, State College for Teachers, 1938.
151. WISE, H. A. *Motion Pictures as an Aid in Teaching American History.* New Haven, Connecticut: Yale University Press, 1939.
152. WITTICH, W. A., and FOWLKES, J. G. *Audio-visual Paths to Learning.* New York: Harper & Bros., 1946.
153. WITTY, PAUL, and COOMER, ANNE. "Reading the Comics in Grades IX to XII," *Educational Administration and Supervision,* XXVIII (May, 1942), 344-53.
154. WITTY, PAUL; GARFIELD, SOL; and BRINK, WILLIAM G. "Interests of High-School Students in Motion Pictures and Radio," *Journal of Educational Psychology,* XXXII, (March, 1941), 176-84.
155. WOELFEL, NORMAN, and TYLER, I. K. *Radio and the School.* Yonkers-on-Hudson, New York: World Book Co., 1945.
156. WOLFE, H. G. "An Experimental Evaluation of the Motion Picture as an Aid in Classroom Teaching." Master's Thesis, University of Rochester, 1930.
157. WOOD, B. D., and FREEMAN, F. N. *Motion Pictures in the Classroom.* New York: Houghton Mifflin Co., 1929.
158. WRIGHTSTONE, J. W. "Conventional versus Pictorial Graphs," *Progressive Education,* XIII (October, 1936), 460-62.
159. ———. "Growth in Reading Maps and Graphs and Locating Items in Reference Books," *School Review,* XLVII (December, 1939), 759-66.
160. WRIGHTSTONE, J. W., et al. "Radio Education," *Encyclopedia of Educational Research,* pp. 879-887. New York: Macmillan Co., 1941.
161. YOUNG, A. L. "Teaching with Motion Pictures," *Peabody Journal of Education,* III (May, 1926), 321-26.
162. YOUNG, W. E. "Methods of Learning and Teaching," *Review of Educational Research,* XI (October, 1941), 446-53.
163. ZYVE, CLAIRE T. "Experimental Study of the Teaching of Arithmetic Combinations," *Educational Method,* XII (October, 1932), 16-18.

CHAPTER XIII

SO THE CHILDREN MAY LEARN

W. A. WITTICH

Director, Bureau of Visual Instruction
University of Wisconsin
Madison, Wisconsin

The first time I gave it any serious thought was as I listened to Bill Williams, our superintendent of schools, as he spoke to our service club and gave us his annual "state-of-the-nation" talk. He told us how, in our community of 10,000, we had almost 1,800 children in school—that education was important—that good teachers are harder and harder to get—something to do about teacher-training agencies not meeting the demand—the need for bigger budget—and so on. Bill Williams concluded by saying that not enough parents knew what was going on in school. "A recent survey of parents' attitudes toward school revealed," Bill went on, "that most adults think about school in terms of the impressions they had of the school they last attended—as children, of course."

This really started me thinking—when had I visited our school last? We have three children—our youngest is in kindergarten; there is one in fourth grade; and the oldest is just finishing up junior high school.

When had I gone to school last? Realization hit me like a bomb! I really hadn't. Oh, yes, there was the time our younger daughter sprained her ankle on the playground and I had rushed right over to bring her in for an examination—couldn't call that a visit. Then the time I was called in to explain why Mrs. Jones' flowers "seemed" to be trampled every time my "kids" walked past. No. . . ., I just had never taken the time to drop in and see what was really going on—what the schools really were doing for my youngsters.

The next thing I knew Chuck Marshall, president of our service club, was beating on the bell announcing adjournment, and Bill,

Chuck, I, and the rest of us walked out thinking about our school but mostly about what we had waiting for us back on our desks. The thought seemed to stay with me—that idea of Bill Williams'—parents didn't know—parents ought to know—I ought to know—me—with three youngsters in school! The least I could do is to go over to the Tenth Street School and see what's going on.

I found myself walking through the portals of the school that I had "visited" on two previous occasions. My visit now was my first with any serious thought about looking in to see what today's school really looked like—what today's educational plan was like!

I went into the principal's office. The principal was out, but the office girl invited me to make myself at home and go anywhere I liked. I did.

I got my bearings and soon found myself standing in the doorway of the kindergarten room where my youngest, my son, was having the time of—better than that—he was acting as if he were "well adjusted to the situation." I guess that is what they call it today. Wraps were being thrown aside. I listened. The talk was about a field trip, or, no, they had just come back from one. Movement outdoors attracted my attention. A big orange-and-black bus picked up speed as it rolled off down the road. Apparently the youngsters had been somewhere.

Soon everything was quiet. The teacher began to talk—about what would they like to do now that they had come back from their field trip? There was a lot of buzzing and a lot of ideas—ideas from the children about stories to tell, pictures to paint, a house to build out of blocks and things, and lots else I didn't quite follow. Before I knew it the whole group just sort of broke apart, and then little groups collected in this corner, over near the playhouse—all over—little knots of interested youngsters with heads turned down over something they were very interested in doing. It looked like cutting and pasting and coloring and painting, and others talking at a great rate.

The teacher—oh, she was just going quietly and unhurried from one group to another, but there was a "hum" in the air, and everyone was busy. I just stood and watched—watched my youngster, but of course didn't let on. I watched for quite a time. A glance at the clock by the teacher, a clap of the hands, a suggestion here and there, and the kindergarteners were just about ready to wind up their short afternoon session.

As the last small boy scurried into the doorway, the room was clear —now just what I'd come for, a chance to talk to Miss Stiller who had had all three of our youngsters.

Miss Stiller made me feel she had been waiting for me to visit. Soon we were in the midst of discussion. We talked about the easels—easels covered with large sheets of paper that bore vivid splashes of orange, greens, reds, and purples. We talked about the panel upon panel of bulletin board that covered the inside walls and which were fantastically decorated with great splurges of color and form. She told me how the children had gathered the small plants that grew so green in the terrarium steaming with moisture. We looked at the aquarium—"balanced" it was, she said—and laced with lush green fronds that seem to wave in the water, and, amid bubbles from the intake pipe, tiny fish of bright gay colors glided before the wondering eyes of a "tag-along" who was too intrigued to be on his way home. I looked up and around me—gay curtains—child-sized furniture—lines of blocks—shelves of bright-covered books met my contemplation. I pulled myself away. "Well, what were the youngsters doing today? How is my son getting along?" This must have been just what Miss Stiller was waiting for. "Do you have a minute?"

I nodded. Miss Stiller walked over to the desk and picked up a blue-covered thing that turned out to be the kindergarten course of study. She hesitated a moment, then walked over to shoo three youngsters out of the playhouse. I couldn't help but look in—a home—all decorated with curtains, furniture, child-size cups and saucers, books and bookcases, pillows and covers—everything! And, right near it—an indoor slide, a teeter-totter, and a little merry-go-round.

Returning, Miss Stiller began, "I hardly know where to start. The first idea of kindergarten is to allow young children who haven't learned to play too well together to get used to each other. We take that job for granted—we really begin when we find ways for the children to have experiences—experiences with things about them, experiences here in school, experiences in this neighborhood, opportunity to 'see,' to touch and examine, to inquire, and smell, and feel, and to be curious about the things that lie all about them."

I nodded my appreciation.

Miss Stiller went right on, "A long time ago a philosopher named Froebel called this *realism in learning*. It was good thinking then. It's even better today because there are so many more 'real' things to be curious about. Consider this room of ours. Isn't it wonderful? It is a living, learning environment. Look at all our opportunities for inquiring, for seeing, for investigating—things we can touch, and handle, and talk about! Look at our terrarium and aquarium, our 'home.' Over there the children are building the 'gas station' we were visiting this afternoon. We wanted to find out what the men over at the corner filling station do in our community—what they do for our parents."

"Isn't it wonderful," I ventured. "I suppose the children were quite thrilled at having an opportunity to talk to the men at the gasoline station."

"Thrilled? Yes!"

Miss Stiller eyed me questioningly—was *I* getting the idea?

"This is the way we learn. It isn't just the gas station—it's the florist and the chicken hatchery, the seed store, the toy shop, the arboretum, the animal hospital, the food store." Miss Stiller paused, "It's learning through experiencing that will bring true understanding to your son—experiencing here in this room and in our community."

I thought that over.

"My goodness," I added, "things have changed. I don't recall going to all these places when I was just starting school. I sat at a desk, and I had a book, and if I squirmed I caught . . . . ."

I turned to the colorful drawings which were drying on the easels, and I remarked that the children of today certainly are clever. "I guess they are just more creative today!"

I liked that term. I had heard it used at a P. T. A. meeting.

"Creative?" questioned Miss Stiller. "It's not as easy as that. There are some people who believe that children today *are* more creative—that all we have to do is give them paints, pens, pencils, crayons, and paper and they'll go ahead and 'create.' It has been my experience, however, that before a child has many original ideas to express, he first has to have a broad background of experiencing, many and varied opportunities to see and to examine. His creativeness, then, is to give original or 'new' expression to these experiential backgrounds. That's why we take the children on these field trips, and, when the children return, they then create their own impressions. That's what you saw the children doing. Some of them were expressing their ideas through play. We call it creative dramatics. I had nothing to do with their ideas but to make an occasional suggestion; they know their responsibility.

"Others were painting. You saw them. And where did they get their ideas? Why, of course, from the experiences they had, and soon these and more background experiences will give them the basis for their reading. Next year we'll find that these children, because they have had these broad firsthand background experiences, will become good readers."

I was impressed. My thoughts turned again to that bus I saw departing, and I added, attempting a joke, "I suppose you must be the principal's favorite to get bus service—that bus I saw drawing away?"

Miss Stiller looked at me thoughtfully, "No, not a favorite at all. Field trips are just one of the ideas we use in our learning and experiencing. A few years ago a committee of teachers presented to the superintendent their ideas on improved learning environments. The superintendent thought it was good. He presented some of the policy problems before the school board."

Miss Stiller looked through her file, and, as she did, she went on to tell me all about the teacher planning committees—how they all worked together in the interest of building a full learning environment for the children. Then she located the thing she had been searching for.

"I'd like to read this to you," she said. "A field trip in our opinion today isn't an excursion—a chance for a holiday. Listen to this resolution the school board adopted at that meeting several years ago.

"'In order to provide a more effective teaching environment, field trips and excursions outside the classrooms and school buildings and grounds, under supervision of the members of the school staff, are to be henceforth considered by the board of education as an extension of the classroom and as an integral part of the education program.'"

Other talk followed—about the filmstrip-projected pictures frequently used in discussions, about good music via radio and records, and about films, films in school. I'd have to return again and see that.

I walked slowly down the hall. Bill Williams was right. My recollection of school was the last impression I had of my own schooling—the little red schoolhouse; discipline; seats in rows; books, dog-eared and tattered, and more books—lucky if I had the teacher's attention for ten minutes a day.

Education today! Why I hadn't even begun to understand it. High time I took an afternoon off to find out. What had Miss Stiller said? Object-teaching—firsthand experiencing—the community as the classroom—a learning environment in the school and beyond the walls of the classroom—ability to create—to express ideas. But, not until lots of experience had become ideas—ideas! Kindergartens certainly have changed. Why, there were no kindergartens when I was a child—and little enough firsthand learning experiencing.

By the time I returned to the office, the principal had returned. John Gavin was his name—a neighbor of mine. I hadn't seen him much in school before. I was invited into the office, and with no little amazement he discovered why I was there.

"Well," he continued, "let me look at my schedule—fourth-grade social studies! You'd be interested in that. Why don't you go up?"

I was interested! My youngest daughter was in there. High time I visited. Again I set aside thoughts of returning to the office.

Carefully I opened the door to Miss Esser's fourth-grade room. There was something "different" going on. The room was not dark, just dim. I heard something that sounded strangely like a radio, but wasn't. It was the narration accompanying a film—a film projected on a type of screen at the front of the room which presented a brilliant image. And yet the surroundings were pleasantly lighted. Every eye attended the moving image. Not a sound came from the children as they listened intently to the narrated description. I soon discovered the reason for their fascination. A fascinating picture story was being revealed.

Here was a procession of Chinese country folk. Pigs dangling from shoulder poles swung not too steadily in rhythm with the porters' bent backs. Others guided wheelbarrows of grain and flocks of geese that waddled zigzag through the ditch along the road. Then we were in the village—a village slowly coming to life, shutters being taken down. Slanting rays of the sun showed it was early morning, and a confusion of sounds revealed the bustle and hurry of their work-a-day world slowly rousing itself. The images faded, and, as they returned, we were again at the village outskirts, on a farm. As if we were unseen observers in the Chinese farm home, we saw breakfast being prepared, the table spread, little children dressing and cleansing themselves for the day. We followed the menfolk, who shouldered crude hoes and spades on their way into the fields. They plodded slowly behind the leisurely-gaited water buffalo.

We followed the children as they went to school, we observed their dress, we heard them converse, and we saw the games they played before their schoolhouse. A moment later, in their Chinese schoolroom, we watched them carefully tracing the intricate outlines of their writing. We listened to their strange-voiced recitations. We watched them in their round of schoolroom activities.

Then we saw father at his work. We saw the fathers of other children as they followed their respective vocations in the villages and in a near-by large city.

At the close of the day we returned to the household. We watched the plodding animals return from the fields and the weary laborers take their places around the tables. We saw the food being spread, the children eating, taking leave of their parents, and preparing for bed.

The day's activities of the village and of the household came to a close. What was this?

One of the children turned off a projector as the last image disappeared. Two other children worked the sun shades into their normal position, and the classroom came to life. I gathered myself—almost shook myself to come back from thousands of miles away—from the startling experience we had been participating in. I was an observer from another land—I was still watching a people dwelling on the other side of the globe.

Miss Esser's voice began. She asked the children what they had liked. The children talked. Pupils and teacher enumerated new information they had learned. The children expressed preferences for things of this experience which were most intriguing and most fascinating to them: the games they saw played, the sports, assisting mother, things of the school. Was it the dress of the children? Was it the foods they ate, the homes they live in? The children's interests were diversified, very different. Cleverly, Miss Esser encouraged the children to become curious about additional problems growing out of their film experience. Some children, banded together by like interests, were planning further activities which involved reading, dramatization, investigation among source books in the library, and other activities which were suited to the individual interests of the child and which seemed to grow naturally and with enthusiasm from the experiencing all had gained from this amazing graphic textbook, the sound motion picture film.

It was wonderfully natural. The children were interested, and there was work to be done—work to be done in the midst of a zeal that I had never known as a student.

Miss Esser spoke again, "What are some important things that we must do whenever we study new information?"

The children, in one way or another, expressed their concern over what each of them had learned from this experience. Quite naturally Miss Esser got the children started on a self-inventory. Each child was to investigate what he personally had received from his learning experience, what he learned, where learning had been less effective.

Short-answer inventories were passed out among the children and as they began work, quiet settled over the room. Miss Esser approached.

"How is my daughter getting along?" I began, thinking this a good way to identify myself and business.

"Oh, very well."

"Was she experiencing any difficulty?"

"Nothing to be concerned over—nothing beyond the inevitable difficulty which all children experience once they begin to investigate things, and people, and ideas that occur thousands of miles away from their own community."

I must have looked puzzled.

Miss Esser continued, "In fourth grade we leave the study of things close at hand and go far away. It isn't easy for children who have lived and experienced here in this community to suddenly study things and people they have never experienced. You see, they have no background—no background for appreciating these people we're studying today."

Recognition came. "A-ha! Readiness again. Has this something to do with the readiness idea that Miss Stiller was telling me about?" Of course, all this to myself.

And, as if anticipating my thoughts, Miss Esser continued, "You see as long as children observe and experience the things that are directly about them, they have little difficulty. They have lots of experiences; they have lots of thoughts about which to express their own opinions, and ideas, and creative art, writing and discussion. But when these young people suddenly begin to study things which occur beyond the opportunity of direct observation, then trouble seems to begin."

"And, I suppose," I added, "that that's where the good teacher gathers about her all these things that I see distributed about the room."

"Exactly. The world is 'bigger'—there's more to know—more we must know! Many of these youngsters are not going to spend their lives in this community. They're going to be citizens of the world. I'm reminded of a speaker we had here recently who said, 'These children are the last of the earthbound generation. They're the ones whose wings will take them far abroad, will intermingle them with the peoples of the world.' Today we no longer can live unto ourselves. What happens in China, in Malaya, in Russia affects us too—we who live right here in our little community."

As Miss Esser spoke, I understood and agreed.

"But how do you do all this? Where do you start?"

My gaze turned to the well-stocked room library where colorful bindings of green, red, orange, and gray gave evidence of dozens—yes, dozens—of books that these youngsters must be using as a part of their work. Then I noticed the radio with its shiny antenna bristling from its top, the sound projector set on a portable stand, the screen already folded and placed to serve as a bulletin board, still another projection device standing on the shelf in the corner, and, again, the inevitable bulletin boards, well-covered with evidences of children's work that had obviously sprung from interest developed in studying this new, far-away country. I "returned" to Miss Esser as she continued her explanations.

"Years ago, you know, we took for granted some of the limitations of learning. We knew that we coudn't do much about history. It was gone in the past, never again to be experienced firsthand. When we studied geography, we were content with the motionless pictures on the bulletin board and in the book. For information we had the words of our geography books. When we studied nature, we went out on short trips from the building to investigate the things about us, but we soon discovered that there were many things not available to us. The world is big, and natural phenomena extend to its very limits."

"And I suppose today," I added, "we're still handicapped with these same problems."

"Oh, no," Miss Esser countered. "Today we have new means of bringing information into this learning environment of ours—our *own* classroom. And what we can't find here, we may find in our library or in our community, and in the factories, and in the stores of our community, which we visit again and again."

Hmmmm, I mused to myself, more field trips. Aloud I ventured, "I suppose you take field trips."

"We certainly do," Miss Esser replied, "and with the school bus which picks us up at our own curb, drives us safely to our destination, and returns us right here at the close of the schoolday. Why, just last week, we took one trip that carried us to a game-farm forty-four miles away."

"That's quite a distance."

"Oh, not when we leave here at eight in the morning, take our lunch along, and return before school dismisses in the afternoon."

"But about these new materials of which I was telling you. We believe that object-teaching is just as important an avenue of new learning here in the intermediate grades as it is for younger children. What we can experience directly, we do. When we can't study at firsthand, we use materials which have recorded firsthand experiences. So, today, in our own school library, we have classroom films, filmstrips, transcriptions and recordings, models, specimens, charts, and maps. Oh, I could go on to name a dozen others. Sound motion picture films in social studies bring the world to us. Today, as we study history, we can 'live' among the children and their parents who settled at Salem in 1636, we can go down the Ohio in a pioneer's flatboat, stay at Fort

Harrod with Boone, or be with the pioneers of the plains as they built their sod huts. Today we have transcriptions which allow us to listen to the voices and speeches of our great statesmen even though they have long since been deceased."

My silent interest was reason enough for Miss Esser to continue.

"I wish you could have been here yesterday as we watched a colony of bees swarming, making their nest, building their combs, feeding their young, and finally cross-pollinating flowers as they brought back pollen to feed the young workers."

"This through films?" I inquired.

Miss Esser nodded, "But please excuse me now. I notice the children have finished, and I must get back to my work with them."

I retired to the back of the room, sat down, and listened as follow-up activities were being planned. One group soon decided they would create a dramatization of some of the activities they had seen in the Chinese school. Another group was more than curious about costumes, food habits, and, in a matter of moments, were soon on their way to the library to investigate for themselves. Another group was fascinated by the possibility of graphically picturing some of the things they had seen. Soon they were off to the art room for materials and supplies which they could carry back here and use in the creation of a mural. And so it went. . . . .

As I walked down the corridor to return to the office, many questions passed through my mind. It was true. My last impression of education was the "little-red-schoolhouse" idea. What a revelation to come here and see the modern learning laboratories that provided a world experience for my children. As I walked down the hall, ideas teemed through my mind—ideas about how children learn most effectively—about the different world of people, places, and events about which our children today must know, and know of clearly, understandably, in order to live effectively in the world of tomorrow. Ideas! Yes, about bulletin boards and maps—maps more attractive and better marked than anything I had used—and globes, and charts, and files for those flat pictures that were attractively displayed on the bulletin boards. And then the projectors—what were they? Miss Stiller had described them—glass slide projectors, 2" x 2" projectors, the motion-picture projector—and the radio, the turntables, both for transcriptions and recordings—even a sound-recording device so that children could speak and read—and then, and best of all devices, listen to themselves and improve through *self* criticism. Then, too, the field trips into the community—forty-four miles and back again.

I wondered if such things happen in all our schools. Is this just an exception? I could see it now—this is the way children everywhere can learn.

I found myself before the office and again in Mr. Gavin's presence. Miss McCombe had just come in from observing the work of the eighth-graders. Miss McCombe, I learned, was our curriculum coordinator. Curriculum? Just what did that mean? I asked Miss McCombe.

"The curriculum?" Miss McCombe considered a moment, then, "Every experience that the school offers to your children. That's what we mean by the curriculum."

"That must be quite difficult to organize and plan," I ventured.

"It is. And more than that, it's constantly changing. It needs constant study. This world environment of ours is constantly expanding, and things which seemed of first importance years ago suddenly seem to be of secondary importance. New ideas, information, cultural patterns suddenly rush into world prominence. People who live in places not even mentioned in our 1940-edition geographies helped us recapture the Pacific. Today our children must understand and know these people who have become so important to us. In science some of the oldest concepts which we once regarded as scientific truths have been challenged since the discovery of the release of atomic power. War discoveries have altered other ideas—our children must learn.

"But, your question. Our curriculum is the subject of *continuing study by everyone of the teachers on our staff.*"

"Continuing study," I pondered aloud, "by the teachers who guide the day-after-day school work these youngsters of mine do?"

"Yes! I just returned from the eighth grade. In the general-science lab the children were in the process of studying earthworms. This is all part of a teacher's planned series of experiences with insects and worms and the part they play in the balance of nature and in our lives. Years ago we read about insects and let it go at that. Now the planning committee studies the best learning approach to the problems the children investigate."

I beamed with recognition, "The object-teaching method?"

Miss McCombe went right on, "Today each youngster was given a laboratory package—a specimen for dissection, knives, pin cards, and other paraphernalia that they need to use as they investigate for themselves. Beforehand, however, they had witnessed a film called 'The Earthworm.' This film shows how the worm serves mankind by continually fertilizing and refertilizing the soil, allowing the oxygen to enter the pores. Explanations in animation and direct photography explain reproductive cycles. During this explanation they watched a skilful biologist dissect and study the structure of a specimen like the one the students would soon work on. Following this the children returned to their worktables and attempted to imitate the techniques they had seen. The model had been presented—and they are up there right now."

"But what about their reading?" I questioned.

"Reading is just as fundamental a source of information today as it ever was. Yes, even more so—only now reading in their own textbooks and in source books in the library takes on added meanings because of the background experience upon which the student will build his word and sentence meanings."

Miss McCombe paused and studied me carefully as if to determine whether I followed her explanation.

"Readiness again—background experience—real experiencing, the basis for all further understanding." I returned a glance of assurance to Miss McCombe.

"That unit on earthworms, together with the suggestion of source materials, the film, charts, the laboratory instruments, and the lists of basic and source books, had been worked out in detail by a committee of junior high school teachers whose responsibility it is to teach science. Similarly the kindergarten teachers meet and will continue to meet frequently to plan better means of bringing experiences with an enlarging environment to the understanding of the child."

Mr. Gavin began, "Don't forget, Miss McCombe, about our faculty representative who works directly with your office and who brings you the thinking of our teachers here."

"I'm glad you mentioned that," Miss McCombe went on. "We have regular meetings during the year during which teachers discuss learning problems and exchange ideas and techniques they have found effective in overcoming problems of instruction. In geography, the teachers have accomplished a great deal."

"And in science," Mr. Gavin interposed, "I still can 'see' those amazing time-lapse motion pictures on plant life, on the life cycle of plants and animals. I think one of the best teaching film series we use is that which explains the development of plant, animal, and bird life. Why, as I watch, I'm taken to within six inches of gorgeously colored birds as they build their nests, lay the eggs, hatch their young, and care for them."

Miss McCombe continued, "At our central curriculum office it is our responsibility to assist the teachers' planning and thinking, to make available to them the latest films, the best slides and filmstrips, the most effectively illustrated books. Oh, the books we have today are simply marvelous! Our librarian tells us that since we have begun the planned use of audio-visual materials in our classrooms, the free reading that children do, the reading that is an outgrowth of their classwork, has increased beyond anything she has anticipated. Last year a study made of the free reading habits of intermediate-grade children who regularly experience audio-visual materials as they supplement regular classwork revealed a 150 per cent superiority over groups not experiencing audio-visual materials while studying the same subjects."

Children passing through the halls caused Miss McCombe to glance at her watch.

"If I'm going to meet the high-school social-studies teachers at the curriculum center, I'll have to be on my way." She glanced at me. "Why don't you come along with me? It's on your way."

Again I thought of my high-stacked desk, but . . . . .

As Miss McCombe swung her car along Tenth Street, she chatted enthusiastically about the new opportunities my children were having of more completely understanding their world, how this year every elementary school regularly used carefully chosen audio-visual materials, how every floor of every elementary school was equipped with a mobile audio-visual cabinet including the sound projector I saw used, how teacher committees were constantly selecting good books, filmstrips, transcriptions, charts, maps, and motion pictures which would help accomplish desired learning experience heretofore not possible.

We drew to the curb before the central administrative offices. As we walked into the curriculum center, there was a display which challenged my interest as a parent and certainly must have been a bonanza to the teacher searching for better means of accomplishing the learning problem which she was working through with her children. We moved from the motion-picture film files to the professional library. We saw the latest books on classroom methods and techniques. I paused before cabinets of filmstrips, racks of transcriptions, cases of intricately wrought models of old tools, sailing vessels, early railroad engines, farm equipment, and too many more to tell about.

A hearty voice interrupted my browsing, "Well, well, my efforts this noon have been rewarded!" It was our superintendent, Bill Williams, "What do you think of our learning laboratory?"

I remarked that it looked something like the better scientific labs that I had visited. Then there was no stopping him. He found out I had been visiting "my" school.

"Well, was I right?" Bill Williams asked. "Any of your impressions been changed? Any of the 'Little-Red-Schoolhouse' ideas still hanging on?"

I admitted that they had been replaced and that he was right.

"I wish there was something I could do to get every one of our parents, and the rest of the townspeople for that matter, to regularly visit and see what's happening to our children.

"Sometimes I even get a little concerned about our school board. Why I remember eight years ago when I first suggested that we equip every one of our elementary schools with the new materials of instruction, they said in so many words 'we refuse to allocate tax monies for the entertainment of our children.'"

I was silent. I'm afraid I might have acted in the same way.

Bill continued, "Well, we overcame that obstacle. Remember, Miss McCombe, what we did?"

Miss McCombe paused a moment then began, "Oh, yes. We let them listen to a few good history transcriptions. I'll never forget what that did to some of the dissenters. And then we showed them a recent film on American history. What was the name of it? Oh, yes, 'Early Settlers of New England.'"

Here John Gavin burst in, "Some of those men on our school board were quick to admit that if they could have seen those pictures when they were children, they'd have a real and understandable grasp of American history."

"And," Miss McCombe continued, "when we showed them some of the films on science, and particularly a few in vocations, that seemed to turn the trick."

"Yes," John went on, "from the day in which we spent virtually nothing for instructional material, we have come to the point now when in our current budget we are spending $8.05 per pupil on instructional materials—'curriculum materials' we call them in the budget, that includes good books, transcriptions, sound films, maps, models, filmstrips."

Here Miss McCombe interjected, "I hope we're not going to have to buy projection equipment out of that."

"You bet we're not," John Gavin added. "That comes under capital expense."

"And my salary? What about that?"

"That's taken out too, Miss McCombe—instructional expense. We no longer have to tuck things away in nooks and crannies. We recognize," John Gavin laughed, "pardon me, our forward-looking board of education recognizes that our most important resource today is our children, and unless we give them the opportunities to learn, to really experience this expanding world of ours, well, they are just not going to be able to take their places intelligently and ably in their world of tomorrow."

"My! my!" I said, half under my breath, "that must cost money."

"Certainly, it costs money. Didn't I hear that you just recently re-equipped your office? Why don't you continue to use the things you bought when you set up for business—wasn't it twenty-one years ago—or have new and improved ideas been attracting your attention?"

"Yes," I said sheepishly, "they have. Cost me a pretty penny too."

I thought of the conversation I had had with some of my colleagues. I would soon lose my clients if I didn't keep abreast with the latest techniques and the latest equipment. Just then a group of teachers walked in.

"You'll have to pardon me now," Miss McCombe said, "our building co-ordinators are beginning to come in, and we have to discuss some of the new materials that we have been trying out experimentally in our classrooms. You see, we really classroom-test all of our learning materials. It's only in that way that we can come away with a real impression of their contribution to the learning situation that the children engage in."

Bill Williams and I walked out and I took my leave. I walked home. I wanted to think—the world is expanding—more to learn, less time—textbooks can't do it all—walls of the classroom—bring the world to the classroom—take class to world—new materials—new techniques—new equipment.

All this—almost like the decisions I make. Why, only last week I had to have some dental work done. I went to the dentist with the most "know-how," with up-to-the-moment equipment. And last year —when I took Sophie over to the hospital for her appendectomy, Dr. Stuart had assured me—best equipment in this section of the state—latest techniques.

And I guess that goes for school teaching! I want my children to have the best. They'll certainly need it. . . . . .

I thought a lot about these things, and we talked it over that evening at the dinner table. The dishes were cleared, and my two older youngsters went up to their rooms to study. I tagged along.

My oldest youngster, in the eighth grade, was looking through her Current Events paper. What was that? A large pie chart— a graph— the heading, "The Way We Spend Our Tax Dollars,"—look at those figures. National defense, 14 billion; education, 4 billion—hold on. National defense 14 billion; education, 4 billion? Why, that's right!

For national defense? For education? Certainly, we've got to have national defense. But what's this about education? Is that the way we are going to keep on year after year, or is there something in this education business? Maybe those figures should be turned around.

Look—here in the next column. Bill S246 slated for passage, federal aid to education, initial grant amounting to $300,000,000 to be divided among the states of the Union on the basis of need. Why, that's more like it—not enough, but a start. That's the kind of thing we need.

Education—how much are we spending? Enough? Let's put, first things first. Those words of John Gavin were still in my ears, "What we're doing is working with our most important resource—children." Coal, iron, and steel, those aren't our resources. No sir-ree. . . . they're our children! And, the best we can do for them is little enough. The best we can do is what we want for them—provide them with a learning environment that is real—understandable, bring out their best—interests and capabilities.

Yes, that's our job—my job to help give these children of mine—all the children—all the children of all the people—the best education experiences the minds of men can plan—can provide—for the children—for tomorrow. The children must learn!

INDEX

Adapting audio-visual methods to different educational levels, 38-41
Adler, Mortimer, 275
Adult education, use of audio-visual materials in, 40-41
Aims of audio-visual specialists, 1
Aims and methods of communication, 4-5
American Council on Education, 47
American Library Association, 40
Armed forces, research on use of audio-visual materials with, 256-60
Arnspiger, V. C., 262, 269
Atyeo, H. C., 277
Audio-visual aids: extension courses in, 112-14; factors affecting teacher education for use of, 110-12; promoting teacher growth in use of, 112-21
Audio-visual center, responsibilities of state agencies and higher institutions for, 248-52
Audio-visual department in local school system, 130-43, 180-92; administration of, 129-30, 192-200; advantages of, 182-84; financial support for, 149-51, 199-200; functions of, 132-44, 184-92
Audio-visual materials: administering programs involving use of, 237-44; bases for determining advantages of renting or purchasing supply of, 212; budgetary procedure for utilization of, 244-47; centralized services to facilitate use of, 40; characteristics of, 53-64; classifying and cataloguing supplies of, 213-14; community use of, 208-9; cost of equipment for use of, 59-61; criteria for selection of, 132-33; definition of, 1, 28-29; distribution of, 141-43; effect of, on teacher's services, 205-6; evaluation of, 215-16; expenditures for, 48-49; implications of, for crowded curriculum, 69-71; improving production of, 214-15; integration of, with curriculum, 35-38; local facilities for distribution of, 57, 58; physical facilities for care and use of, 232-37; preparation and care of different types of, 134-41; present practices in use of, 38-45; production of different types of, 45-46; provisions for individual classroom use of, 207-8; quantitative standards for use of, 211-12; relation of, to learning experiences, 29-35; research on use of, in World War II, 255-61; role of, in education, 203-9; role of state agencies in distribution of, 57-59; school preparation of, 225-32; selection of, in relation to educational objectives, 209-10; sources of information on, 210-11; use of, at different educational levels, 38-41; use of, in different subject areas, 41-45, 206; use of, in teacher training, 46; use of, in various school situations, 216-25
Audio-visual methods in the schools, 38-45; in rural areas, 149-52; in city schools, 130-92
Audio-visual programs for state school systems: operation of, in California, 168-79; present status of, 165-68
Audio-visual specialists, diversity of aims of, 1

Bell, Reginald, 273
Blumer, Herbert, 274
Brooker, F. E., 260, 273
Brownell, William A., 254
Buffalo, New York, Museum of Science, 281
Buswell, G. T., 279

California program in audio-visual education, 168-79
Cantril, Hadley, 284
Cataloguing audio-visual materials, 213-14
Chambers, M. M., 259
Chappell, Matthew N., 284
Charters, W. W., 274
City school systems: audio-visual department in, 130-43, 180-92; N.E.A. study of audio-visual programs in, 38-39; qualifications of personnel for, 193-96; responsibilities of audio-visual staff in, 130-31
Classroom use of audio-visual materials, providing facilities for, 207-8
Class size: effect of, on teachers' decisions with respect to objectives and methods of instruction, 93-94; relation of audio-visual materials to, 69-70
Cleveland, Ohio, radio programs for classroom listening, 34

INDEX

College instruction, use of audio-visual materials in, 40
Communication: aims and methods of, 4-5; definition of, 5; media and forms of, 6-10; recent developments in, 16-18; relation of languages to, 6-7; role of education in, 24-26; social significance of, 4-6; teaching languages and skills of, 20; use of pictorial forms in, 14-19
Community use of audio-visual aids, 208-9
Concepts of learning, relation of audio-visual materials to, 65-66
Conferences and institutes for promoting teacher growth in use of audio-visual aids, 114-15
Connecticut, University of, extension course in audio-visual aids, 112-13
Consitt, Francis, 262, 266, 270
Contrived experiences, as related to learning, 30
County systems of audio-visual programs for rural schools, 156-60
Curriculum: integration of audio-visual materials with, 35-38; overcrowded condition of, as obstacle to use of audio-visual materials, 66-68

Dale, Edgar, 28, 30, 147, 274
Dane County, Wisconsin, audio-visual program for rural schools, 150
Day, Daniel, 284
DeKieffer, Robert E., 96, 98, 166
Demonstrations, use of, in various learning experiences, 30
Dewey, John, 7
Dictionary of Education, 28
Direct experience, use of audio-visual materials in, 29
Distribution of audio-visual materials, 141-43; local facilities for, 57, 58; responsibility of state agencies for, 57-59
Dramatic participation as basis of learning experiences, 29-30

Educational Film Library Association, 150, 216
Equipment required for use of audio-visual materials: cost of, 59-61; designing school buildings for installation of, 62-64; operation and maintenance of, 61-62
Evaluation of audio-visual materials, 215-16
Evaluation of outcomes of learning experiences, 91-93
Expenditures for audio-visual materials, 48-49
Extension courses in audio-visual aids, 112-14

Federal Communications Commission, 284
Field, Harry, 284
Field trips, research on educational values of, 277-78
Film Council of America, 41, 48
Film libraries, services of, 42
Films: care and distribution of, 136-37; effects of price level on utilization of, 54-56
Filmstrips, research on educational uses of, 279-80
Financing audio-visual program: budgetary procedures for, 199-200; in California, 173; in rural schools, 149-51; in the St. Louis school system, 132
Freeman, Frank N., 262, 263, 265

Gatto, F. M., 263
Graphic materials: educational uses of, 34-35; research on educational uses of, 282-83

Hansen, J. E., 262
Harris, William T., 127
Health education, use of audio-visual materials in, 44-45
Higher institutions, responsibilities of, for audio-visual center, 248-52
Hite, Herbert, 105
Hoban, Charles F., 34
Hoban, Charles F., Jr., 34, 215, 256, 258
Hooper, C. E., 284

Industrial-arts instruction, use of audio-visual materials in, 44
Industrial training, research on use of audio-visual materials in, 260-61
In-service teacher education in audio-visual field: contribution of the workshop to, 117, 172; evaluating results of, 121-23; factors contributing to success of, 110-12; materials and facilities needed for, 112; providing leadership for, 110; role of audio-visual co-ordinator in, 117-18; services of audio-visual center for, 120-21; teacher participation in plan-

ning for, 111; value of bulletins and handbooks for, 118-20
Instructional motion pictures: effect of prices on utilization of, 54-56; research on the use of, 261-73
Integration of audio-visual materials with school curriculum, 35-38; in rural areas, 147-48
International relations, use of audio-visual materials in connection with, 47-48

Journal of Applied Psychology, 284

Katz, Elias, 280
Kindergarten, use of audio-visual materials in, 38-39
King County, Washington, co-operative film library for rural schools, 157-58
Knowlton, D. C., 262
Krasker, Abraham, 272

Lantern slides, research on educational uses of, 279-80
Larson, L. C., 254
Lazarsfeld, Paul F., 284
Learning experiences: effects of, on learner's behavior, 72-76; relation of audio-visual materials to, 29-35; selecting instructional materials for, 89-91; types of, 29-30
Learning situations, use of, in promoting desirable changes in pupil behavior, 77-93
Leonard, J. P., 273
Lewin, William, 276
Local school system: financing audio-visual services in, 149-51, 199-200; functions of audio-visual department in, 132-44, 184-92
Luckiesch, Matthew, 254

McClusky, F. D., 262, 263, 270
Miles, J. R., 257, 259
Motion Picture Association of America, 216
Motion pictures as used in communication of ideas, 31-32
Motivation, teachers' decisions in relation to, 84-89
Mumford, Lewis, 15
Museum materials, research on educational uses of, 280-82

National Education Association, 38, 42, 165

Nebraska experiment with audio-visual program for rural schools, 159-60
New York Times' investigation of history teaching, 82-83
Noel, Elizabeth G., 273
Noel, F. W., 273

Observational situations, as related to learning experiences, 30
Ohio State University Project in Evaluation of Radio Broadcasts, 47
Oregon state system of higher education plan of extension courses in audio-visual aids, 113-14
Overcrowded curriculum as obstacle to use of audio-visual materials, 66-68

Payne-Fund Studies of Theatrical Motion Pictures, 274-76
Phonograph records, care and use of, 140-41
Physical education, use of audio-visual materials in, 44-45
Powel, Lydia, 281
Preservice audio-visual courses: content of, 95-99; place of, in teacher-training program, 100-105; services of college audio-visual center in, 105-6; trends of, in teacher-training institutions, 104
Price, R. H., 277
Prices for different types of audio-visual materials, 54-56
Primary grades, use of audio-visual materials in, 38-39
Production of audio-visual materials, 214-15
Psychological Test Film Unit of the Army Air Forces, 257
Public Opinion Quarterly, 284
Pupil assignments as evidence of teacher's objectives, 72-73
Pupil responses as result of learning experiences, 73-76
Purchasing audio-visual materials, bases for determining need of, 212

Radio broadcasts, educational uses of, 33-34
Radio, research on educational uses of, 283-84
Ramseyer, L. L., 262, 270
Recordings: educational uses of, 33-34; research on educational uses of 283-84
Reid, Seerley, 284

Renshaw, Samuel, 254
Renting audio-visual matériel, bases for determining advantages of, 212
Research evidence supporting approved utilization of audio-visual materials, 255
Research on use of audio-visual materials with armed forces, 256-60
Roberts, A. B., 254
Role of audio-visual materials in education, 203-9
Rulon, P. J., 262, 268
Rural schools: availability of audio-visual materials for, 146-47; co-operative audio-visual programs in, 150-52; county systems of audio-visual programs for, 156-60; methods of improving audio-visual programs in, 149-52, 160-61; Nebraska experiment with audio-visual program for, 159-60; objectives of audio-visual programs in, 146-48; status of audio-visual programs in, 152-56; utilization of community resources for curriculum enrichment in, 148

Safety education, use of audio-visual materials in, 44-45
St. Louis, Missouri, program of audio-visual education, 127-32
Sargent, Stansfeld, 14
School buildings, installation of audio-visual equipment in, 62-64
Science instruction, use of audio-visual materials in, 43
Selection of audio-visual materials for different educational uses, 209-10
Sherif, Muzafer, 14
Social-science instruction, use of audio-visual materials in, 43-44
Solar system, teaching unit on, as illustration of curricular integration of audio-visual materials, 36-38
Spain, C. R., 257, 259
Standards for use of audio-visual materials, 211-12
State agencies, responsiblities of, for audio-visual center, 248-52
State audio-visual unit, principles directing operation of, 162-65
Stenius, A. C., 280
Sterner, Alice P., 276
Still pictures: projected and nonprojected types described, 32-33; research on educational uses of, 279-80

Sumstine, David, 261
Surveys of audio-visual field, 254

Tabler, C. H., 48-49
Teacher education for use of audio-visual aids, 110-12
Teacher growth, promotion of, in use of audio-visual aids, 110-12;
Teacher load, effect of, on teachers' decisions relating to objectives and methods of instruction, 93-94
Teacher-training courses in audio-visual field, 46
Teaching objectives, relation of instructional materials to, 79-84
Television broadcast, values of, for learning, 30-31
Theatrical motion pictures, research on social effects of, 273-77
Thomas, Katheryne C., 282
Transcriptions, educational uses of, 33-34
Tyler, I. Keith, 283
Tyler, Ralph W., 254

United Nations film unit, 48
University of Chicago Center for Study of Audio-visual Materials, 47
Utilization of audio-visual materials, 216-25; budgetary procedure for, 244-47

Verbal symbols, role of, in learning, 35
Vocational education, use of audio-visual materials in, 44

Watkins, R. K., 262
Weber, J. J., 262
Weinman, Constance, 105
Western Illinois State Teachers College report on functions of the audio-visual center, 105-6
Westfall, L. H., 265
Wittich, W. A., 269, 272, 294
Woelfel, Norman, 283
Wood, Ben D., 262, 265
Workshop, use of, in teacher education in audio-visual field, 117, 172
World War II, research on use of audio-visual materials in, 255-61
Wrightstone, J. W., 282

Young, W. E., 277, 279

INFORMATION CONCERNING THE NATIONAL SOCIETY FOR THE STUDY OF EDUCATION

1. PURPOSE. The purpose of the National Society is to promote the investigation and discussion of educational questions. To this end it holds an annual meeting and publishes a series of yearbooks.

2. ELIGIBILITY TO MEMBERSHIP. Any person who is interested in receiving its publications may become a member by sending to the Secretary-Treasurer information concerning name, title, and address, and a check for $4.00 (see Item 5).

Membership is not transferable; it is limited to individuals, and may not be held by libraries, schools, or other institutions, either directly or indirectly.

3. PERIOD OF MEMBERSHIP. Applicants for membership may not date their entrance back of the current calendar year, and all memberships terminate automatically on December 31, unless the dues for the ensuing year are paid as indicated in Item 6.

4. DUTIES AND PRIVILEGES OF MEMBERS. Members pay dues of $3.00 annually, receive a cloth-bound copy of each publication, are entitled to vote, to participate in discussion, and (under certain conditions) to hold office. The names of members are printed in the yearbooks.

Persons who are sixty years of age or above may become life members on payment of fee based on average life-expectancy of their age group. For information, apply to Secretary-Treasurer.

5. ENTRANCE FEE. New members are required the first year to pay, in addition to the dues, an entrance fee of one dollar.

6. PAYMENT OF DUES. Statements of dues are rendered in October or November for the following calendar year. Any member so notified whose dues remain unpaid on January 1, thereby loses his membership and can be reinstated only by paying a reinstatement fee of fifty cents. levied to cover the actual clerical cost involved.

School warrants and vouchers from institutions must be accompanied by definite information concerning the name and address of the person for whom membership fee is being paid. Statements of dues are rendered on our own form only. The Secretary's office cannot undertake to fill out special invoice forms of any sort or to affix notary's affidavit to statements or receipts.

Cancelled checks serve as receipts. Members desiring an additional receipt must enclose a stamped and addressed envelope therefor.

7. DISTRIBUTION OF YEARBOOKS TO MEMBERS. The yearbooks, ready prior to each February meeting, will be mailed from the office of the distributors, only to members whose dues for that year have been paid. Members who desire yearbooks prior to the current year must purchase them directly from the distributors (see Item 8).

8. COMMERCIAL SALES. The distribution of all yearbooks prior to the current year, and also of those of the current year not regularly mailed to members in exchange for their dues, is in the hands of the distributor, not of the Secretary. For such commercial sales, communicate directly with the University of Chicago Press, Chicago 37, Illinois, which will gladly send a price list covering all the publications of this Society and of its predecessor, the National Herbart Society. This list is also printed in the yearbook.

9. YEARBOOKS. The yearbooks are issued about one month before the February meeting. They comprise from 600 to 800 pages annually. Unusual effort has been made to make them, on the one hand, of immediate practical value, and, on the other hand, representative of sound scholarship and scientific investigation. Many of them are the fruit of co-operative work by committees of the Society.

10. MEETINGS. The annual meeting, at which the yearbooks are discussed, is held in February at the same time and place as the meeting of the American Association of School Administrators.

Applications for membership will be handled promptly at any time on receipt of name and address, together with check for $4.00 (or $3.50 for reinstatement). Generally speaking, applications entitle the new members to the yearbook slated for discussion during the calendar year the application is made, but those received in December are regarded as pertaining to the next calendar year.

5835 Kimbark Ave. NELSON B. HENRY, *Secretary-Treasurer*
Chicago, 37, Illinois

PUBLICATIONS OF THE NATIONAL HERBART SOCIETY

(Now the National Society for the Study of Education)

POSTPAID
PRICE

First Yearbook, 1895	$0.79
First Supplement to First Yearbook	.28
Second Supplement to First Yearbook	.27
Second Yearbook, 1896	.85
Supplement to Second Yearbook	.27
Third Yearbook, 1897	.85
Ethical Principles Underlying Education. John Dewey. Reprinted from Third Yearbook	.27
Supplement to Third Yearbook	.27
Fourth Yearbook, 1898	.79
Supplement to Fourth Yearbook	.28
Fifth Yearbook, 1899	.79
Supplement to Fifth Yearbook	.54

PUBLICATIONS OF THE NATIONAL SOCIETY FOR THE STUDY OF EDUCATION

POSTPAID
PRICE

First Yearbook, 1902, Part I—*Some Principles in the Teaching of History.* Lucy M. Salmon........$0.54

First Yearbook, 1902, Part II—*The Progress of Geography in the Schools.* W. M. Davis and H. M. Wilson........ .53

Second Yearbook, 1903, Part I—*The Course of Study in History in the Common School.* Isabel Lawrence, C. A. McMurry, Frank McMurry, E. C. Page, and E. J. Rice.... .53

Second Yearbook, 1903, Part II—*The Relation of Theory to Practice in Education.* M. J. Holmes, J. A. Keith, and Levi Seeley........ .53

Third Yearbook, 1904, Part I—*The Relation of Theory to Practice in the Education of Teachers.* John Dewey, Sarah C. Brooks, F. M. McMurry, et al........ .53

Third Yearbook, 1904, Part II—*Nature Study.* W. S. Jackman........ .85

Fourth Yearbook, 1905, Part I—*The Education and Training of Secondary Teachers.* E. C Elliott, E. G. Dexter, M. J. Holmes, et al........ .85

Fourth Yearbook, 1905, Part II—*The Place of Vocational Subjects in the High-School Curriculum.* J. S. Brown, G. B. Morrison, and Ellen H. Richards........ .53

Fifth Yearbook, 1906, Part I—*On the Teaching of English in Elementary and High Schools.* G. P. Brown and Emerson Davis........ .53

Fifth Yearbook, 1906, Part II—*The Certification of Teachers.* E. P. Cubberley........ .64

Sixth Yearbook, 1907, Part I—*Vocational Studies for College Entrance.* C. A. Herrick, H. W. Holmes, T. deLaguna, V. Prettyman, and W. J. S. Bryan........ .70

Sixth Yearbook, 1907, Part II—*The Kindergarten and Its Relation to Elementary Education.* Ada Van Stone Harris, E. A. Kirkpatrick, Maria Kraus-Boelté, Patty S. Hill, Harriette M. Mills, and Nina Vandewalker........ .70

Seventh Yearbook, 1908, Part I—*The Relation of Superintendents and Principals to the Training and Professional Improvement of Their Teachers.* Charles D. Lowry........ .78

Seventh Yearbook, 1908, Part II—*The Co-ordination of the Kindergarten and the Elementary School.* B. J. Gregory, Jennie B. Merrill, Bertha Payne, and Margaret Giddings........ .78

Eighth Yearbook, 1909, Parts I and II—*Education with Reference to Sex.* C. R. Henderson and Helen C. Putnam. Both parts........ 1.60

Ninth Yearbook, 1910, Part I—*Health and Education.* T. D. Wood........ .85

Ninth Yearbook, 1910, Part II—*The Nurse in Education.* T. D. Wood, et al........ .78

Tenth Yearbook, 1911, Part I—*The City School as a Community Center.* H. C. Leipziger, Sarah E. Hyre, R. D. Warden, C. Ward Crampton, E. W. Stitt, E. J. Ward, Mrs. E. C. Grice, and C. A. Perry........ .78

Tenth Yearbook, 1911, Part II—*The Rural School as a Community Center.* B. H. Crocheron, Jessie Field, F. W. Howe, E. C. Bishop, A. B. Graham, O. J. Kern, M. T. Scudder, and B. M. Davis........ .79

Eleventh Yearbook, 1912, Part I—*Industrial Education: Typical Experiments Described and Interpreted.* J. F. Barker, M. Bloomfield, B. W. Johnson, P. Johnson, L. M. Leavitt, G. A. Mirick, M. W. Murray, C. F. Perry, A. L. Safford, and H. B. Wilson........ .85

Eleventh Yearbook, 1912, Part II—*Agricultural Education in Secondary Schools.* A. C. Monahan, R. W. Stimson, D. J. Crosby, W. H. French, H. F. Button, F. R. Crane, W. R. Hart, and G. F. Warren........ .85

Twelfth Yearbook, 1913, Part I—*The Supervision of City Schools.* Franklin Bobbitt, J. W. Hall, and J. D. Wolcott........ .85

Twelfth Yearbook, 1913, Part II—*The Supervision of Rural Schools.* A. C. Monahan, L. J. Hanifan, J. E. Warren, Wallace Lund, U. J. Hoffman, A. S. Cook, E. M. Rapp, Jackson Davis, and J. D. Wolcott........ .85

Thirteenth Yearbook, 1914, Part I—*Some Aspects of High-School Instruction and Administration.* H. C. Morrison, E. R. Breslich, W. A. Jessup, and L. D. Coffman........ .85

Thirteenth Yearbook, 1914, Part II—*Plans for Organizing School Surveys, with a Summary of Typical School Surveys.* Charles H. Judd and Henry L. Smith........ .79

Fourteenth Yearbook, 1915, Part I—*Minimum Essentials in Elementary School Subjects —Standards and Current Practices.* H. B. Wilson, H. W. Holmes, F. E. Thompson, R. G. Jones, S. A. Courtis, W. S. Gray, F. N. Freeman, H. C. Pryor, J. F. Hosic, W. A. Jessup, and W. C. Bagley........ .85

Fourteenth Yearbook, 1915, Part II—*Methods for Measuring Teachers' Efficiency.* Arthur C. Boyce........ .79

PUBLICATIONS

	POSTPAID PRICE
Fifteenth Yearbook, 1916, Part I—*Standards and Tests for the Measurement of the Efficiency of Schools and School Systems.* G. D. Strayer, Bird T. Baldwin, B. R. Buckingham, F. W. Ballou, D. C. Bliss, H. G. Childs, S. A. Courtis, E. P. Cubberley, C. H. Judd, George Melcher, E. E. Oberholtzer, J. B. Sears, Daniel Starch, M. R. Trabue, and G. M. Whipple...	.85
Fifteenth Yearbook, 1916, Part II—*The Relationship between Persistence in School and Home Conditions.* Charles E. Holley...	.87
Fifteenth Yearbook, 1916, Part III—*The Junior High School.* Aubrey A. Douglass....	.85
Sixteenth Yearbook, 1917, Part I—*Second Report of the Committee on Minimum Essentials in Elementary School Subjects.* W. C. Bagley, W. W. Charters, F. N. Freeman, W. S. Gray, Ernest Horn, J. H. Hoskinson, W. S. Monroe, C. F. Munson, H. C. Pryor, L. W. Rapeer, G. M. Wilson, and H. B. Wilson.....................................	1.00
Sixteenth Yearbook, 1917, Part II—*The Efficiency of College Students as Conditioned by Age at Entrance and Size of High School.* B. F. Pittenger...............................	.85
Seventeenth Yearbook, 1918, Part I—*Third Report of the Committee on Economy of Time in Education.* W. C. Bagley, B. B. Bassett, M. E. Branom, Alice Camerer, J. E. Dealey, C. A. Ellwood, E. B. Greene, A. B. Hart, J. F. Hosic, E. T. Housh, W. H. Mace, L. R. Marston, H. C. McKown, H. E. Mitchell, W. C. Reavis, D. Snedden, and H. B. Wilson...	.85
Seventeenth Yearbook, 1918, Part II—*The Measurement of Educational Products.* E. J. Ashbaugh, W. A. Averill, L. P. Ayers, F. W. Ballou, Edna Bryner, B. R. Buckingham, S. A. Courtis, M. E. Haggerty, C. H. Judd, George Melcher, W. S. Monroe, E. A. Nifenecker, and E. L. Thorndike..	1.00
Eighteenth Yearbook, 1919, Part I—*The Professional Preparation of High-School Teachers.* G. N. Cade, S. S. Colvin, Charles Fordyce, H. H. Foster, T. W. Gosling, W. S. Gray, L. V. Koos, A. R. Mead, H. L. Miller, F. C. Whitcomb, and Clifford Woody..	1.65
Eighteenth Yearbook, 1919, Part II—*Fourth Report of Committee on Economy of Time in Education.* F. C. Ayer, F. N. Freeman, W. S. Gray, Ernest Horn, W. S. Monroe, and C. E. Seashore...	1.10
Nineteenth Yearbook, 1920, Part I—*New Materials of Instruction.* Prepared by the Society's Committee on Materials of Instruction...	1.10
Nineteenth Yearbook, 1920, Part II—*Classroom Problems in the Education of Gifted Children.* T. S. Henry..	1.00
Twentieth Yearbook, 1921, Part I—*New Materials of Instruction.* Second Report by the Society's Committee..	1.30
Twentieth Yearbook, 1921, Part II—*Report of the Society's Committee on Silent Reading.* M. A. Burgess, S. A. Courtis, C. E. Germane, W. S. Gray, H. A. Greene, Regina R. Heller, J. H. Hoover, J. A. O'Brien, J. L. Packer, Daniel Starch, W. W. Theisen, G. A. Yoakam, and representatives of other school systems....................	1.10
Twenty-first Yearbook, 1922, Parts I and II—*Intelligence Tests and Their Use.* Part I—*The Nature, History, and General Principles of Intelligence Testing.* E. L. Thorndike, S. S. Colvin, Harold Rugg, G. M. Whipple. Part II—*The Administrative Use of Intelligence Tests.* H. W. Holmes, W. K. Layton, Helen Davis, Agnes L. Rogers, Rudolf Pintner, M. R. Trabue, W. S. Miller, Bessie L. Gambrill, and others. The two parts are bound together..	1.60
Twenty-second Yearbook, 1923, Part I—*English Composition: Its Aims, Methods, and Measurements.* Earl Hudelson..	1.10
Twenty-second Yearbook, 1923, Part II—*The Social Studies in the Elementary and Secondary School.* A. S. Barr, J. J. Coss, Henry Harap, R. W. Hatch, H. C. Hill, Ernest Horn, C. H. Judd, L. C. Marshall, F. M. McMurry, Earle Rugg, H. O. Rugg, Emma Schweppe, Mabel Snedaker, and C. W. Washburne..................................	1.50
Twenty-third Yearbook, 1924, Part I—*The Education of Gifted Children.* Report of the Society's Committee. Guy M. Whipple, Chairman...	1.75
Twenty-third Yearbook, 1924, Part II—*Vocational Guidance and Vocational Education for Industries.* A. H. Edgerton and others..	1.75
Twenty-fourth Yearbook, 1925, Part I—*Report of the National Committee on Reading.* W. S. Gray, Chairman, F. W. Ballou, Rose L. Hardy, Ernest Horn, Frances Jenkins, S. A. Leonard, Estaline Wilson, and Laura Zirbes................................	1.50
Twenty-fourth Yearbook, 1925, Part II—*Adapting the Schools to Individual Differences.* Report of the Society's Committee. Carleton W. Washburne, Chairman..........	1.50
Twenty-fifth Yearbook, 1926, Part I—*The Present Status of Safety Education.* Report of the Society's Committee. Guy M. Whipple, Chairman.....................................	1.75
Twenty-fifth Yearbook, 1926, Part II—*Extra-curricular Activities.* Report of the Society's committee. Leonard V. Koos, Chairman...	1.50
Twenty-sixth Yearbook, 1927, Part I—*Curriculum-making: Past and Present.* Report of the Society's Committee. Harold O. Rugg, Chairman.....................................	1.75
Twenty-sixth Yearbook, 1927, Part II—*The Foundations of Curriculum-making.* Prepared by individual members of the Society's Committee. Harold O. Rugg, Chairman	1.50
Twenty-seventh Yearbook, 1928, Part I—*Nature and Nurture: Their Influence upon Intelligence.* Prepared by the Society's Committee. Lewis M. Terman, Chairman..	1.75
Twenty-seventh Yearbook, 1928, Part II—*Nature and Nurture: Their Influence upon Achievement.* Prepared by the Society's Committee. Lewis M. Terman, Chairman..	1.75
Twenty-eighth Yearbook, 1929, Parts I and II—*Preschool and Parental Education.* Part I—*Organization and Development.* Part II—*Research and Method.* Prepared by the Society's Committee. Lois H. Meek, Chairman. Bound in one volume. Cloth	5.00
Paper..	3.25

PUBLICATIONS

POSTPAID PRICE

Twenty-ninth Yearbook, 1930, Parts I and II—*Report of the Society's Committee on Arithmetic.* Part I—*Some Aspects of Modern Thought on Arithmetic.* Part II—*Research in Arithmetic.* Prepared by the Society's Committee. F. B. Knight, Chairman. Bound in one volume. Cloth.................................... 5.00
Paper 3.25
Thirtieth Yearbook, 1931, Part I—*The Status of Rural Education.* First Report of the Society's Committee on Rural Education. Orville G. Brim, Chairman. Cloth...... 2.50
Paper..... 1.75
Thirtieth Yearbook, 1931, Part II—*The Textbook in American Education.* Report of the Society's Committee on the Textbook. J. B. Edmonson, Chairman. Cloth........ 2.50
Paper..... 1.75
Thirty-first Yearbook, 1932, Part I—*A Program for Teaching Science.* Prepared by the Society's Committee on the Teaching of Science. S. Ralph Powers, Chairman. Cloth 2.50
Paper..... 1.75
Thirty-first Yearbook, 1932, Part II—*Changes and Experiments in Liberal-Arts Education.* Prepared by Kathryn McHale, with numerous collaborators. Cloth......... 2.50
Paper..... 1.75
Thirty-second Yearbook, 1933—*The Teaching of Geography.* Prepared by the Society's Committee on the Teaching of Geography. A. E. Parkins, Chairman. Cloth....... 4.50
Paper..... 3.00
Thirty-third Yearbook, 1934, Part I—*The Planning and Construction of School Buildings.* Prepared by the Society's Committee on School Buildings. N. L. Engelhardt, Chairman. Cloth... 2.50
Paper..... 1.75
Thirty-third Yearbook, 1934, Part II—*The Activity Movement.* Prepared by the Society's Committee on the Activity Movement. Lois Coffey Mossman, Chairman. Cloth 2.50
Paper..... 1.75
Thirty-fourth Yearbook, 1935—*Educational Diagnosis.* Prepared by the Society's Committee on Educational Diagnosis. L. J. Brueckner, Chairman. Cloth............ 4.25
Paper..... 3.00
Thirty-fifth Yearbook, 1936, Part I—*The Grouping of Pupils.* Prepared by the Society's Committee. W. W. Coxe, Chairman. Cloth................................... 2.50
Paper..... 1.75
Thirty-fifth Yearbook, 1936, Part II—*Music Education.* Prepared by the Society's Committee. W. L. Uhl, Chairman. Cloth.. 2.50
Paper..... 1.75
Thirty-sixth Yearbook, 1937, Part I—*The Teaching of Reading.* Prepared by the Society's Committee. W. S. Gray, Chairman. Cloth............................. 2.50
Paper..... 1.75
Thirty-sixth Yearbook, 1937, Part II—*International Understanding through the Public-School Curriculum.* Prepared by the Society's Committee. I. L. Kandel, Chairman. Cloth.. 2.50
Paper..... 1.75
Thirty-seventh Yearbook, 1938, Part I—*Guidance in Educational Institutions.* Prepared by the Society's Committee, G. N. Kefauver, Chairman. Cloth................... 2.50
Paper..... 1.75
Thirty-seventh Yearbook, 1938, Part II—*The Scientific Movement in Education.* Prepared by the Society's Committee. F. N. Freeman, Chairman. Cloth............. 4.00
Paper..... 3.00
Thirty-eighth Yearbook, 1939, Part I—*Child Development and the Curriculum.* Prepared by the Society's Committee. Carleton Washburne, Chairman. Cloth....... 3.25
Paper..... 2.50
Thirty-eighth Yearbook, 1939, Part II—*General Education in the American College.* Prepared by the Society's Committee. Alvin Eurich, Chairman. Cloth........... 2.75
Paper..... 2.00
Thirty-ninth Yearbook, 1940, Part I—*Intelligence: Its Nature and Nurture. Comparative and Critical Exposition.* Prepared by the Society's Committee. G. D. Stoddard, Chairman. Cloth... 3.00
Paper..... 2.25
Thirty-ninth Yearbook, 1940. Part II—*Intelligence: Its Nature and Nurture. Original Studies and Experiments.* Prepared by the Society's Committee. G. D. Stoddard, Chairman. Cloth.. 3.00
Paper..... 2.25
Fortieth Yearbook, 1941—*Art in American Life and Education.* Prepared by the Society's Committee. Thomas Munro, Chairman. Cloth....................... 4.00
Paper..... 3.00
Forty-first Yearbook, 1942, Part I—*Philosophies of Education.* Prepared by the Society's Committee. John S. Brubacher, Chairman. Cloth.................... 3.00
Paper..... 2.25
Forty-first Yearbook, 1942, Part II—*The Psychology of Learning.* Prepared by the Society's Committee. T. R. McConnell, Chairman. Cloth...................... 3.25
Paper..... 2.50
Forty-second Yearbook, 1943, Part I—*Vocational Education.* Prepared by the Society's Committee. F. J. Keller, Chairman. Cloth............................ 3.25
Paper..... 2.50
Forty-second Yearbook, 1943, Part II—*The Library in General Education.* Prepared by the Society's Committee. L. R. Wilson, Chairman. Cloth.................. 3.00
Paper..... 2.25

PUBLICATIONS

	POSTPAID PRICE
Forty-third Yearbook, 1944, Part I—*Adolescence*. Prepared by the Society's Committee. Harold E. Jones, Chairman. Cloth	3.00
Paper	2.25
Forty-third Yearbook, 1944, Part II—*Teaching Language in the Elementary School*. Prepared by the Society's Committee. M. R. Trabue, Chairman. Cloth	2.75
Paper	2.00
Forty-fourth Yearbook, 1945, Part I—*American Education in the Postwar Period: Curriculum Reconstruction*. Prepared by the Society's Committee. Ralph W. Tyler, Chairman. Cloth	3.00
Paper	2.25
Forty-fourth Yearbook, 1945, Part II—*American Education in the Postwar Period: Structural Reorganization*. Prepared by the Society's Committee. Bess Goodykoontz, Chairman. Cloth	3.00
Paper	2.25
Forty-fifth Yearbook, 1946, Part I—*The Measurement of Understanding*. Prepared by the Society's Committee. William A. Brownell, Chairman. Cloth	3.00
Paper	2.25
Forty-fifth Yearbook, 1946, Part II—*Changing Conceptions in Educational Administration*. Prepared by the Society's Committee. Alonzo G. Grace, Chairman. Cloth	2.50
Paper	1.75
Forty-sixth Yearbook, 1947, Part I—*Science Education in American Schools*. Prepared by the Society's Committee. Victor H. Noll, Chairman. Cloth	3.25
Paper	2.50
Forty-sixth Yearbook, 1947, Part II—*Early Childhood Education*. Prepared by the Society's Committee. N. Searle Light, Chairman. Cloth	3.50
Paper	2.75
Forty-seventh Yearbook, 1948, Part I—*Juvenile Delinquency and the Schools*. Prepared by the Society's Committee. Ruth Strang, Chairman. Cloth	3.50
Paper	2.75
Forty-seventh Yearbook, 1948, Part II—*Reading in the High School and College*. Prepared by the Society's Committee. William S. Gray, Chairman. Cloth	3.50
Paper	2.75
Forty-eighth Yearbook, 1949, Part I—*Audio-visual Materials of Instruction*. Prepared by the Society's Committee. Stephen M. Corey, Chairman. Cloth	3.50
Paper	2.75
Forty-eighth Yearbook, 1949, Part II—*Reading in the Elementary School*. Prepared by the Society's Committee. Arthur I. Gates, Chairman. Cloth	3.50
Paper	2.75

Distributed by
THE UNIVERSITY OF CHICAGO PRESS
CHICAGO 37, ILLINOIS
1949

www.ingramcontent.com/pod-product-compliance
Lightning Source LLC
Chambersburg PA
CBHW050838230426
43667CB00012B/2045